RELEVANCE OF ENVIRONMENT

RELEVANCE OF ENVIRONMENT

A Critique on International Relation Theories

Narottam Gaan

Publications

KALPAZ PUBLICATIONS

DELHI-110052

Relevance of Environment
A Critique on International Relation Theories

Rs. 890

ISBN: 81-7835-411-X

Published in 2005 in India by
Kalpaz Publications,
C-30, Satyawati Nagar, Delhi-110052
E-mail : Kalpaz@hotmail.com

Laser Typesetting at : Master Computers, Delhi
Printed at : Salasar Imaging System, Delhi

Dedication

to

Paramahamsa Prajnanananda

The bee of my mind is engrossed in the blue-rayed lotus of Thy feet. I drink the nectar of Thy tender love. This royal bee of Thine sips only from the blossom that exudes Thy perfume.

Contents

Prologue

When the cold war was at its height anus race and the theories of deterrence interwoven with it dominated the security discourse of both the superpowers. One wanted to domesticise the universe, the other to universalize its domestic working class militancy. In the middle of the eighties, a new awareness emerged to questioning the relevance of mindless military build up as a means to define national security on a maximum minimum continuum paradigm. In the United States a discontentment of the public brewed over the military expenditures that could be expended on maximizing their domestic imperatives in terms of inordinate consumption, exorbitant life style and production of wealth-Similarly in Soviet Union, questioning the logic of military expenditure without providing the minimum needs to its people came to the fore with the winding down of its bamboo or iron curtains.

Besides, the growing awareness that war was disappearing from the scene and in some cases had disappeared, as an option in relations amongst a substantial group of states, caused a decline in politico military construct of national security issues. The emergence of detente and effectiveness of nuclear deterrence between East and West took kindly to the outlook that the Soviet Union could be included in the emergent security core group consisting of Western Europe, Japan, and North America an outlook that grew stronger with Gorbachev enthroned in power in Soviet Union supporting an explicit demilitarization of the cold war. With Vietnam debacle driving a nail in the coffin of American supposed military arrogance and supremacy, a growing tendency in the west to question whether war was a cost effective method for achieving what said above a wide range of political and economic objectives, took strong roots. In the broadening of this outlook war as a predominant apparatus of national security faded away to question the realistic assumption about the primacy of this military apparatus in the national security construct. Territorial exclusivity, boundary making and spatial distancing were thought no longer the key words dominating the realist assumption of security. The security shifted away from boundary or territory to people, individuals, the economy and the interspaced and external environment. What had traditionally been thought of as low politics: the international economy and the environment rose to the core of the securitization. Only during the last decade of the cold war when it was to be flickered out, the wider agenda reemerged to give prominence to the non-military aspects of national security.

In case of the environment the concept 'securitization' can be harked back to 1960s when a number of popular books such as Rachel Carson's controversial 1962 best seller 'Silent Spring' riveted to the growing impact of humankind on environment calling for a rethinking of the entire established relationship between nature and civilizations. What was a background constant in terms of a bountiful heap of lifeless raw materials to be transformed endlessly into consumptive parts of human commodious living, became a foreground variable to redefine and broaden the national security. The hitherto conventionally understood and misperceived relationship between man and nature is not just mechanical but more complex and delicate. Viewed from a Judeo-Christian perspective, and putting nature at the beck and call of human rapacious behaviour for mere exploitation starkly put future of humanity at stake.

By 1970, the observance of Earth Day, was the largest environment demonstration in history" because it could spur millions of Americans to participate in this event smacking of their rising awakening to the impact of industrialization on human life, the psychological stresses of nuclearisation, environmental disasters, advancement in scientific knowledge and the compatibility of environmentalism with other anti war and women's movements.[1] This movement could point to the issue of environmental politics finding their way into the national security agenda. Further, a host of books by writers such as Paul Ehrlich (1969) Garret Hardin (1968), Barry Commoner (1971), Donella, Meadows et al (1972 and Lester Brown (1972) erupted a public debate about the issue such as exponential population growth, the tragedy of commons, the negative externalities of production technology, the potential limits to industrial growth and the complex global interdependencies of the late twentieth century. These authors could be able to adorn the environmental politics with new analytical and normative discourse. In recognition of the growing importance of environmental issue forming the core of international debates, the United Nations Conference on the Environment held in 1972 in Stockholm put the environmental issue at the core of the agenda of world politics. Even during the century prior to 1972, many governmental and nongovernmental member of international community met sporadically all ineffectively to discuss a range of environmental issues. It was at Stockholm an international and official status was accorded to environmental issues through the creation of United Nations Environment Programme (UNEP). Since then taking a leaf from this, the number of agreements, conventions and treaties among and between states on air pollution, climate change, forest, ozone layer, the use of nuclear weapons, protection of flora and fauna, transboundary flow of hazardous materials, has grown up as yet with many states failing either to sign or implement these agreements. A corpus of international environmental laws now exists to guide and monitor state actions. The United Nations has acted to incorporate environmental law issue into its specialized agencies such as UNDP, World Bank, International Labour Organization, World Health Organization, International Maritime Organization, and UNESCO.

Public concern about environmental issues climbed so high backed by many scientific findings about air pollution, deforestation, and acid precipitation that compelled state policy makers to take environmental issues seriously. The result was the creation of World Commission on Environment and Development in 1983 Chaired by Gro Harlem Brundtland, former Prime Minister of Norway, and the release of its report 'Our Common Future'.

Ensconcing its attention on the global and interlocking process of population growth, food production, ecosystem protection, energy use, industrialization and urbanization with a wide ranging proposals and recommendations woven into its broad framework. The concept of sustainable development, it defines it as to meet the needs of the present without compromising the ability of future generations to meet their own needs. The elaboration of sustainable development bridging the diverse interests of developed and developing states, found its culmination in 1992 conference on Environment and Development held in Rio. This has also been integral to discussion at other UN conferences on issues such as population and development held in Cairo in 1994. Thus from Stockholm to Rio's Agenda 21, the world has traversed a long way during these last decades to include the impending environmental issues into its security agenda in recognition of the gravity and magnitude of the crisis.

What was a moral outrage at the impact of pesticides on human health grew steadily during these years into a wide range interconnected issues, including climate change, biodiversity, resource depletion, pollution and the threat from meteorites. The underlying problem was a combination of burgeoning human numbers and rising industrialization within a finite planetary ecosystem. The entire global concern for environmental issues can be split into two: one was the Arcadian desire to securitize the environment and to make a restitution of what has been done to the environment. The second was a pragmatic survival thinking that if human beings exceeded the carrying capacity of the ecosystem in too many ways, they would peril the supporting conditions of their own prosperity, civilization, and possibly existence. Aware that the despoliation of nature in combination with growing population could strike a threatening blow against humanity making it vulnerable to disruption in production, and economic sufficiency, the entire political segment of the world decided to give primacy to the environment-no longer the evaded sector. In other words, three broad and interconnected issues emerged to occupy the attention and concern of practitioners and policy makers of world politics: environmental ethics, sustainable development and environmental security.

Given the severity of the crisis, what it needs is a systemic change or an overhaul of the system that is solely responsible for such an environmental impasse. The way it has entered into the academic realm gaining legitimacy and into the mainstream of international relation shows that policymakers and scholars are very much keen on providing compromised, and short-term solutions to maintain the status quo based on a symptom cure paradigm. That means they are interested in removal of symptoms not in cure of the roots. As alleged by some critics like Vandana Shiva, Maria Mies and Carolyn Merchant including the author, this symptom cure approach has suited the interests of the rich industrialized North. By co-opting environmental issues into their hegemonic mainstream of international relations, as dependable and subordinate variables, these rich industrialized countries have succeeded in marginalizing the concern of the poor developing world and at the same time in exaggerating its contribution to the environmental crisis. In this way, this policy of cooption and shifting of the responsibility of the America led North countries put a veneer on their own historic nuisance to the environment These approaches further divested the environmental movement of their potential revolutionary ethos, which are essentially required to herald systemic changes.

At the other extreme is a minority of thinkers like Julian Simon, Herman Kalm, Ronald Bailey and Wallace Kaufman who challenge the mainstream thinking of environmental politics. In their views, the assertion that certain human activities affect the environment in adverse ways that threaten both the existence and welfare of human beings, and the ecosystem's complex evolutionary process, is ill founded and exaggeratingly alarmist. These critics rely on scientific uncertainty and inconclusive studies and findings of the academic world to contest the grounds on which an overarching primacy has been put on environment over and above other factors.

In the middle of these expostulations is the environment-conflict linkage approach made by Homer Dixon and others. From an array of case studies such as in Rwanda, Somalia, Pakistan, Philippines they unearthed the environmental causes of conflict. According to their studies, environmental scarcity of resources has produced many social effects in terms of economic decline, poverty, decrease in agricultural productivity, migration and weakening of state structure which in turn result in violent intra, or inter state conflicts such as simple scarcity, group-identity conflict and insurgencies and relative deprivation conflicts. These studies are diagnostic in the sense that these have brought to the centre stage the environmental causes of conflict which are independent variables not subordinate to what conventionally held as primary-political, social and economic factors. Central to their model was the notion of an ingenuity gap or a disparity between the solutions required to cope with environmental scarcity and the human, social and institutional capital that could be mustered to provide these solutions. This ingenuity gap undermining human adaptive responses in combination with resource scarcity generates violent conflicts in a number of regions. Critics of this model like Richard A. Matthew, Ted Gaulin and Bryan Mc Donald disagreeing with what environment-conflict linage models propound, concede environmental stress only becomes an important explanatory variable when the level of environmental stress exceeds the adaptive capacity of a state. In their view, this rarely happens because societies almost always find ways to cope. These scholars also view that human adaptive capacity is neither completely stalled out as suggested by Homer Dixon nor do Julian Simon and Herman Kahn suggest it ubiquitous as. Rather in the vast majority of cases, human adaptive capacity lies somewhere between two unrealistic extremes.

The author in this book accepting the stand taken by Homer Dixon enlarges its scope by conceptualizing that environmental security addresses the very roots of what wrecks such disastrous consequences on humanity. Neither Dixon, nor Matthew has touched the ethnocentrism of Western pattern of development, its life style and approach to life and nature. Endorsing the stand taken by Dixon and others the author holds that environmental scarcity of resources can cause intra and inter state violent conflict in interaction with its various social effects. But violence is not a solution to the crisis. In order to ensure positive peace, environmental security envisages finding out alternatives, and overhauling the dominant pattern of development and life style that has been responsible for environmental degradation.

Disagreements over causes, effects, and responses as to the environment exist with differential focus prioritizing their environmental concerns. Deep ecologists advocate a biocentrism and holistic approach in which all forms of life are intrinsically valuable and interrelated-It is preservationist and concerned with defence of wilderness, ecosystems and biospecies. It is perceived as a social being solely concerned with the health of plants and animals. It puts blame on technology, pride and greed which are the forces encouraging mankind to exploit after and try to control the great web of life of which it is a part. A product of nineteenth century preservationalist battles, deep ecology faded to cast the ecological crisis within a wider social context. Its ecological holism describes, humanness as a mere biological component of the interdependent biosphere has no necessary purpose but to serve the cycle of life; as they are at the top of the food chain, humans do not appear very important to the long-term sustainability of life. In other words deep ecologists can be accused of dissolving humanness, either through biological reductionism or through the doctrine of larger self. Social ecologists on the other hand adopt an anthropocentric perspective. They understand and address environmental change in terms of its relationship to forms of social injustice and violence. They entwine the fate of the people with the environmental degradatiom Social ecology and its ecoanarchist branch under Murray Bookchin unlike the deep ecologists stressing on unicellular earth and its ecological holism, put emphasis on political and economic aspects of the ecological crisis and construction of an ecologically proper ethic/polis theory for human kind. Inspired by Peter Kropotkin's rejection of the facile interpretation of Darwinism as a theory of struggle in nature, and his advocacy of self empowered commune, Bookchin argued for ecology of freedom, which is a defence of both the individual and community. The liberty of one is ensured by egalitarian and democratic relationship with the other Solution to the ecological crisis is quite dependent on the democratic reconstruction of society, with a sensibility of sociality to freedom, peace, and ecology extending to a municipal confederalism, which will bind the sovereign communities through non-representational democratic rules. The respect for life, human and non-human is premised on his advocacy of equality of unequal and recognition of differences not indiscriminate attribution of rights in the name of justice.

Ecofeminism, a branch of social ecology drawing impetus from the coincidence between women's subjugation and the control of the nature, in both cases by men, aims at disabusing the political theorists of a world view of both women and nature as useful and expendable matter to be controlled, exploited and discarded to satisfy the male needs. It defends a particular constituency by reflecting on the modem killing of nature, on the deadly cumulative impact of science, monopoly capitalism and the global suites system.

The challenges of climate change due to emission of CO_2 to the atmosphere mostly a doing of the rich industrialized North-to the sovereign state system, its legitimacy and the security system built around it have gained momentum calling for a review of Westphalian sovereign state system.

The developments in the field of science considering everything both animate and inanimate as objective unconnected particles, faith in instrumentality of reason, centrality of technology and progress replacing what is sacred and premium on matter over divine-all these came as a threat to the global ecology. Thus the traditionally established cosmic worldview came in clash with a secular modernist worldview resulting in a crisis situation. The secular worldview having its roots in Renaissance and science became the dominant western worldview represented by the US and other European countries from a global perspective. It is not cosmic laws but mechanical laws as discovered and subject to control and manipulation by the scientists as well human beings that became the guiding metaphor for human progress and modernization. Viewing the entire planet as an external mechanical object to be exploited, and measuring progress in terms of inordinate and luxurious life style, exorbitant consumption, industrialization based on fossil fuel technology, and holding wealth production and richness as synonym for happiness, have become universally accepted norms of a secularist view of progress. Science played a key role in the emergence of a secularist world view which shifts human faith in the Ultimate Reality to matter, scripts the triumph of human reason over the vagaries of nature and usurps the space and time not in a timelessness but linearity frame for material progress. The secular portrayal of the world resulted in the spread of western democracy, market economy and globalization to all parts of the globe as standard of development and modernity.

Today there is a wide measure of agreement which on the physical side of science approaches almost to unanimity; that the stream of knowledge is heading towards a non mechanical reality; the universe begins to look more like a great thought than like a grew machine. The ever expanding universal self heading towards that Incomprehensible ultimate reality has been reduced by the secularist world view to an individualized self thinking the entire universe as a mechanical lifeless other to be expended for satisfaction of its brute desires. The western view of the universe as framed by science has been able to sustain secularism as a globally viable culture dismantling what ancient sages and saints and the present scientists have viewed about the universe. Not transcending beyond the cocoons of body, mind, intellect based reason and rationality, to get comprehension of the ultimate reality, and to enlarge one's atomized self into the universal self, the humans learnt from the western dominant secularist paradigm to apply the instrumentality of, ea. in the service of their desires. The ever growing consumption, inordinate life style and wealth production facilitated by secularist world view created a world of ever deepening contrast between conspicuous consumption in the North and grueling poverty in the South. Myriad forms of pollutions threatening air land, water, seas, and oceans have plagued the entire universe plunging the entire living system into the abyss of insecurity. Whereas from a conventional international relation Perspective these general problems are taken as distinct fields of study within the existing realist paradigms, they may also be understood more systematically as interrelated symptoms and causal connections of the global problematique.

From a cosmological perspective, the roots of the global problematique lie embedded in the mode of consciousness that is born out of the secular materialistic worldview. But the consciousness that is born out of the enlarged universal self is what the global ecology envisions to put humanity in the larger cosmos. Since the western secular worldview has been irreversibly global the danger it poses by destroying the environmental functions has also become global. For the first time in history, humanity has become a geophysical force capable of undermining Earth's life support systems. The contemporary ecological crisis poses a serious challenge to the secular worldview. The concept of expanded self does not mean return to undifferentiated oneness of humanity with nature or pre-rational modes of consciousness. It means realization of the oneness of spirit in both nature and human beings. It means ascension to a higher stage of consciousness, which enables human beings to perceive spirit or sacredness in both animate and inanimate. Having shared the same ontological foundation with science that human beings are mere particles of motion in quest for material welfare, the International Relation theories are becoming one-sided and inadequate to meet the impending challenges from the environment, since the ultimate truth or reality is not matter. There have been changes in the findings of scientists in recent years coming in proximity to the Eastern mysticism that from cosmic self have come forth all physical, biophysical and psychophysical energies, all worlds, all gods, and all beings. Thus, based upon the neglected understanding of the oneness of spirit the international relation theories need to be reinvented from a rather different perspective: a cosmic view of the world as the unfolding of spirit. This view integrates all the disparate and divergent and synthesizes them into the web of larger universal self. Constructism, sovereignty, secularism, and post modernism have been interpreted and weaved into the cosmic whole as a foundation of international relation theories to countervail the excesses of materialism and move humanity towards a higher plane of consciousness. While describing sovereignty as a historical construct and secularism as a discourse it understands constructs which is an important moment of truth in its recognition of inter subjective dimensions of reality. Secular materialism has reduced the world to a mere instrumentality and observable objectivity, and undermined for centuries together the internal subjective aspects of reality. A deeper, vaster, and more meaningful dimension of reality exists above the sensate and material level.

Since environmental degradation is a crisis of consciousness born of materialistic worldview, the cosmic worldview acknowledges humanity's special position and unique responsibility in the cosmos to redress the environmental Political and international relation theories always put primacy on institutions and structures, which they believe, can be manipulated to redound to the materialistic needs of the individuals. In these theories little importance is accorded to ethical and moral build up of individuals in owning responsibility for what they have done to the environment But the environmental insights and ethics require individual responsibility and an ethical resurgence in human beings. The cosmic worldview can bridge the hiatus between these two approaches. The global environmental crisis necessitates a heightened consciousness born of the realization of unity and oneness of spirit in both animates and inanimate. The onus is on individuals to evolve consciously into the realm of expanded self The theories and practices in international relations and world politics have been determined by the secular materialistic worldview represented by the western powers led by the United States. The destructive consequences of such a view have already been writ large on the human life. In the context of western culture the hegemonic representation of such a materialistic view, the orientation has been so strongly towards creative physical activity to change, action, acquisition and expansion of power, and whose basic understanding of the world therefore involves conceiving of reality as tangible and object like, in order to be able to manipulate and get a grasp on it for our own benefit in this materialized form. The fundamental responsibility lies in awakening the humans to the devastating implications of the exterior and fragmented view of the reality of the materialistic view and to the desideratum of being spiritually motivated to comprehend the ultimate reality. The main theme of the theories and practices of world politics has been to legitimize and reinforce the matter centric view deeply penetrated into western culture and civilization and clamped its hegemony over all nations, people, societies, and nature.

If the modernity's notion of secular sovereign state and its political authority remains confined to the acceptance of non interference of political authority into the religions domain of human beings, then possibility of human beings risen to super conscious stage remain galore. But secularism understood as being mirrored of a fragmented and mechanical material world consisting of multitude of different objects assembled into a huge machine, stands in the way of individuals being transcended from the limitation of atomized egoistic self into super consciousness stage. This is the secular problematique of the sovereign state system based on Cartesian and Newtonian view of matter. Sharing the same ontological edifice with science, the political authority was based on promotion of possessive individualism in terms of production of wealth, inordinate consumption and profligate life style at the expense of nature, other individuals, society and nations. The fulfillment of these materialistic goods remained the criteria of individuals while tendering consent to the sovereign state system. But the future generations' consent to the rightness of political authority to exploit nature, even at their expense taken for granted remained lacking in the legitimation to sovereign state system. At present the focus on intergenerational responsibility and inter species accountability in many regimes, particular those addressing issues with less temporal horizons, such as climate change, ozone depletion and the extinction of species points to the relevance of cosmic view questioning the secular worldview. Thus a shift from one sided and single pointed confinement to matter under secular worldview to a universal episteme. Causing new spatial ordering principles, new temporal understandings and new norms of legitimation, is evident in increasing proliferation of a plethora of international agreements on environmental issues since 1970. These agreements put a limit on freedom of authority of sovereign state to continue promoting wealth production, inordinate consumption and profligate life style at expense of nature and others. The states are free to abrogate these agreements but cannot do so at their peril and ignoring pressures from the internal and external sources exerted on them to adhere to the principles of environmental protection. The single point perspective of the sovereign state is being transformed into the multilateral governance, a multi perspective form of organization. The cosmic worldview suggests a movement beyond the multi perspectival and matter confinement to the universality and oneness of spirit The present globalization ushering in colonisation of the parts by the western view of universe as all matter or economy should not be termed as evidences of an approximation to cosmic worldview. It is an odyssey of transcendence from within and beyond on the part of human beings and their institutions thinking all as subjectivities interconnected and interrelated in the web of spirit. The current shift in the meaning of sovereignty away from a sole emphasis on rights and towards an in corporation of accountability and responsibility also suggests that secularism's single point perspective is giving way to more inclusive approaches. To hold all, both inanimate and animates as the living presence of spirit is one of the important aspects of cosmic worldview. The extension of rights to non-human species, and recognition of urgency to protect the inanimate represents a rudimentary yet significant shift from secularism's self atomized and individualized human centeredness and anthropocentric presumption in the direction of recognizing the web of interdependence among species and embeddedness of humans within that web. Unless the human beings realize the oneness of spirit in transcendence of matter-spirit dichotomy characteristic of secular worldview, the full-scale shift towards the cosmic worldview cannot be effected.

The rightfulness of political authority of the sovereign state to promote material prosperity and universalize matter as ultimate reality not the spirit was derived from the premise provided by science. This faith in science to ensure a materially glittering world is ruptured in the face of deep ecological, social and cultural crisis it fostered. A leap of faith of all scientists, policymakers and human beings in the Cartesian split and mechanistic world for human liberation needs to be shifted to faith in cosmic worldview and its idea of unity and oneness between matter and spirit Though a shift in the twentieth century science is perceived from this fragmented, mechanized and distorted view of matter to the idea of unity advocated in Eastern Philosophy, it has not been universalized and yet to form the premise of modern sovereign state system. To persist in such an old Cartesian mechanized, fragmented and distorted view of the universe comes as a testament to our immaturity and failure to identify ourselves with the Real self From this arrogant rational instrumentality of secular world view emerges the creeping ecological crisis challenging us, the individual human beings and collectivities to evolve body, mind and soul consciously towards the realization of the ultimate truth. The experience of the universe in modem physics as a dynamic, inseparable whole makes the traditional concepts of space and time, of isolated objects, and of cause and effect loses their meaning. Such an experience however is very similar to that of the Eastern mystics, but very seldom has it been realized that this seems to lead in the same direction, towards a view of the world, which is very similar to the views held in Eastern mysticism.

The ecological crisis born of such a materialist and secular worldview puts the daunting challenges to the established frame of mind about international relation theories. The realist and liberal theories dominating the global politics have been challenged by the ecological thought. The shift of modem science towards a view akin to the Eastern mysticism necessities a review of what so far has been defined as development and modernization. This book while taking up the challenges from the ecological crisis, has made an attempt at rethinking the established international relation theories, and suggests a cosmic approach replacing the old mechanical portrayal of the world.

Dolapurnima
Author

25 March, 2005

Acknowledgements

This book assumes the present form as a result of the extraordinary help of some celebrated scholars upon whom I depended over the last few years. I have synthesized and built upon material that I have published in journals and books since 1990. Without the help and cooperation from others it could not have been possible to bring out this book. My unbounded thanks and gratitude go to Dr. Arthur H. Westing, Dr.Thomas F Homer Dixon of Toronto University, Dr. Richard A Matthew of California University who have played a key role in shaping my views and vision about the multidimensional aspects of environmental security from different perspectives. Dr. Westing deserves my heartfelt gratitude for having agreed to contribute a paper to this book. From the core of my heart I always convey my sense of gratitification to these erudite scholars for the materials, articles and books they have provided me without exhibiting even a slightest evidence of their being reluctant. My joys know no bounds when I feel to extend my sense of heartrendering gratitude to Marilyn Weiner and Hal of Screen scope of Washington for air dashing to India from such a far off place to take an interview with me for their documentary film on environmental security. It is really they who introduced me to Prof. Richard A Matthew. I am equally grateful to a host of critics of environmental security such as Daniel Deudney, Richard A Moss and Barry Buzan for having opened my horizon and my outlook to the neglected and not yet scrutinized aspects of environment, through their papers, articles, books and comments. I will fail in my duty if I do not give my heart felt and heart rendering thanks to the authorities of European University Center for Peace Studies, (EPU), Stadtschlaining, Austria and the Austrian Government for having privileged me with a much coveted scholarship to go to Austria and Hungary and to have higher studies on International Relation. This helped me a lot come in contact with a number of great scholars like Westing, Gunther Bachler and Johan Galtung whom I consider as yet the very prominent authorities in this field to have provided different perspectives to my critical outlook. I also thank the authorities of Jawaharlal

Nehru University Library, Indian Council of World Affairs, Teenmurti Library, United Nations Library and American Centre for having allowed me to work and collect materials in the past.

I am extremely grateful to my parents, my life partner Reena in our eternal journey, and my two loving beautiful flowers Tattwamasi and Yogeswar who have always spurred me inspiringly to the ethos of trailblazing and emerging shining, and withstand difficulties in the preparation of the book. Behind all these and the sole doer, but for who it was not possible to write such a book are Paramahamsa Prajnanananda and my Gurudev Paramahamsa Hariharananda. I deem it a God given priviledge to sing in paeans of their Beatific Bliss and Glory, which I always keep with me as treasure trove.

Narottam Gaan

1

Introduction Nature Back in International Relation

It is enunciated in Taitariya Upanisad[1] (II, I-3) that first there was space, from space came air, from air came fire, from fire came water, and from water came the earth, then all living beings. So all these elements of creation are found immanent within human beings, the latest and last creation of God. Nature constituted of both living and nonliving is the external manifestation of what is found in microform in human beings. Inextricably correlated and symbiotically related, both nature and human beings seem to be part of the same Universal self, the Creator of the universe. Delineated as such in India philosophy, culture and religion this does not jibe with the mainstream of western thinking which views that both nature and human beings are two separate, disjointed and unconnected categories and extraneously related only when the former is held subordinate, the lifeless other, and solely exists for the purpose of the latter.

The relationship between nature and human beings was shot into prominence only recently when the disastrous impacts of the decline in quality and quantity of the flora and fauna of nature on human beings, their social relationship and political – economic fabric were seriously felt and factorized into explaining many of the political events, crises and conflicts. It was a divagation from what was conventionally held in post Second World War mainstream of International Relation that social events were to be explained by social factors or causes.

Notwithstanding this differentiated view of nature, the very fact that the natural environment shapes human behaviour and political institutions finds acceptability in every age. Natural environment, which was a neglected area of study, has occupied in recent years center stage in national and international politics with literatures proliferating on environmental security and conflict to explain the environmental causes of conflict.

The very analysis of nature as a cause of political outcome can be harked back to Aristotle and Montesquieu. The Greek geographer-philosopher Strabo during 64 BCE-23 CE believed that geography was destiny, even that particular geographical circumstances conducted to certain political orders. Aristotle famously remarked, in the Politics, on the impact of climate on men's characters and, ultimately, their politics. The ancients were true ecologists, for they assumed a strong organic relationship between environment and society. Long before 'green house effect' came to limelight, let alone having to come to grips with politics, Montesquieu had declared the "empire of climate is the first and greatest empire."

Contrary to what Jean Bodin writing in 1566, said reason as exercised by statesmen could overcome the tyranny of geography, Napoleon Bonaparte stated that "the politics of a state is its geography".[2] Long before the term "geopolitics" was coined by Swedish academic Rudolf Kjellen, political scientists tried to understand nature as a cause of political events. With nature coming back into the arena of political analysis, political science returns to its earliest and most basic theories.[3]

Nature as Cause of Social Events

That nature is the cause of social and human events has become the main focus of naturalist theorists, which are though of various types such as cosmic naturalism, analogical naturalism, anthropological naturalism and functional-materialistic naturalism.

Cosmic naturalism believes in cosmic astrology to be the guiding factor of human events. Astrologists locate the cause of human events in astronomical patterns. Here the links between causes and consequences are mysterious and not subject to scientific or empirical investigation.

The analogic naturalism agrees with analogous linkage between the human social processes and natural ones, but does not claim that non-human physical nature is the cause of human outcomes. By borrowing various metaphors, languages, images and models from nature, these theorists try to understand the logic of human social systems. This borrowing has been mutual, for example, Charles Darwin applied" the doctrine of Thomas Malthus... to the whole animal and vegetable kingdoms".[4]

Deudney states "there is no convincing reason to believe that deeply recurrent patterns in non human nature...must serve as a model for human interactions, because human beings differ in so many important ways from other animal and all plant life".[5]

Sometimes a close resemblance between human brings and animals is struck. Human beings are endowed with a rare power of discrimination and wisdom without which humans are just like animals. There is no dearth of literature to demonstrate an analogy between human beings and plants. In the Bhagavad-Gita it is said

Urdhvamulam adhahsakham asvattham prahur avyayam' Chandamisi yasya parnani yas tam veda sa vedavit." (Chap XV, I)

They (The wise) likened human life to an imperishable Asvattha tree with its root above and branches below. It leaves are the Vedas; he who knows it is the knower of Vedas. Paradoxically, though the ashvattha tree is here referred to as eternal, the word itself in one commonly accepted derivation means that which does not remain tomorrow, from a-svas. The metaphorical ashvattha tree in this sense alludes to the world of transitoriness and its beings, which are ever in the process of change-nothing remaining the same from the present moment to the next.[6]

So allegories and metaphors are used to be derived from plant kingdom to understand the philosophy of human life and unravel the mystery behind the creation. The halo of sacredness that is strewn around the planet kingdom has something to say above threat stage of human life where he/she does not find day distinction between human beings, animals and plants and realizes the eternal immanent in them like the life and seed of the ashvattha tree being eternal. In order to make the planet earth worth living in, what this school of thought suggests is to find a symbiotic and organic relationship that exists between human beings, animals and plants and all elements of the creation.

The anthropological naturalist theories discover the causes of human behaviour in intrinsic human nature – factors such as race, intelligence, genetic endowment, and deep psychology.[7] Though such theories have largely disappeared from the domain of international relations and political science, but have strong footholds in other social sciences.

Functional-materialist naturalist theories are very much relevant to the issues of environmental security and conflict. The interaction of human beings with the non-human natural environment results in specific human behaviour and institutions about which these theories provide behavioural social scientific propositions. These theories try to forge a link or bond between specific physical constraints and opportunities provided by nature with alternatives in the performance of very functional tasks of human beings. The very nature and process of human activity towards survival, sustenance or development in the form of organizing society, group and political institutions and human behaviour is very much shaped by the diverse ways in which the differing material environments present themselves to human beings.

It is not only the presentations of specificity of natural environment to human beings, but the very understanding of the intricacies of nature and its relation with human beings in particular historical and cultural contexts that set the goal, objectives and nature of human activity. As such theories are not exclusively about political outcomes, but encompass sociological, economic and cultural outcomes as well.[8]

The main objective of these early theories is to demonstrate that the natural environment and its resources are independent variables such as climate, soil, water mineral resources, topography and population to shape patterns of human political life in many important and recurrent ways.

Nature absent in Social Sciences

In the late nineteenth and early twentieth century and more particularly after the Second World War, the development and researches in the realm of social science witnessed expulsion of nature from their studies. Whereas the naturalist social scientists were wont to explaining human activities and political tendencies in terms of nature as causal variables, the social scientists sought social causes of social outcomes. Thus, the absence of nature in the explanatory analysis of social scientists made the social science denatured. This occurred at a time when Western liberalism, pattern of development, and masculine understandings of power understood the nature as the other a repository of lifeless raw materials to be harnessed for the betterment of human beings. But in this pattern of development, cultural hegemony and thinking was expressed a little concern for the natural environment. The speed with which the global environment is deteriorating and catapulting the attention of policy makers to the center stage of reviewing the hegemonic cultural pattern and developmental thinking requires the earliest back of nature into the realm of social sciences. Thus what was at the earliest a natural social science needs to be appended to the present social-social science.

The proclivity of social scientists to give a short shrift to natural variables in favour of human institutions and historical variables was strengthened after the Second World War. As the sociologist Samuel Klausner has observed, "in part social science has asserted its independence as a discipline by demonstrating the limited explanatory power of physical concepts of human behaviour".[9] The analysis of natural environment as an independent and causal variable is largely absent in the field of international relations defined as a branch of political science. Kenneth Walz finally sealed the ouster of natural environment from the realm of social science as found in his "three images" typology of theories of the causes of war.[10] First image explanations locate the causes of international outcomes, say the cause of war, "in the nature and behaviour of men wars result from selfishness, from misdirected aggressive impulses, from stupidity."[11] Second image explanations locate causes in the internal structure of the state. Imperialism, for example results from a particular internal economic structure like capitalism; similarly, international peace results from a particular form of government like democracy.[12] In order to explain what the actors will do in international relations, then in addition to looking at the attributes of the actors, we must also look to the constraints that define the strategic settings in which the actors interact. The third image locates causes within the state system.[13]

Marking a departure from the actor centered history and also from the tendency of the present social scientists, some historians like Fernand Braudel, William McNeill, Alfred Crosby and G. Barraclough pronounced in their writings the intimacy of human beings with their environment. As Geoffrey Barraclough observed, "the prevalent tendency is to adopt a broadly materialistic position in the sense that their central theme is man's conflict with his environment."[14] Similarly depicting a historian's enterprise, Braudel stated, the mountain as more important than the ruler. His study encompasses the entire material realities of "man in his intimate relationship to the earth which bears and feeds him."[15]

Nature deterministic or Puppet?

At one extreme of geopolitical theorists is found a tight and inevitable relation between the material forces and institutional structure. Human beings are held as the puppets of material forces. At the other extreme is Lucian Febvre's concept of possibilism, which emphasized human freedom in responding to material forces.[16] According to this view material forces are of marginal importance in explaining human affairs.

Between the two extremes can be made a middle synthesized view which holds that natural environment significantly defines the consequences of the choices humans make, but does not dictate which choice they desire or pursue. It is also inevitable that they will bear the consequences of not making an appropriate choice. Human institutions are not passive before nature, or the puppets of nature, but it is nature and not humanity that significantly determines whether human actions achieve their goals.

Geopolitical Theory: Role of Climate in Shaping the Fate of Nations

Prior to industrial revolution climate was a prominent topic in geopolitical theory. Hippocrate's Airs, Waters, and Places[17] attested to such a view followed by Aristotle and Montesequieu. In his Politics Aristotle delineates three zones and argues that people in cold northern regions were prone to an excess of spiritedness (thumos) and as a result were ungovernable, but free.[18] At the other extreme, people in the torrid zones of Asia and Africa were prone to an excess of bodily desires (eros). Pursuing wants of the body, Asian and Africa lived in a condition of material sophistication. But the absence of spiritedness made them relatively passive politically, and more willing to accept despotic rule. In Aristotle's view the middle temperate zone is the golden mean between two extremes. The Greeks living in it could enjoy the benefits of material civilization without despotism. Carrying further the arguments, Aristotle stated that the Greeks had a natural prosperity, and right to rule over lesser peoples. On the basis of this natural factor, he explained why one group of humans dominated the other groups.[19]

Later on Montesquieu's views stand just a restatement of what Aristotle had said about the impact of climate upon the temperament of human beings, which in turn affects the type of custom and law of society. Unlike Aristotle, who emphasized the superiority of balanced or middle climatic conditions, Montesquieu argued that colder Northern conditions are most conducive to the advance of civilization. Like Aristotle, Montesquieu linked colder climates with a love of liberty, and argued that warmer climates retards materials progress, induces political prosperity and a predisposition towards despotism. Like Aristotle, Montesquieu did not attribute all political outcomes to climate.

This natural social science based on nature as the causes of social outcomes declined giving rise to social science that gave importance to social causes of social outcomes in the 19th century. Few researches like Markham and Huntington continued the Aristotelian tradition, and argued that tropical regions of the world are economically and politically retarded relative to the temperate regions because of the enervating effects of humidity and heat.[20]

The above analysis relates to arguments about the deterministic role of climate in shaping the character and destiny of the nation. Nature remained an independent variable or factor to explain political and social behaviour of human beings.

Development in the field of science and technology reduced natural environment to a repository of raw materials to be exploited for the betterment of human beings. Nature no longer remained independent or deterministic rather because a puppet in the hands of the human beings. Today, a country is considered more advanced, progressed or civilized, having highest rates of economic growth, only because it has overexploited the resources of the earth at the expense of other nations, or other peoples, and overtaxed the atmosphere by emitting carbon dioxide more than what other nations put together had done to the atmosphere. Ironically, the polluters in the world today to the utmost are the richest. The pattern of development, life style and consumption as decided by the western people since the day of industrialization and development of science, based on burning of fossil fuels have been responsible for global climate change with disastrous consequences like global warming, sea level rise, ozone hole and other changes upon survivability and existence of not only human beings but of the entire creation. As yet no other change to the environment has been more challenging to the existing dominant pattern of development, way of life, political and economic thinking than the climate change.

Nature in an Unequal World

Geopolitical theories about the role of environmental factors in shaping the very uneven patterns of economic and political development during the emergence of global system remain relevant. Emergence of Europe over the last half millennium as the dominant free in world history has been the most far-reaching development. Through its network of trade, exchange and interaction on a worldwide scale European occupied almost all the earth. With the end of colonialism, the European dominance ended, but a "great rift" between the North and South continues to be one of the salient features of the world politics.[21]

According to Deudney, three clusters of arguments can be launched to explain the disparity and great hiatus between the North and South. Out of these two arguments are both social-social scientific in the sense that these put emphasis on social causes for explaining social outcomes. The third one is geopolitical. External social systemic explanations based on Marxism and World-system theory argue that North's progress is based on exploitation and plundering of the rest of the world. Most arguments on the "development of underdevelopment" emphasize that the source of South's impoverishment is external and located in the logic of a world system of capitalism and imperialism dominated by the North.[22]

The internationalist social systemic theories argue that domestic institutional and cultural factors, market institutions and incentives, cultural disposition towards work and savings are of crucial importance for development. These two clusters of arguments do not give credence to the geopolitical theory that nature is important. Pushed to the marginal status by the decay of geopolitics in the political science, the third clusters of arguments hold that the great difference in the pattern of development and economic growth can be explained as the product of ecological and climatic factors.

The environmental degradation in all sectors of nature with its disastrous impact on existence and survival of the living beings on earth has again brought to fore the importance of ecological factor in political analysis. What was once neglected and given a low status comes to be considered important in view of the fact that the environmental degradation due to human activities has come in challenging the conventionally understood political theories and ideas on security, development and political organization, etc. The social science's ascent on social causes of social outcomes needs to be supplemented by returning to the natural-social science approach. The impact of natural environment and human – nature interactions remain the basis on which such a journey back to the geopolitical traditions should take place. That does not mean that natural environment is always independent of social practice, but a rethinking of the role of nature in social practice and human evolution needs to take place. In the words of Deudney, "unfortunately, the recent turn of social theory away from structuralism to an emphasis on the socially constructed nature of reality, while offering many insights and correctives to mechanistic structural arguments could exacerbate the incapacity of social science to deal with environmental issues."[23] It is western view of life, political and economic constructions that have perceived nature in a particular way and accordingly being acted upon for its social purpose. Such a social construction of nature has been at the root of the environmental crisis afflicting the entire globe. So such a particularistic perception and construction of nature and weaved into its political and economic design has been universalized and hegemonic at the cost of other's perception and construction. Social science theories guided by this particularistic turned universalistic logic and arguments in their social construction of nature and weaving into their overall socio-politico design have been impervious to the other aspects of the diversely enriched human life, as well to the beauty and bounty of nature. "Social constructions inevitably shape how nature is perceived and acted upon, but nature itself is not socially constructed, and any social science that assumes so will inevitably be blind to important aspects of human life. Nature constitutes a structuring reality for human beings that is not socially constructed."[24]

The relationship between nature and civilization harks back to the day the creation came into being on this earth. But the arrogance with which the human beings-the dominant creature of the universe-wreak havoc on its nature is a very recent phenomena and started with industrial age. Rachel Carson's controversial 1962 bestseller 'Silent Spring' highlighting the impact of pesticides on human health and her moral outrage at the rapacious behaviour of Homo sapiens, could forsage a revolutionary change in the manner in which the relationship between nature and civilization would henceforth be perceived. No longer could nature be regarded as simply a compendium of lifeless raw materials-the other-to be endlessly transformed by human ingenuity and labour into commensurable commodities. The relationship was more complex and beyond the mechanical portrayal of the Newtonian age. Succinctly put, the environmental life support system upon which all life depends is being depleted and degraded by human actions-at stake is the future of humankind.

The scientific world during 16th and 17th century through its enormous discoveries and inventions promised the human beings the Heavenly city to be brought down to the Earthly city by inclining humans to materialistic aggrandizement, goods driven pleasures, exorbitant consumptions, inordinate life style. In its endeavour it partly succeeded but failed in that it became unwittingly an accomplice in the hands of human beings in destroying the nature. The faith of the science in ingenuity of human beings to create a Heavenly city on earth came to be reviewed with its being not able to find alternative or other roads to what so far has been defined as development. In the early euphoric ambience of industrial revolution and march of science could not be heard the murmurs, protestations and concerns about the deleterious impact of industrial pollution, and fears of scarcity-induced conflict and misery. Even the environmentalist Lester Brown's arguments for a redefinition of national security in 1977 and six years later Richard Ullman's support to this initiative created little interests among the students of world politics. These voices for a second look were silent springs but could not be washed away completely by turbulent waters of the imperatives of cold war. Environmental issues were placed squarely on the agenda of world politics at the United Nations Conference on the Environment held in Stockholm in 1972. Through the creation of the United Nations Environment Programme at this conference an officially recognized institutional setting was accorded to environmental issue. Public concern about the immediate and cumulative effects of environmental change compelling state officials to take environmental issues seriously reached its crescendo when Brundtland Commission released its report, 'Our Common Future' in 1987, established by the United Nations General Assembly. The findings of the report caught the immediate attention of the policymakers because its redefinition of development was designed to meet the needs of the present without compromising the ability of future generations to meet their own needs. By the late 1980s and early 1990s environmental security became a broad movement. Numerous environmental advocates including Michael, Renner, Jesica Tuchman Mathews, Norman Myers and Gwyn Prins wrote in favour of redefining national security to encompass resources and environmental threats. Homer Dixon and others brought out a link between environmental degradation and conflict. With the end of cold war, the environmental movement got prominence and moved into the political mainstream and gained legitimacy in the academic world.

Many important theories in International Relation such as liberalism, realism and post modern theories like critical theory seem to be anachronistic and inadequate to deal with the impending environmental crisis in the sector of land, water, atmosphere, ocean and seas with disastrous consequences on the political, social and economic life of the individuals.

This book is an endeavour in the direction of the putting the challenges; the environmental crisis throws open to the established theories in International Relation, in their proper perspectives. In stead of confining itself to the periphery of the crisis, diagnosing the symptoms it goes deep into the crisis and strikes at the very root to start building anew the conventionally understood theories with insights and thoughts derived from time immemorial civilized values and ethics. It calls for a review of the core western centric and liberal assumptions upon which the normative structure of the contemporary international society is based. A moral and ethical reconstruction of society and human beings is emphasized upon in their awareness of the transcendental that unites all the animate and inanimate, the present and future with the bond of divine. It carries human beings beyond the standardized normative structure of western determined global market society and its values. It questions the very conception of the world as a complex of phenomena controlled by certain scientifically identifiable laws. The solution to the environmental crisis, it does not seek in some technical tricks but in the ethical resurgence of human beings with a transcendental vision and wisdom.

Standing on the bedrock of ecological issues, the present work is a milestone in that it attempts at explaining how realism, liberalism and post modern critical theories in International Relations needs to be reinvented. The first chapter brings to limelight the inadequacies of traditional concept of security and conflict between and among nations. It shows, how environmental degradation appears as an independent variable to explain the many of violent conflicts occurring at present around the globe. It questions the very adequacy and logic of powers of states to be measured in terms of military to combat the non-military threats stemming from the environmental sector. A theoretical build up of environmental security and conflict with examples has been made in this chapter to reinforce the point that the traditional concept of security and conflict needs to be reexamined.

The second chapter exposes the reader to the limitations of understanding environmental security and conflict within the framework of Westphalian concept and logic of sovereign state system. Going beyond the authoritative works on environmental security, the present work redefines environmental security in a more comprehensive way than is evident in many renowned literatures that carries it beyond the road to sovereignty. Standing at the confluence of sustainable development, intergenerational responsibility and environmental ethics, environmental security redefines itself while responding to the critics of environmental security.

Postmodern critical theories challenge the established theories and ideas hegemonically dominating the world. These aim at reconstruction or deconstruction of the social and political world. The third chapter comes in to supplement critical theories what they were lacking with environmental aspects. Without the environment, the critical theories are halfway emancipatory. How social construction or deconstruction is possible and be emancipatory with a language that is not yet devoid of western logic and arguments? New insights offered by the ecological thought challenging realism and liberalism will cast critically theory within the larger emancipatory critique of mainstream International Relation theories.

The fourth chapter strikes at the very root of western liberal democracy and its legitimacy within broader perspective of sustainable development, accountability to future generation and redefining the very pattern of development and way of life.

The fifth chapter questions the very foundation of liberal democracy from an ecological perspective. Based on unlimited consumerism, individualism and judo chiristian tradition of anti nature, liberal democracy and its legitimacy does not take into account the interests of future generations and other living and non-living. This chapter questions the very foundation of legitimacy, as it has not reflected in it the interests of the future generation. In order to make sustainable development possible and include the interest of the future generations in the mode of legitimation this chapter makes a valuably prescriptive study.

The sixth chapter delineates the politics of climate change and its challenges to the sovereign state system, established economic and political thinking, and way of life. It shows how the present climate change talks, negotiations and treaties remain ineffective before the adamancy of the United States. Unless and until the western concept of development based on burning of fossil fuels, pattern of life and consumption style gets reviewed; all hopes and aspiration of humanity fixed on a treaty will remain chimerical.

The seventh chapter from a South's Perspective reviews, the right to development and other rights. It challenges the western constructed concept of development and rights from an ecological perspective.

The western doctrine of progress based on industrialization has been considered as sources of an environmental destructive dominant cultural tendency clamping on all the diverse cultural multi literalism. This dominant view of development resulting in materialism forms the foundation of secular world view. This reduced reality to matter. Taking insights from eastern philosophy, western idealism and recent developments in physics, the eighth chapter challenges the secular sovereign state based on matter and propounds a cosmic whole approach.

The ninth chapter specifically contributed by Dr. Arthur H. Westing points to the ecological consequences of war. The very instrumentality of war as a means to resolving interstate or intrastate conflicts has been contested from ecological grounds.

The conclusion chapter makes a synoptic review of all chapters and adds guidelines fors new planetary ethics and wisdom to be followed by policy makes while defining their national interests on the anvil of realism.

References

1. Eight Upanisads Vol. I translated by Swami Gambhirananda (Calcutta: Advaita Ashrama, 1998), fourth edition, pp. 323-25.
2. Quoted in Adam Garfinkle, Geopolitics: Middle Eastern Notes and Anticipations, ORBIS Vol. 47, No. 2, Spring 2003, p. 264.
3. *Ibid.*

4. Charles Darwin, The Origin of Species (Original 1859), (New York: Oxford University Press, 1979).
5. Daniel H. Deudney, "Bringing Nature Back in: Geopolitical Theory from the Greeks to the Global Era," in Daniel H. Deudney and Richard A. Matthew ed., Contested Grounds (Albany: State University of New York Press, 1999), p. 28.
6. Sri Sri Paramahansa Yogananda, God Talks With Arjuna, The Bhagavad Gita: Royal Science of God realization Vol. II, Kolkata: Yogada Satsanga Society of India, 2002), p. 927.
7. Melvin Konner, The Tangled Wing: Biological Constraints on the Human Spirit (New York: Harper and Row, 1982); Mary Midgley, Beast and Man: The Roots of Human Nature (Ithaca, N.Y.: Cornell University Press, 1978).
8. Marvin Harris, Cultural Materialism: The Struggle for a Science of Culture (New York: Random House, 1979); and Martin F. Murphy and Maxine L. Margolis, eds., Science, Materialism, and the Study of Culture (Gainescille University Press of Florida, 1995).
9. Samuel Z. Klausner, "Social Science and Environmental Quality", The Annals, of the American Academy of Political and Social Science Vol. 389, May 1970, p. 4.
10. Kenneth Waltz, Man, the State and War (New York: Columbia University Press, 1959).
11. *Ibid*, p. 16.
12. *Ibid*, pp. 80-164.
13. *Ibid*, p. 12.
14. Geoffrey Barraclough, Main Trends in History (expanded and updated by Michael Burns) (London: Holmes & Meier, 1991), p. 158.
15. Fernand Braudel, On History, trans, Sarah Matthews (Chicago: University of Chicago Press, 1980), p. 185.
16. Lucian Febvre, A Geographical Introduction to History (London: Kegan, Paul, 1925).
17. Hippocrates, "Airs, Waters and Places", in G.E.R. Lloyd ed, Hippocratic Writings (London: Penguin, 1978).
18. Aristotle, The Politics. Barker ed., (Oxford: Oxford University Press, 1948), Paragraph 1327, p. 298.
19. See David Livingstone, The Geographical Tradition (Oxford: Blackwell, 1993), pp. 1-32, 216-59; and David Arnold, The Problem of Nature: Environment, Culture and European Expansion (Oxford: Blackwell, 1996)

20. Ellsworth Huntington, Civilization and Climate (New Haven, Conn.: Yale University Press, 1915); Ellsworth Huntington, The Mainsprings of Civilization (New York: John Wiley and Sons, 1945).
21. L.S. Stavrianos, Global Rift (New York: Morrow, 1981).
22. See Thomas Richard Shannon, An Introduction to the World System Perspective (Boulder, Colo.: Westview Press, 1989).
23. Daniel H. Deudney, "Bringing Nature Back in Geopolitical Theory from the Greeks to the Global Era", *op. cit.*, p. 50.
24. *Ibid.*

2

Violent Environmental Conflict: A Critique on National Security

The late 1970s witnessed a spurt of activity resulting in a myriad of calls to redefine security in non military terms that include rising poverty, rapid population growth, spread of infectious diseases, and environmental degradation. The realist understanding and definition of security was state centric connected with state secrecy, nuclear and military power. The realist framework of national security as a function of the successful pursuit of interstate power competition through military means continued right through the cold war. According to Dalby, "cold war versions of security have usually been understood in spatial terms as moves of exclusion and protection is a spatial exercise in distancing and boundary making".[1] This means in geopolitical parlance, the spatial limitation of Soviet political control. During the last half century, security has been primarily a matter of concern for states and their military alliances. The legitimacy of the governments is generally understood in terms of provision of internal security for the inhabitants residing within its territorial jurisdiction. Where stability of the regime has been held synonymous with national security serious inroads into the realm of human rights, and internal repressions have been rationalized in the name of national security. Where political instability has been identified as threat, national security is understood as containing and limiting political change and legitimizing the status quo. The intensification of cold war climaxed in the proliferation of nuclear weapons and in the Reagan administration's Strategic Defence Initiative and Star wars merely exposed the paradox of security where the enhancement of nuclear power does not mean the enhancement of security to the people. The problems plaguing the entire humanity in terms of grinding poverty, burgeoning population growth, spread of diseases, scarcity of resources and environmental degradation could not be comprehended within the realist framework based on state centric military capability. Thus, the dominant realist paradigm to understand the current realities seems to be inadequate. It has "become an anachronism that has lost much of its explanatory and prescriptive power."[2]

Environmental Security

The state-centric and military perspective of security has lost both practical relevance and intellectual credibility in the context of a number of historic forces and events in the contemporary age. These include the end of cold war, global integration of national economies, erosion of national identifies and cultures, the shift in priority from military rivalry to economic competition, and the diminishing role of state as the dominant actor in international politics. On the other hand, there has emerged diverse new issues-ranging from poverty to refugees crises, information privacy to cyber-terrorism, environmental problems to natural disasters – which requires non-state and non-military policies and strategies. These newly emerging security concerns have been characterized as non-traditional, and are now considered a major component of what is christened as comprehensive security. Among these emergent problems replacing the threat of East-West ideological divide, military aggression and struggle for global preponderance is the global environmental crisis. It looms large in terms of global warming, sea level rise, acid rain, greenhouse effect, diminishing capacity of the agricultural system, depletion of earth's finite resources, punching holes in the ozone layer, and biodiversity loss. Simply put, the global agenda has expanded since the demise of cold war, as has the need for urgent attention to these problems for solution. It is thus seen that "welfare not warfare, will shape the rules and global threats like ozone holes and pollution will dictate the agenda."[3] It is within this context that the environmental question has gained worldwide significance as a security issue. In fact, environmental security stands out as perhaps the most widely debated issue, especially due to its all-pervasive nature, cross national scope and inter generational implications.[4]

While many of the past, present and future causes of conflict and war may seem to have little or no direct connection with the environment or with resources, a strong argument can be made for linking certain resource and environmental problems with the prospects for political frictions and tensions, or even war and peace. At the centre of ongoing debate is the assertion that resource scarcity and certain forms of environmental degradation are important factors contributing to political instability or violent conflict at local, regional and interstate levels. There is a growing perception that local, regional and global environmental deficiencies or resource scarcities will increasingly produce conditions that may lead to conflict.[5]

This conceptual shift towards environmental security in the context of collapse of Soviet Union and diminution of security threats associated with cold war, pitch forked into the mainstream security debates urging the policymakers to cast about for a new security focus. Despite contentious debates within the field of environmental security, a wide variety of recent comments by senior diplomats and policy makers are symptomatic of the recognition that issues related to environmental security have ascended to the highest levels.

In 1987, the General Secretary of the Soviet Union, Mikhail Gorbachev stated:

> [The World] is not secure in the direct meaning of the word when currents of poison flow along river channels, when poison rains pour down from the sky, when an atmosphere polluted with industrial and transport waste chokes cities and whole regions, when the development of atomic engineering is justified by unacceptable risks…The relationship between man and the environment has become menacing. Problems of ecological security affect all the rich and the poor.[6]

In November 1989, Prime Minister Margaret Thatcher gave a speech to the United Nations General Assembly-saying: While the conventional political dangers – the threat of global annihilation, the fact of regional war-appear to be receding, we have all recently become aware of another insidious dangers. It is as menacing in its way as these more accustomed perils with which international diplomacy has concerned itself for centuries. It is the prospect of irretrievable damage to the atmosphere, to the oceans, to earth itself.[7]

In April 1997, as United States secretary of state, Ms Albright went on to say:

> Not so long ago, many believed that the pursuit of clean air, clean water, and healthy forests was a worthy goal, but not part of our national security. Today, environmental issues are part of the mainstream of American foreign Policy.[8]

It was in this backdrop of future non-military threats that a number of studies and research institutions undertook works to determine if and how environmental factors were related to the intra and inter state conflicts or violence that appeared to be surfacing around the globe.[9] These studies varied in their approach, their terminology, and their specific findings and consistent in their explanations suggested that environmental stress, operating through a set of intervening variables, could contribute to violent conflicts, and thus constituted a threat to national and international security. Furthering this argument that the mounting environmental problems and the associated issues need an attention with which the conventional outlook of national security appears to be incongruent, Jeremy Rifkin points out: "The environmental threats facing the planet are not simply the result of scientific miscalculation. Nor are they merely the consequences of ill-conceived management decisions. Ironically it is the notion of security upon which our entire morden worldview is based that has led us to the verge of ecocide… In less than a century the practice of geopolitics thus pushed the world to the brink of both nuclear Armageddon and environmental catastrophe forcing us to reconsider the basic assumption of security that animate the modern world view".[10]

Similarly, Lodgaard feels that "the concept of environmental security challenges established frames of mind and political conflicts. It conveys a message that environmental problems have a legitimate claim for status as military problems have."[11]

Another proponent of environmental security in the same vein opines:

> …national security is not just about fighting forces and weaponry. It relates to watersheds, croplands, forests, genetic resources, climatic and other factors that rarely figure in the minds of military experts and political leaders, but increasingly deserve in their collectivity to rank along side military approaches as crucial to a nation's security.[12]

The growing significance of environmental security is quite evident in major international forums. Some well known examples include the UN Conference on Human Environment (1972), Ottawa Conference on Conservation and Development (1986), United Nations Conference on Environment and Development (1992), World Summit for Social Development (1995) and UN symposium on the Global Environment in the 21st Century (1997). These conferences and symposia eventually resulted in various international conventions and protocols for environmental protection or security, such as the Vienna Convection for the Protection of the Ozone Layer, the Convention on Biological Diversity, the Framework Convention on Climate Change, the convention to combat desertification, and the Kyoto protocol.[13] Harking back to as far as 1987, for example, The World Commission on Environment and Development (Brundtland Report) entitled 'Our Common Future", stresses the factor of environmental degradation causing the violent relationship between states:

> "Environmental stress is both a cause and effect of political tension and military conflict...nations have fought to assist or resist control over raw materials, energy supplies, land, river basin, sea passages and other key environmental resources. According to the report, such conflicts are likely to increase as these resources became scarcer and competition for them will increase."[14]

Environmental security as a concept encompassing non-military aspects was officially mentioned for the first time in the International conference on the Relationship between Disarmament and Development convened by the UN General Assembly in New York from 24 August to 11 September 1987. The final document adopted by consensus states:

> Recently non-military threats to security have moved to the forefront of global concern. Underdevelopment and declining prospects for development as well as mismanagement and waste of resources, constitute challenges to security. The degradation of the environment presents a threat to sustainable development.... Mass poverty, illiteracy, diseases, squalor and malnutrition affecting a large proportion of world's population often become the cause of social strain, tension and strife.[15]

Two distinct features of environmental security are: first, the environmental causes of conflict, i.e. environmental factors behind potentially violent conflicts; second, the impact of environmental degradation on overall political economy, health and life of the people. If environmental degradation or deficiencies create the conditions that render conflicts, act as multipliers that aggravate core causes of conflict[16] or act as a catalyst factor in creating conflicts, then environmental degradation or scarcity of resources becomes a national security issue.[17]

Environmental Conflict

In spite of these criticisms, the most influential arguments in the field have concluded that environmental stress is linked to conflict indirectly, but significantly. While the precise character of the linkage varies from case to case, it is made possible environmental stress is supposed to overwhelm the adaptive capacity of some societies while simultaneously introducing and reinforcing forms of conflict and instability. While division and debates characterize the field of environmental security, there is a strong degree of theoretical consensus among researchers. The most prominent and dominant thread that runs through the entire environmental security literature is that the environmental stress simultaneously reduces adaptive capacity and engenders conflict.

The dominant paradigm in the environmental security literature harks back to writers like Thomas Malthus, but it has obtained its contemporarily influential formulation in the work of Thomas Homer Dixon and Toronto Group. From a myriad of empirical case studies conducted by them on Haiti, Chiapas, Gaza, Pakistan and Bangladesh – India, they concluded that environmental scarcity of renewable resources viz., water, forest, fisheries and cropland give rise to a number of deleterious social effects including economic decline, social segmentation and human migration – these social effects in interaction with other political, economic and social factors, can generate conflict and instability. Central to their model was the notion of supply of ingenuity gap or a disparity between the solutions required to cope with environmental scarcity and the human, social and institutional capital that could be mustered to provide these solutions. This ingenuity gap essentially undermines human adaptive responses. That means, according to their studies, resource scarcity and limited or inadequate adaptive capacity coalesce together to generate violent conflicts in various regions.[18]

Dominant Paradigm

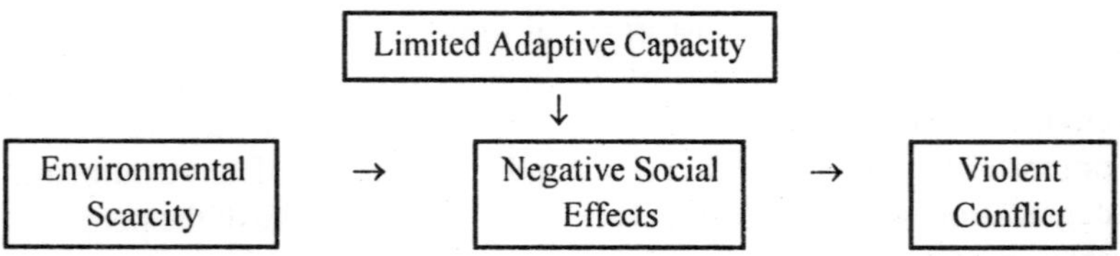

A theoretical representation is made in this figure[19] to understand the linkage between environmental stress and conflict. On theoretical ground it is criticized that even if resource scarcity plays a causal role in conflict, there are other more convincing explanations for conflict. Further, the prospects for adaptation, cooperation or resolution are not as completely bleak as are often presented. At the very prospects of an unlikely nuclear war, the fear of destructibility by the use of nuclear weapons has not any way diminished the universality of nuclear weapon as a main national security issue. It is that fear of destruction, which may have brought many nuclear powers to negotiating table for cooperation or disarmament. The resultant cooperation should not be cited to underrate the holistic perception of nuclear weapons as being a national security concern. Similarly, environmental scarcity of resources with its disastrous social effects may not be everywhere a direct cause of violent conflict, sometimes in combination with other factors causes conflict. For example, sea level rise, a consequence of global warming due to North's mindless pursuit of industrialization based on fossil fuel technology will affect low-lying areas such as Bangladesh below the sea level turning millions of them as refugees fleeing to Indian territories that is likely to exacerbate the already infested ethnic conflict in North-Eastern states. That it would not affect other countries does not any way diminish the environmental causes of conflict not less than the universality of nuclear weapons as a security concern. The consequences of environmental scarcity of resources on political, economic and social life of a state or states may prompt states or nations to cooperate to avoid the negative effects of war on environment. So the environmental co-operation syndrome as argued by some should not be overrated to diminish the role of environmental scarcity of resources causing conflict or violence. No nuclear war has ever been fought in this world after American's dropping of hydrogen bombs on Japan's Herosima and Nagasaki during the course of Second World War. This would be as preposterous to say that nuclear weapon lack the potential or prospects for conflict as to say that the environmental scarcity of resources lacks the potential for conflict as it has not resulted in conflict in some areas or has resulted in cooperation. Adaptation means the involvement of all state apparatus, institutions, scientific community, even the social system and value structure including the affected to take steps that would obviate the negative effects of environmental scarcity. The poor developing countries may not have the economic and scientific wherewithal as argued by Dixon to cope with the situation. Even the developed countries will not find it a smooth sailing while responding to the environmental crisis. For example, in regard to stabilization of CO_2 in the atmosphere American steps to renege on its commitment agreed to at Kyoto were a capitulation to the petroleum, and coal industrial lobby. What has threatened the world is the Western inordinate life style and pattern of development causing global warming, sea level rise and ozone layer depletion. To ensure environmental security what it requires is to make an overhaul of its pattern of life and development, which is not possible with strong protestations from high-class people. So Bush, American President caving in to the pressure of the industrial class justified his rejection of Kyoto protocol on the ground that countenancing the Kyoto commitment would hamper its economy and life style of its people. [20] Environmental security means overhauling the entire economic development pattern and existing social values related to liberal capitalism that is not possible without politico-socio-economic disruption. So the potential for conflict lies as much in the environmental scarcity of resources as in the very remedies and adaptive measures – a part of fulfillment of environmental security.

Inspite of the criticisms above, the main thrust of the studies showing the linkage between environment and conflict, remains paramount: the environmental scarcity operates through a set of intervening variables, contexts or ideational factors that directly cause conflict, and that environmental social effects and stress, as such outstrips attempts to cope with the crisis.

Another study undertaken by Swiss Peace Institute's Environment and Conflicts Project (ENCOP) was in the direction of what the Toronto group suggests. Gunther Bachler belonging to this group in his study used the term transformation by which he meant "the introduction of a heuristic concept in recording those interactions between the three levels – nature, human beings and the economy in a regional context-which have led to conflicts between human communities and will ... increasingly lead to such conflicts." [21]

Degradation is used in this context as an indicator of the degree of environmental transformation. In the words of Kates et al, "the biosphere has accumulated or is on its way to accumulating such a magnitude and variety of changes that it may be said to be transformed." [22] In other words, "transformation conflicts are caused by fundamental authropogenic changes in the environmental media and by the interactions between the processes of change and their consequences in the eco-regional context." [23]

Another authority Stephan Libiszewski belonging to ENCOP, making a distinction between traditional resource wars and environmental causes of conflict is of the view that 'an environmental conflict is a conflict caused by the environmental scarcity of a resource, that means: caused by a human made disturbance of its normal regeneration rate. Environmental scarcity can result from the overuse of a renewable resource or from the overstrain of the ecosystem's sink capacity, that is pollution. Both can reach the stage of destruction of space of living. Conflicts caused by physical, geopolitical or socio-economic resource scarcity are not environmental conflicts but traditional conflicts of resource distribution." [24]

As found in the Toronto Group's research, the ENCOP also walks on the same furrow that scarcity gives rise to conflict. Also it is alleged to be silent about human adaptation to resource scarcity. In these studies, it is mal-development, a condition similar to Homer Dixon's ingenuity gap that undermines human responses and enhances conflicts.[25] Though the

ENCOP model is more complex than the Toronto group's general model, but the theoretical argument presented by both is very similar.[26]

In a 1999 NATO pilot study this dominant environmental conflict paradigm was found in the line with the other studies.[27] According to this study, "[i]t is not environmental stress in isolation that characterizes the nature of the conflict between groups but other factors".[28] Here too political, economic and social factors intervene between environmental stress and conflict. The State Failure Task Force (SFTF), another research group marking the same dominant paradigm as with the preceding studies, reiterates the causal weight of environmental stress through intervening variables.[29] While the researches did find that massive environmental damage in a short time frame could directly cause political collapse, the far more common scenario was that environmental stress operates through the intervening variable of quality of life to generate conflict. Though highly critical of Toronto group, recent work by Gleditsch and de Soysa appears to have been co-opted by the dominant paradigm. According to their studies, resource scarcity, one component of a multifaceted development problem that they call" poverty" reduces agricultural production that in turn leads to conflict. That is, scarcity leads to a negative social outcome that becomes the proximate cause of conflict.[30] Beyond this; however, the Gleditsch and de Soyasa model is similar to the Toronto Group in that there is little room for human adaptation to conditions of scarcity. Indeed, their key independent variable, poverty, is defined by a lack of social and human capital. "Like Homer Dixon's ingenuity gap, Gleditsch and de Soyasa's explanatory variable appears to lock in negative social outcomes, leaving little room for human adaptation." [31] There is some variation in these models and terms presented by these research groups. But in each case the general theory linking resource scarcity and conflict is the same. Homer Dixon focuses on an "ingenuity gap", ENCOP on" mal-development" and Gleditsch and de Soysa on "poverty". Nevertheless, all these phrases describe a similar process-a limited capacity to respond to scarcity. The model which is critical of all the above models adopted by Richard A Matthew et al, finds flaws in current theory in environmental security on two counts. "First, it focuses on too short a time frame. Second, and relatedly, it underestimates human adaptive capacity." [32] They were averse to accepting the two extremes, Homer Dixon's lack of adaptive capacity in the poor countries, and Julian Simon and Herman Kahn's faith in the infinite capacity of individuals to adapt. To them, human adaptive capacity lies somewhere between these two extremes. Julian Simon writes, "there is no physical or economic reason why human resourcefulness and enterprise cannot forever continue to respond to impending shortages and existing problems with new expedients that, after an adjustment period, leave us better off than before the problem arose."[33]

Homer Dixon responds to this saying, "while I acknowledge the extraordinary potential of human resourcefulness and enterprise, I nonetheless argue that some societies – especially poor societies – will not be able to supply the unprecedented amounts of ingenuity they will need to solve their emerging scarcity problems."[34] This clearly demonstrates, Homer Dixon never maintains that all societies will not be able to cope with the situation. It is some poor societies because of various factors will be in dearth of required supply of ingenuity to adapt to the situation. This brings Homer Dixon closer to the position taken by Richard A. Matthew and his associates. If adaptation is a dynamic and continuous process, then there may be adaptation failure in some and adaptation success in others visited with trauma, travails and hardships. When such individual trauma, travails and ordeals while adapting to the environmental stress becomes a collective or group phenomena in a particular political context or in the face of growing incapability of state, the potential for violent conflict exists. Taking a departure from this, Matthew group holds that from a longer time perspective even if the adaptive failures through feedback will result in adaptive success, thus avoiding the prospects for environmental conflicts. Contrary to what Neo-Malthusians such as Paul Ehrlich, Robert Kaplan, and Thomas Homer Dixon contend, "adaptive mechanisms do not simply stall or become overwhelmed while levels of environmental stress continue to escalate."[35] To quote Richard A Mathew further: "This is not to say that all forms of adaptation are socially desirable. Adaptation can mean people of the developing would going further and further into the hinterland to gather fuel, wood and water; parents sending their children to work in factories because of crop failure; and simple belt-tightening people eating less,"[36] or as happened in Kalahandi district of Orissa people eating the dried up kernel of ripen mangoes died while adapting to food scarcity, or people in these tribal areas of Orissa are forced to sell their children as bonded labours as a mark of adaptation to the environmental scarcity of crop land and food. These latter examples are certainly unsettling and portent of potential for violent behaviour in an organized form depending on the nature of political system prevailing. If to use the language of Matthew, these starvation, death, or going without food, or half fed situations are the genuine form of adaptation, then conflict arising out of these situations created by environmental scarcity in the form of collective or group behaviour or response can be a genuine version of adaptation with a view to develop new legitimate and representative political authority and institution and new value structure that would reinvent the political-economic thinking which so far has contributed to environmental scarcity. As Walzer argues, conflict is a normal and important aspect of social development.[37] Then the portrayal of environmental crisis as an environmental conflict paradigm from a broader perspective does not lose its significance or acceptability, as a theoretical framework as argued by Richard Matthew and his group. The conclusion that this group arrived at is not to deny the linkage between environmental scarcity and conflict but stresses on "longer term studies "that" might provide deeper understanding of the ways in which concerns about environmental stress and degradation are relevant not only to the those concerned with international security, but also those worried about human rights, social justice and sustainable development.[38]

On the one side the economic deprivation, decreased agricultural production, health hazards, poverty, starvation or half fed or even death situation due to pollution and water scarcity-part of the adaptive success as propounded by Matthew – may cause indirect conflict in association with other factors as nuanced by Volker Boge[39] or Homer Dixon[40]. The other side is the situation of direct conflict or violence arising out of the environmental scarcity of resources-a case of adaptive failure. Hence the conflict emanates directly from the overuse and or pollution / destruction of a renewable natural resources. For example, if a downstream riparian threatens to go to war against an upstream riparian, because the latter pollutes river water so gravely that it cannot be used by the inhabitants of the downstream riparian, who are highly dependent on this water, then the environmental character of conflict is evident.[41] An array of evidences can be cited to show such threats of conflict over environmental scarcity of water all over the globe.[42] That in some cases it has led to cooperation to avoid war does not divest the environmental conflict of its theoretical appeal. Another example of direct violent conflict over environmental scarcity of resources like fish can be cited. The decline in fish catch due to environmental degradation all over the globe and in South Asian regions in particular could result in a series of violent conflict between Tamil Nadu fishermen of India, and Sri Lanka over fishing in waters of Kachchativu Island ceded by India to Sri Lanka as a gesture of friendship and good will in 1974.[43]

The two aspects of environmental scarcity induced situation in terms of adaptive failure and adaptive success can dovetail together into what is called environmental security in a broader sense. What is called as adaptive success at micro level along with adaptive failure in terms of poverty, food scarcity, health hazards or suffering due to environmental degradation at macro level, for example the impact of global warming due to western pattern of development based on fossil fuel industrialization and inordinate life style, poses challenges to redefine development and the vision of and approaches to life. Dixon says, "Highly unequal social arrangements make it much more likely that environmental scarcity will cause severe social friction. Such arrangements, in other words, often interact with severe scarcity to generate destructive social competition that impedes technological and institutional adaptation." [44] A serious ingenuity gap will cause major social changes like constrained agricultural and economic productivity and large population movements, igniting the simmering dissatisfaction among the people into orgy of widespread and chronic civil violence." [45] What remains pivotal to defining environmental security in a broader sense that will remove the causes of environmental conflict as well the causes of environmental scarcity that inflicts on the individuals in terms of health hazards, suffering, economic deprivation, poverty or starvation as undergone by them as a part of adaptation. Thus, at the confluence of the morally and ethically required nuances of sustainable development, economic rethinking, new planetary principles and new vision of, and approach to life, stands the environmental security. Thus, the very basis of environmental security challenges the established frame of mind about what so far has been defined as development, pattern of life style, and geopolitical security of the sovereign state system. It is not the national security in terms of military but the planetary security that will be the foundation of environmental security on this confluence.

Environmental Scarcity of Resources

Starting from 1st world war not only to the Falkland war as enumerated by Westing, but to the latest Gulf war all wars have been fought over access to natural resources such as minerals, fuels, fish stocks, products of the land and the land itself. The whole history of humanity has borne a testimony to the congeries of violent conflicts, contentions and wars that had taken place over access to and distribution of natural resources. In view of this, many scholars exhibit a tendency to interpret the linkage between environment and conflicts as a question of struggle for scare natural resoures.[46] Though environmental conflicts can manifest themselves as conflict over resources, in fact these multitude of wars are not really coming within what the term 'environmental' is understood. Human ecology poses questions about the nature of the relationship between the humans and the environment. The basic problems of this relationship under the study of social ecology are the limits of the utilization of the natural resources and of pollution of air and landscapes. This also implies a number of limits in the demands made of, and burdens laid on the human body and on the social life of the community.[47] A human made environmental change does not simply mean any interaction between humans beings and their environment. It means a destabilizing interference in the ecosystem's equilibrium. The pollution of atmosphere by emission of carbon dioxide, for example from fossil fuels based industries, overtaxes the ecosystem's absorption capability and causes the so called green house effects. This climate warming, in turn changes among other things, the balance between ice sheets and liquid water on the earth's surface, causing a rise of the sea level. In a similar way, the process of desertification can be explained as consequences of the devegetation, and overuse of the soil causes a decline of precipitation and soil erosion. As water supply is the prerequisite of nearly every ecosystem's functioning, serious manipulation in river flows is another example of human interference, which often affects the ecological equilibrium in the concerned regious. The environmental degradation is only about these affected life supporting conditions, the negative impact on human beings and society. Environmental change can mean a loss of quality; a degradation.[48] Environmental degradation is thus, understood as a human made environmental change having a negative impact on human society. Gunther Bachler, in the place of degradation used the word 'transformation'. The term 'global human – ecological transformation' is meant the introduction of a heuristic concept in regarding those interactions between the three levels-nature, human beings and the economy in the regional context-which have led to conflicts between human communities and will increasingly lead to such conflicts." [49]

To know the critical differentiation between renewable and non renewables-surprisingly not highlighted by many of the participants in this long debate-is necessary to understand the concept of environmental change and degradation. Natural resources can be roughly divided into two groups: non-renewables, like fresh water, soil, forests, air, climate, oceans and biodiversity. Renewable resources can be further divided into two groups: those that provide goods and those that provide services. Ocean fisheries supply fish that are a good while the stratospheric ozone layer renders a service by protecting life from high levels of ultraviolet radiation. Some renewables provide both goods and services; forests supply timber (a good) while also maintaining regional hydrological cycles (a service). They are renewable because they are ecologically integrated in a feedback circle system, which guarantees their replacement or the preservation of their quality. On the other hand, non-renewable resources as they are, cannot be integrated in such an ecosystem.[50] Therefore, they can be depleted but they cannot be degraded. Their depletion causes degradation of the renewable resources. Further to distinguish, a non-renewable consists of a stock, which is the total quality of the resource available for consumption. A renewable resource has both a stock and flow, which is the incremental addition to or restoration of the stock per unit of time.[51] To draw an analogy between the stocks and flows of renewable resources and money in bank, a renewable resource's stock is the resource's capital or principal, which generates a flow of interests or income that can be tapped for human consumption and well-beings.[52]

A further characteristic of renewable resources is that they can be less substituted than non-renewable ones, and in several cases not substituted at all. Food, fresh water, clean air and life supporting climatic conditions are not just sources of wealth in an economic sense but also biological prerequisite of life. In addition to environment as a bank of material resources and a sink for wastes, a third dimension of environment, as a space of living should be considered.[53] The loss of settlement areas due to the rise of the sea level, to desertification, or to industrial accident or project or dams, means more than just a shortage of resource 'land'. It includes an existential dimension and in certain dramatic cases of environmental degradation, it implies an aesthetic dimension of environment's impoverishment.[54]

The concept of environmental degradation in order to be understood correctly, leads to another important differentiation concerning the concept of resource scarcity that are of four distinct types.[55]

1. Physical scarcity means that resource is available in finite amounts.
2. Geopolitical scarcity means that resources are often distributed unequally on the surface of the earth so that some countries depend on deliveries from others.
3. Socio-economic scarcity concerns the unequal distribution of purchasing power and of property rights to provide natural resources between or within societies.
4. Environmental scarcity caused by environmental degradation means those resources that have traditionally been regarded as plentiful and naturally renewable but are becoming scarce now because of this failure of human beings to adopt sustainable methods of their management.

Unequal geopolitical and socio-economic distribution are often a source of degradation behaviour and the physical scarcity of a renewable resource can be a reason for the depletion of resource's capital stock. These are causally interrelated. Here the main focus is on the environmental scarcity of renewable resources that has the potential to seriously undermine human well-being. It can arise in three ways: through a drop in the supply of a key resource, through an increase in demands, and through a change in the relative access of different groups to the resource. Homer Dixon calls these respectively supply induced, demand induced and structural induced scarcities. Depletion and degradation produce a decrease in total resource supply or in other words, a decrease in the size of the total resource stock. But population growth and changes in consumption behaviour can also cause greater scarcity by boosting the demand for a resource. Thus, if a rapidly growing population depends on a fixed amount of cropland, the amount of cropland falls inexorably. Finally, scarcity is often caused by a severe imbalance in the distribution of wealth and power that results in some groups in a society getting disproportionately large slices of the total resources, where as, others get slice that are too small to sustain their livelihoods. This is what is called structural scarcity.

Analysts and policymakers in the past have usually addressed these three sources of scarcity independently. Neo Malthusians and economic optimists have given importance to supply and demand induced scarcity while generally ignoring the political economy of resource distribution. According to Dixon, these three scarcities interact and reinforce each other in an extraordinarily pernicious ways.[56] One type of interaction is resource capture. The degradation and depletion of renewable resources can interact with population growth to encourage powerful groups within a society to shift resource distribution in their favour by manipulating laws and institutions governing resource access. These powerful groups tighten their grip on the dwindling renewable resources while subjecting the marginal groups to greater scarcity.[57]

Thus, in Bangladesh, worsening land scarcities, partly caused by rapid population growth and human induced natural disasters, encouraged powerful landowners to exploit weakness in the state's land inheritance laws in order to seize lands from the poor farmers. These peasants have been forced to migrate to Indian territories for better livelihood. This happens also in Chiapas where the peasants were forced deeper into the state's lowland rain forest, farther away from the state's economic heartland, and deeper into poverty.

Process of Resource Capture

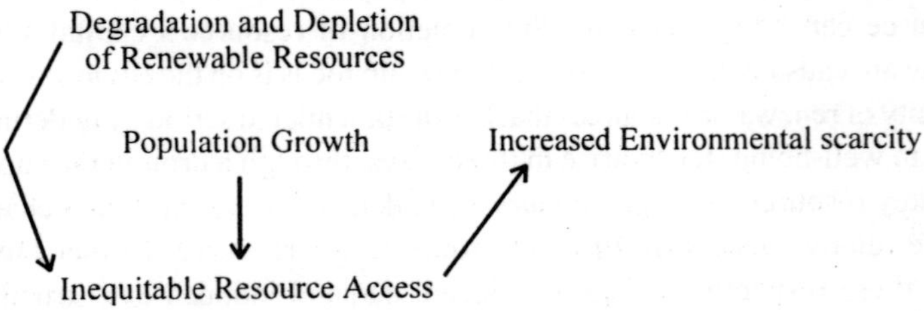

This figure is a representation of the process of resource capture as outlined by Homer Dixon.[58]

In the early 1990s, Israel's average annual supply of renewable fresh water was about 1950 million cubic meters against its demand including that of settlements in the West Bank and Golan Heights which was 2, 150 cubic meters. [59] The annual deficit of about 200 cubic meters is covered by overpumping aquifers, which has already plummeted water tables in some parts of Israel and West Bank. This decline has caused the exhaustion of some wells and the infiltration of sea water from the Mediterranean.[60]At the same time Israel's population is expected to increase from the present 6.0 million to around 7.5 million in the 2020.Accordingly, the country's water demand by 2020 is estimated at 2, 800 cubic meters.[61]

Ground water constitutes sixty per cent or about 1200 cubic meters of annual sustainable supply of water. The rest comes from the river flow, flood water, and waste water cycling. Two of the three main aquifers on which Israel depends lie principally underneath the West Bank. About 475 cubic meters or about 40 per cent of the ground water Israel uses originates in this territory. To protect its water interests Israel strictly restricted water use by Jewish settlers and Arabs on the West Bank. On a per capita basis in the early 1990s, settlers consumed four times as much as Arabs. Of the 650 cubic meters only 125 cubic meters were allowed to be used by the Arabs. Israel also restricted the number of wells Arab could drill in the territory, the amount of water Arabs were allowed to pump, and the times at which they could draw irrigation water. During occupation after 1967 Arabs were not permitted to drill new wells for agricultural purpose, although the Mekorot, Israel Water Company drilled more than thirty wells for settler's irrigation. The area of irrigated Arab farmland on the West Bank dwindled from 27 per cent of the total cultivated area to 3.5 to 6 per cent.[62] Arab agriculture in the regions got a setback because some Arab wells became dry or saline as a result of Israeli wells being drilled deeper nearby. These Israel water policies restricting water use to Arabs combined with the confiscation of agricultural land for settlers as well as Israeli restriction on Palestine agriculture propelled many West Bank Arabs to abandon farming and flee to towns to find either unemployed or become day labourers within Israel. No doubt many political, economic and ideological factors, operate to explain the present conflagration in this region but the links between these processes and unrest in West Bank appears reasonable to conclude that water scarcity and its economic effects contribute to the present crisis in the region.[63] Rising frustration in Palestinian community due to this factor appears to lie underneath the long ongoing Israeli Palestine territorial war.[64]

Ecological Marginalisation

It is a process resulted out of a structural imbalance in resource distribution, which in association with rapid population growth forces resource starved people into ecological marginal areas, such as upland hillsides.[65]

The Process of Ecological Marginalization

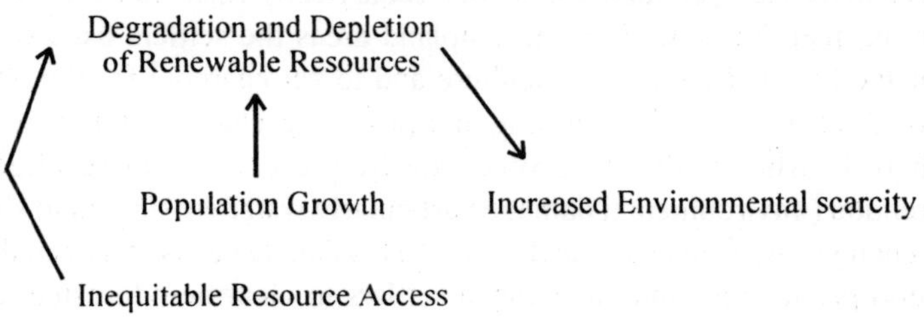

This figure as pointed out by Dixon represents the process by which poor people due to inequitable resource distribution, population growth and land degradation are forced to migrate to marginal regions.[66] As happened in Bangladesh, the people living in low lying areas affected by inequitable distribution of land, high density of population growth, soil erosion, and natural disasters such as cyclone, flood and storms have been settled in Chittagong Hill Tracts (CHT) which in turn, has not only caused massive deforestation because of slash and burn agriculture but also driven the indigenous tribal people Chakmas into Indian territories.[67] This process is visibly seen in the Himalayas, Indonesia, Central America, Brazil, Rajastan and the Sahel. Overtime, the process "causes environmental degradation and intractable poverty to become more and more closely intertwined in particular geographic areas with fragile environmental degradation. The world's poorest people are thus increasingly clustered in two types of areas: remote and ecologically fragile rural areas and the edge of growing urban areas." [68] A grossly unfair distribution of good cropland in lowland regions a colonial heritance bequeathed to Philippines by its former Spanish and American colonial rulers continues to be reinforced since independence by a powerful landowning elite.[69] Introduction of green-revolution and modern technologies in agriculture from 1960s into the 1980s resulted in a hike not only in the lowland production of grain for domestic consumption but also in cash crops. The proceeds from the cash crops helped the country pay its huge external debt. This unusual increased production opened the prospects of demand for agricultural labourers in large farms but it was not enough to compensate for a population growth rate at over 2.5 per cent. In combination with this population growth, unequal land access produced a surplus in agricultural unemployment. Daily wages demonstrated a downward slide with rural and urban industrialisation lacking sufficient capability to employ the excess labour. Thus, economically impoverished millions of poor agricultural labourers and landless peasants migrated to urban areas such as Mamila, already overburdened with shanty towns, and millions others moved to the least productive and often ecologically vulenerable territories such as steep hill sides.[70] In these upland areas the settlers used fire to clear the forested land for agriculture and to get charcoal for the cities. Thus, the slash and burn farming and procuring charcoal for the cities with little wherewithal to protect the fragile ecosystem resulted in horrendous environmental damage particularly water erosion, land slides and changes in the hydrological cycle.[71] This damage caused a dismal fall in food production, and encouraged settlers to clear new-forested land, thus ensuring massive land degradation. The often-sought for marginally fertile land is no longer in sight in many places and economic conditions remain as desperate as before for many peasants.[72]

Significance of Context

Not in all cases environmental scarcity or degradation has been a direct cause of conflict or violence. In cases of scarcity of renewable resources like water, fish, the conflict may be direct or where the environmental cause is found to be dominant. In case of environmentally induced migration the conflict is in association with social, political or economic contexts. These contexts are to be taken note of while studying the environmental causes of conflict. For example, some find behind the 1994 Rwandan genocide, the rapid population growth, severe land scarcity and the resulting food shortfalls-as the key factors. According to

Washington Post in its editorial comment: while the Rwandan civil war was; military, political and personal in its execution", a key underlying cause was "a merciless struggle for land in peasant society whose birth rates have put an unsustainable pressure on it." [73] On close scrutiny, the genocide in Rwanda was nothing but "a struggle among elites for control of the Rwanda state. Land scarcity played at most a peripheral role by reducing the regime legitimacy in the countryside and restricting alternatives for elite enrichment outside of government." [74]

While putting a premium on contexts, one should not swing to the opposite extreme saying the causal role of environmental scarcity is entirely subordinate to that of contextual factors. To some skeptics, scarcity is wholly a result of political, economic and social factors, such as failed institutions and policies, and needs a little independent attention.[75] Homer Dixon refutes this argument on the following grounds:[76]

First, environmental scarcity is not only influenced by social factors like institutions and policies, it can itself affect these institutions and policies in harmful ways. For example, the Mauritanian government built a series of dams along the Senegal river to avoid food shortages and drought, as a result the land prices hiked in these areas, given the critical land scarcities elsewhere in the regions. Being controlled by Moors of Arab region, the government in order to get profit modified the existing laws relating to land ownership, even abrogated the traditional right of black Mauritanians to farm, herd and fish along the river. This harmed the interests of large sections of the country's population.

Second, the environmental scarcity is not wholly a result of economic, political and social factors. It is also partly a function of particular physical characteristics of society's surrounding environment. These characteristics are, in some respects independent of human activities. For example, the depth of soils in the Filipino uplands prior to land clearing and features that make Israel's aquifers vulnerable to salt intrusion and Bangladesh's physical environment are physical givens of these environmental resources. Third, once environmental scarcity is irreversible, and then the scarcity is an external influence on society (Hait's top soil washes away into the sea). Even if new policies are undertaken to remove the underlying political and economic causes, the scarcity remains irreversible and remains a continuous burden on society. For example, chronic instability in Haiti and insurgency and violence elsewhere around globe such as in Filipino cannot be understood and remedied unless and until the independent causal role of environmental scarcity is understood and accepted not subordinate to contextual factors.

On the basis of preferential values, beliefs, social and political institutional behaviour, domestic and international arguments can be advanced in favour of not resorting to nuclear brinkmanship. These contexts are no doubt important and become effective in avoiding a nuclear holocaust but these do not in any way diminish the independent importance of possession of nuclear weapons on the part of a state as a security threat. Similarly, in some cases for example as argued, adaptation is a measure that people undertake by suffering a hardship in the form of starving, or death hazards in response to environmental stress, thus avoiding the slide into the loop of environmental conflict. Here, adaptation may not have resulted in a conflict as conceptualized by the dominant environmental conflict paradigm school of thought, but the threats posed by environmental degradation, say due to global warming or green house effect – the result of a policy and function of some governments remain irreversible, because scientific study on the causal role of nations on the region basis and their impact on nation wise has remained to a greater extent uncertain. For example, a scientific study is yet to be made out, pointing out what quality of emission of CO_2 from US to the atmosphere causes what amount of global warming, effects on agricultural, health, food etc on how many poor countries. This kind of scientific uncertainty, and study in general has not been able to muster and organize the affected people politically against the cause nations. Even if there is adaptation or adjustment or surrender the threats to the people from the environmental degradation continues unabated. Thus environmental security is a broad and comprehensive spectrum which includes both the environmental causes of conflict and the adaptive measures, so that a review of policies, values and social and political preference of institutions can take place to ensure human security not in terms of adaptive suffering or resorting to conflict for resolution but in terms of an affirmative, positive proactive policy, renewed vision and new planetary ethics.

Scenarios of Environmental Scarcity

Cropland Scarcity

At present total global cropland stands at about 1.5 billion hectares, which is about twice, the area of the lower forty-eight states in the US. Total arable land on the planet including current and potential cropland amounts to 3.2 to 3.4 billion hectares. Most of the best land has already been exploited and the rest is less fertile, rain starved and not easily irrigable and infected with pests. A country is described as land scarce when 70 per cent or more of arable land is under production. In Asia the most populous continent, the per cent of all arable land stands at 82. Though the percentage is lower in Africa and Latin America, the poor quality of much of remaining land is indicative of the fact that the previously high rates of cropland expansion cannot be continued.[77] Land scarcity has already reached a critical proportion in some areas such as Sahel, semi arid region of East and South East Africa, Southern Mexico, Andean highlands and Central America. World's largest untapped agricultural land lies under the rain forests of Congo and Amazon basins-two of the world's main repositories of biodiversity. Soils here being thin and readily eroded by tropical rains, are generally fragile and vulnerable to abrupt degradation.

During the 1980s, cropland grew at just 0.26 present a year in developing countries less than half the rate of the 1970s. More importantly arable land per capita plummeted to 1.9 per cent a year.[78] According to an estimate by experts, in the absence of a major increase in the arable land in developing countries, the world average of 0.26 hectare of cropland per capita will come down below 0.20 hectares by the year 2025 in view of the growing rate of world population growth. The benchmark to plumb the severity of land scarcity remains at 0.07 hectares of land per capita, though contentious because they depend on assumption about prevailing resource use technologies, capital availability, and other inputs to production. In 1990 Egypt was well below the threshold, at about 0.055 hectares per capita, and by 2025 population growth alone will push the countries such as Bangladesh, Kenya and Israel far under the threshold. The inequalities of land distribution existing in every society mean that the weaker and marginal groups will be subjected to much deepening scarcity. As is revealed, tens of millions of marginalized peasants in the developing world already subsist on very small, often fragmented plots of low quality land. It is estimated that more than 70 per cent of all rural households in these developing countries are either landless or nearly landless. According to Jeffrey Leonard, in the late 1980's "935 million rural people live in households that have too little land to meet the minimum subsistence requirements for food and fuel." [79] This excludes China, which at present could add as many as 100-200 million people to the category.

Tracts of land around the globe every year are being lost to a congeries of problems, including encroachment by cities, erosion, depletion of nutrients, acidification, compacting, and salinization and waterlogging from over irrigation.[80] A known conservative in assessment of environmental damage, Vaclav Smil estimates that 2 to 3 million hectares of cropland are lost annually to erosion, perhaps twice as much land goes to urbanization and at least 1 million hectares are abandoned because of excessive salinity.

In addition, about one-fifth of the world's cropland is suffering from some degree of desertification. Taken together, he concludes the planet will have lost about 1 million hectares of arable land between 1985 and 2000, equal the area of California and Texas combined.[81] A study made by the International Soil Reference and Information Center and the United Nations Environment Programme in association with over 250 soil and environmental scientists in 1990, gives a general impression about the state of land degradation in the world according to which, 38 per cent of world's current cropland, 65 per cent in Africa, 51 per cent in Latin America and 38 per cent in Asia are affected by land degradation.[82]

Deforestation

The study made by the UN Food and Agriculture Organisation (FAO) suggests that the already high rate of global tropical deforestation of the early 1980s has gone up again. In the early 1980s, the world was losing 11.3 million hectares of tropical forest annually. By 1991 the FAO put the figure at 17 million hectares.[83] Between 1960 and 1990 Asia is estimated to have lost nearly a third of its tropical forests, while Latin America and Africa lost almost a fifth.[84] At present, Brazil, Indonesia and Malaysia these three countries alone account for over half of the world's tropical rain forests.[85] Other countries experiencing high rates of deforestation include Costa Rica, Cameroon, India, Myanmar, the Philippines, Thailand, and Vietnam.

It is not that in developing countries only deforestation has taken place. The impression has been created to show that it is the developing countries and their growing population that have been responsible for the present heightened rate of deforestation. The fact is that after decimating their forest cover, the industrialized countries now shift the responsibility and burden to the developing countries to protect the forest cover. So use of phrases like "common heritage of mankind", and global commons is used to make forests in developing countries as carbon sinks. According to Gregg Marland, indeed out of the 800 million hectares of woodlands, about 300 millions hectares – well over a third – has taken place only in the industrialized countries.[86]

Water Scarcity

Heightened competition for fresh water poses a major threat to human security the world over. It could well prove to be the major source of conflict in the 21st century, not unlike oil in the present century.[87] Water depletion or degradation is supply induced. Water scarcity crisis is gravest when viewed in terms of rising demand. Reduced and degraded water quality has a direct impact on human health; about 250 million new cases of water borne diseases are reported every year causing about 10 million deaths.[88]

Water Availability in 1995 and 2025

Countries	*Percapita water availability 1995 m3 / person and year*	*Projected Per Capita Water Availability 2025 m3/person /year*
Africa		
Algeria	527	313
Burundi	594	292
Comorous	1667	760
Egypt	936	607
Ethiopia	1950	807
Kenya	1112	602
Libya	111	47
Malawi	1933	917
Morocco	1131	751
Rwanda	1215	485
Somalia	1422	570
South Africa	1206	698
Tunisia	434	288
The Americans		
Canada	98, 667	79, 731
United States	9, 277	7, 453
Barbados	192	169
Haiti	1, 544	879
Asia/ Middle East		
Bahrain	162	104
Cyprus	1, 208	947
Iran	1, 719	916
Israel	389	270
Jordan	318	144
Kuwait	95	55
Oman	874	295
Qatar	91	64
Saudi Arabia	249	107
Singapore	180	142
Yemen	346	131

In 1999 human beings were estimated to draw about 4, 250 cubic kilometers of fresh water a year from various sources returning about 1, 700 cubic kilometers often in polluted conditions.[89] This consumption is growing at a rate of 2 to 3 per cent a year. The annual quantity of water available from rivers is probable closer to 40, 000 cubic kilometers.[90] Though this suggests water supply is in abundance, great difference in water availability is marked among regions. In a number of arid developing countries burgeoning population growth threatens to reduce water availability below 1, 000 cubic meters of water per capita per year, a benchmark regarded by experts as about the minimum necessary for an adequate quality of life in moderately developed countries.[91] Such average can further slide down, as such are deceiving, as large disparties in water access that exists in all societies are kept hiding in working out this average. In such a situation of water average dwindling below 1000cubic meters in a developing country, a bulk of its population is likely to confront serious water scarcity. Then, this would result in restricting irrigated agriculture to a greater extent, and slum dwellers and urban squatter settlements will have insufficient water for basic hygiene, and rural families will have to walk a long distance to fetch water from streams and ponds.

The following table[92] identifies regions where water scarcity is likely to take place in the next decades as a result of population growth. Green house induced climate change is likely to affect these estimates because it would shift precipitation patterns and therefore the overall water supply.

Despite the uncertainty introduced into the estimates of water scarcity by the green house gases emitted into atmosphere by the industrialized nations, the Middle East and parts of Africa are likely to be affected severely by water scarcity. In these countries, populations are expanding rapidly and water is already extremely scarce.[93] According to a study, the number of people living in countries severely affected by water stress or chronic water scarcity in 1997 stands at 430 million. This number is expected to rise to 3 billion or over a third of the planet's population projections.[94]

Disputes over river water becoming scarce day by day with growing population it is held, would become more frequent among or between nations in coming decades.

Decline in Fish stocks

There are widespread evidences – from Maine to Newfoundland, to Southern India-of regional over exploitation of fish. Many fisheries are reported to have suffered from eutrophication, coastal pollution and destruction of mangrove swamps – the breeding grounds of prawns. Tropical fisheries especially in South East Asia are being ravaged by a combination of dynamite and cyanide fishing. These large swings in productivity are related to global climate changes, in particular EI Nino oscillation in the South Pacific.[95] As early as 1987, the FAO commented: "The time of spectacular and sustained increases in fish catches is over.... Almost all-important stocks of demersal species are either fully exploited or overfished. Many of the stocks of more highly valued species are depleted. Reef stocks and those of estuarine / littoral ones are under special threat from illegal fishing and environmental pollution." [96] In a 1995 report, the FAO concludes that about 69 per cent of the World's conventional species are "fully exploited, over exploited, depleted, or in the process of rebuilding as a result of depletion.' Further it notes that," this situation is globally non-sustainable and major ecological and economic damage is already visible".[97]

Total world sustainable fish both marine and fresh water fish production, which has quintupled since 1950, from 20.75 to 101.27 million metric tons in 1993 stands at 100 million metric tons.[98] To maintain current per capita human fish consumption the world will have to produce about 91 million metric tons of food fish by the year 2010.[99] Of the approximately 86 million metric tons of fish caught from marine and inland fisheries, about 57 million metric tons went to human consumption. It is unlikely that the quantity of food fish caught from marine and inland fisheries will exceed 60 million metric tons annually.[100] The remaining 31 million metric tons will have to come from aquaculture, which means doubling of aquaculture production from its 1993 levels of 16 million tons. This seems highly improbable. In such a situation, increasingly sophisticated fishing fleets may be used to push fish production beyond sustainability to meet the fish requirement of the people. This is likely to affect the marginal communities and small-scale fishers along the coasts of developing countries who entirely depend on traditional fishing.

In addition to increasing human numbers overfishing using high tech electronics to track fish, and competition among fishermen to catch as quickly as possible without any regard to the long term maintenance of the fisheries is one of the primary reasons for their decline.[101] A big contributor to the pollution of ocean and seas is the growing urban population, of which one third live within 60 kilometers of the coastline. Heavy metals, sewage, indiscriminate use of fertilizers, solid wastes from industries, run off from agricultural, and mining of sands and coral reefs have seriously affected sea life, overfeeding algae and causing it to bloom in a rapid growth that uses up the oxygen fish need to breathe.[102] The stratospheric ozone hole radiating more ultraviolet rays to the earth affects the sea life causing an increasingly mortality of fish. Global warming is very much likely to affect the sea life because it could alter water currents, which circulates heat and vital nutrients. The photosynthesis and growth of phytoplankton at the lowest link of the food chain, have decreased by as much as 20 per cent near the surface of Antarctic waters-at the surface where most marine growth and reproduction takes place.[103] Not only decline in fish catch but also their contamination has been a serious problem for fish consumers.

Loss of Biodiversity

Another important casuality of human activity inflicting damage on Earth's renewable resources is the priceless bio diversity. The estimates of number of species on the planet cover a wide range, from 5 to more than 30 million. The current best estimate known to science is 1.75 million[104] and only 13 per cent of the species on Earth has yet been described.[105] The tropical forests is the largest repository of genetics information, the majority of it contained in insects and microbes not yet identified. The world's biodiversity is a priceless resource for the development of new crops, medicines and a wide range of industrial products from paints to lubricants. With the destruction of tropical forests, the earth is robbed of most of its genetic information. Industrialization of agriculture, planting of trees and croplands to obtain high yields of products in grain and woods have resulted in simplification of ecosystem which in turn has reduced ecosystem stability and the availability of services such as soil nutrients and pest control.[106]

With the rapid destruction of tropical forests and other species' habitats around the Earth, both animal and plant species are vanishing at an extraordinary speed. According to an entomologist, the global loss from tropical deforestation alone could range from four to six thousand species a year, a rate ten thousand times greater than the natural background rate of extinction prior to the advent of human beings on earth.[107] The Global Biodiversity Assessment similarly concludes that "recent rates of deforestation translate into a rate of extinction of about 0.25 per cent per annum."[108] Though this is a crude estimate "the current extinction rates are dramatically higher than background extinction rates."[109] Urban growth, population growth, pollution, human predation and loss of habitats to loggers all contribute to the crisis. If climate change stress is an indication, then "an estimate of a 25 per cent reduction in planetary biodiversity in the next one hundred years is plausible. Such a loss would rival four of the five previous mass extinctions on earth. From both a moral and practical point of view, it could be the single greatest calamity human beings inflict on the planet." [110]

Global Warming

A world heavily dependent on carbon based fuels for economic growth and development finds that their use causes a build up of carbon dioxide in the atmosphere, which heats up the planet like a garden green house. It is the western pattern of development based on fossil fuel based industrialization that has been solely responsible for accumulation of CO_2 in the atmosphere. Industrialized countries owe their current prosperity to years of historical emissions, which have heaped up in the atmosphere since the very inception of industrial revolution, and also to a high level of current emissions. The use of these fossil fuels and hence carbon emissions are closely linked to economic growth and life style. Every human being contributes to the carbon dioxide concentration in the atmosphere, though the person's life style decides the amount that is emitted. The more prosperous a country's economy and higher its per capita income, the higher its fossil fuel consumption for power generation and transport, and the higher its GHG emissions. The following tables [111] shows a comparative statement of emissions of CO_2 to the atmosphere by both industrialized and the developing countries:

Percentage and distribution of net emissions of Green house gases (GHG) by industrialized and developing countries.

Country	*WRI formula*	*CSE calculation*
United States	17	27.4
Soviet Union and Eastern Europe	16	17.6
Western Europe	14.3	11.9
Japan	3.9	2.5
Other industrialized countries	1.4	7.5
India and China	10.3	0.6
Brazil	10.3	18.2
Other developing countries	26.7	14.3

The WRI report was widely quoted to point out that developed and developing countries have contributed almost equally to the global warming problem. On the contrary, WRI's own data and methodology showed, when reinterpreted by CSE that developing countries as a group contributed to only 33 per cent of the net emission in 1987. This was when the unused emissions of developing countries were traded with all countries including industrialized countries on an equal per capita basis. But when the unused emissions were traded only with other developing countries, which were emitting in excess, the industrialized countries' share increased to 91 per cent while that of the developing countries dropped to nine per cent.[112]

Comparative figures of total emissions of GHG s of WRI's top ten emitting nations as calculated by CSE (million tonnes of carbon equivalent)

Country	*Accumulation in the atmosphere*		*Absorbed by natural sinks*	
	WRI	*CSE*	*WRI*	*CSE*
US	1000	1532	1368	836
Soviet Union	690	730	882	842
West Germany	160	155	144	149
United Kingdom	150	132	160	178
Japan	220	140	202	281
France	120	69	121	173
Brazil	610	1017	826	418
China	380	32	793	1141
India	230	0.7	643	871
Indonesia	140	9.5	240	370

In an analogy to national financial debt, Kirk Smith calls these cumulative emissions the 'natural debt of a nation'. Just as the nations take on a financial debt over the years in order to grow faster, they also take on a natural debt for the same reason. In the latter case economics borrow the assimilative capacity of the environment by releasing waste gases faster than they can be removed naturally. His calculation shows that the developed countries are the holders of the largest natural debts. 260 t/capita for the US compared to six t/capita for India in 1990. The United States seems to be responsible for some thing like one-third of the global natural debt, mainly because of its heavy use of fossil fuels starting early in the century. If annual US per capita emissions were to remain at their present value 5.2 t/y and India's per capita emission 0.22 t/y were to continue, India would reach the level of one t/y in the year 2024-a level that was surpassed by the US well before 1900. During the 35 years between 1990 and 2024, the per capita Indian natural debt would have quadrupled six to 24 tons / capita in India while an America's per cent capita natural debt would have increased by 70 per cent.[113] From the standpoint of global warming, however the US would have added ten times as much debt... In terms of total atmospheric accumulation, India would be responsible for less than five per cent of that of the US.

The industrialized countries to show that not only the effects but also the causes belong to all have used science in the past. The methane gas emitted from paddy cultivation in South particularly in India and Thailand is highlighted to gloss over the historic responsibility that lies with the industrialized North to stop emitting CO_2 to the atmosphere right now, by making no distinction between the survival emission of the South and the luxury emission of the North.[114] In all international negotiations relating to climate change US insistence on meaningful participation of the South exposes American double standard and negation of equity while propounding this in dealing with the task of cleaning the atmosphere which the industrialized world in a sense colonized it to the peril of the South. Since emission of CO_2 to the atmosphere is closely related to economic development and life style, the high level accumulation of CO_2 by industrialized North suggests that it is the inordinate life style and consumption pattern of the North people and the continuing persistence of development paradigms based on fossil fuels in the North that has been responsible for global warming and its consequent effects on human life. Thus, the climate change negotiations have already been sucked into the deep-water politics of their respective national interest defined in terms of economic growth and consumptive life style. America's rejection of Kyoto protocol which it signed to reduce CO_2 to the agreed level, is on the same ground that reduction of its level of CO_2 would mean acceptance of a lower standard of living on the part of its citizens, and a challenge to its existing life pattern and above all winding up of some fossil fuel based industries which America is not prepared to do being influenced by the powerful coal automobile industrial lobby in US.[115]

There has been a welter of scientific uncertainty about positive and negative feedbacks that may accentuate or diminish human perturbations of the global heat balance. And also very little research has been conducted on the possible impacts of climate change on different countries and regions. However over the last few years, a consensus has developed among the experts: assuming no major changes in the trend of human emission of green house gases, We will likely see a global warming between one and three and one-half degrees Celsius by 2100, with a best estimate of two degrees warming.[116] This seems not to be a much of an increase to create panic in view of the fact that the earth has warmed only about five degrees since the coldest period of ice age, around 18, 000 years ago. But what is of concern to mankind is the predicted rate of warming which during the next hundred years will "probably be greater than any seen in the last 10000 years.[117] Already global mean surface air temperature has risen by 0.3 and 0.6 degrees celsius since the late nineteenth century, and the last decade has witnessed a number of the warmest years on record.[118] There is a growing consensus among the scientists about "a discernible human influence on global climate." [119]

According to the second report of the Intergovernmental Panel on Climate Change (IPCC), global mean surface air temperature (the Earth's surface temperature) has increased between 0.3-0.6° C. since the late 19th century. It estimates that global mean surface temperature would be about 2°C above pre industrial levels by the year 2030, and about 4°C above pre-industrial levels by 2090. Global sea level has risen by 10-25cm over the past 100 years. It is projected to rise between 9cm and 29cm by 2030 and 28cm and 96cm by 2090.[120]

The consequences of global warming according to this report are as follows: [121]

- ***Changes in weather patterns*** – more floods and droughts in some areas, and far reaching effects on agriculture and forestry.
- ***Scarcity of drinking water and sanitation***-millions would be affected.
- ***Food crisis*** – decline in food production in the tropics and subtropics, despite steady global production.
- ***Flooding***-rise in sea levels would submerge small island states and low-lying deltas, such as in Bangladesh, Egypt and China. Millions would be driven out of their houses as refugees.
- ***Deaths and diseases*** – heat stress and vector borne diseases would claim more lives as the tropical habitat of insects expands northwards.
- ***Loss of biodiversity*** – species adapted to cool climates would become extinct as habitats disappear and they are unable to migrate.

Ozone Layer Depletion

The ozone issue was first noticed worldwide in1985 when a British scientist reported that a hole in ozone layer had been occurring over Antarctica every spring since 1979. The scientists who then sprang into action confirmed that the ozone layer was being depleted far more rapidly than had been forecast and the cause of this being the presence of human made chemicals chloroflurocarbons (CFCs) in the upper reaches of the stratosphere. The ozone layer provides a fragile shield for the earth against harmful ultraviolet radiation (UV-B) from outer space. Ever since its discovery, this hole has been growing steadily. In the Antarctica spring of 1998, the ozone hole reached the largest ever covering an area of 2.6 billion hectares more than two and a half times the area of Europe, and even covered some populated areas of the Southern hemisphere. In 1999, the ozone hole had an average of 2.2 billion hectares, only slightly smaller, attributed rare to climatic changes than any significant reversal of the phenomena. While no hole has appeared elsewhere, the Arctic spring has seen the ozone layer over the North Pole thin by up to 30 per cent, while the depletion over Europe and other high latitudes varies between 5 per cent and 30 per cent.[122] Scientists have warned that if this hole is not sealed in the sky, it could lead to enormously increased penetration of ultraviolet rays which would increase skin cancers, cataracts and depress the human immune systems. Satellite observations show that since 1972, the amount of UV radiation has increased an average of 6.8 per cent per decade in the northern hemisphere and 9.9 per cent per decade in the South.[123] According to a study, on average a 1 per cent decrease in stratospheric ozone produces about 1.6 per cent increase in the incidence of carcinogenic UV radiation on the surface of the earth, which in turn produces about a 2.7 per cent increase in nonmelanoma skin cancer rates.[124] A ten per cent reduction in ozone is predicted to result in 24 per cent increase in incidence of non-melanoma skin cancer, a 30 per cent reduction will lead to a doubling and a 50 per cent reduction in quadrupling of such cases. Dramatic increases in all forms of skin cancer have been reported worldwide over recent decades but rates of non-melanoma skin cancers have increased so significantly that it has been labeled "a quiet 20th century epidemic." [125] What is of greater concern is the deleterious effects of increased UV radiation on crops, forests, amphibians, ocean phytoplankton and human and livestock health.[126]

The problems of rising cropland scarcity, tropical deforestation, growing fresh water scarcity and depletion of fish stocks when interact with the aforementioned effects of climate change, will very much threaten the well being of the many developing states. The global inequities in CFC use are enormous. The global consumption was and remains lopsided with the developed world in 1986 using more than 85 per cent of the total. The United States alone consumes roughly 30 per cent of the World CFC total followed by Japan and Europe. The developing countries' share is miniscule with India and China together consuming about 2 per cent.[127]

The Montreal ozone protocol signed in 1987 by the industrialized nations, instead of having set out a system in which a global common resource is shared and managed equitably, with equal rights for every citizen, the treaty operates within the context of existing inequities.[128] While this agreement suited the economic interests of the North, where the major producers of CFCs were based, it was unfair on the South because it froze existing and unequal consumption patterns. Its 1987 version therefore gave richer countries the right to pollute more. Even after this version was implemented, industrialized countries were allowed to have a higher per capita consumption of ozone depleting substances than developing countries. While all developing countries had to restrict their use to 0.3 kilogram per capita, the per capita consumption for US for instance was at 0.85kg per capita.[129] Its compliance mechanism is only effective against developing countries, which depend on the protocol for funds. It does not cover any industrialized country's commitments, and any efforts to hold industrialized countries responsible for their actions have failed.[130] This is a flaw that needs to be addressed in view of the damaging effects of ozone hole on human life.

In spite of a decline in production and consumption of CFCs because of the industrialized countries' abiding commitments to the treaty, the challenges remain. In the words of Topfer, contrary to popular impression, the protection of ozone layer is far from assured at present." [131] The Montreal Protocol envisages peak ozone depletion around 2000-2005 following, which a steady improvement culminates in full recovery around 2050. But a 1998 study by NASA scientists suggests that this production might have been too optimistic. According to NASA, the depletion of Arctic ozone will not peak until 2010-2019, between 10-20 years later than expected. It also warns of likely development of a severe Arctic ozone hole, tripling the levels of UV radiation hitting Northern countries perhaps due to the impact of global climate change on the ozone layer.[132]

Energy Consumption

During the past two decades, humankind's primary energy consumption has gone up steadily by 2 to 4 per cent a year. Today it stands at 8.8 billion metric tons of oil.[133] In many developed countries, per capita energy consumption is thirty or more times than in developing countries. Currently oil makes up 38 per cent of global commercial energy consumption; coal 30 per cent, natural gas 20 per cent, hydropower about 7 per cent; and nuclear power 5 per cent. As accessible and cheap petroleum reserves are depleted, this percentage will change. Around 60 per cent of the world's population depends on non-commercial sources of energy for cooking and heating such as fuel wood, twinges, branches and straw. These people mostly living in Africa, Indian subcontinents and China will face scarcity of these resources as the forests are getting degraded day by day, they have had to go miles daily for fetching these fuels.[134] As pointed out by Dixon, "the level of global energy consumption in coming decades will depend on a wide array of factors, including whether energy prices are adjusted to reflect the costs of pollution and global warming to our societies, whether new technologies allow more efficient production and use of energy, and whether international agreements are achieved to restrict releases of carbon dioxide." [135]

In 1993, the World Energy Council (WEC) published four scenarios for primary energy demand, each using different assumptions about economic growth, energy intensity of production, energy efficiency, technology transfer and institutional improvements. The predicted energy demand in 2020 for these scenarios ranges from 11.3 to 17.2 billion metric tons of oil equivalent.[136] A 1992 study by the MITRE Corporation suggests that global commercial energy demand in 2025 will be about 13 billion metric tons of oil equivalent, which is roughly in the middle of the WEC range. This study also estimates that oil shortage will begin around 2030 or sooner, because of the depletion of oil resources.[137] In 1995, the WEC and IIASA published a joint report that extended the time horizon of 1993 WEC estimates to 2050.They judged that world economic output would increase by 3-5 times by 2050 and that global demand for energy services could rise by as much as ten times. But because energy intensities will continue to decrease, primary energy requirements would rise by only one and a half to three times (to 14 to 25 billion metric tons of oil equivalent)[138]

What gets clear is the realization that energy security will not come with more drilling. According to one study, "one of the ironies at the turn of the century is that, in an age when the pace of technological change is almost overwhelming, the world will remain dependent, out to the 2020 at least, essentially on the same sources of energy-oil, natural gas, coal-that prevailed in the twentieth century." [139]

Recourse to nuclear energy appears not the viable alternative. Expansion of nuclear power is definitely not worth the high level waste it would generate. The Kyoto Protocol cannot be used to promote nuclear energy. Nuclear energy is not clean till a way is found to deal with nuclear waste.[140] Any strategy that seeks to obtain least cost carbon emission reduction options will inevitably focus on improving energy efficiency in the carbon energy sector. But will energy efficiency within the fossil fuel energy scenario help solve the global warming problem? Dennis Anderson, a senior adviser in the World Bank's industry and energy department, warns:

"It will not be possible to prevent the accumulation of carbon in the atmosphere unless non-carbon (or non-net carbon emitting) alternatives become available. Improving energy efficiency will help, and is important for economic as well as environmental reasons, but it will not prevent carbon accumulations from growing exponentially or indefinitely, so long as carbon emissions from the burning of fossils fuels exceed 2-3 billion tons per year-the current estimate of the 'natural' net rate of absorption of carbon by the earth's oceans and land masses. Presently, the rate of emissions is around 6 billion tons per year, and emissions are growing almost in direct proportion to world energy demand; it is conceivable that emissions will exceed 10 billion tons in 20 years, and 20 billion tons in 50 years-and this would be in an energy efficient world."[141]

If the world waits for a large part of its oil and coal resources to be exhausted before the shift to zero carbon energy transition occurs, which will not be before the 22nd century, then the certainty of serious climate change occurring becomes inordinately high almost definite. According to a major study by WEC and IIASA (International Institute for Applied Systems Analysis) the gross global carbon emissions from fossil fuel combustion could rise from 6.23 gtC in 1990 to anywhere between 5.93 gtC to 16.00 gtC in 2050 and per capita carbon emission from 1.18 tC in 1990 to anywhere between 0.59 tC to 1.59tC. Gross carbon emissions of OECD countries could rise from 3.03 gtC in 1990 to anywhere between 4.2 gtC to 9.02 gtC in 2050[142]. Despite focus on renewable sources of energy, the renewables are still unable to penetrate the market. For example, despite 30 years of public discussion and environmental support, renewable energy technologies have failed to emerge as a prominent component of the US energy infrastructure. The Natural Resources Defence Council, a prominent public interest group in US, said, the Bush-Cheney energy plan is the culmination of a process that hinged on cosy business connections, silent deals and oil and energy industry campaign contributions.[143] The biggest obstacles in the way of renewable technologies today are low fossil fuel prices and fossil fuel subsides in many countries; declining public sector research and development, and plummeting private sector research and development as the deregulation of energy markets increasingly focuses attention on short term returns.[144] In the absence of focusing on renewables as the primary objective of national energy policy by the developed world since they owe a historic responsibility of having wrought a drastic climate change in terms of global warming, sea level rise and other green house effects by emitting maximum amount of CO_2, the continuous focus on carbon based energy will further intensity the climate change with diabolic consequences on the developing world.

Population Growth

The above environmental scarcity of resources is not always the result of a natural process but often the result of an interaction with the population. Population size can be a key force driving supply-induced scarcity. In combination with prevailing social structure, technologies, and consumption patterns population growth makes environmental degradation and depletion worse.[145] Conflicting views on population and the environment exist. The Malthusian concept of population as a central factor can be considered. The left of the centre radicals stress on poverty, inequality and over consumption by the North, or technology as the causes of environmental degradation. The right wing radicals ensconce their faith in the unlimited capacity of human ingenuity to respond to the need of the free markets, which would enable it to resolve the problems of environmental decay. Whereas population explosion has not been a central concern in the North, it has become predominantly a central concern in the South.

More conveniently the North has been putting the blame far what they have wrought to the environmental on the South's population explosion in a bid to continue the perpetuation of their economic exploitation of the poor South. On the other hand, it is held that the environmental problems lay more with the high consumption levels in the developed countries than with the supposed population levels in the South. The ethnocentrism of Western paradigms of development based on fossil fuel based technology, and Western economic structure dominating the entire globe with the South occupying the periphery, have resulted in decimating the environment. The role of North in causing global warming and ozone layer depletion is indubious. South's imitating Western pattern of development and life style as a model of development, exploitations of the renewable resources for repayment of debts or to earn more foreign currencies redounded to the economic prosperity of the North at perils of nature.

The latest United Nations medium projections suggest the total human population will grow from the current 6.0 billion to about 8 billion in 2025 and 9.4 billion in 2050.[146] Although the rate of global population growth has dropped from 2.1 per cent to about 1.3 per cent over the last decades, the human population is still expanding by about 80 million a year. It is estimated that the growth will average about 80 million people a year during the entire four decades from 1980-2020. About 50 per cent of the anticipated growth in the developing world's population will result from the age structure of today's population, especially the large number of girls still to reach the reproductive age which guarantees a much larger population in developing world in future even if all these countries make the best use of the available family planning methods.[147] In such a situation where over 90 per cent of today's population growth is taking place in the developing world, the ratio of poor people to rich is rapidly growing. In 1950 the ratio was about two to one, today the ratio is about four to one and in 2025, it will be almost six to one.[148]

It is also held that the population issue is no longer a concern.[149] The inequal economic structure of the world presided over by the North and the inordinate life pattern and consumption of the industrialized World are often glossed over to magnify the population explosion in the South as the key cause of environmental degradation. As some views, the environmental problems lay more with high consumption levels in the developed countries than with the supposed population growth in the South.[150]

Due to population growth, the surplus populations in the South are migrating to cities to form slums and shanties raising the prospects of violence. Questions may be raised whether the highly populous states in South such as India, China, Pakistan, and Egypt have the required natural resources and economic capability to sustain their populations. As a result, these countries' population will perpetrate a huge toll of their natural environment.

Social Effects, Adaptative Failure and Ingenuity Gap

Environmental scarcity of renewable resources in its interaction with other factors can cause various social effects on the developing countries. According to various research studies there are five main identifiable social effects.[151]

- Decrease in agricultural production
- Economic decline
- Population Displacement or Migration
- Greater segmentation of society, usually along existing ethnic cleavages and divides
- Disruption of institutions, especially the state

These social effects often found interlinked have feedback relationships.

Decline in Agricultural Productivity

Food production is crucial to the livelihood of most of the people in developing countries. Any shortfall in food production is likely to affect theirs lives, as they spend half of their income on food. There is a causal connection between environmental degradation or scarcity of resources and agricultural output, as suggested by researchers. Effects of land degradation, water scarcity or degradation, deforestation and global warming on food production are obvious in many cases. Coastal cropland in countries such as Bangladesh and Egypt is vulnerable to storms and cyclones, because as predicted, global warming will cause sea level rise, and might intensify storms. The green house effects will also change precipitation patterns and soil moisture. Lower precipitation will most severely affect regions that already have degraded and eroded soils, because lost rooting depths makes plants vulnerable to droughts.[152] Laboratory experiments under ideal conditions hold out better prospects for increased crop yields, efficient use of water and larger and faster growing of plants in a warmer climate. But these studies have ignored the influence on yields of more frequent extreme climate change caused by global warming, increased pest infestations and the decreased nutritional quality of crops grown in a carbon enriched atmosphere.[153]

The impact of deforestation on food production is well known. Logging and clearing of lands accelerate soil erosion, change hydrological cycle, precipitation patterns, and decrease land's ability to retain water during rainy season. The flash floods resulting from this damage irrigation works fill the irrigation channels with silt and plug the reservoirs. Degradation and scarcities of cropland and water affect agricultural production to a significant extent.

It is statistically shown that during eighties world has witnessed an increase in food production due to introduction of green revolution, new technologies, intensive use of irrigation, chemical fertilizers and pesticides. But what is note worthy is that these statistics have hidden the wide disparties in food availability among and within developing countries, and ignored the socio-economic consequences of green revolution. At the end of 1980's, for example, twenty five poor countries could not provide sufficient food calories for the health, growth and productive work of their population.[154] Because of a combination of production and distributional problems, and disparties in access to natural resources, some 840 million people around the world-about 15 per cent of the world's population-currently suffer from chronic hunger.[155] Although both the percentage and absolute number of hungry people have slided globally in the last twenty years, Latin America, South Asia and especially Sub-Saharan Africa have not shown improvement in these statistics. Around the world, 34 per cent of the world's children are malnourished, about eleven thousand die everyday from malnutrition or related problems; and tens of millions of children suffer from sickness or learning disabilities because of deficiencies of micronutrients like iron, vitamin A and iodine.[156]

Technological ingenuities such as the green revolution to meet the problems of growing population and food scarcities have not proved to be panaceas. For example, green revolution introduced into two states of India, Haryana and Punjab by the scientific community in the 1960s raised in the beginning hope of rise in food production, through whether it was irrigation, energy, chemical fertilizers or pesticides. For decades down, the line more has brought in more problems. Lost of production has spiralled, but the rate of increase in production has not shown a similar trend. Heavy withdrawal of nutrients from soils through intensive cropping patterns has brought down the levels of micronutrients to a point of deficiency. The cost of production has disregarded the ecological and social cost.[157] Thus, the green revolution has turned a nightmare. The regional scarcities of land and water will be having serious effects on food production in developing countries as these countries' food demands grow up and as they reach the limits of potential gains from green revolution. As projected, increased per capita consumption of grain combined with population growth will increase annual consumption of grain of developing countries from 875 million metric tons in the 1980's to 2.35 billion metric tons by 2030, world consumption will rise from 1.68 billion tons to 3.3 billion tons.[158]

To meet the food demands of the growing population in the face of environmental scarcity of land and water what is needed is to increase food production, which is to come from higher yields. By 2030, grain yields in developing countries will need to average nearly 7 metric tons per hectare. Yet the current world average is only 2.8 tons.[159] and many farmers in countries like India and Pakistan do not reach half this average.

According to a study, "many regions will experience virtually no improvement in food security", although the aggregate global supply and demand picture is relatively good. This study further shows that, "there will be very little reduction in the number of malnourished children" in the developing world as a whole; the number will actually increase in sub-Saharan Africa and parts of South Asia.[160]

As figured out by Homer Dixon, the possible effects of environmental change on agricultural productivity can be studied.[161]

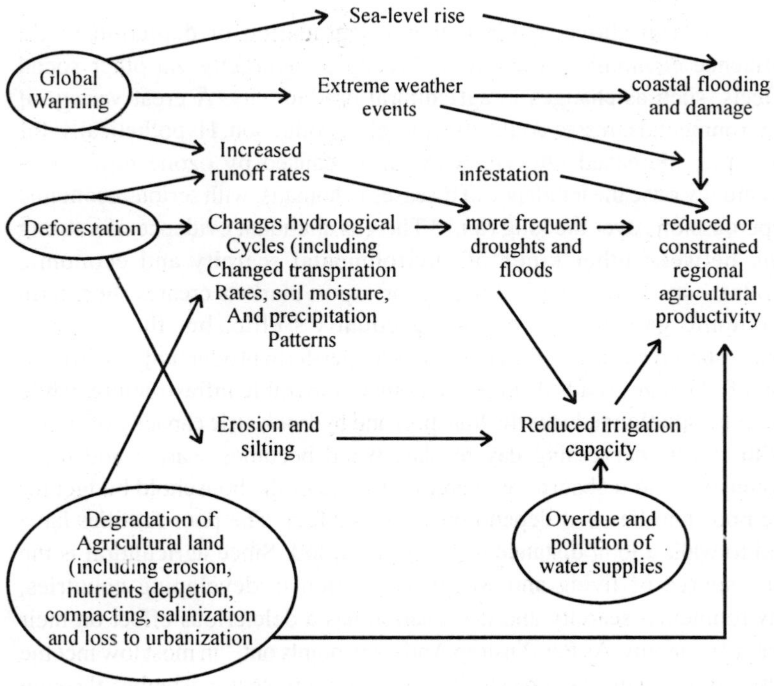

Possible Effects of Environmental Change on Agricultural Productivity

Economic Decline

According to Volker Boge, economic decline may take the following forms due to overuse, and pollution or destruction of renewable resources.[162]

- Decrease in agricultural production
- Insufficient supplies of basic goods (e.g. fuel wood) for the population
- Problems regarding industrial production, transportation systems, traffic etc
- Decline of production for the world market and associated effects
- Production of industrial toxic waste, and waste in general
- Industrial accidents/ catastrophes and their economic repercussions
- Large negative effects on human health

As seen above, environmental degradation or depletion might influence economic productivity directly or indirectly via other social effects, such as changes in agricultural productivity. A great variety of environmental stresses could affect wealth production. Hypothetically, for example, increased ultraviolet radiation caused by ozone hole could eventually raise the incidence of diseases in humans, with serious economic repercussions over the long run.[163] There is abundant evidence of a strong link between other kinds of environmental scarcity and economic productivity. For example, logging for export markets creates short-term economic gain for the exporting country's elite, but the resulting deforestation can affect the economy's longer-term productivity. Increased run off damages roads, bridges and other vulnerable infrastructure, while the extra siltation reduces the transport and hydroelectric capacity of rivers. With forests decreasing day by day, wood becomes scarcer and more expensive, and it absorbs an increasing share of the household budget for the poor families that depend on wood for fuel. The poor families have had to walk a long distance to fetch fuel wood. Since agricultural is the only source of living and wealth generation in developing countries, environmental scarcity and degradation has a deleterious effect on their overall economy. As Per Pinstrap Anderson points out, "in most low income developing countries, growth in the agriculture sector whether through food or non food agricultural commodities, is the most effective and often the only viable lead approach to sustainable economic growth and poverty alleviation." [164] Some experts predict that the economic relief brought by the green revolution within many poor countries will be short lived. Jeffrey Leonard notes: "Millions of previously poor families that have experienced less than one generation of increasing wealth due to rising agricultural productivity could see that trend reversed if environmental degradation is not checked." [165]

Robert Repetto of the World Resources Institute noted in regard to the impact of environmental degradation of land on economy: "With erosion, farm output and income have fallen in some regions without major changes in farm practices; other farmers have been induced to change cropping patterns and input use; and in extreme cases, erosion has led to the complete withdrawal of land from cultivation." [166] According to his estimate, erosion in upland Indonesia annually cost the country's agricultural economy nearly half a billion dollars in discounted future income.[167] Gaza offers a particularly stark example of the impact of supply induced scarcities of fresh water on agricultural productivity, on health and, ultimately, on economic development.[168] To buttress his point, Homer

Dixon has quoted the Chinese researcheres study of the combined effects of supply induced environmental scarcity on China's economic output.[169]

Migration

One of the consequences of the interaction of the sources of environmental scarcity of resources is the migration of the people from one region to another region within a state or from one state to another as environmental refugees with destabilizing effects on both domestic order and international security.[170]

In 1985 the United Nations Environment Programme introduced the concept of environmental refugees. They were defined as those people who have been forced to leave their traditional habitat temporarily or permanently because of marked environmental disruption. This is due to reason both natural and anthropogenic that jeopardized their existence and/or seriously affected the quality of their life.[171] So it is ascertained that environmental degradation has been a major and predominant cause of flight or migration of people both intra and interstate. Among a complex web of factors responsible for migration, environmental degradation may act as a precipitating event that "disrupts the normal functioning of the system and thus destroys the capacity of a population to survive under the prevailing conditions." [172] Environmental degradation in the natural processes by human activities in the face of what Giddens calls the" high consequences of modernity", [173] may collapse the very social systems, which provide people with an ongoing sense of ontological security. Not only environmental scarcity of resources but their consequences in the form of global warming, greenhouse effect, sea level rise, flood, cyclone, storm and droughts have impelled the people to migrate as refugees." [174]

While explaining the distinction between migrants and refugees many experts emphasize the importance of both push and pull factors in the decisions of potential flight of people. Push factors are defined as characteristics of the current place of residence, such as low economic development that encourages people to leave. Pull factors are characteristics of a potential home that attracts people to go there. While drawing the line between refugees and migrants, the experts say, refugees are motivated mainly by push factors, migrants are motivated by a combination of both push and pull factors. According to Astri Suhrke, the environmental problems are more likely to produce migrants than refugees, because such problems usually develop gradually, which means that the push effect is not sharp and sudden and that pull factors can therefore clearly enter into potential migrants' calculation.[175]

While doubting the push/pull distinction as a helpful analytical tool, Homer Dixon instead notes that, "the real motivator of migration is the gap between the potential migrants' current level of satisfaction and the level they expect to attain in a new land. The larger the gap, the greater is the incentive to migrate. And this gap is not determined by an additive function of push and pull factors but by the relationship between the perceived quality of life in the home region and that in the receiving region."[176]

The Bangladesh – Northeast India region is a good illustration of land scarcity having caused millions of people to move from Bangladesh to the Indian states of Assam, Tripura, West Bengal and Orissa and other metropolitan cities. According to estimates, migrants from Bangladesh have expanded the population of neighbouring areas of India by 12 to 17 milllion.[177]

Domestic Cleavages and Social Segmentation

Economic decline and population movement induced by the environmental scarcity of resources can create many fissures and cleavages in the political and social structure of the states. Severe environmental scarcity can aggravate divisions or segmentation among ethnic, religious, and linguistic groups.[178] Homer Dixon has cited the example of South Africa to explain how environmental scarcity can create division and segmentation within a society. According to him, "scarcity sharpens distinction between winners and losers-between groups that profit from scarcity and those that are hurt. It encourages competitions among groups for control of resources critical to survival and prosperity, and it encourages resource-dependent groups to turn inward and to focus on narrow survival strategies.'[179] This insularity reduces interactions among these groups and between them and the state. Apartheid in South Africa concentrated millions of blacks in some of the country's least productive and most ecologically sensitive territories where population densities were further increased by high natural birth rates. These black populations in these homelands were forced to subsist on local cropland, water and fuel wood. Lack of resource management skill, high population growth and low capital investment further eroded the available resource base. The corrupt local elites captured the best local resources throwing the weaker groups to the most ecologically sensitive parts of the homelands. As a result, wide areas of these territories were completely stripped of trees for fuel wood, grazed down to bare dirt and eroded of topsoil. A 1980 report concluded that rarely 50 per cent of Ciske's land was moderately or severely eroded, and nearly 40 per cent of its pasturage was over grazed.[180] With the tumbling down of apartheid's strict urban migration laws, environmental scarcity in the homelands contributed to an annual migration of up to 750, 000 blacks to the country's urban areas.[181] Severe population pressures in these areas damaged and depleted local streams, community cropland and fuel wood stocks. The concentration of many people on a degraded resource base in the context of weak local governments, again caused resource capture: powerful warlords secured community support in part by controlling basic environmental resources, such as land and water through their own paramilitary forces.[182]

Division and segmentation took place among the ethnic groups, among family based clans, and among residents of township, informal settlements, and work hostels as communities withdrew into themselves to protect access to these resources. As resources were degraded within their territories, warlords often tried to maintain power by pointing to resources in neighbouring townships and informal settlements and mobilizing their communities to seize them. This mobilization often set in motion a cycle of appalling violence among African communities. "Squatters are mobilized to fight for access to resources in neighbouring townships, and township youth organize military style units to defend their areas and counter attacks squatter areas." [183] These processes exacerbated inter group segmentation, broke down social networks and weakened community norms resulting in a loss of the society's social capital.

Similarly in Bangladesh, land scarcity caused population growth and environmental degradation and its consequences in the form of flood, cyclone and storms resulted in settlement of Bangladeshis in Chittagong Hill Tracts. This brought Chakmas the original inhabitants of CHT into direct conflict with Bangladeshis, as the demands on the resource base increased [184] and the Bangladeshis occupied the traditional resource base of the Chakmas forcing them to environmentally marginalised slope hill areas.

Disrupted Institutions and Growing Weakening of the State

The social effects described above are likely to tear the fabric of legitimized, accepted and authoritative institutions that guide and pattern social behaviour.[185] Homer Dixon and his group have identified the links between rising environmental scarcity and declining state capacity.

First, environmental scarcities increase financial and political demands on the state. For example, as they have cited China, Pakistan, SouthAfrica and Philippines, environmental scarcities put pressure on the countries to meet the needs of the expanding marginal people. The Chinese government must spend huge sums on new infrastructure such as wells, dams, canals, pipelines and irrigation system.[186] The study of the impact of environmental scarcities on state capability in these states shows that" environmental scarcities expand marginal groups that need help from government by constraining rural economic development and by encouraging people to move into cities where they demand food, shelter, transport, energy, and job."[187] As J.D. Kasarda and A.M.Parnell note rapid population growth in cities contribute to "high rates of unemployment and under employment, ... soaring urban poverty, insufficient shelter, inadequate sanitation, inadequate or contaminated water supplies, serious air pollution and other forms of environmental degradation, congested streets, overloaded public transportation systems, and municipal budget crises."[188] In response, the subsidies of urban services introduced by governments eat away their revenues causing misallocation and distortion of prices and capital. Second, resource scarcities affect the state via their effects on elites. On one hand, scarcities threaten the incomes of elites that depend on resource extraction. They often compete among themselves for cornerning the shrinking resource rents, and try to obstruct any institutional reforms that would distribute more fairly the costs of rising scarcity. As seen in China, water scarcities have engendered sharp divisions between Beijing and the provinces and among the provinces themselves.[189] Philip Shenon of the New York Times notes that critical land scarcities have emboldened these powerful groups to ignore the instructions of the state. According to him, "huge profits from land sales... tend to overwhelm any fear of the central government. With the prospect of millions of dollars in profits on even a small plot of land, developers and corrupt officials are often willing to take the risk of ignoring instructions from Beijing."[190] They often lobby to change the property rights and other laws governing the use of scarce resources such as water, land and forests. In many societies these rent seeking elites influence the state through bribery, kickbacks and other forms of corruption.[191]

Third, in such a situation of resource scarcity, and the elites trying to corner the resource pie, struggle for resource control takes place between the powerful elite group and the weak groups. This infighting and struggle for shrinking resources worsens social segmentation, and weaknes the cohesive fabric of civil societies. State's failure to meet the needs of the marginal people weakens its legitimacy. Fourth and finally, if resource scarcity affects the economy's general productivity, tax revenues to local and national governments can decline. Such a revenue decline hurts elites that benefit from state largesse and reduces the state's capacity to meet the increasing demands of the people arising from environmental scarcity. Charles Barber shows that the proliferations of local conflicts over forests depress the legitimacy, coherence and reach of the Indonesian state at the local level.[192]

Lack of Ingenuity Supply and Adaptive Failure

According to Homer Dixon and his group, the environmental scarcity of resources and its various social effects can make the developing societies vulnerable to the extent that they would not be able to adapt to the situation and find out solutions as they are plagued by lack of supply of ingenuity. What adds to their disadvantage is the very fact that many of them are not adequately endowed with the social institutions including the productive research centers, efficient markets and capable states which are necessary for an ample supply of both social and technical solution to environmental scarcity. As argued by this group, environmental scarcity sometimes diminishes these countries' ability to create and maintain such institutions.[193] But the proponents of new economic growth theory or endogenous growth theory, overlooking the fact that environmental scarcity can stymie the supply of ingenuity, argue that ideas are a factor of economic production in addition to capital, labour, and land.[194] In their views scarcities will boost the supply of ingenuity. In other words necessity will often be the mother of invention. This will help alleviate scarcity's severity and social impacts. These economists focus mainly on ideas embodied in new technologies. Homer Dixon's concept of supply of ingenuity is not confined to mere technological and scientific innovations. That environmental scarcity and its social impacts need only the attention of scientists and engineers has been reviewed. According to Homer Dixon, "the supply of this technical ingenuity depends on an adequate supply of social ingenuity at many levels of soviety. Social ingenuity is key to the creation, reform and maintenance of public and semipublic goods such as markets, funding agencies, educational and research organizations, and effective government." [195] Social ingenuity is thus a precursor to technical ingenuity and key to adaptation strategies. Countries afflicted by environmental scarcity of resources need sophisticated and stable systems of markets, legal regimes, financial agencies, and educational and research institutions to promote the development and distribution of new grains adapted for dry climate and eroded soils, of alternative cooking technologies to compensate for the loss of firewood and of water conservation technologies. In the words of Dixon, "it is both an input to and output of the economic system." [196] It is not that the ingenuity required to adapt to the crisis created by environmental scarcity is produced always at the top of the social hierarchy, it is also produced at the community and household levels.

Burgeoning population growth and increasing per capita resource consumption are causing a steady increase in the ratio of the consumption of resource per unit of time to the total amount of resource available. Thus, the scarcity has in turn increased the requirement for ingenuity. The increased pace of resource depletion means that societies have less time to adjust their institutions and technologies. Since human beings are consuming a very broad spectrum of renewable resources at very high rates, serious scarcities can affect many resources simultaneously or in quick succession. This multiplicity of scarcities can make it harder to find relatively abundant resources to substitute for scarce ones. Further, the ingenuity requirement to compensate for scarcities of renewable is generally greater than that of non-renewables. The economists have ignored the difference between the two. These can be no substitute for renewables. For example, nothing can substitute for water in the tissues of a living organism. Thus, the options for responding to scarcity of renewables are restricted, and society's need for ingenuity rises. Even if the requisite is supplied, the systems will still be vulnerable to sudden shocks, because many environmental scarcities are interconnected and unpredictable. Further more, even if societies manage their resource systems exceptionally well, fundamental physical, biological, and social constraints may make it difficult to fully compensate for the effects of scarcity. These constraints include inescapable time lags that affect a society's ability to mitigate scarcities, like the time needed for a new forest to grow, for a new technology to be disseminated, or for cultural change to take place.[197]

Constraints on Supply of Ingenuity

But optimists like Aaron Wildavsky, Todd La Porte, Dennis Avery, and Thomas Schelling ensconce faith in the ingenuity and resourcefulness of man to find solution to the crisis. Julian Simon has abiding faith in the resourcefulness and capability of human beings to respond to the scarcity of resources and the concomitant consequences with new ingenuity that will keep him invulnerable to the crisis and leave them better off [198] Homer Dixon does not harbour a slightest doubt of the extraordinary potential of human resourcefulness and enterprise, but nonetheless argue that some poor developing societies will not be able to supply the unprecedented amounts of ingenuity required to solve the impending environmental scarcity. He has identified four factors that can limit the supply of social and technical ingenuity: market failure, social friction, shortage of capital, and constraints on science.[199]

Market Failure

Many resources especially renewable like hydrological cycles and productive seas cannot be physically controlled or divided into salable units for the exclusive use of specific consumers. It is therefore hard to assign clear property rights, and they remain open access resources that are vulnerable to over exploitation. As Repetto notes, "Prices can guide market adjustment processes only if resources can be brought and sold which presupposes that they can be owned. Many important resources are not privately owned, usually because it is impossible to segregate one person's portion from another's and reserve it for exclusive use." [200] At best their scarcity is indirectly reflected in the prices of marketable resources that are dependent on them. For example, damage to ocean ecosystems can cause fish prices to rise.

Even if property rights are clear, market prices may still not fully reflect the costs of resource use. Resource extraction or use can produce negative externalities-such as river siltation from upstream deforestation-that is not incorporated in the resources price. The World Bank notes that "clear property rights may induce private users to adopt the correct pattern of timber extraction, taking into consideration the current and future benefits from logging, but give no incentive to take into account the costs of deforestation to those living outside the forests-for example, increased soil erosion or lost biodiversity." [201] Poor countries are particularly disadvantaged because they start with underdeveloped economic institutions. The state which is to play a key role in increasing ingenuity supply through research, development, and extension services is very much stymied in developing societies because of economic and other constraints.

Social Friction

As analyzed above, environmental scarcity of resources produces frictions, cleavages and social segmentation among various groups. Mancur Olson's work [202] is cited by Dixon to understand his analysis. First, Olson shows that small coalitions can generally organize themselves more quickly and purse their interests with greater force than larger groups. They therefore have political power disproportionate to their size, and they can be more nimble, focused and effective in their lobbying. Second, this proportionate power will be particularly acute in unstable societies, because large coalitions need time and social stability to establish them and grow. The governments of unstable countries are therefore "systematically influenced by the interests, pleas and pressure" of small coalitions.[203] Third, small coalitions are always guided by their narrowly defined self-interests in total disregard of the common well being. Olson writes, there is "no constraint on the social cost such an organization will find it expedient to impose on the society in the course of obtaining a larger share of the social output for itself." [204]

It has been pointed out earlier that increased environmental scarcity of resources exacerbated social segmentation, sharpens cleavages among groups, and provokes action by group to protect their interests in terms of resource capture and rent seeking. Building on Olson's argument, Homer Dixon points out that the smaller groups purse their interests better than larger ones in developing countries, because their possession of wealth, power and status well informed by their position in the social order had made this minority well advantaged while pursing their narrow self interests, the small coalitions often impede the process of institutional building that reflect the broader interest of society. They hamstring all efforts to reform existing or establish new social institutions, laws and structural arrangements, if these effects run counter to coalitions interests, as they often do.[205] This social friction arising out of environmental scarcity makes it harder to focus and coordinate social activities, talents, and resource in response to scarcity. As Olson points out, narrow coalitions "interfere with an economy's capacity to adapt to change and to generate new innovations." [206] Thus, the coalitions provoked to action by scarcities will sometimes block solutions to the very same scarcities. Increasing social friction affects incentives for political entrepreneurs to produce and deliver the social ingenuity needed for new institutions, Ruttan and Hayani opine that "the supply of institutional innovations depends critically on the power structure or balance among vested interest groups in the society." [207] As seen, scarcities of cropland and water in Bangladesh – scarcities arising from both skewed resource distribution and populations growth – induce some agricultural innovation, but they also inflame existing distribution struggles among coalitions. These struggles in turn have obstructed reform of water control institutions and the deployment of irrigation technologies.[208] A society that is very much informed by a culture of selfishness will soon slip into narrow coalitions as scarcity worsens. For example, Filipino culture encourages cooperation within groups rather than among groups resulting in what is often remarked, clannishness of the society and undermining the concept of national welfare.[209] To the contrary, a society where there is prevalence of culture of good will, reciprocity, civic mindedness, and trust can impede the rise of narrow coalitions as scarcity worsens.

Thus, Homer Dixon cited these two contextual factors, which will especially influence the degree of social friction caused by environmental scarcity and the extent to which this friction hamstrings the supply of ingenuity. In his words, "if narrow coalitions have already penetrated the state, social friction will have a particularly strong effect on society's capacity to reform and build institutions." [210]

Capital Availability

Capital both financial and human is necessary to respond to the environmental scarcity of resources. Availability of capital is generally lower in developing societies. To undertake any scientific and technological research in response to scarcity needs huge finance. Political entrepreneurs need financial capital to provide selective incentives and side payments to coalitions that block institutional change. The state needs capital to provide public goods like infrastructure and resource monitoring. Many societies afflicted by severe resource scarcity are poor; moreover, the often-predatory behaviour of their elites further reduces general capital availability.[211] Dearth of adequate and required laboratory equipments, computers, journals and books impedes the efforts to build indigenous research capability in developing societies.[212] In addition to shortage of finance, lack of human capital also cripples the supply of ingenuity. For example, the United Nations reports that by 1987 nearly a third of Africa's skilled labour had left for Europe and that the continents as a whole lost sixty thousand middle and high-level managers between 1985 and 1990.[213]

Constraints on Science

As said above, the economic and technological optimists exude faith in human kind's ability to manage the resource scarcity. Homer Dixon outlines four constraints on science that will hinder ingenuity's supply.[214] First are human cognitive limits. Humans do not have the infinite ability to understand and manage the complex, multivariate, nonlinear and often chaotic processes of ecological –social systems. The relationship in some of these systems are" simply too numerous and complex to be grasped, much less controlled, by the human intellect." [215] Many natural, social systems are probably computationally intractable, which means they cannot be accurately modelled using any realistic amount of computational power.[216] Scientists are additionally handicapped because they cannot conduct controlled experiments with large-scale natural and social systems.

The cognitive features of human brain evolved in ecological circumstances restrict human ability to supply ingenuity. Second is the escalating cost of research in the field of science and technology. To probe deeper into the labyrinthine nature has become a very costly affair. The poor societies plagued by resource scarcity need the help of advanced science like molecular biology, which they cannot afford, especially when faced with resource crunch. A third constraint arises from the cumulative nature of scientific knowledge: each new discovery must build on a host of earlier ones. "The pace of discovery is marked by jumps and lags as scientists make breakthroughs or lose time pursing fruitless leads. This pace cannot be easily forced, especially in basic science where the work's ultimate practical use is not clear." [217]

A final constraint is science's vulnerability to social control. It needs a great variety and abundance of resource inputs, a non-hierarchical institutional structure, a dense network of connections between like-minded innovators, and a popular culture for promotion of science. For example, the development in former Soviet Union in 1990s crippled its vast research establishments and led to the rise in occult and anti science movements causing a decline in respect for analytical thought.[218]

Violent Environmental Conflict

The environmental scarcity of resources and its main negative social effects contribute to violent conflict. If there is a decline in agricultural productivity, decline in economic well-being, poverty stalks their way of life in developing societies, if a large number of people move from their homelands, if societies segment and fractured and institution disrupted and state weakened, what types of conflict are likely to occur? A host of theories on the nature and types of conflict can be dependent upon to answer this question. Three sets of theories in particular are key: one each at the individual, group, and systemic level of analysis.

Based on the study of individual psychological behaviour, frustration-aggression theories are generally used to explain civil strife, revolution, insurgencies, strikes, riots and coups. These theories propound that people get aggressive when they feel frustrated at not getting their things or wishes fulfilled or being hindered by some one from fulfilling a strong desire. An important subset of these theories suggests that this frustration and aggression can be caused by relative deprivation, which means that when people perceive a widening gap between the level of satisfaction they have achieved and the level they believe they deserve. Deprivation is therefore relative to some subjective judgement of equity or fairness, and the size of the perceived gap obviously depends on the beliefs about economic justice held by individuals.[219]

Using social psychological theories of group behaviour, group-identity theories explain inter group conflicts on the basis of nationalism, ethnicity, and religions. These theories explain on what basis the individual members identify themselves with a group ultimately to be bound by itself distinguishing it from other groups and resulting in a 'we vs. they' syndrome. Identifying with a group bestows on them a psychological sense of camaraderie or 'we ness', which is reinforced and satisfied in a group when it is directed against and attacks another group. Similarly a person's sense of self worth may be strengthened when his or her group's status is enhanced in relation to that of other groups. By attacking or denigrating outside or the other groups the leaders of a group exploit the psychological need of its members for feeling of 'we ness', to enhance their political power and pelf within their own groups.[220] Structural theories premised on the assumption of microeconomics and game theory, explain conflicts arising from the rational calculations of actors in the face of perceived external constraints. The structure of an actor's social situation is the perceived set of possible interactions with other actors and the perceived likely outcomes of these interactions. This structure is determined by physical factors such as the number of actors in the system, resource limits, and barriers to movement or communication; by social factors such as shared beliefs and understandings, rules of social interactions, and the set of power relations among actors in the system; and by psychological factors, in particular, the beliefs and preferences of other actors.[221] As Wendt notes, the view of structure as constraint is only one of three possible positions on the issue. Structure can also be thought of as generating the actors rather than constraining them, or structure and actor can be seen as dialectically related-that is, generating but not reducible to each other as Gidden suggests.[222]

Divided into two parts general and civic strife – the general structural theories are often applied to inter state war. These theories suggest that external constraints such as power imbalances in the international system can encourage or compel countries to go to war. Scholars who emphasize such constraints usually also acknowledge the causal importance of internal factors, such as the actor's particular interests and beliefs. By stressing power relations almost exclusively perhaps Waltz comes closest to presenting a purely structural theory of international behaviour and war. De Mesquita contends that the geographic proximity of actors is an important structural determinant of international conflict; where as Choucri and North emphasizes differences in states' resource endowments.[223] Structural theories of civic strife suggest that revolution, insurgency, rioting, and coups de'tat are a function of the opportunity structure that confronts groups challenging the authority of the state. In the words of Homer Dixon, "serious civil strife is not likely unless the structure of political opportunities facing challenger groups keeps them from expressing their grievances effectively and peacefully, but offers them openings for violence against authority." [224] This opportunity structure depends on the relative power and resource of challenger groups or the state, on the power of groups that might ally themselves with challenger groups or the state, and on the costs and benefits that groups believe they will accrue through different kinds of collective action in support of or in opposition to the state.[225] On the basis of these theories, Homer Dixon and his group have identified three main kinds of conflict that might arise from environmental scarcity: simple scarcity conflicts, group identity conflicts, and insurgencies.

Simple Scarcity Conflict

Here the use of the adjective 'simple' does not mean 'unimportant'. It distinguishes this type of conflict from others that involve psychological and social processes more complex than those posited by rational – choice theorists. Volker Boge terms these conflicts in a narrower sense that emanates directly from the overuse and/ or pollution/destruction of a renewable natural resource.[226] For example: If a downstream riparian threatens to go to war against an upstream riparian, because the latter pollutes river water so gravely that it cannot be used by the inhabitants of the downstream riparian, who are highly dependent on this water, then the 'environmental' character of conflict is evident. Four environmental resources such as agriculturally productive land, forests, river water and fish would appear to ignite simple-scarcity conflict. Evidences can be culled from history showing the number of wars among or between nations over non-renewable resources. For instance, prior to and during Second World War, Japan was bent on securing coal, oil, minerals, and other resources in China and South East Asia. Hitler's forces before capturing Caucasian oil fields were stopped at Stalingrad in 1942. The Gulf wars in 1991 and in 2003 launched by the U.S. and its allied forces against Iraq were at least partly motivated by the desire for oil.[227] The lateral pressure theory as argued by Nazli Chourci and Robert North suggests that countries facing high resource demands and limited resource availability within their territories would seek the needed resources through trade or conquest beyond their boundaries.[228] It has been the conventional wisdom based on the realist paradigm of international relations theory, that critical scarcities of natural resources can cause war. Realism focuses on states as rational maximizers of power in an anarchic international system. State behaviour including conflictual behaviour is mainly a function of the structure of power relations among states in the system, not of events or pressures operating inside these states. Because environmental scarcity's most important social effects unfold inside countries, realism therefore encourages scholars to ignore or downplay the consequences of environmental problems for peace and conflict. If these scholars do consider environmental problems, they focus disproportionately on simple scarcity conflicts among states over strategic environmental resources such as water.[229]

While accounting for causes of international conflicts, these scholars have not been able to distinguish between the scarcities of renewable and non-renewable resources. They have overlooked two reasons why modern states do not generally fight over renewable resources. If power is understood in a dispositional sense, then renewable resources such as cropland, forests and fish seized from a state cannot be easily translated into power. These resources may eventually generate wealth that can be harnessed by the state for its own ends; this outcome is uncertain and remote in time. In contrast, states can quickly use non-renewable like oil and iron to build and fuel the military machines of national aggression. The more easily fungibility of non renewable resources into state power than the renewables in a political and economic order based on fossil fuel industrialization and militarization, has enhanced the chances of interstate wars over the non-renewable resources. That does not in any way denude the renewable resources of their potential to state power and for violent conflict among nations. In the seventeenth through nineteenth centuries, for example, shortage of timber for naval ships contributed to serious, and sometimes violent conflict among European powers.[230]

The second reason is that the countries with agrarian economies highly dependent on renewables tend to be poor and poor countries cannot easily buy large and sophisticated weapons to attack their neighbours.

According to Homer Dixon, "for these reasons, both the incentives and the means to launch resource wars are likely to be lower for renewables than for non-renewables." [231]

The exception is water particularly river water. Water is a critical resource for personal and national survival. It is essential to the production and use of military power, and rich countries are as dependent on water as poor countries.[232] About 40 per cent of the world's population lives in the 220 river basins shared by more than one country. At a meeting in Stockholm in August, 1995 Ismail Serageldin, the World Bank's Vice President for Environmentally Sustainable Development, declared that the 'wars of the next century will be over water not oil.[233] The same words were echoed by Wally N Dow, Secretary General of the United Nations Conference on Human Settlements, held in 1996 in Istanbul when he stated: "I suspect that in the next 50 years, we will see a shift from oil to water as the cause of great conflicts between nations and people".[234] In a similar vein, Peter Gleick stated: "As we move into the twenty first century, water and water supply systems are increasingly likely to be both instruments of political conflict and the objectives of military action as human populations grow, standards of living improve, and global climate changes make water supply and demand more problematic and uncertain." [235] The likelihood of water being the object of military or political actions depend on the degree of water scarcity; the extent to which the supply is shared by two or more groups; the relative power of these groups; and the ease of access to alternative sources.

Water is unevenly distributed throughout the world. Some regions receive enormous amounts of rainfall or river flow, while others are extremely dry and suffer from absolute scarcity. Human factors, such as high population densities or intensive industrial development, may cause conditions of relative scarcity. In the past, absolute scarcity was a more important factor in regional water issue. Increasingly, however, relative scarcity is the problem leading to water disputes, as population pressures come up against resource limits.[236] Water has been used as a military and political goal not only in the past but also in the modern era. The Jordan River Basin has been the scene of a wide variety of water disputes among Israel, Syria, Egypt and Lebanon. The Jordan River is formed by the convergence of three tributaries-the Hasbani, Dan, and Banjas that rise in Lebanon, Israel, and Syria respectively. The three meet in Israel territory and flow southward into the Sea of Galilee (Lake Tiberias) and then into the Lower Jordan River. The Yarmouk tributary, which rises in Syria forming boundary between Syria and Jordan, and then between Jordan and Israel, enters the Lower Jordan a few kilometers South of Lake Tiberias. The lower Jordan, which flows into the Dead Sea, forms the boundary between Israel and Jordan for some of its distance. In the late 1950s when Israeli government began work on its National Water Carrier to take fresh water from Lake Tiberias and transport it Southward, outside the Jordan basin and throughout Israel, and announced to complete its first phase by 1964, the Arab countries strongly protested as violation of their security.[237] In response to Israel's diversion plan, the Arab League adopted a proposal to divert the Hasbani River into Lebanon, channel its surplus waters to the Banias in Syria, and divert the surplus waters of the Banias to the Yarmouk for the benefit of Jordan. In 1964, within weeks of the work on the Arab diversion project, a series of military responses to river water projects involving Israel, Syria, Jordan and Egypt took place. It became a cardinal political issue of interstate relations in the Middle East. Israeli's Premier Levi Eshkol stated that "water is a question of life for Israel," hence any attempt to prevent Israel from using a portion of the Jordan waters would be considered a violation of its right to exist. He warned the Arabs that "Israel would act to ensure that the waters continue to flow" into its territory.[238] Border clashes, and arms race between Israel and its Arab neighbours continued throughout 1966 till all these resulted in Arab-Israeli war of 1967. The Jordan water crisis of 1964 and Arab-Israeli war of 1967 were two distinct crises in a protracted conflict. In the analysis of Lowi, in the years leading up to war, water related issues-specially, the depletion, degradation or altered allocation of water resources, or the threat there of – were definitely part of the larger picture "forming" part of the package of issues that established conditions that made war likely." [239] The 1967 war in the Middle East resulted in Israel winning control of all the headwaters of the Jordan as the ground water of the West Bank. Water remains an important factor in the politics of the region. The multilateral and bilateral peace talks conducted in the 1990s, which led to the interim agreement between the Israelis and the Palestinians and to the Peace Treaty between Israel and Jordan explicitly included negotiations and agreements on the shared water resources of the Jordan River. Israeli and Syrian concerns over the Banias, which originates in the Golan Heights, remain an important unresolved issue. Jordanian concerns about Syrian dams on the Yarmouk, the major tributary to the Jordan, are still unanswered.

The use of water as an instrument or tool of conflict and as both offensive and defensive weapons, which has a long history, can be seen at present. For example, North Korea announced plans in 1986 to build a major hydroelectric dam on the Han River upstream of South Korea's capital, Seoul. The project would provide much needed electricity to the North, but South Korea perceives its potential as a military weapon. In the perceptions of South Korean hydrologists, the destruction of the dam by the North would destroy most of Seoul. In response to this South Korea has built a series of levees and check dams above Seoul to defend against any such threat.[240]

During the Persian Gulf War in 1991, the coalition forces discussed the possibility of using the Ataturk dam in Turkey on the Euphrates river to shut off the flow of water to Iraq solely dependent on flows of the Euphrates river.[241] Both Syria and Iraq continue to have an ongoing dispute with Turkey over the operation of Ataturk and the level and quality of flows in the Euphrates reaching both downstream countries.

Singapore not self sufficient in water because of its high population density and small size, depends on piped water from Malaysia for nearly half of all its needs. In addition, Singapore imports water from Malaysia that it then treats and sells back under an agreement signed in 1965.[242] Their relations have been strained by economic competition, religious, political and ethnic differences. In early 1997 these relations soured again when ruling political party urged its government to review the basis of its water agreement with Singapore.[243] Singapore clearly worried that Malaysia might use water as a political and strategic weapon against Singapore. In response to this Singapore has launched also a campaign to increase water and reduce consumption through an aggressive conservation program, which includes new desalination plants that would produce water at about eight times the cost of current supplies.[244] Whether this exorbitant cost is worth risking the strained relations with Malaysia remains to be seen.

Where water resources and water supply systems are a strategic resource with economic, political or military importance, they become targets during war or conflicts. The United States targeted irrigation levees in North Vietnam. Syria tried to destroy Israel's National Water Carrier while it was under construction in the 1950s. The Iraqis in1991 Gulf war intentionally destroyed the water desalination plants of Kuwait, and in turn suffered from the destruction of their water supply system by the allied forces assembled to liberate Kuwait.[245]

Group – Identity Conflict

Here the ecological issues lead to conflict in a broader sense, i.e. the conflict results from the social effects of ecological degradation. Group identity theories described above explain the group identity conflict. In general group identity conflicts often emanate from the large-scale migration of population that can be caused by the environmental scarcity. As different ethnic, religious and cultural migrants meet an indigenous group due to environmental stress, an intergroup hostility and violent clash with a strong identity dynamic takes place. When the people started to move because their homeland has been severely damaged and depleted by deforestation, soil erosion, salinization etc, and came in contact with a different group, violent clash occurs which can be termed as an environmental conflict in a broader sense.

Group-Identity Conflict: Bangladesh – Assam Region

Bangladesh represents a Malthusian nightmare with too 'little food, or too many people on too little land". It is one of the world's most densely populated and impoverished states having 128 million people and GNP production capita equivalent to 170 dollars. The country's population density of 930 per square kilometer is the world's highest. As studies show, nearly 56.5% of rural households comprising 7.8 million people without land and it is estimated that the proportion of landlessness has grown faster than the population.[246] In the words of development economist of Bangladesh" the economic viability of Bangladesh has long been in question because of its over population, poor natural resource base, vulnerability to natural disasters and undiversified economy dependent on the production of crops, rice and jute.[247]

Their economy deprivation and poverty is further compounded as seen before, by the region's vulnerability to frequent floods and cyclones. Bangladesh passes through recurring vicissitude of floods, cyclones, drought and famine destroying hundred and thousand human lives in the process. Floods have killed more than one million people since 1961. The 1988 flood, the most devastating in terms of human lives and economy reduced rice production by 1.6 million tonnes and caused 1.3 billion dollars worth of damage to Bangladesh's economy.[248] Experts in Bangladesh opine that the single most harmful environmental factor in the country is flooding resulting in temporary and permanent migration not only across districts, but also across international frontiers.[249] Each year in Bangladesh 18 to 19 million people are affected by floods.[250] The displacees of the river bank erosion are the worst of the landless poor.[251]

The search for land due to increased landlessness caused by population growth and flooding has resulted in massive migration of landless to urban areas within the country and to India. It is seen in

Bangladesh "land has always been almost as fluid as the water that shapes it. The geography of the delta changes like a speeded version of continental drift." [252] Every year new lands are formed due to river erosion by eating into the existing land. This is perceptible in Hatia and South of Noakhali. These lands are known as 'charland', the scramble for which has reached a crisis proportion in Bangladesh. People dispossessed by erosion have no automatic right to these newly accreted land. All these newly deposited charland belongs to the government. The landless as they are illiterate and ignorant and incapable of bureaucratic appeasement, are deprived of their lands with no access to this new land. Jotdars and rich landowners get hold of legal titles to charland under fictitious names, through their nexus with political and bureaucratic leadership. Apart from the woes which the poor landless peasants and fishermen suffered at the hands of landowners, jotdars, the absence of mangroves which are to stabilize their charland results in another human tragedy when tens of thousands of people are swept away by tropical storms sometimes with their islands disappearing into the sea.[253] This search for land has resulted in-group clashes in Bangladesh with the state alternately supporting the landowners. This only reinforces the existing social divides and relative deprivation among the landless and poor people in rural and urban areas. The growing number of squatters around urban centres as in Bangladesh due to the migration of landless people has also resulted in clashes for jobs and economic sustenance.

Taking advantage of this feeling of relative deprivation among the people, military dictatorships frequently come to power. In Bangladesh frequent political instability punctuated by military dictatorships may be attributed to this growing sense of relative deprivation among the poor who are promised in return for their upliftment, votes. One of the primary reasons of the likelihood of democratic regimes being not successful in Bangladesh can be traced to the deepening poverty and internal calamities like floods, cyclones and surges. Poverty induced by environmental change leads to severe internal strike, including coup de tat, revolutions and insurgencies.[254] It is envisaged that these regimes that succeed to power through these means will probably be more extremists, authoritarian, corrupt and abusive of human rights.[255] In the absence of any concrete poverty alleviating measures to blot out relative deprivation existing among the poor upon whom the ruling regimes cash in to come to power, could search other rhetorics to legitimize their continuity in power, and divert people's attention from the existing domestic failures. In Bangladesh, rising anti-India feelings of water issue or Babri Masjid demolition at Ayodhya in December 1992 or pandering to fundamentalist Muslims have been observed in the recent years. This creates a feeling of continuous animosity towards the neighbouring state.

Induced by poverty and environmental degradation between 12 to 17 million landless poor people in their search for land and economic livelihood, have been migrating to neighbouring states of India, viz. Assam, West Bengal, Tripura, Orissa, and urban centres like Delhi and Bombay creating a" sub nation, the size of Australia within India." [256] Though Bangladesh continues to proclaim that it has no illegal aliens in India, Bangladesh communities have sprung up in Delhi and Bombay under the shelter of flyovers and in Muslim dominated regions. The political parties in India resort to political use of Bangladesh settlers as potential vote banks. While the Government of India put the Bangladeshi migrants figures at about 100, 000, the intelligence sources estimate it at 200, 000.[257] Providing advantage to political parties during hustings, these refugees receive patronage in terms of education, development and health facilities even at the cost of the local inhabitants. This contains the seeds of further local conflicts.

An estimate suggests that as many as 1, 000 people a month are coming to West Bengal.[258] Most drift to Calcutta where their living conditions are marked by squalor, overcrowding and abysmal poverty. After the destruction of the Babri Mosque, many in the squatter communities were involved in the rioting and carnage that enveloped the city for several days.[259] It is seen that rioters were driven more by class hatred, envy and need to plunder and pillage the middle class than by any religious fanaticism.[260] Such rioting and clashes have domestic political fall out with some Hindu dominated political parties being inclined to reap political dividends. In their search for vote banks among the refugees, the political parties particularly the Congress and Communist Party have down played the number of refugees settled in West Bengal.

The migration of Bangladeshis is not confined only to Northeastern states of India but also has spread to Orissa's coastal areas. The ninety kilometre long coastal belt spreading from Dhamara of Bhadrak district to Paradeep of Jagatsingpur district has been littered with the illegal settlement of Bangladeshis including Mahakalapada, Dangamala and Ekakola of Kendrapara district. With the active connivance of local politicians, they have settled along these coastal areas destroying twenty five thousand hectare of reserved forest cover and converting these either to cultivable land or for prawn cultivation.

The destruction of mangrove forests for agricultural activities, unplanned and illegal habitation, and illegal prawn culture by these migrants could be one of the factors that helped super cyclone in Orissa in1999 grow in intensity and severity to surpass the previous cyclones. As Assam and Central governments are confronted with the problems of law and order, terrorism and insurgencies, the Orissa government is likely to face similarly these problems in near future. As reported, thousands of Bangladeshis are settling near the defence establishment at Bhadrak and understood to have been employed as daily wagers in the works of the defence institution in the night. These Bangladesh migrants are seen permanently settling in the nearby areas and getting BPL cards and other government facilities with the active support of politician to turn them into a potential vote bank. In these coastal areas if reports of their being involved in narcotic traffics, ISI activity on behalf of Pakistan and other nefarious activities like smuggling, murder and burglary, are to be believed, then government's sitting silently putting the issue of illegal migration on the backburner has drawn broadside from the local people. This has irked the local people and their fear that this could convert the coastal belt of Orissa into a mini Bangladesh has resulted in strong resentment against the government failure to send back these migrants. A total of 1200 refugees of Bangladesh legally settled in1957 has now touched 1 lakh 80 thousand after 46 years causing a feeling of being reduced to minority in the local people.[261] One should not underestimate the fact that the settlement of Bangladeshis along the coastal line cutting deep into the forest cover-the natural bulwark against storm and cyclones-and the local people's economic livelihood, could one day turn into a violent conflagration between the migrants and local people with the considerable involvement of the Orissa government, like the violent one, which happened recently in Raighar and Rangabhati of Nabarangapur district between the local tribal people and Bangladesh refugees settled in these areas by the central government over land. This has claimed the lives of 10 people, and injured 55 people. This is not a new one, adding to this, 56 times the local tribal people have been in skirmishes with the Bangladesh refugees. With strong pressure on the government not to show short shrift to the migration of Bangladeshis, the government has decided to deport some Bangladeshis to their homeland.[262]

This has already created a political uproar in the state with various political parties demanding an abrupt halt to this.

Due to the constant stream of migrants from Bangladesh to Assam, "the problem the Assmese face today is that it soon may be themselves who constitute an island within a sea of Bengalis".[263] The demographic structure of Assam has already been in a danger of having transformed the once dominant Assamese into a minority within Assam.[264]

There has been a spate of data raising controversies about the exact number of illegal Bangladeshi migrants settling in Assam.[265] Estimates indicated that Assam's population increased from 14.6 million to 22.9 million during 1970s.This increase of 65.6% in one decade could not be attributed to a natural population growth alone, especially when the rest of India, showed an increase of 24.7% during the same period.[266] Illegal migration is the only reason for that unexpected growth. Conservative estimates put it at over 6 million persons.[267]

The most recent study on this shows that the Indian government has been faltering in giving the correct estimate in order to reap political dividends by using them as legitimate voters. The Bangladesh government similarly for political reasons has been down playing the number, which may create conflict with India. Taking into account many expert estimates, this study is of the view that Bangladesh refugees have expanded the population of the neighbouring Indian states by 12 to 17 million of which 1 to 2 million may have been caused by the 1971 war. The population of Assam has gone up by at least 7 million people to its current total of 22 million.[268] Some accounts put the figure as high as 13 million and accuse the Bangladesh government of pursing a policy of lebensraum in northeast India.[269] The Assamese people however reluctantly accepted these migrants so long as the latter preferred to be mere labourers. Social tensions and violent conflict soon began to erupt when the migrants made serious inroads into their economy and put pressures on existing resource base. Along with this Assamese fear of being reduced to a minority within their own homeland leading to the extinction of their culture and identity, accentuated the problems.

The Assamese legitimate fear, discontentment and lowered standard of living was accomplished by the failure of both the central and state government's disinclination to stem the tide of flow of Bangladeshis who were settled by them for their votes.[270] This led to the first popular movement by All Assam Students Union (AASU) against these illegal immigration. Their main demands were mainly the detection of foreign nationals on the basis of the 1952 National Register of Citizens, their disenfranchisement and deportation. Strikes, demonstrations, blockades, civil disobedience and boycott of elections paralyzed the administration. A series of governments rose and fell, political instability continued to invite the intervention of central government and its rule. From 1981 to 1983, illegal immigrants swelled in numbers in Assam from Bangladesh resulting in a number of communal clashes and riots killing hundreds and thousands of people. The initial ethnic tension simmered for years due to the government's negligence and continued Bangladesh influx had suddenly turned into a fury of human carnage. It was the worst ethnic riots in India since independence, and the number of human lives lost in these riots surpassed even the anti-Sikh riots of 1984, or the anti-Muslim riots of Bombay in January 1993 or religious rioting in 1990 and 1992 over the Babri Mosque demolition.[271] The holding of elections in Assam in 1983 without fulfilling the AASU's demands resulted in extreme violence claiming lives of many thousands. A study of the reasons behind the riots underlines a common factor, i.e. land between Bangladesh and northeast India.[272]

The first step towards a solution to the ethnic conflict in Assam was the 1985 Assam Accord that outlined (I) the expulsion of all immigrants entering Assam after 24 March 1971, (ii) a ten-year disenfranchisement of illegal immigrants entered between 1966 and 1971, (iii) and those who came before 1966 to be granted Indian citizenship. 2[73] In the general election Assam Gana Parishad created out of the AASU won the election ousting Congress party from power.[274] The Congress party ruling at the centre delayed in implementing the Accord, which contributed to the continuance of the instability.[275] Renewed agitation by the AASU started again with United Liberation Front of Assam (ULFA) and Bodo Land tribal movements against the Bengalis joined in making revolutionary demands for balkanization of Assam.

The issue of migration of Bangladeshis has already soured the relations between India and Bangladesh. Erecting a fence along the parts of the border and the forced repatriation of refugees at any point on the border have contributed to continued conflict with Bangladesh. Despite a series of meetings at the ministerial and secretarial levels, illegal migration remains, and continues unabated.

The ULFA and Bodoland movements, which continue in their demands for separatism, are militarily encouraged by Pakistan and Bangladesh. As Hiteswar Saikia, the former Chief Minister of Assam revealed, the underground member of the United Liberation Front of Assam, the Bodo Security Force and other insurgent organizations active in Manipur, Nagaland and Tripura were getting shelter, weapons and arms training in Bangladesh and Tripura with the help of Pakistan's ISI.[276] The outgoing BSF director general, D.K.Arya of India in his 10-page press release statement disclosed that insurgent groups operating in North East were acquiring sophisticated weapons from Thailand with the active connivance of Bangladesh's intelligence agencies. Bangladesh is providing all possible help in terms of shelter and training, and the ISI of Pakistan is also actively involved in encouraging the Indian insurgent groups operating from the Bangladesh soil.[277]

The press release further accused Bangladesh of fanning religious fundamentalism and disruptive forces, and deliberately facilitating migration of its nationals to India. He further implied that rise of insurgency in North East and growing migration to India with Bangladesh and Pakistan actively involved in encouraging morally and materially such centrifugal forces, have serious implications on India's security and unity.

By the year 2020, there will be 220 million Bangladeshis and one billion Indians competing for land and jobs.[278] In the case of sea level rise, as predicted due to global warming, Bangladesh will be worst hit thus, forcing some more million environmental refugees to enter India. This will compound the problems for India, and will further downgrade Indo-Bangladesh relations.

If the influx is not stopped, there will be a sharp decline in communal harmony and centre-state relations will be vitiated giving rise to separatist tendencies and ethnic crisis in the north eastern part of India on a scale larger than what is seen at present. Any drastic measure to stop the flow of Bangladesh immigrants on the part of India will aggravate the conflict between India and Bangladesh. With the BJP party in India drawing attention to the issue of illegal Muslim migrants to enhance its sphere of influence especially in communist ruled West Bengal and northeastern states, the ruling party will capitalize on the anti-India feelings of fundamentals Muslims in Bangladesh in order to legitimize its authority. The former BJP government's decision to complete fencing on the border already raised a hornet's nest in Bangladesh.

Insurgencies

The third type of violent conflict in the form of rebellion or guerrilla war against state according to Dixon, can be explained and predicted by a combination of relative-deprivation theories and structural theories of civil strife.[279] These two theoretical perspectives in combination suggest that insurgency is a function of both the level of grievance motivating challenger groups and the opportunities available to these groups to act violently on their grievances.[280] Multiple pressures exerted at different levels in society interact to produce the grievance and opportunity simultaneously and raise the chance of insurgency. Environmental scarcity and degradation of resources plays a key role in exacerbating economic hardship and dislocation, intergroup segmentation and weakening of institutions such as the state. These factors combine to cause insurgency. Economic decline-one of the social effects of environmental scarcity – as suggested by relative deprivation theory, will result in some groups being increasingly frustrated and aggrieved by the widening gap between their actual level of economic achievement and the level they feel they deserve. The faster the growth of the gap, the greater is the intensity of the grievance of the disadvantaged groups prompting them to act violently against those groups perceived to be the agent of their economic deprivation and misery. There is no clear correlation between economic hardship and violence.[281] Whether or not people get aggrieved and turn violent in the face of severe economic difficulty depends on their notion of economic justice. People belonging to a culture may adapt to situation of economic deprivation and unequal distribution of wealth, and will not be prone to violence. Relative deprivation theory incorporates this contextual factor because deprivation is always relative to an individual or group's notion of economic justice. Economic crisis must be severe, persistent and pervasive enough to erode the legitimacy of the dominant social order and system of government. Group identity conflict and insurgency are the most important types of conflict likely to arise from severe environmental scarcity. It also contributes to several other types of conflict. Under certain circumstances, for example, scarcity can stimulate coup de'tat as aggrieved and conflicting elites take advantage of a weakened state. Drought and a severe food shortfall in Ethiopia opened up structural opportunities for the 1974 coup against Emperor Haile Selassie.[282]

In some cases environmental scarcity stimulates a form of insurgency that combine both group – identity and relative deprivation motivations. If a historically defined identity of a group is linked to a particular set of natural resources or a particular pattern of resource use, degradation of that resource can engender a feeling of relative deprivation. This relative deprivation may be expressed through aggressive assertion of group – identity. Sporadic violence in South Eastern Nigeria in1994 and 1995, when the Ogani people protested pollution of the Niger delta by multinational oil companies, and the secessionist rebellion on the island of Bougainvillea in Papua New Guinea from the late 1980s to mid 1990s against a foreign owned copper mine, which damaged the island's environment, are good examples to show the relative deprivation conflict.

Environmental Scarcity, Relative Deprivation and Tamil Separatism in Sri Lanka

The incongruities between the ecogeographical region and political boundaries have often led to conflict within a state or between states. When political and territorial boundaries are superimposed upon ecogeographical regions, the incongruities between these are noticed frequently. In some cases, several states occupy parts of a single-ecoregion; in other cases states encompass more than one ecoregion. In case of states with more than one ecoregion, conflict can be stimulated for two reasons. First, multi-ecogeographical states are more often multi-ethnic states and some ethnic group within a state are often politically weaker than others, often lacking sovereignty over the territories they occupy. Second even if different ecoregions are ethnically homogenous they often support populations of different densities. A more populous region may have the power to control the resources of other regions to the extent of exploiting the resources of one ecogeographical region for the benefit of people who live elsewhere. A kind of inter-state colonialism takes place.[283] Over-exploitation and degradation of the region warrants calling it "a national sacrifice area".[284]

Sri Lanka provided an example of this kind of conflict in a small state. It has a wet zone centred in the Southwest, and a dry zone located in the east and north. The wet zone is inhabited mainly by Sinhalese, while most of the Tamil ethnic groups live in the dry zone. Sinhalese dominate the state government. Government sponsored water projects in the dry zone benefited mainly the Sinhalese, many of whom resettled in areas occupied by Tamils. Thus the dry zone being a national sacrifice area has been one of the complex roots of civil war in Sri Lanka.[285]

Two reasons can be accounted for this kind of conflict. One is the apparent incongruity between the ecogeographical region and the territorial boundaries within the state inhabited by different ethnic groups. This superimposition of ethnic demarcated territorial boundaries on the ecogeographical region has led to the expatriation of the resources and the environment of the region by the ethnic dominant Sinhalese group ruling the state at the expense of the other Tamil groups. Second, is the exceeding carrying capacity and the natural threshold of the region beyond its regeneration. In Sri Lanka, the dry zone has been overexploited beyond its capacity to benefit the Sinhalese at the cost of the Tamil.[286] There are a number of reasons and theories put forward for Tamil separatism in Sri Lanka.One significant cause being underplayed is the consequence of a grim situation aggravated endemically by the burgeoning population growth, and its pressures on scarce land. With the advent of the British, education came to be considered an avenue for survival in the view of the limits placed on land by the environment in terms of both productivity and increasing landlessness. Within Sri Lanka, the Tamils came to occupy extensive and dominant positions in the bureaucracy, university and business, decreasing the population's competition over additional exploitable land.

Aside from other strategic steps, the Sinhalese majority's compelling poverty and unemployment pressurized their governments to take steps to thin down the Tamil dominance. Thus, followed the imposition of Sinhala as the official language, constriction of university admission for Tamils and adoption of a new constitution devoid of any federal structure.[287] What came as harsh set back to the Tamils was the land colonization of Sinhalese in the Eastern province considered by Tamils as an integral part of their traditional homeland.[288]

From 1950 onwards, the Sinhalese government sponsored attempts at, and encouraged settlement of Sinhalese from the south to the north central and northeastern dry zone. These canal colony settlers in larger irrigation schemes began to form a reason for discontentment among the Tamils.[289] This was considered a further attempt at cutting deep into the already limited and scare Tamil resources. The main motive behind such a settlement was Sinhalese landlessness, which was more acute than among the Tamils.[290] This Sinhalese colonization of the Tamil ancestral homeland not only brought about a drastic transformation of the demographic structure reducing Tamils to a minority in their own land, but also resulted in a dependent population coming under tension and rebellion due to scarcity of resources, made worse by the incoming settlement.

There is evidence to prove that the agrarian policies of successive governments and state sponsored colonization schemes have brought about a demographic transformation in the Trincomalee and Amparai districts. While the Sinhalese were mainly 3% of the population in 1921, they rose to 33% in 1981. Similarly in Amparai, an increase of 78 per cent in Sinhalese population was seen by 1981.[291]

The Tamils were also affected by land colonization in other districts, viz. Mannar, Vavunia and Batticola. It is also alleged that the Sinhala fishermen are being inducted to threaten the very way of life and source of living of Tamil fishermen.[292]

Group Vs Group

The Tamil youth disenchanted with the political process, which gave priority to Sinhalese interests resorted to violence, murder, robbery and assassination. Riots in 1983 provided the turning point. Started by the killing of 13 Sinhalese army men by Tamil militants, the Sinhalese in turn retaliated in Colombo and other parts of the island killing hundreds of Tamils.

Group Vs State

A group vs group ethnic conflict turned into a conflict between a group and a state, which supported the Sinhalese majority. By early 1980s, Sri Lanka found itself in the midst of what can be termed a civil war or secession, as several militant Tamil organizations led by the youthful Liberation Tigers on Tamil Eelam (LTTE) resorted to violence as a means to remedy their plight. Nothing short of an autonomy or separate state was considered as conducive for safeguarding their interest. Guerrilla warfare on the part of Tamil militants and military crackdown on them by Sri Lankan became a regular phenomenon.

State vs State

A group vs. state conflict, a national problem of Sri Lanka was externalized with the influx of Tamil refugees in 1983 into India. Fleeing the military atrocities in Sri Lanka, the Tamil refugees crossed over into the ethnically similar state of Tamil Nadu in India. Tamil Nadu housing about 200, 000 Sri Lankan Tamils has empathized with the cause of the Sri Lankan Tamils. Due to the rivalry between the DMK and AIADMK political parties in Tamil Nadu, each party has vied to be perceived as supporting fellow Tamils. Each is motivated both by genuine concern as well as by pure political pragmatism. The very dynamics of working of the Indian federal system have urged upon the centre not to minimize the Tamil cause, in the context of the state's penchant for independence. The ruling parties in Tamil Nadu and in New Delhi provided Tamil militants sanctuary, military and material help. Tamil Nadu was an important factor pressurizing New Delhi to support the Tamil insurgents. After the assassination of Prime Minister Indira Gandhi, Rajiv Gandhi tried to steer clear of interfering in the affairs of Punjab, Kashmir and Assam. In this attempt to settle the internal problems, the policy on Tamils of Sri Lanka changed. On failing to solve the issue peacefully, the Indian government air lifted humanitarian aid in May 1987 with fighter jets as protection, into the territory of Sri Lanka.The internationalization of the issue took place as Sri Lanka tried to seek the support of the United States and other powers.[293]

Subsequently, Rajiv Gandhi signed an agreement with President Jayawardene on 29 July 1987, which empowered India to military intervene to disarm militants and maintain a cease-fire with a quid pro quo for Sri Lanka promising a modicum of autonomy to Tamils in North East Sri Lanka. This outraged both the Tamil militants for not being satisfied with the deal, and the Sinhalese for having conceded too much to the Tamils.

This aggravated the situation and widened the difference between the Indian government and Tamil militants. Rajiv Gandhi was assassinated in Tamil Nadu while electioneering by the Tamil militants. Premadasa, who succeeded Jayawardene, stressed that the Indian Peace Keeping Forces return to India.The ethnic conflict continues, despite assurances of solutions by successive Governments in Sri Lanka. At this stage the Sinhalese again started colonizing the eastern sector. With the deepening of the crisis, it has been ironic to note that just five years after the Indian troops were unceremoniously asked to quit Sri Lanka, the island's majority Sinhalese population, which cheered the withdrawl, wishes, New Delhi would once again come to their country's rescue.[294]

As seen from the problems of environmental degradation and social effects in Sri Lanka, the resource base is gradually declining with land man ratio dwindling to an alarming extent. In a complex system of causes of ethnic conflict in Sri Lanka, environmental scarcity of resources appears to be one of its primary constituents. In the absence of a satisfying and enduring solution to the Tamil ethnic conflict, any military solution on the part of the Sri Lankan government is bound to arouse Tamil sympathy in India.In view of the stranglehold the Sinhalese Buddhists have had in Sri Lankan political decision making, the Sri Lanka government cannot give the Tamils more than what the Sinhalese want the government to concede.

As the age structure shows, large number of unemployed youths will enter the job market by AD 2010. The deteriorating economic base, declining environment and growing population would reinforce the Sinhalese masses' psychological and social sense of backwardness by the invidious comparison with the advanced Tamils in terms of disparaging evaluation of self worth which has often manifested in anxiety, violence and hostility.[295] In the absence of any truce satisfying the Tamil demands, hostility and violence that will increase between the Tamil militants and the Sri Lanka Government may compel many Tamils to migrate to Tamil Nadu in India, posing security threats to India as the engagement of these Tamils in illegal activities like smuggling, and fratricidal murder of other militants have already become a law and order problem in the state. Tamil tigers appear to have a free run of the place in several villages on the Tamil Nadu coastline. As former Union Minister Chidambaram admitted, saying that the Tamil Nadu coastline is dotted with villages where the LTTE appears to have a free run.[296] The overwhelming task of settling Tamil refugees will be a strain on Tamil Nadu's economy and resources.

The Sri Lanka Tamil refugees came from a poor country to a poorer country like India. What were not easily available to the poor Indians were made available to the refugees at subsidized rates and also free of costs on humanitarian grounds. Approximately, 15 crores of rupees are spent annually on the maintenance of the refugees by Tamil Nadu government to be finally reimbursed by the Indian government.

Being prone to water scarcity, [297] refugee settlement will aggravate the crisis sometimes resulting in group fighting and conflict with the increasing military activities on the part of Sri Lanka government, the Tamil Nadu government may be more empathetic to the Tamil cause than what central government would want Tamil Nadu to be. So India's evincing greater interests for these reasons in solving the crisis cannot be certainly "an independent Tamil Eelam, which could have easily become a safe sanctuary and staging area for Sikhs, Assamese and other militant separatists in India.[298] The present continuing Sri Lankan military onslaughts on LTTE and establishing its stranglehold in North East peninsula has aroused strong reaction from the Tamil Nadu state of India with its government, people and opposition parties observing 'bondh' and asking the Indian government to intervene in order to stop decimation of innocent Tamil people by Sri Lankan military forces.

The Tamils in Sri Lanka lost Indian sympathy following the assassination of Rajiv Gandhi by LTTE. The Indian Government sincerely wants a political solution to the ethnic crisis in Sri Lanka. Continuation of the crisis has serious implication on Indian security, unity and integrity. From a recent interrogation of NSCN militants caught in Nagaland early November, the LTTE's well established connections within Bangladesh with insurgent groups in North East and the United Liberation Front of Assam (ULFA) in terms of military weapons supply and traning, were corroborated by the Indian Home Ministry to the greater security concerns of India.[299]

As found from the study of environmental degradation and various social effects, the people in Sri Lanka including the landless, rural and urban poor and the growing unemployed youth would be affected by an increasing sense of relative deprivation, caused by faulty government economic policies as well as environmental degradation and environmental scarcity of resources, it may result in situations manifesting violence, murder and conflict. Eventually, the government may depend on the Buddhists clergy to highlight the Tamil Sinhalese ethnic crisis, keeping in view the need, first, to reinforce.their legitimacy in power and secondly, to drive the depraved people's attention away from the immediacy of the situation by internationalizing the already existing ethnic crisis.

Environmental Degradation, Relative Deprivation, Ethnic Conflict in Pakistan

Ethnoregional sentiments have been growing stronger among the Pathans, Baluchis and Sindhis against the Punjabi dominated Pakistan. This has increased ever since Pakistan attempted at Punjabization of all regions regardless of their distinctive culture and language with Punjabis ruling the roost in all spheres whether it is industry, military, bureaucracy or economic or politics.

Extensive influx or refugees from India (Muhajirs) during partition and from the other provinces of Pakistan to Sind was the primary reason to create feeling of deprivation and subordination in Sind people when those aliens contributed to the economic and commercial prosperity of Karachi without bestowing corresponding benefits on the indigenous Sindhis.[300] Their demands for more autonomy in terms of political and economic representation in military and bureaucracy remain still potential sources of conflict. The current riots in Karachi decimating Muhajirs may point to a sense of deprivation among the Sindhis. The migration to Karachi from other provinces has reduced the Sindhis to a minority.[301] Besides diversion of the Indus Water to Punjab at the cost of Sindh, the influx of people from India (Muhajirs) and from Punjab has resulted in abysmal decrease in land-man ratio, resource base and economic opportunities for the local people. To the resentment of Sidhis some of the best and most fertile land in the Ghulam Mahammad barrage area of Sind from which they have been ousted, have been allotted to the ex-servicemen who are mostly Punjabis. As pointed out, large tracts of vulnerable land in Sindh brought under irrigation since independence have been allotted to Punjabis, member of armed forces, senior bureaucrats and their relatives.[302] This, further shrinked the land for the local Sindhis. As a result of this infiltration, it is natural that it resulted in a conflict between the locals and the non-locals. Sindhis's initial demand for a homeland targeted at Muhajirs who contributed a lot to the economic and commercial expansion of Karachi. In the NWFP, the call for an independent entity of Pakhtunistan comprising the Pathan areas of both sides of the Afghanistan-Pakistan border predates independence. Being extremely conscious of their distinct, ethnic and cultural identities, they are also strongly discontent with the growing dominance of Punjabi in all spheres to their despair and impoverishment. The politics of preference for Punjabi in matters of land and water as seen earlier, was the bone of contention between NWFP and Pakistan.

Baluchistan is Pakistan's largest and poorest land most sparsely settled province. It constitutes 40% of Pakistan's landmass but only 5% of its population. What is the bone of contention is that a majority of Baluchistan's population is non-Baluch. In the northern areas of the province, Pathans predominate and in Las Bela and Sibi districts, Sindhi and Siraiki are spoken more frequently than Balchi or Brohi, whereas in Quatta District, Punjabi or Pustho is more often spoken. The struggle of the Baluchis against what they call the tyranny of the Punjabi elite has been going on for the last three decades. The Sindhi elite's fear of discrimination in career advancement and other economic opportunities is similar to the threat which the locals of Baluchistan and NWFP feel from Punjabis, who have continually migrated to Quetta in Peshawar and to other cities.

A perusal of ethnic consciousness of the Pathanas, Baluchis and Sindhis will indicate a feeling of 'relative deprivation. This has existed all along among all the three groups. Without being sensitive to the development of these people, Pakistan policy of giving predominant position to Punjabis in education, service, and bureaucracy, economic and military has created the relative deprivation among them. The ethnocentrism of Punjabis in Pakistan's political economy has given rise to sharpening the ethnic identities among these groups. What has been strongly opposed to, are the assimilationist and redistributional policies. Given the dominance of Punjabi, the assimilationist policies are viewed as clever subterfuge to weaken the minority, and strengthen the Punjabi domination. Its distributional policies are resented because by these, the majority community redistributes resources to minority communities.[303]

Besides, with Bangladesh being independent, "Pakistan has been the victim of a successful secessionist movement and 'would be opponents' of the continued integrity of Pakistan are encouraged by their predecessor's success".[304]

To these feelings of 'relative deprivation' among the disgruntled in Pakistan will be added equally the deteriorating environmental and resource depletion in these regions. Growing population, its pressures on land which has already been degraded due to various reasons like siltation, salinity and water scarcity, urbanization, transmigration of people from rural to urban, competing with them for the basic human needs, need for more productivity on marginal land and dependence on fertilizers, for this, are some of the grave problems afflicting these regions, 27 million hectares of land in Pakistan are already affected by desertification. Water scarcity, desertification and degradation of land have had deleterious effects on productivity on which teeming millions depend. The Kalbagh dam project, which will displace 250, 000 and submerge vast areas in NWFP and Baluchistan, with adverse effects on the Indus delta system in terms of increasing salinity, siltation and water scarcity, has been a subject of conflict between the central government and the regions. Though the Indus Water Apportionment Accord has been signed distributing water among these regions, a further considerable reduction in the flow of Ganges water will happen due to this project and will aggravate the resentment of these regions against the Punjabi dominated Pakistan. The influx of 3.4 million Afghan refugees as a result of the Afghan war into NWFP, of same ethnic background, i.e. Pushtun, with their 3 million livestock, apart from having ethnic rivalry, law and order problems and a drain on scarce resources, have degraded the environment in terms of overgrazing, deforestation and erosion of water courses. It is alleged that due to watercourses being eroded, the lifespan of the important Mangla dam is estimated to be halved with other concomitant-disastrous consequences for irrigation and power generation.[305]

Link Between Urban Growth and Violence

Between 1950 and 1990, there was a fivefold increase – to 1.5 billion – in the number of urban residents in developing countries; about 37 per cent of the population of the developing world now lives in cities. By 2025, the United Nations projects a future tripling of the total to 4.4 billion, at which point nearly two thirds of the citizens of the developing world will live in cities.[306] Apart from natural growth, reclassification, contribution of permanent migration from rural areas to urban growth is huge, though below 50%.[307] Rural – urban migrants tend to be relatively young which accentuates the youth bulge in urban population in poor countries. This age distribution contributes to natural population growth in cities, because a younger population has more children and fewer deaths compared to an older population.[308]

During the 1960s, some scholars suggested that rural to urban migration in the developing world could cause a spurt in urban violence. According to Wayne Cornelius there are three hypotheses on this linkage.[309] First, migration could breed economic frustration, migrants' expectations could not be fulfilled and the exorbitant and inordinate consumption of the elites could enhance the migrants' awareness of their marginal status. Second, cultural incongruity, conflicts and disruption of past living habits and custom of the migrants would cause personal identity crisis. This would increase the chance of primary group breakdown and weakening traditional social controls on deviant behaviour. As migrants sought entry into new protective groups, they would be easily recruited into extremist political activity. Third, the urban environment provides an opportunity for high levels of social communication, increased political awareness, and mobilization of radical opposition to go hand in hand. This would politicize migrants and encourage mass involvement in political action.[310]

Little empirical research has been done in recent years on this to prove these hypotheses. It needs to be studied whether the links are strengthened when large migrants interact with many factors like economic crisis, poverty and environmental scarcity of resources.

Pakistan's Cities Such as Karachi-An example of this Linkage

In Pakistan, the migration from rural areas to urban areas has been constantly rising. A growing number of shanties are seen around Karachi. As predicted, sea level rise submerging Karachi may result in flight of people for food and shelter to relatively secure urban areas and other places. The new level of conflict will spawn up among various groups. Competition for jobs, economic benefit and basic modern amenities among the urban population will entwine migrants and the original inhabitants in various conflicts. Government's attention is concentrated on urban areas and for meeting their basic modern demands such as provisions for water, education, electricity, health and sanitation by diverting a sizeable part of the total budget. The disillusioned rural people and poor urban people will be thus disenchanted with the government setting the stage for political instability. An analyst of rural urban relationships in developing countries describes the conflicts that may arise thus.

That most important class conflict in the poor countries of the world today is not between labour and (those who control) capital, nor is it between foreign and national interests. It is between the rural classes and urban classes. The rural sectors contain most of the poverty and most of the low cost sector of potential advance. But the urban sector contains most of the articulateness and power... As a result, the urban classes have been able to win most of the rounds of struggle with the countryside; but in doing so they have made the development process needlessly slow and unfair.[311]

Karachi grows by about 400, 000 people per year. Where as its population rises at around 5 per cent per annum, urban services expand by only 1.2 per cent.[312] Government and development authorities cannot provide residents with basic services; the city's aging infrastructure is over taxed and does not properly serve new communities. Housing problem, acute shortages of electricity, and water, disarranged transport system and trafficking in narcotics and arms has plagued Karachi. High demand for water along with rampant corruption and mismanagement in the Karachi Water and Sewage Board has created a tanker mafia cornering all the profits by selling water to customers at exorbitant prices, often on credit.[313] Frustration stemming from the lack of urban services has prompted attacks on the offices of the Karachi Electricity Supply Corporation and the Karachi Water and Sewage Board.[314] The inability of state institutions to address diverse demands accentuates latent ethnic and class tensions. Immigration and high urban population growth further boost grievances, highlight the impotence of the state, and reduce state legitimacy. This strong urban bias in terms of provision of services such as education, health, electricity and water widens social inequities and increases social conflicts. Though some studies show little historic correlation between rapid urbanization and civil strife, [315] Pakistan has recently been affected by an orgy of riots in Karachi.

As evident from the above analysis, the environmental degradation may not be the root cause of ethnic disputes in Pakistan but however, appear to exacerbate the problems. The existing feelings of relative deprivation among various ethnic regions in Pakistan may be further aggravated by the environmental degradation along with its social effects. In the case of such ethnic crisis and rise of separation in Pakistan, the Pakistani government being unable to address these problems will find a convenient hypothesis to raise the bogey of Indian involvement as in recent riots in Karachi, Pakistan alleged Indian role.[316] The Indian involvement was emphasized to secure legitimacy by the ruling elite in its domestic front. This would gain support of its fundamentalist Muslim population. These as usual orchestrated allegations of Indian premeditated plan to dismember Pakistan, are believed to have happened in case of Bangladesh, by the Pakistani government. This factor could potentially bedevil Indo-Pak bilateral relations.

The unchecked build up of carbon dioxide and other greenhouse gases in the global atmosphere due to industrialization would cause, as predicted, far reaching disruption in temperature and rainfall patterns.[317] As said above the impact of global warming on agricultural production and the overall economy of developing countries has been enormous. As predicted, in agricultural terms Pakistan would find itself worse off than India – in turn possibly affecting their relations.[318] The prospective of food insecurities and declining economy for a growing population would very much question the credibility and legitimacy of Pakistani state and government to rule. Further the existing ethnic crisis and this growing sense of relative deprivation among the poor, deprived and depraved people will exacerbate separatist tendencies among various regions. Pakistan in order to divert domestic attention could draw India into the conflict.

The Philippines has also demonstrated clear links between ecological marginilazation and conflict. According to Daniel Lascon, in the early 1990s there are two sources of poverty and injustice behind the country's chronic insurgency: the accumulation of land in the hands of a few who failed to deal with the problems of poor, and land degradation that affected small farmers and was not alleviated by government action.

References

1. S. Dalby, "American Security Discourse: The Persistence of Geopolitics," Political Geography Quarterly, 9, 1990, pp. 171-88.
2. O.R. Holsti, "International Systems, Systems Change and Foreign Policy," Diplomatic History, 15, 1991, p. 94.
3. J.Joffe, "Entangled for ever", in C.W.Kegley Jr. and E.R.Wittkoff, eds., The Future of American Foreign Policy (New York: St. Martin's Press, 1992), p. 35.
4. M.Shamsul Haque, "Non-Traditional Security and the Environment in North east Asia", Work in Progress Vol. 16, No. 3, Summer 2002, p. 24.
5. Peter H.Gleick, World's Water: The Biennial Report on Fresh Water Resources (Washington D.C.: California: Island Press, 1998), pp. 105-106.

6. M.Gorbachev, "Reality and guarantees for a secure world", Moscow News, No. 39, 1987, p. 3287.
7. Quoted in Peter H.Gleick, World's Water, *op. cit.,* p. 106.
8. U.S. Department of State, "Environmental Diplomacy: The Environment and U.S. Foreign Policy", U.S. Department of State, Washington, D.C.: 1997.
9. Ted Gurr, Minorities at Risk: A Global view of Ethnopolitical Conflicts (Washington DC: US Institute of Peace Press, 1993).
10. J.Rifkin, Biospheric Politics: A New Consciousness for a New Century (New York: Crown, 1991), p. 2.
11. Sverre Lodgaard, "Environmental Conflict Resolution," paper presented at the UNEP meeting on Environmental Conflict Resolution, Nairobi, 30 March 1990, p. 18.
12. Norman Myers, "The Environmental Dimension to Security Issues", The Environmentalist Vol. 6, Winter 1986, p. 251.
13. See M.Shamsul Haque, "The Fate of Sustainable Development Under the Neoliberal Regimes in Developing Countries", International Political Science Review 20/2 (1999), pp. 199-222.
14. World Commission on Environment and Development, Our Common Future (Brundtland Report (New York / London: Oxford University Press, 1987)) p. 290.
15. Quoted in Dietrich Fisher, Nonmilitary Aspects of Security: A System's Approach, United Nations Institute for Disarmament and Research (UNIDIR), (Aldershot: Dartmouth Publishing Company Ltd, 1993), p. 10.
16. Norman Myers "The Environmental Dimension to Security Issues," The Environmentalist Vol. 6, Winter 1986, p. 253.
17. Gareth Porter "Environmental Security as National Security Issue", Current History, May 1995, p. 218.
18. Thomas F.Homer Dixon, Environment, Scarcity, and Violence (Princeton, New Jersy: Princeton University Press, 1999); Thomas F.Homer Dixon and Jessica Blitt, Evidences: Links Among Environment, Population, and Security (New York: Rowman and Littlefield, 1998); Thomas F.Homer Dixon, "Environmental Scarcities and Violent Conflict: Evidence from Cases", International Security Vol. 19, 1994, pp. 5-40.

19. Thomas F. Homer Dixon, Environment, Scarcity, and Violence, p. 7 and Daniel Esty et. al., "The State Failure Task Force Report: Phase II Findings", Environmental Change and Security Project Report 5, 1999, p. 63; S.C. Lonergan, ed., Environmental Change, adaptation and Security, (Boston: Klewer, 1999); David Dessler, "Review of Environmental Scarcity and Violence", Environmental Change and Security Project Report 5 (1999), pp. 100-101.
20. David L. Lhevy and Daniel Egan, "Capital Contests: National and Transnational Channels of Corporate Influence on the Climate Change Negotiations", Politics and Society Vol. 26, No. 3, September 1998, pp. 337-361. See also N.Gaan," Politics of Governance of Global Climate change: Not on Equity but on North's Interests", India Quarterly Vol. LVIII, No. 4, October-December 2001, pp. 89-112.
21. Gunther Bachler, Conflict and Cooperation in the Light of Global Human-Ecological Transformation, ENCOP, occasional paper 9, October 1993, p. 5.
22. Robert W.kates and B.L. Turner II and William Clark, "The Great Transformation", In B.L. Turner II, and William C. Clark, Robert W.Kates, John F.Richards, Jessica T. Mathews, William B. Mayer, eds. The Earth as Transformed by Human Action: Global and Regional Changes in the Biosphere over the Past 300 years (Cambridge: Cambridge University Press with Clark University, 1990), p. 1.
23. Gunther Bachler, Conflict and Cooperation, *Ibid.* p. 16.
24. Stephan Libiszewski, What is an Environmental Conflict? ENCOP, Occasional paper No. I, July 1992, p. 6.
25. Richard A. Matthew, Ted Gaulin, and Bryan McDonald, "The Elusive Quest: Linking Environmental Change and Conflict" submitted to Canadian Journal of Political Science, Revised Manu-script submitted; Dec 21, 2001, File Number: 01-12, p. 7.
26. See for details Nancy Peluso and Michael Watts, ed., Violent Environments (Ithaca: Cornell University Press, 2001), pp. 15-24.
27. Committee on the challenges of Modern Society, NATO, "Environment and Security in an International Context", NATO Report 232, 1999.

28. *Ibid*, p. 22.
29. Daniel Esty et.al., "The State Failure Task Force Report: Phase II Findings", Environmental Change and Security Project Report 5, 1999.
30. Ted Gaulin, "To Cultivate a New Model: Where do Soyasa and Gleditsch Fall Short", Environmental Change and Security Project Report 6, 2000, pp. 104-107.
31. Richard A. Matthew, et al., "The Elusive Quest", *op. cit.,* p. 9.
32. *Ibid*, p. 25.
33. Julian Simon, The Ultimate Resources (Princeton, N.J.: Princeton University Press, 1981), p. 345; and Julian Simon, The Ultimate Resource 2 (Princeton, N.J.: Princeton University Press, 1996).
34. Thomas F. Homer Dixon, Environment, Scarcity and Violence, p. 114.
35. Richard A. Matthew, et.al., The Elusive Quest, p. 21.
36. *Ibid*, p. 16.
37. Michael Walzer, Just and Unjust Wars: A Moral Argument with Historical Illustrations (New York: Basic Books, 1992); Michael Walzer, Spheres of Justice: A Defence of Pluralism and Equality (Oxford: M. Robertson, 1993); Michael Walzer, Thick and Thin: A Moral Argument at Home and Abroad (Notre Dame: University of Notre Dami Press, 1994); and Michael Walzer, "The Politics of Rescuse", Social Research 62, 1995, pp. 53-67.
38. Richard A. Matthew, *et. al*, "Elusive Quest, p. 24.
39. Volker Boge, "Proposal for an Analytical framework to grasp environmental conflict", ENCOP, occasional paper No. I, July 1992, Swiss Peace Foundation. p. 5.
40. Homer Dixon, Environment, Scarcity and Violence, *op. cit.*
41. Volker Boge, *op. cit.*
42. Peter H.Gleick, World's Water: The Biennial Report on Fresh Water Resources (Washington D.C.: Covels, California, Island Press, 1998); Haleh Hatami and Peter H.Gleick, "Chronology of Conflict over Water in the Legends, Myths and History of the Ancient Middle East", Report of the Pacific Institutes of the Studies in Development, Environment, and Security," Oakland, California, October 1992; Helga Haftendorn, "Water

and International Conflict", Third World Quarterly Vol. 21, No. 1, 2000, pp. 51-68; Marq De Villiers, Water Wars, London: Weidenfeld and Nicolson, 1999) ; World in Transition: Ways towards Sustainable Management of Fresh Water Resources, German Advisory Council on Global Change, Annual Report 1997 (Heidelberg: Springer – Verlag Berlin, 1999).

43. Megan, Environmental Scarcity of Fish and Conflict: The Case of India and Sri Lanka over Kachchativu Waters", International Studies Notes Vol-22, No. 3, Fall 1997, pp. 17-23.
44. Homer Dixon, Environment, scarcity and violence, *op. cit.*, p. 43.
45. *Ibid.*, p. 44.
46. See for example, Lothar Brock, "Peace through parks: The Environment on the Peace Research Agenda," Journal of Peace Research Vol. 28, (40), 1991, pp. 408-409.
47. Joseph Huber, Eine Sozialvissen schaftliche Interpretation der Humanokologie, Glaeser 1989, p. 65.
48. Stephan Libiszewski, "What is an Environmental Conflict?, ENCOP, Occasional paper No. 1, July 1992, p. 4.
49. Gunther Bachler," Conflict and Cooperation in the Light of Global Human-Ecological Transformation", ENCOP, occasional paper No. 9, October 1993, p. 5.
50. Stephan Libiszewski, What is an Environmental Conflict? *op. cit.,* p. 4.
51. See for several definitions, David Pearce and Kerry Turner, Economics of Natural Resources and the Environment (Baltimore: John Hopkins University Press, 1990), pp. 52-53.
52. Thomas F.Homer Dixon, Environment, Scarcity, and Violence (Princeton / NewJersey: Princeton University Press, 1999), p. 47.
53. United Nations Population Fund: The State of World Population (Oxford: Oxford University Press, 1992), p. 23.
54. Stephan Libiszewski, *op. cit.,* p. 5.
55. Judith Rees, "Resources and the Environment, Scarcity and Sustainability", in Robert Benneth and Robert Estall, ed., Global Change and Challenge: Geography for the 1990's (London / New York, 1991).

56. Thomas F.Homer Dixon, Environment, Scarcity, and Violence, p. 15.
57. Homer Dixon, and Valerie Percival, Environmental Scarcity and Violent Conflict: Briefing Book (University College, University of Toronto and America Association for the Advancement of Science, 1996), p. 6.
58. *Ibid*, p. 7.
59. Miriam Lowi, West Bank Water Resources, *op. cit.* ; Miriam Lowi, "Bridging the Divide: Transboundary Resource Disputes and the Case of West Bank Water", International Security Vol. 18, No. 1, 1993, pp. 113-38; Stephen Lonergan and David Books, Watershed: The Role of Fresh Water in the Israeli – Palestinian Conflict (Ottawa International Development Research Centre, 1994), Miriam Lowi, Water and Power: The Politics of a Scarce Resource in the Jordan River Basin (Cambridge: Cambridge University Press, 1995).
60. See Fred Pearce, "Wells of Conflict on the West Bank," New Scientist 130, No. 1777 (1 June 1991), pp. 37-38.
61. Miriam Lowi, West Bank Water Resource and the Resolution of Conflict in the Middle East, Occasional paper No. I, Project on Environmental Change and Acute Conflict (Cambridge, Mass: American Academy of Arts and Science and University of Toronto, 1992), p. 34.
62. Natasha Beschorner, Water and Instability in the Middle East, Adelphi Paper 273, International Institute for Strategic Studies (London: Brassey's 1992), p. 14, p. 78.
63. Thomas F. Homer Dixon, Environment, Scarcity and Violence, p. 76.
64. N.Gaan, "Water and Conflict in West Bank and Golan heights: Are Environmental Issues and National Security Linked", India Quarterly, July-December, 2002.
65. Homer Dixon, Environment, Scarcity, and Violence, *op. cit.*, p. 16.
66. Homer Dixon, and Percival, *op. cit.,* p. 7.
67. See Narottam Gaan, The Environmental Degradation and Conflict: The Case of Bangladesh – India (New Delhi: South Asian Publisher, 1998), pp. 100-107.

68. Jeffrey Leonard, "Overview", in Environment and the Poor: Development Strategies for a Common Agenda (New Brunswick, N.J: Transaction, 1989), p. 5.
69. See Richard Kessler, Rebellion and Repression in the Philippines (New Haven, Conn.: Yale University Press, 1989), p. 18.
70. See for fall account, Maria Conception Cruz et al., Population Growth, Poverty, and Environmental Stress: Frontier Migration in the Philippines and Costa Rica (Washington, D.C: World Resources Institute, 1992).
71. World Bank, Philippines: Environment and Natural Resource Management Study (Washington, D.C.: World Bank 1989).
72. Robin Broad with John Cavanaugh, Plundering Paradise: The Struggle for the Environment in the Philippines (Berkeley: University of California Press, 1993).
73. Washington Post," From Rwanda to Cairo", 25 August 1994, p. A18.
74. Thomas F.Homer Dixon and Valerie Percival, "Environmental Scarcity and Violent Conflict: The Case of Rwanda", Journal of Environment and Development No. 3, 1996, pp. 270-91.
75. See Ronnie Lipschutz, "Environmental Conflict and Environmental Determinism: The Relative Importance of Social and Natural Factors", in Nils Petter Gleditsch, ed., Conflict and the Environment (Dordrecht: The Netherlands: Kluer, 1997), pp. 35-50. See also Wenche Hauge and Tanja Ellingsen, "Beyond Environmental Scarcity: The Causal Pathways to Conflicts", Journal of Peace Research Vol. 35, No. 3, 1998, pp. 299-317.
76. Homer Dixon, Environment, Scarcity, and Violence, *op. cit.,* pp. 17-18.
77. World Resources Institute (WRI), World Resources 1990-91(New York: Oxford University Press, 1990), p. 5.
78. Nafis Sadik, The State of the World Population 1990(New York: United Nations Population Fund, 1990), p. 8.
79. See Jeffrey Leonard, "Overview", in Environment and the Poor: Development Strategies for a Common Agenda (New Brunswick, N.J.: Transaction, 1989), p. 13.

80. See Sara Scherr and Satya Jadav, Land Degradation in the Developing World: Implication of Food, Agriculture, and the Environment for 2020, IFPRI Food, Agriculture, and Environment Discussion paper 14 (Washington, D.C.: International Food Policy Research Institute, 1996).
81. Vaclav Smil, Energy, Food, Environment: Realities, Myths, Options (Oxford: Oxford University Press, 1987), pp. 223, 230.
82. Global Assessment of Soil Degradation, World Map on Status of Human Induced Soil Degradation (Nairobi, Kenya/ Wageningen, The Neatherlands: United Nations Environment Programme/ International Soil Reference Centre, 1990).
83. World Resources Institute (WRI), World Resources 1992-93(New York: Oxford University Press, 1992), p. 118.
84. World Resources Institute (WRI), World Resources 1996-97(New York: Oxford University Press, 1996), p. 205.
85. World Resources Institute (WRI), World Resources 1994-95(New York: Oxford University Press, 1994), pp. 130-35.
86. Gregg Marland, "The role of forest in addressing the carbon dioxide greenhouse in James C. White, ed., Global Climate Changes Linkages (New York: Elsevier, 1989).
87. Mikiyasu Nakayama, "Water: The 21st Century's Oil", Work in Progress Vol. 15, No. 2, The United Nations University, Winter 1998, p. 18.
88. Nicholas Kristof, "For Third World, Water is still a Deadly Drink", New York Times, 9 January 1997, p. 41; See also Linda Nash, "Water Quality and Health", in Peter Gleick, ed., Water in Crisis: A Guide to the World's Fresh Water Resources (New York: Oxford University Press, 1993).
89. WRI, World Resources 1990-91, *op. cit.,* pp. 170-171.
90. Thomas.F.Homer Dixon, Environment, Scarcity and Violence, *op. cit.,* p. 67.
91. Peter Gleick, "Water in 21st Century", in Gleick ed., Water in Crisis, *op. cit.,* p. 105. Malin Falkenmark. Fresh," Water: Times for a Modified Approach", Ambio Vol. 15, No. 4, 1986, pp. 192-200.
92. Tom Gardner Outlaw and Robert Engelman, Sustaining Water, Easing Scarcity: A Second Update (Washington, D.C.:

Population Action International, 1997); Homer Dixon, Environment, Scarcity, and Violence, *op. cit.,* p. 68.

93. Malin Falkenmark "The Massive Water Scarcity Now Threatening Africa –Why Is not it Being Addressed," Ambio Vol. 18, No. 2, 1989, pp. 112-18.
94. Tom Gardner-Outlaw and Robert Engleman, Sustaining Water, Easing Scarcity, Op.cit; and Malin Falkenmark and Asit Biswas, "Synopsis further Momentum to Water Issues: Comprehensive Water Problem Assessment in Being", Ambio Vol. 24, No. 6, 1995, pp. 380-82.
95. Food and Agriculture Organisation (FAO), The State of World Fisheries and Aquaculture (Rome: FAO, 1995), p. 2.
96. Food and Agriculture Organization (FAO), World Fisheries Situation and Outlook (Rome: FAO, 1989), p. 6.
97. FAO, The State of World Fisheries and Aquaculture, *op. cit.,* p. 6.
98. *Ibid*, p. 47.
99. *Ibid*, p. 5.
100. Homer Dixon, Environment, Scarcity and Violence, *op. cit.,* p. 70.
101. Michael Satchell, "The Rape of the Oceans", US News and World Report, 22 June 1992.
102. Hal Kane, "Fish catch is no longer growing", in Lester R.Brown, et.al eds., Vital Signs:The Trends That are Shaping our Future 1993-94(London: Earthscan, 1993), p. 32.
103. Testimony of Susan Weiler, Executive Director, American Society of Limnology and Oceanography, Department of Biology, Whitman College, Walla, Walla, Washington before Hearing of Global Change Research: Ozone Depletion and its Impacts, US Senate Committee on Commerce, Science, and Transportation, 15 November 1991.
104. D.Wawksworth and M.Kalin-Arroyo "Magnitude and Distribution of Biodiversity", Section 3 in V.H. Heywood and R.T Watson ed., Global Biodiversity Assessment (Cambridge: Cambridge University Press, 1995), p. 111.
105. *Ibid.*
106. S.Naeem et.al., "Declining Biodiversity can Alter the Performance of Ecosystems," Nature Vol. 368, No. 6473, 21

April 1994, pp. 734-37 ; D.Tilman, et.al., "Productivity and Sustainability Influenced by Biodiversity in Grassland Ecosystem", Nature Vol. 379, No. 6567, 22 February 1996, pp. 718-20.

107. Edward O.Wilson, "Threats to Biodiversity", Scientific American. Vol. 261, No. 3, September 1987, p. 111.

108. R.Barbault and S.Sastrapradja, "Geneneration, Maintenance and Loss of Biodiversity", in V.H. Heywood and R.T. Watson ed., Global Biodiversity Assessment, Section 4. *Op. cit.,* p. 198.

109. *Ibid.*

110. Homer Dixon, Environment, Scarcity, and Violence, *op. cit.,* p. 72.

111. Anil Agrawal and Sunita Narain, Global Warming in an Unequal World: A Case of Environmental Colonialism, (New Delhi: Centre for Science and Environment, 1991), p. 22-23.

112. Anil Agrawal and Sunita Narain, Towards a Green World (New Delhi: Centre for Science and Environment, 1992), p. 33.

113. Kirk Smith, "The Greenhouse index," Environment (Washington D.C.: Heldref Publication, 1991).

114. Anil Agrawal and Sunita Narain and Anju Sharma, Globgal Environmental Negotations I (New Delhi: Centre for Science and Environment, 1999), p. 20.

115. Narottam Gaan," Politics of Governance of Global Climate Change: Not on Equity but on North's Interests", India Quaterly Vol. LVIII, No. 4, October-December 2001, pp. 89-112; See also David L.Lhevy and Daniel Egan, "Capital Contests: National and Transnational Channels of Corporate Influence on the Climate Change Negotaition", Politics and Society Vol. 26, No. 3, September 1998, pp. 337-361.

116. J.T. Houghton et.al. Climate Change 1995-The Science of Climate Change (Cambridge: Cambridge University Press, 1996).

117. *Ibid*, p. 6.

118. Willam Stevens, "Global Climate Stayed Warm in 1996, with Wet, Cold Regional Surprises," New York Times, 14 January 1997, P.B9.

119. Houghton et. al., eds., Climate Change 1995, Science of Climate Change, *op. cit.,* p. 4.
120. See Anil Agrawal et.al., Global Environmental Negotiations I, *op. cit.,* p. 19.
121. R.T. Watson, M.C.Zinyowera and R.H. Moss eds., The Regional Impacts of Climate Change: An Assessment of Vulnerability, IPCC Working Group II Special Report, 1998 ; see also Down to Earth Vol. 6, No. 15, 31 December 1997, p. 30.
122. United Nations Environment Programme 2001, Basic Facts and Data on the Science and Politics of Ozone Protection, Press background, Nairobi, Http:// www.unep.org/ozone/pressBack/ as viewed on August 2, 2001.
123. "Ultraviolet Radiation on the Rise", Scientific American, Vol. 275, vo.4, October 1996, p. 28.
124. Gert Kelfkens, Frank de Gruijal, and Jan Van der Leun, "Ozone Depletion and Increase in Annual Carcinogenic Ultraviolet Dose" Photochemistry and Photobiology Vol. 52, No. 4, 1990, pp. 819-23.
125. Gavin Hayman et.al., Chilling Facts about a Burning Issue: CFC Smuggling in the European Union, London Environmental Investigation Agency, 1997, p. 2.
126. "Environmental Effects of Ozone Depletion: 1994 Assessment", Special issue of Ambio Vol. 24, No. 3, 1995.
127. Cynthia Pollock Shea, Protecting Life on earth: Steps to save the Ozone layer, Washington D.C.: World Watch Paper 87, 1988.
128. Anil Agrawal and Sunita Narain, Towards a Green World, *op. cit.,* p. 8.
129. Anil Agrawal and Sunita Narain, Anju Sharma and Achila Imchen eds., Global Environmental Negotiation 2 ; Poles Apart, (New Delhi: Centre for Science and Environment, 2001), p. 13.
130. *Ibid*, p. 80.
131. Quoted in Julian Newman and Steven Trent, A Crime Against Nature, (London: Environmental Investigation Agency, 1998), p. 1.

132. *Ibid.*, p. 2.
133. World Energy Council, Energy For Tomorrow's World: The Realities, the Real options, and the Agenda for Achievement (New York: St. Martin's Press, 1993), P.III ; and World Energy Council and International Institute for Applied Systems Analysis, Global Energy Perspectives to 2050 and Beyond(London: World Energy Council, 1995), p. 45.
134. Dan M.Kammen, "Cookstoves for the Developing World", Scientific American Vol. 273, No. 1, July 1995, pp. 72-75.
135. Thomas F.Homer Dixon, Environment, Scarcity and Violence, *op. cit.,* p. 59.
136. World Energy Council, Energy For Tomorrow's World, *op. cit.*
137. S.W. Gouse, et.al., (MI TRE Corporation) "Potential World Development Through 2100: The Impacts of Energy Demand, Resources and the Environment", ın World Energy Council Journal, (London: World Energy Council, 1992), pp. 18-32.
138. Quoted in Homer Dixon, Environment, Scarcity and Violence, *op. cit.,* p. 60.
139. The Geopolitics of Energy into the 21st Century, Centre for Strategic and International Studies, February 15, 2001.
140. Down to Earth, Vol. 11, No. 11, October 31, 2002, p. 36.
141. Dennis Anderson, "Energy and Environment: Technical and Economic Possibilities", Finance and Development, IMF, Washington D.C., June 1996, pp. 10-13.
142. Nebojsa Nakicenovic et al.ed., Global Energy Perspectives (Cambridge: Cambridge University Press, 1998).
143. Down to Earth, 31 October 2002, p. 30.
144. Sivan Kartha, et.al., Meaningful Participation for the North and South, Presented at a Workshop conducted by SEI and CSE on Towards Equity and Sustainability in the Kyoto Protocol, Buenos Aires, 8 November 1998.
145. Richard Bilsborrow and H.W.O Okoth Ogendo, "Population Driven Changes in Land Use in Developing Countries," Ambio Vol. 21, No. 1, 1992, pp. 37-45 ; and Tom Rudel and Jill Roper, "Regional Patterns and Historical Trends in Tropical Deforestation, 1976-1990: A Qualitative Comparative Analysis", Ambio Vol. 25, No. 3, 1996, pp. 160-66.

146. United Nations Population Division, World Population Prospects: The 1996 Revision, Demographic Indicators 1950, 2050, Diskettes 1-4 (New York: United Nations, 1996).
147. John Bongaarts, "Population Policy Options in the Developing World", Science Vol. 263, No. 5148, 11 February 1994, pp. 771-76.
148. See Nathan Keylitz's review of Alfred Sauvy's article in Population and Development Review Vol. 15, No. 2, 1989, pp. 359-62.
149. Ben Wattenberg, "The Population Explosion is Over", New York Times Magazine, 23 November 1997, pp. 60-63; Nicholas Eberstadt, "The Population Implosion", Wall Street Journal, 16 October 1997, P.A22.
150. Kerstin Kiessling and Nathan Keylitz, "The Population Debate: Urgency of the Problem", Paper presented at the Population Summit of the World's Scientific Academics held in New Delhi from October 24-27, 1993; See also Down to Earth Vol. 2, 30 November 1993, p. 15.
151. Thomas F.Homer Dixon, Environment, Scarcity and Violence, (Princeton, New Jersey: Princeton University Press, 1999), p. 80, and Volker Boge," Analytical Framework to grasp environmental conflict," ENCOP, Centre for Security Studies and Conflict Research and Swiss Peace Foundation, Zurich/Bern, Occasional Paper No. I, July 1992, p. 4.
152. Vaclav Smil, Energy, Food, Environment: Realities, Myths, Options (Oxford: Oxford University Press, 1987).
153. Fakhri A. Bazzaz and Eric D. Fajer, "Plant Life in a CO_2 Rich World", Scientific American Vol-266, No. I, January 1992, pp. 68-74 ; Harold A. Mooney and George W. Koch, "The Impact of Rising CO_2 Concentrations on the Terrestrial Biosphere", Ambio Vol. 23, No. I, 1994, pp. 74-76.
154. Per Pinstrup-Anderson, World Food Trends and Future Food Security, Food Policy Report (Washington, D.C.: The International Food Policy Research Institute, 1994, p. 3.
155. Celestine Bohlen, "Conference on Food Aid Starts in Rome," New York Times, 13 November 1996, P.A5.
156. Thomas F. Homer Dixon, Environment, Scarcity and Violence (Princeton, New Jersey: Princeton University Press, 1999), p. 84.

157. Down To Earth Vol. 9 No. 6, August 15, 2000, pp. 30-40: See also Peter Hazell and C. Ramasamy, The Green Revolution Reconsidered: The Impact of High Yielding Rice Varieties in South India (Baltimore: Johns Hopkins University Press, 1991).
158. Pierre Crosson and Jock Anderson, Resources and Global Food Prospects: Supply and Demand for Cereals to 2030. World Bank Technical Paper Number 184(Washington, D.C.: World Bank, 1992), p. 12.
159. WRI, World Resource 1996-97, p. 238.
160. Mark Rosegrant, Mercedita Agcaoili-Sombilla, and Nicostrato Perez, Global Food Projections to 2020: Implications for Investment, IFPRI Food, Agriculture, and the Environment Discussion Paper 5 (Washington, D.C.: International Food Policy Research Institute, 1995).
161. Homer Dixon, Environment, Scarcity and Violence, *op. cit.*, p. 82.
162. Volker Boge, Proposal for an Analytical Framework to Grasp Environmental Conflict, p. 4.
163. J.D.Longstreth et al., "Changes in Ultraviolet Radiation Reaching the Earth's Surface," Ambio Vol. 24, No. 3, 1995, pp. 153-65: Harry Slaper et al., "Estimate of Ozone Depletion and Skin Cancer Incidence to Examine the Vienna Convention Achievements," Nature Vol. 384, No. 6606, 21 November 1996, pp. 256-68.
164. Per Pinstrup-Anderson, "Global Perspectives for Food Production and Consumption," Tidsskrift for Land Okonomi Vol. 4, No. 179, 1992, pp. 145-69.
165. Jeffrey Leonard, "Overview", in Environment and the Poor: Development Strategies for a Common Agenda (New Brunswick, N.J.: Transaction, 1989), pp. 27.
166. Robert Repetto, "Balance Sheet Erosion How to Account for the Loss of Natural Resources", International Environmental Affairs Vol. 1, No. 2, 1989, p. 129.
167. *Ibid.*, pp. 103-37.
168. Kimberley Kelly and Thomas Homer Dixon, Environmental Scarcity and Violent Conflict: The Case of Gaza, Occasional Paper of the Project on Environment, Population, and Security

(Washington, D.C.: American Association for the Advancement of Science and the University of Toronto, 1996).

169. Vaclav Smil and Mao Yushi, The Economic Cost of China's Environmental Degradation, Occasional Paper of the Project on Environmental Scarcities, State Capacity, and Civil Violence (Cambridge, Mass: American Academy of Arts and Science and the University of Toronto, 1998).

170. See Jodi Jacobson, Environmental Refugees: A Yardstick of Habitability, Worldwatch Paper 86(Washington D.C.: Worldwatch Institute, 1988); Arthur H.Westing, "Environmental Refugees: A Growing Category of Displaced Persons," Environmental Conservation 19, No. 3 1992, pp. 201-7; Norman Myers, Ultimate Security: The Environmental Basis of Political Stability (New York: W.W. Norton, 1993); Norman Myers, "Environmental Refugees in a Global Warmed World", BioScience 43, No. II 1993, pp. 752-61 ; and Norman Myers and J.Kent, Environmental Exodus: An Emergent Crisis in the Global Arena(Washington D.C.: Climate Institute, 1995).

171. E.EI Hinnawi, Environmental Refugees, UN Environmental Programme, Nairobi, 1985, p. 4.

172. Anthony H.Richmond, "Reactive Migration: Sociological Perspectives on Refugees Movements", Journal of Refugee Studies Vol. 6, 1993, p. 6.

173. A. Giddens, The Consequences of Modernity (Cambridge: Polity Press, 1991), p. 171.

174. V.Sahrke and A. Vinsentin, "The Environmental Refugees: A New Approach", Ecodecision, September 1991, pp. 37-74.

175. Astri Suhrke, Pressure Points: Environmental Degradation, Migration, and Conflict, Occasional Paper No. 3, Project on Environmental Change and Acute Conflict (Cambridge, Mass.: American Academy of Arts and Sciences and the University of Toronto, 1993); and Astri Suhrke," Environmental Degradation and Population Flows", Journal of International Affairs Vol. 47, No. 2, 1994, pp. 473-524.

176. Thomas F. Homer Dixon, Environment, Scarcity and Violence, *op. cit.,* pp. 93-94.

177. Homer Dixon, Environment, Scarcity and Violence, p. 95; Sanjoy Hazarika, Bangladesh and Assam: Land Pressures,

Migration, and Ethnic Conflict, Occasional Paper No. 3, project on Environmental Change and Acute Conflict, (Cambridge, Mass.: American Academy of Arts and Science and the University of Toronto, 1993), pp. 52-54 and N.Gaan, Environmental Degradation and Conflict: The Case of Bangladesh – India (New Delhi: South Asian Publishers, 1998), pp. 62-63.

178. Valerie Percival and Thomas Homer Dixon, "Environmental Scarcity and Violent Conflict: The Case of South Africa," Journal of Peace Research 35, No. 3, May 1998, pp. 279-98.
179. Homer Dixon, Environment, Scarcity and Violence, *op. cit.,* p. 96.
180. Francis Wilson and Mamphela Ramphele, Uprooting Poverty: The South African Challenge (New York – Norton, 1989).
181. Lesley Lawson," The Ghetto and the Greenbelt", in Jacklyn Cock and Eddie Koch, ed., Going Green: People, Politics, and the Environment in South Africa (Capetown: Oxford University Press, 1991), p. 47.
182. Anthony Minnaar, "Undisputed Kings: Warlordism in Natal", in Anthony Minnaar ed., Patterns of Violence: Case Studies of Conflict in Natal (Pretoria: Human Science Research Council, 1992), p. 92.
183. Doug Hindson, Mark Byerley, and Mike Morris, "From Violence to Reconstruction: The Making, Disintegration, and Remaking of an Apartheid City", Antipode 26, No. 4, 1994, p. 341.
184. N.Gaan, Environmental Degradation and Conflict, *op. cit.*
185. Douglass North, Institutions, Institutional Change and Economic Performance (Cambridge: Cambridge University Press, 1990), p. 3.
186. Elizabeth Economy, Reforms and Resources: The Implications for State Capacity in the People's Republic of China, Occasional Paper of the Project on Environmental Scarcities, State Capacity, and Civil Violence (Cambridge, Mass.: American Academy of Arts and Sciences and the University of Toronto, 1997).
187. Thomas Homer Dixon, Environment, Scarcity and Violence p. 101.

188. J.D. Kasarda and A.M. Parnell, eds., Third World Cities: Problems, Policies and Prospects (London: Sage, 1993).
189. Elizabeth Economy, Reforms and Resources, *op. cit.*
190. Philip "Shenon Gincum Journal: Good Earth is Squandered. Who will Feed China?" New York Times, 21 September 1994, P.A10.
191. See Charles Barber, Indonesia Case Study, Occasional Paper of the Project on Environmental Scarcities, State Capacity and Civil Violence (Cambridge, Mass: American Academy of Arts and Science, and the University or Toronto, 1997).
192. Barber, Indenesia Case Study, *op. cit.*
193. Homer Dixon, Environment, Scarcity, and Violence, p. 108.
194. See Paul Romer, "The Origins of Endogenous Growth," Journal of Economic Perspective Vol. 8, No. 1, 1994, pp. 3-22.
195. Homer Dixon, Environment, Scarcity and Violence, p. 110.
196. *Ibid.*
197. *Ibid*, p. 114.
198. Julian Simon, The Ultimate Resources (Princeton, N.J.: Princeton University Press, 1981) p. 345.
199. Homer Dixon, Environment, Scarcity and Violence, *op. cit.* p. 117-118.
200. Robert Repetto, "Population, Resources, Environment: An Uncertain Future", Population Bulletin Vol. 42, No. 2, 1987, pp. 6-7.
201. World Bank, World Development Report 1992(New York: Oxford University Press, 1992), p. 70.
202. Mancur Olson, The Rise and Decline of Nations: Economic Growth, Stagflation, and Social Rigidities (New Haven, Conn.: Yale University Press, 1982).
203. *Ibid*, p. 165.
204. *Ibid*, p. 44.
205. Elinor Ostrom, Larry Schroeder, Susan Wynne, "Institutional Incentives and Sustainable Development," World Development Vol. 17, No. 9, 1989, pp. 1375-87; Also see David Reed's review of the World Bank's World Development Report 1992 in International Environmental Affairs Vol. 4, No. 4, 1992, pp. 367-71.

206. Olson, Rise and Decline, p. 62.
207. Vernon Ruttan and Yujiro Hayami, "Towards a Theory of Induced Institutional Innovation," The Journal of Development Studies Vol. 20, No. 4, 1984, P213.
208. James Boyce, Agrarian Impasse in Bengal: Institutional Constraints to Technological Change (Oxford: Oxford University Press, 1987) see also Homer Dixon, Environment, Scarcity and Violence, Chapter-3.
209. Richard Kessler, Rebellion and Repression in the Philippines (New Havan, Conn.: Yale University Press, 1989), p. 18.
210. Thomas Homer Dixon, Environment, Scarcity and Violence, p. 120.
211. Peter Evans, "The State as Problem and Solution: Predation, Embedded Autonomy, and Structural Change," in Stephan Haggard and Robert Kaufman (Princeton, N.J.: Princeton University Press, 1992), p. 144.
212. See Mamman Aminu Ibrahim, "The Information Drain: Obstacles to Research in Africa", Gatekeeper Series No. 32 (London: International Institute for Environment and Development, 1992).
213. United Nations Development Program, Human development Report 1992, (New York: Oxford University Press, 1992), p. 57.
214. Homer Dixon, Environment, Scarcity and Violence, pp. 123-24.
215. E.O. Wilson, "Is Humanity Suicidal? New York Times Magazine, 30 May 1993, p. 29; Michael Manning and David Rejeski," Sustainable Development and Risk: A Fit? Paper presented at the Conference on Comparative Risk and Priority Setting of Air Pollution Issues, Keystone, Colo., 7-11 June 1993.
216. See Joseph Traub and Henryk Wozniakowski, "Breaking Intractability", Scientific American Vol. 270, No. 1. January 1994, pp. 102-7.
217. Thomas Homer Dixon, Environment, Scarcity and Violence, p. 124.
218. Robert Wright, "The Experiment That Failed: Why Soviet Science Collapsed", The New Republic 205, No. 18, 28

October 1991, pp. 20-25 ; and Sergei Kapitza, "Anti Science Trends in the USSR", Scientific American 265, No. 2, August 1999, pp. 32-38.

219. John Dollard et al. Frustration And Aggression (New Haven, Conn.: Yale University Press, 1939); Lenoard Berkowitz, Aggression: A Social Psychological Analysis (New York: McGraw-Hill, 1962). On relative deprivation, see James Davies, "Toward a Theory of Revolution", American Sociological Review 27, No. 1, 1962, pp. 5-19; Ted Gurr, Why Men Rebel (Princeton, N.J.: Princeton University Press, 1970); and Ted Gurr and Raymond Duvall, "Civil Conflict in the 1960s: A Reciprocal Theoretical System with Parameter Estimates", Comparative Political Studies Vol. 6, No. 2, 1973, pp. 135-69.

220. Henri Tajfel, ed., Differentiation between Social Groups (London: Academic Press, 1978); Edward Azar and John Burton, International Conflict Resolution: Theory and Practice (Sussex: Wheatsheaf, 1986); Lewis Coser, The Function of Social Conflict (London: Free Press, 1956) and Donald Horowitz, Ethnic Groups in Conflict (Berkeley: University of California Press, 1985).

221. See Thomas F. Homer Dixon, Environment, Scarcity and Violence p. 137.

222. Alexander Wendt, "The Agent-Structure Problem", International Organisation Vol. 41, No. 3, 1987, pp. 335-70, and Anthony Giddens, The Constitution of Society: Outline of the Theory of Structuration (Berkley: University of California Press, 1984).

223. See Kenneth Waltz, Theory of International Politics (Reading, Mass: Addison-Wesley, 1979); and Bruce Bueno de Mesquita, The War Trap (New Haven, Conn.: Yale University Press, 1981).

224. Thomas Homer Dixon, Environment, Scarcity and Violence, p. 137.

225. Charles Tilly, From Mobilization to Revolution (Reading, Mass: Addison-Wesley, 1987); and Sidney Tarrow, Power in Movement: Social Movements, Collective Action and Politics (Cambridge: Cambridge University Press, 1994).

226. Volker Boge, "Proposal for an analytical framework to grasp environmental conflict", Environmental Conflicts Project (ENCOP), Centre for Security Studies and Conflict Research, Swiss Federal Institute of Technology, Swiss Peace Foundation, Zurich/Bern, Occasional paper No. 1, July 1992, p. 4.
227. Nazil Choucri and Robert North, Nations in Conflict (San Francisco: Freeman, 1975).
228. For general analysis of the role of scarcity of nonrenewable resources in interstate conflict, see Ronnie D.Lipschutz, When Nations Clash (Cambridge, Mass.: Ballinger Publishing, 1989).
229. Waltz, Theory of International Politics; Robert Gilpin, War and change in World Politics (Cambridge: Cambridge University Press, 1981): For views of political change in realist theory, see R.B.J Walker, "Realism, Change and International Political Theory", International Studies Quarterly Vol. 31, No. 1, 1987, pp. 65-86.
230. See Robert Albion, Forests and Sea Power: The Timber Problem of the Royal Navy, 1652-1863 (Cambridge, Mass; Harvard University Press, 1926).
231. Thomas F.Homer Dixon, Environment, Scarcity and Violence, p. 139.
232. Peter Gleick, Water and Conflict, Occasional paper No. 1, Project on Environmental Change and Acute Conflict (Cambridge, Mass: American Academy of Arts and Science and the University of Toronto, 1992); Peter H.Gleick, World's Water: The Biennial Report on Fresh Water Resources (Washington D.C.: California, Island Press, 1998), pp. 105-153.
233. Ismail Serageldin, "Earth Faces Water Crisis", Press Release, World Bank, Washington, D.C.: 6 August 1995.
234. Quoted in Mikiyasu Nakayama, "Water: The 21st Century Oil," Work In Progress, A Review of Research Activities of the United Nations University Vol. 15, No. 2, Winter 1998, p. 18.
235. Peter H.Gleick, World's Water, p. 107.
236. United Nations, Comprehensive Assessment of the Freshwater Resources of the World.Prepared for the Commission for Sustainable Development and the General Assembly. Stockholm Environment Institute and the United Nations,

Nations, New York 1997; P.H. Gleick, "Water and Conflict", International Security Vol. 18, No. 1, pp. 79-112.

237. M.R.Lowi, Water and Power: The Politics of a scarce resource in the Jordan River Basin (Cambridge: Cambridge University Press, 1995) pp. 115-144.
238. *Ibid*, p. 125.
239. Mariam R.Lowi, "Water and Conflict in the Middle East and South Asia: Are Environmental Issues and Security Issue Linked?, The Journal of Environment and Development" Vol. 8, No. 4, December 1999, pp. 387-88.
240. S.Chira, "North Korea dam worries the South", The New York Times, 30 November 1986, p. 3; and N.Koch, "North Korea dam seen as potential water bomb", Washington Post/ San Francisco Chronicle, September 30, 1987, p. 3.
241. P.H. Gleick, "Water and conflict", *op. cit.,* pp. 79-112.
242. A.Dupont, "The Environment and Security in East Asia", The Adelphi Paper, Research School of Pacific and Asian Studies, Strategic and Defence Studies Centre, Australian National University, Canberra, Australia, 1998.
243. J.Lee, "KL uses water as a political tool", The Jakarta Post, 7 July 1997.
244. G.P.Zachary, "Water Pressure: Nations Scramble to defuse fights over supplies", The Wall Street Journal, 4 December 1997, P.A17.
245. Peter H.Gleick, World's Water, p. 111.
246. Towards Sustainable Development: National Conservation Strategy of Bangladesh, Ministry of Environment and Forest, Government of Bangladesh/IUCN, 1991, p. 69.
247. Mohabab Hossein, "Briefing Paper (Bangladesh)" (London: Overseas Development Institute, November 1990), p. 1.
248. *Ibid.*, p. 3.
249. Atiur Rahman, Impact of Riverbank Erosion: Survival Strategies of Displacees (Dhaka: Bangladesh Institute of Development Studies, 1985), p. 11.
250. John R.Rogge, Riverbank Erosion: Flood and Population Displacement in Bangladesh (Dhaka: Jahangirnagar University, October 1990), p. 35.
251. Atiur Rahman, *op. cit.,* pp. 19-20.

252. Paul Harrison, The Third Revolution: Environment, Population and a Sustainable World (London/ New York: Tauries and Co. Ltd., 1992), p. 230.
253. Don Hinrichsen, Our Common Seas: Coasts in Crisis (London: Earthscan Publication Ltd. In association with United Nations Environment Programme, Nairobi, 1990), chapter 9, p. 127.
254. Jessica Tuchman Mathews, "Redefining Security", Foreign Affairs Vol. 68, No. 2, Spring 1989, pp. 162-177.
255. Thomas F.Homer Dixon, "Environmental Change and Economic Decline in Developing Countries", International Studies Notes Vol. 16, No. 1, Winter 1991, p. 22.
256. Sanjoy Hazarika, Bangladesh and Assam: Land Pressures, Migration and Ethnic Conflict, Occasional Paper series of the Project on Environmental Change and Acute Conflict, A Joint Project of the University of Toronto and the American Academy of Arts and Sciences, No. 3 March 1993, p. 52.
257. *Ibid.*
258. Shika Mukharjee, Special Correspondent of Times of India, Calcutta, December 1992, quoted in Sumit Ganguly, "Ethno-religious Conflict in South Asia", Survival Vol. 35, no, 2, Summer 1993, p. 100.
259. Raj Chengappa and Ramesh Menon, "The New Battle Fields", India Today, 31 January 1993, pp. 28-29.
260. Sumit Ganguly, "Ethno-religious Conflict in South Asia", Survival Vol. 35, No. 2, Summer 1993, p. 100.
261. Times of India, 26 November 2001; Samaj, November 1 2001; Pragatibadi, 28 September 2001.
262. Prajatantra, 14 January 2001; Sambad, 2 December 2000; Sambad, 13 February 2001.
263. Robert G.Gosselink, "Minority Rights and Ethnic Conflict in Assam, India", Boston College Third World Journal Vol. XIV, Winter 1994, p. 91.
264. *Ibid.*
265. Sharifa Begum, Population, Birth, Death and Growth Rates in Bangladesh: Census Estimates (Dhaka, Bangladesh Institute of Development Studies), 1990, p. 56; Marcus Franda, Bangladesh: The First Decade (New Delhi: South Asian Publishers, 1981) p. 235; Census of India, 1991.

266. Amiya Kumar Das, Assam's Agony: A Socio-Economic and Political Analysis, 1982, p. 38, quoted in R.G. Gosselink, *op. cit.,* p. 90.
267. Sanjoy Hazarika, Assam: A Crisis of Identity (1980), p. 10, quoted in Gosselink, *Ibid.* ; see also Mynor Weiner, Sons of the Soil: Migration and Ethnic Conflict in India (New Delhi: Oxford University Press, 1988) pp. 80-81.
268. Thomas F.Homer Dixon," Environmental Scarcities and Violent Conflict: Evidence from Cases," International Security Vol. 19, No. 1, summer 1994, p. 22; see also Sanjoy Hazarika, *op. cit.,* pp. 52-54.
269. Prasun Sonwalkar, "Exodus of Bangladesh to India", Times of India, 6 December 1991, p. 4; Amulya Ganguli, "Bangladesh Lebensraum", Times of India, 13 July 1992.
270. Sanjoy Hazarika, "India Admits Failure to Cut Bangladesh Influx", New York Times, 16 December 1992.
271. Sanjoy Hazarika, *op. cit.,* n 256, p. 58.
272. *Ibid.*, p. 59.
273. Ruben Banarjee, "The NorthEast: Returns to Arms", India Today, 30 November 1992, pp. 36-37.
274. Jonathan S.Landay, "Gandhi Loses an Election to Party Favouring Expelling Moslems", UPI, 18 December 1985, available in Lexis, Nexis Library, UPI File.
275. Mani Deb, "Assam's Patience with Delhi Grows Increasingly Thin", Financial Times, 3 February 1988.
276. Times of India, 29 August 1995, p. 6.
277. Times of India, 1 December 1995. See also Nitin A.Gokhale," Power Keg: What makes the North-east of the Country's Hottest Trouble Spots for Alleged Hands of External Powers like Bangladesh and Pakistan, Sunday Vol. 23, No. 12, 24-30 March 1996, pp. 14-22.
278. Sanjoy Hazarika, "Bangladesh and Assam: Land Pressures", *op. cit.,* p. 61.
279. Homer Dixon, Environment, Scarcity and Violence, p. 142.
280. Kurt Schock, "A Conjunctural Model of Political Conflict", Journal of Conflict Research Vol. 40, No. 1, 1996, pp. 93-133.
281. Mark Lichbach, "An Evaluation of Does Economic Inequality Breed Political Conflict Studies", World Politics Vol. 41, No.

4, 1989, pp. 431-70; See also Raj Desai and Harry Eckstein," Insurgency: The Transformation of Peasant Rebellion", World Politics Vol. 42, No. 4, 1990, pp. 441-465.

282. Peter Wallensteen, "Food Crops As a Factor in Strategic Policy and Action", in Arthur H. Westing ed., Global Resources and International Conflict: Environmental Factors in Strategic Policy and Action (New York: Oxford University Press, 1986), pp. 154-55.

283. Bruce Byers, "Ecoregions, State Sovereignty and Conflict", Bulletin of Peace Propasals Vol. 22 (1) 1991, p. 69.

284. See Christoper McLeod, Randy Hayes and Glenn Switkes, "The Four Corners: A National Sacrifice Area", reprinted from The Workbook Quarterly Journal of the SouthWest Research and Information Centre, P.O. Box 4524, Albuquerque NM.87106, USA, April –June 1985.

285. See Chelvaduari Manogaran, Ethnic Conflict and Reconciliation in Sri Lanka (Honolulu: University of Hawaii Press, 1987).

286. See Bruce Byers, *op. cit.,* p. 71.

287. Robert N.Kearney, "Ethnic Conflict and Tamil Separatist Movement in Sri Lanka", Asian Survey Vol. 25, No. 9, September 1985, pp. 904-905; James Manor, ed., Sri Lanka in Change and Crisis (New York: St Martin Press, 1984), p. 1.

288. Mohan Ram, Sri Lanka: The Fractured Nation (New Delhi: Penguin Books, 1989), p. 33.

289. K.M.de Silva, Managing Ethnic Tensions in Multi-Ethnic Societies: Sri Lanka, 1880-1985(Lanham, MD: University Press of America, 1986); C. Manogaran, Ethnic Conflict and Resolution in Sri Lanka (Honolulu, HI: University of Hawaii Press, 1987).

290. S.V. Kodikara, "The Separatist Eelam Movement in Sri Lanka: An Overview", India Quarterly Vol. 37, April-June 1981, pp. 194-212.

291. M.Y.Mohammad Siddique, "Land and Colonization Problems in Aparai Districts", Cintanai (Jaffana) Vol. 1, July 1983, pp. 94-212.

292. V.Suryanarayana, "Ethnic Conflict in Sri Lanka", in Urmila Phadnis, S.D. Muni and Kalim Bahadur, ed., Domestic

Conflicts in South Asia Vol. 1, Political Dimensions (New Delhi: South Asia Publishers, 1986), p. 140.

293. See, New York Times, June 1987, p. 9.
294. Times of India, 11 May 1995.
295. Donald Horowitz, Ethnic Groups in Conflict (Berkeley and Los Angeles: University of California Press, 1985), p. 167.
296. Quoted in Times of India, 4 September 1995.
297. Paul P.Appasamy, "City of Thrist", Down to Earth Vol. 2, No. 20, 15 March 1994, pp. 34-35.
298. Marshall R.Singer, "Prospects for Conflict Management in the Sri Lankan Ethnic Crisis", in Joseph V. Montvile, ed., Conflict and Peace Making in Multi-Ethnic Societies (New York: Lexington Books, 1991), p. 27.
299. "LTTE has Major Role in Arms Supply to Militants: Government", Times of India, 6 December 1995, p. 9.
300. Charles H.Kennedy, "The Politics of Ethnicity of Sindh", Asian Survey Vol. 31, No. 10, October 1991, p. 9.
301. See Shahid Jaded Burki, "Migration, Urbanization and Politics in Pakistan" in Howard Wriggins and James Guyot, ed., Population and Politics of South Asia (New York, 1983), pp. 147-148, quoted in Uma Singh, "Ethnic Conflicts in Pakistan: Sind as a Factor in Pakistani Politics" in Urmilla Phadnis, S.D. Muni and Kalim Bahadur, ed., Domestic Conflicts in South Asia, *op. cit.,* p. 156.
302. Nahid Islam, "Ethnicity and Environment in South Asia", p. 53.
303. Donald Rothchild, "State and Ethnicity in Africa: A Policy Perspective" in Nevitte and Kennedy, Ethnic Preference and Public Policy in Developing States (Boulder, Co: Lynne Rienner Press, 1986), pp. 47-48.
304. Craig Baxter, Yogendra K.Mallik, Charles H.Kennedy and Robert C.Oberst, Government and Politics in South Asia (Boulder and London: Westview Press, 1987), p. 185.
305. Sandy Gordon, "Resources and Instability in South Asia", Survival Vol. 35, No. 2, Summer 1992, p. 76.
306. John Kasarda and Allan Parnell," Introduction: Third World Development Issues" in John Kasarda and Allan Parnell ed., Third World Cities: Problems, Policies and Prospects (New York: Sage 1993), pp. IX-X.

307. A.S.Oberai, Population Growth, Employment and Poverty in Third World Mega-cities (New York: St. Martin's Press, 1993), p. 26.
308. *Ibid.*, p. 28.
309. Wayne A. Cornelius, Jr., "Urbanisation as an Agent in Latin American Political Instability: The Case of Mexico", American Political Science Review, 63, No. 3, 1969, pp. 833-57.
310. Kenneth F.Johnson, "Causal Factor in Latin American Political Instability", Western Political Quarterly, 17, No. 3, 1964, p. 441.
311. Michael Lipton, quoted in Lestern R.Brown and Jodi L.Jacobson, "The Future of Urbanization: Facing the Ecological and Economic Constraints", World Watch paper 77, May 1978, p. 13.
312. Farida Shaheed, "The Pathan-Muhajir Conflict, 1985-6: A National Perspective", in Veena Das, ed., Mirrors of Violence: Communities, Riots and Survivors in South Asia (New York: Oxford University Press, 1990), p. 205.
313. Ahmed Rashid, "Mean Streets: Chaos and Violence Rule in Karachi", Far Eastern Economic Review, 157, No. 43, 27 October 1994, p. 19.
314. Arif Hasan, "Karachi and the Global Nature of Urban Violence", Urban Age 1, No. 4, 1993, p. 5.
315. Wayne Cornelius Jr. "Urbanization As an Agent in Latin American Political Instability: The Case of Mexico", American Political Science Review Vol. 63, No. 3, September 1969, pp. 833-57; Abdur Lodhi and Charles Tilly, "Urbanization, Crime and Collective Violence in 19th Century France", American Journal of Sociology Vol. 79, No. 2, September 1973, pp. 296-318.
316. Times of India, 2 January 1995, "Pakistan Cries Wolf Again," M.B.Naqvi from Karachi, p. 15.
317. See W. W. Kellog, "Society, Science and Climate Change", Foreign Affairs Vol. 60, 1982, pp. 1076-1109.
318. Norman Myers, "The Environmental Dimension to Security Issues", *op. cit.*, p. 253.

3

Politics of Environmental Security and Traversing Beyond The Westphalian Thematic

Although many recent approaches, such as constructism, critical geopolitics, postmodernism and historical sociology have strongly disavowed the idea of 'state security' propounded by the realists, neorealists, and the neoliberals, they have not been able to dilute the centrality of security in International Relations.

The analysts favouring the realist paradigm hold that the international system is fundamentally anarchic in the sense that political life therein is dominated by states not subject to any authority superior to their own sovereignty. Within this anarchic system, states will purse relentlessly their respective national interests in order to ensure their survival in the face of formidable forces trying to deny this. The core concept of national interest is to be defined in terms of power as the only means of attaining national prosperity and security. Within the anarchic system, states are in constant competition, which, however, does not prevent them from accommodating their respective interests through cooperation where it directly serves them in their quest for national security and prosperity.

The central assumption of Kenneth Waltz's Theory of International Politics (1979) is typically Hobbesian. He wrote: "The state among states, it is often said, conducts its affairs in the brooding shadow of violence. Because some states may at time use forces, all states must be prepared to do so – or live at the mercy of their militarily more vigorous neighbours. Among states, the state of nature is state of war."[1] Waltz conceives the international system as self help system and treats states as defensive actors, in as much as their primary, though not exclusive, intention is self preservation. Thus, while states are not necessarily self-aggrandizing, they are compulsively self-help units, looking for their own security amidst an anarchical milieu where the probability of threats to their survival is always real. Thus states are primarily concerned about their own security and forced to view other states as potential threats. States are basically self-help units within an anarchical system devoid of an authoritative or commanding sovereign regulator.

The end of cold war and disintegration of Soviet Union in the 1990 and 1991 led many idealists to dream about the outlines of a New World Order that would give a quietus for ever to the anarchic international system. These significant events could make a toll of the usefulness of realist paradigm especially as these laid bare some of its weaknesses and contradictions like the fact that it failed to foretell or give hints about the collapse of cold war and the tumble of mighty Soviet Union.[2] But the euphoria about the envision of a New World Order did not last long and as the subsequent events such as the unexpected failure of the Somalia intervention, the disasters in the former Yugoslavia, events in Haiti and Rwanda, plight of refugees in Zaire and American military intervention in Iraq bypassing UN, showed, the New World Order, the contour and contents of which could have supposedly fleshed into a shape, instead buried in the oblivion, again giving rise to the strengthening of age old held view that the realist paradigm still dominates the international system. No doubt the delivery was a still born New World Order baby but the birth pangs it left resulted in the shaking up the global agenda, the surfacing of hitherto neglected and side tracked issues such as environment, human rights, human security and protection of minorities in the center stage, resurgence of regionalism, universalization of liberal market economy and evolution of international institutions and regimes, and the growing importance of non state actors.[3] While attending to these turbulent changes in the international system, the states again stuck to the pursuit of national interest as their dominant stake understood on realist paradigm. American involvement in Afghanistan crisis and in Iraq for the second time ousting Saddam Hussain in the face of stiff opposition from world public opinion, United Nations and other dominant powers such as German, France, Russia and China, only attested to this, and American President Bush rejection of Kyoto protocol reinforces the view that the realist paradigm of national interest and security remains still dominant. Over recent decades, the environmental crisis has brought to the center stage the "non military dimension of security as an important feature of state behaviourism." [4]

This led to many strategic analysts to redefine the concept of national security as to broaden its scope,[5] as the traditional approach reflected too narrow a vision not only of the problems but also of the solutions available to cope with threats.[6] A broader definition instead is felt essential that would take into consideration the fact that a threat to national security exits once an action or sequence of events "threatens.... to degrade the quality of life for the inhabitants of a state or ...threatens significantly to narrow the range of policy choices available to the government of a state or private non governmental entities within the state".[7] The preceding chapter describes in details about the efforts at defining the concept of environmental security. "The emergence of the concept of environmental security became inevitable once national security became associated with 'quality of life' within a sociopolitical context marked over recent years by the introduction of environmental questions into overall national and international concerns." [8]

Environmental Security: not a Dependable Variable

Realists as argued by Michel Frederick are of the view that the unreliability of international institutions, mechanism and rules, regulations and law to manage the environment has recapitulated to state's primacy in providing security to its people against the environmental threats. For example, despite existence of over twenty international and regional agents on the prevention of marine pollution, each year finds tens of millions of tons of waste and polluting substances being dumped into the sea. Over these years, adduced as a priority concern for the international community, quality of the environment has remained yet elusive and not incorporated into a genuine right to a safeguarded environment. International environmental regimes such as agreements and conventions on climate, forest, biodiversity, pollution, WTO, signed over these recent years have not been able to halt the slide in environmental deteriorations, let alone manage it for human safety. Emission of carbon dioxide into the atmosphere goes on increasingly with the prospects of global warming looming large. As argued by Frederick, the unreliability of the existing mechanisms, environmental regimes and institutions for managing the environment has introduced an element of uncertainly into the international system, putting primacy on state as the only security paradigm against the perils of nature and environmental degradation. He writes, "Consequently, it is through the prism of their own national security and hence their national interest, that states will analyze the impact of global environmental problems along with state behaviour apt to upgrade the situation or further harm it. Within such a context, the environmental security concept will then take all the importance that states will effectively grant it" [9]. On realist parlance this means reducing the environmental factor not an independent but dependable and subordinate variable to the politico-military construct of national security.

From the realist perspective the environmental security being a dependable variable thus, takes on the meaning of security of the environment, which involves three elements: (1) the sustainable use of renewable and non renewable resources, (2) protection of the elements-air, water, soil-so as to prevent pollution from stifling natural regeneration; and (3) the maximum reduction of hazards related to industrial activities.[10] According to Arthur Westing, its scope covers the overall problems associated with the protection and use of the environment. In his words, "environmental security has two basic sub components. The first of these – environmental protection has three parts: protection from wartime and similar vandalism; protection from medically unacceptable environmental pollution; and protection for special areas, from all permanent human intrusions. The second sub component of environmental security is the sane resource utilization, whether non-extractive or extractive depends upon exploitation, use or harvesting at all levels, and employing procedures that either maintain or restore optimal resource services or stocks... exploitation of renewable resources must be carried out strictly on the principle of sustained use or sustained discard, with exploitation of non-renewable resources strictly on the principle of frugality."[11] The use of the words "sustained use or sustained discard and frugality suggests impliedly the challenges to the established notion of development within the dominant social-cultural context and the security system built around it. At the same time it calls for an ethical resurgence in human beings impinging on them the need to moderate and delimit their inordinate consumption and life style. Thus, rethinking the dominant view of development and the ethical imperatives comes within the ambit of what is redefined as environmental security, as described in the preceding chapter. The realist interpretation of environmental security ignores these imperatives for reviewing the dominant ethnocentric definition of what so far has been universalized as development. The realist view of environmental security devoid of the development-security syndrome, aims at the security of the environment for the perpetuation of the dominant paradigm of development. The realist understanding of environmental security does not envisage any plan or proposal to end its self-help, divided, hierarchical and anarchic inside/ outside construction of international

from others as the causation of conflict. The case studies made by the environmental conflict schools stand a testimony to the interactive linkages between environment and violent conflict. When Barry Buzan in 'People, States and Fears' divagates from the military sector to discussing security in the four other sectors, political, economic, ecological and societal – the logic clearly says that security began as military but the military definition is increasingly challenged by the new sectors; but what was it that made the military sector conspicuous, and what is that now qualify the other to an almost equal status? This is not really addressed squarely by Buzan but he does actually give the answer or hints at it.[20] He argues more extensively like this:

> **"Because the use of force can wreak major undesired changes very swiftly, military threats are traditionally accorded the highest priority in national security concerns. Military action can wreck the work of centuries in all other sectors. Difficult accomplishments in politics, art, industry, culture and all human activities can be undone by the use of force. Human achievements, in other words, can be threatened in terms other than those in which they were created, and the need to prevent such threats from being realized is a major underpinning of the state's military protection function. A defeated society is totally vulnerable to the conqueror's power which can be applied to end ranging from restructuring the government, though pillage and rape, to massacre of the population and resettlement of the land. The threat of force thus stimulates not only a powerful concern to protect the socio-political heritage of the state, but also a sense of outrage at the use of unfair forms of competition."** [21]

This used to characterize the military sector. When the same can be done through economic or political means overturning the political order there will be security problems too. Thus, the basic definition of security problems is that they can undercut the political order and there by "alter the premises for all other questions" [22] – therefore they have to be addressed before all other questions. Because if they are not; there will not be any other questions because the unit will cease to exist as a sovereign unit. Thus, the environmental security is not mere narrative diagnosis of the causative linkage between environmental degradation and violent conflict affecting the security of the state and international system, or halting at the use of military apparatus of the state for settling the environmentally induced and caused conflict. It challenges the premises of the dominant existing socio-politico economic system that identifies with the state, which have been a nuisance to the environment and ultimately to the people. The defect both with the realist and environmental conflict school is that they incline to make the state the referent for security not the individuals, people, and the alternative premises that question the established dominant western paradigm of development and security thinking.

According to the realist framework, "environmental security represents an absence of non conventional threats against the environmental substratum essential to the well-being of its population and to the maintenance of its functional integrity."[23] On the basis of this realist definition the environmental security must be understood within a state perspective. In chime with realism, within which the concept of environmental security cannot simply be given a "security of the environment" meaning without the risk of distorting the very notion of security since the latter remains the state's prerogative. The notion of security can be understood as such under all its aspects be they political, economic, social, military or environmental. This means notion of security under state perspective remains supreme and all-inclusive and the environmental security is subsumed within it contrary to what environmental security has been defined in this work. It is the other way round that the environmental security is the overall vast design that challenges the premise on which the traditional notion of security rests and goes beyond the framework of state security. Realist thinking has not recognized that environmental security is the key and foundation of all other security. According to Taylor, under International law there is no such thing, as the idea of world environmental order common to all does not exist. The world has been divided on the basis of politically earmarked territorial units. The concept of sovereignty and territorial integrity in which are ingrained the notion of national security, are the very foundations of international law. In this picture of the realist territorially and politically divided sovereign state systems, "there is no direct protection of the environment per se".[24] If modernity is understood as the rendering of nature into territorially and politically carved out states, then these are incongruent with the ecogeographical region. An ecogeographical region can be terrestrial or aquatic or both. It may be conceived of essentially as an ecological subsystem made up of living and non-living components of the environment that interacts to form a life support system. It is by no means fully self-contained because it has numerous feedback relationships with subsystems in the adjoining areas and beyond. Thus, it is a part of the global ecosystem. But then it has a dynamic of its own so that it may also function independently of the contiguous and more distant regions as well as of the globe as a whole.[25] The various sorts of socially and politically determined territorial regions such as ethnic, linguistic, religious ones and so forth are superimposed upon the ecogeographical region. However, lack of correspondence and congruence between the two has often in the face of environmental degradation generated situation of conflict between and among these ethnic, religious or linguistically divided societies and states. Force or war within the military apparatus of the state has never been a solution to these conflicts.[26] So long as the root causes of these conflicts mainly embedded in environmental factors, remain unaddressed, and determine what constitutes security not with state as the referent, force or war will only aggravate the situation dealing not with causes but with symptoms. The very threats that stem directly from environmental degradation and indirectly in combination with other factors are lost sight of or downplayed in the analysis of realism. On the other hand, what the realists suggest is that in the core of the environmental security states need to be given preponderance. Given the nature of the existing international system as a power game, and the little role that the transnational forces, public opinion, ideologies, international organizations and small developing nations play for the preservation of the power equilibrium, to give preponderance to power maximizing states, as argued by realists is not only necessary but natural. Since the environmental crisis is global in terms of climate change, global warming, thinning of ozone layer and loss of biodiversity, the proponents of environmental security advocate not for a conventional statist military approach. But the realists are of the view that the state is the only referent for security to make its own judgement as to what constitutes the threat to its security and survival. Further, the notion of security is tied with state, which is in an advantageous position to translate in terms of issues. "It can be considered that a threat to state's environmental security exists once an action or sequences of events directed in a non-military perspective against its environmental substratum, threatens the quality of life of its population and / or the range of policy choices available to the government in its main areas of activity."[27]

In realist notion of security is involved subjective variation as the propensity to perceive events through the prism of a security threat varies from state to state. What is considered a threat to one state may not be a threat to another. A close link is always found between security and the population's quality and style of life, social and political way of thinking. A sovereign state's prerogative to secure that identity is what comes within the purview of realism as security. For example, the underpinnings of western power maximizing state for security are based on the western life style, pattern of development and inordinate consumption. To secure that commodious living, which is the identity of western populace distinguished from that of other continents, has been the main objective of national interest defined always in terms of power which will enable it to secure resources from other parts of the world even by the use of force. The traditional wars over resources, and raw materials in the past and in the present over oil can be explained by this realist logic. What is perceived as a threat to the luxurious and rich people in the North is the scenario of non-availability of resources or any kind of compromise on their way of life. Thus, America is not in a position to reduce emission of CO_2 to the atmosphere, as it believes that it will put a compromise on their way of life. So in realism's notion of security is involved the subjective and differential analysis of security based on a hierarchical, divided and power maximizing world. All these situations presuppose a state of war as well as an armed intervention by the state under attack. Where as considerations of oil played a significant part in the security thinking of America in relation to Middle East and Iraq, denial of it is perceived as a security threat, where as other nations and world public opinion and even the UN could not buy American idioms and logic to define security threats in the case of American attack on Iraq. So in realist framework of security consideration there would be no question of perceiving or analyzing even the environmental issues other than within the diagnostics of military security. In other words, the realist notion of security cannot be greenized.

On the other hand environmental security does recognize the link between population's quality of life and environment or nature. Nature is not a heap of raw materials, an object and a lifeless other to be exploited for what has been defined ethnocentrically as prosperity and development. A coordinated, symbiotic and organic view of the evolutionary process of the entire nature where both animate and inanimate play a significant role to sustain livelihood is required to found the basis of what should constitute the paradigm of development and security. It is not a hierarchically divided and disjointed world based on exploitation and inequity, and widening hiatus between rich and power, but a scheme of development and security where equity is established between and among the present generations but also between the present and future generations both living and nonliving. It is not the realist notion of security that views the ecosystem, resources and natural cycles not only within its territory but also in other parts of the globe to be exploited for the prosperity and security which is the identity referent for its populace. Thus, what is sustained and conducive to security is unsustainable and security threats to other people. On the other hand, environmental security challenges the very basis of the realist framework of security and its logic. It does not acquiesce in statist frame of security based on duality, division between rich and poor, nature and the universe and the present and future generation. It is universalistic, planetary and cosmic view of security that will determine not only the national security of each and every state, but also security of the people. Contrary to this logic of environmental security, the realist definition of security centers round the state's social well being and the maintenance of its functional integrity. These two criteria are not any way to be compromised in the name of environmental security. In realist thinking these two criteria provide the frame of reference to map out the notion of security on militarist and statist denominations. If states act first and foremost in line with their national self-interest defined on these above two criteria, and in terms of power and security, then pollution problems, environmental scarcity and degradation of resources such as water, fish, air etc can be measured in terms of national securities thus threatened. This is to reiterate what many scholars on environment and conflict such as Homer Dixon and others have tried to prove culling from many case studies that environmental security and degradation of resources directly or indirectly in combination with other factors depending on the severity and magnitude of environmental crisis, social effects and adaptive failure of the people, can contribute to violent conflict both interstate and intrastate having serious implications on the stability and security of the international system. In the realist framework the criteria of social well being and preservation of functional integrity remain uppermost while perceiving the threats from environmental degradation, where as in the analysis of Homer Dixon and others environmental factor remains preponderant and determinant to challenge the established conventionally understood meaning of security. War or use of force in response to environmental threats in terms of statist and military framework does not provide the solution and ensure environmental security. Environmental security traverses beyond this, recognizing the environmental threats to security as the frame of reference to provide a second look at what so far constitutes the copingstone of development, security and prosperity so that security to all, both animate and inanimate and future generations can be ensured taking all as subjectivities important players in a cosmic vision of the universe.

Deudney's Critique of Environmental Security

According to Daniel H. Deudney[28] in three major ways the linkage between environmental degradation and military violence can be established. The first point is that the states in the pursuit of their national security to secure freedom from violence through military means spend a lot on resources which can be diverted towards conservation of environment.

There is no guarantee that the money saved from reducing military expenditures could be spent on environment. Without any cutback on military expenditure the world can afford environmental restoration. It is preposterous to assume that the states would prefer to tighten the strings of their purses in the face of deteriorating environmental degradation in various sectors such as land, water, forest and biodiversity. Popular upsurge and mass discontentment against government showing short shrifts to impending environment crisis should not be ruled out. If the world can afford expenditures on environment even without many cuts on military expenditure then why the conditions of the environment have been getting depleted day by day?

Second, war is destructive of the environment, which is both unintentional and intentional. He cited examples showing how the military destruction of olive groves in Mediterranean land, led to the long lasting destruction of the land's carrying capacities, [29] the US' bombardment and use of defoliants in Vietnam caused significant environmental damage, [30] and more recently during the Gulf war of 1991, Saddam Hussian's forces set the oil fields of Kuwait on fire causing massive ecological damage, and resource wastages.[31] Further extensive use of nuclear weapons would have significant ominous impacts on the global environment in terms of altered weather pattern i.e. nuclear winter and depletion of the ozone layer.[32] Even the conventional war in industrialized countries can be environmentally devastative with release of radiation from civilian nuclear plants.

Third, preparations for war and production of both nuclear and conventional weapons have also deleterious effects on environment. Literatures are not wanting to show how "over the last century, the nuclear weapon states, particularly the United States and the former Soviet Union, generated enormous quantities of radioactive waste as a byproduct of the nuclear weapons development and production."[33] According to Deudney as put forth by the proponents of environmental security, the resources and costs used for preparation and use of nuclear and conventional weapons can be invested for improving the environmental conditions. The costs involved in terms of loss of life and destruction of the environmental biodiversity questions the very logic and raison detre of the international system and state system's dependence on use of force and violence both nuclear and conventional for resolution of conflict. Nobody can deny the fact that war and preparation for it has environmentally ruinous effects. Production and use of weapons of mass destruction has been a major cause of environmental degradation, which in turn comes as a predominant threat to human life. Environmental security deals with all the causes of environmental degradations out of which war and preparation for it is one. The proponents of environmental security depict analytically showing many case studies how the environmental degradation leads to violent intrastate and interstate conflict. Besides, the present work while defining environmental security stresses on rethinking the socio-political basis which has given rise to such a mindset, and established framework of realism looking at the rest other than the self as the other to be exploited for one's own interests. No doubt, elimination of war as a means of resolving conflict would not bring an end to environmental degradation in other sectors. What environmental security suggests is to rethink the western pattern of development, extravagant life style, and consumption and approach to life that has given rise to such a mindset about war, the relation between man and man, man and nature and, the present international system.

To equate environmental degradation with diseases, aging, crime or accidents as equally security threats as done by Deudney, is highly erroneous. Diseases, aging, crime etc are natural processes of human evolution. Even in the absence of environmental degradation, decay, diseases and aging will occur to all forms of life whether human or non human. If these occur naturally and by the process of evolution, nobody considers these as security threats to human beings. The way Deudney applies this logic to question why environmental degradation can be considered a security threat shows that he failed to show the difference between the natural process of evolution, and the human being made disturbance into this natural process. Environmental degradation is not natural, it is anthropogenic and created by human beings, their way of life, pattern of organization, development, and social –political –economic thinking. Studies show, environmental degradation and scarcity of resources and their social effects have intensified and spread the frequency of diseases, created new diseases, brought aging faster than its natural occurrence, increased the number of accidents, crimes and violent conflict. Consequently, there is nothing wrong in terming these recrudescence of diseases, aging, accidents, crimes and violence as security threats if factored by environmental degradation occupying the status of national security not in the sense of being required to be resolved within the realist military apparatus of the state. If the main objective of national security is to provide a good life, and establish social cohesion and stability, then these threats assume very much the character and status of national security. Environmental security is thus, assurance of human security against the environmentally induced diseases, aging, crime and violence in a broader and more comprehensive sense occupying the status of national security not through military means as these however invincible may be, cannot stop their recurrence, hastening and recrudescence. Despite changes and growing interdependence due to revolutionary steps in the field of communication to end distance, the irony is that the international system is tried to be understood in Westphalian logic to fit into western strait jacket in the 21st century. Persistence of this attitude is found in Deudney when he opines that "there is nothing distinctively national about either the causes, the harms or the solutions that warrants privileging the national grouping" on the grounds that environmental problems, causes, and effects are confined to the boundary of a state.[34] He has ignored how the environmental degradation or development activities in one state have been a security threat to another nation. For example, the scientists predicted sea level rise submerging low-lying areas of Bangladesh, Maldives, Egypt affecting millions of people is not the doing of these affected countries. Sea level rise is the result of global warming caused by the rich North countries' mindless historic emission of CO_2 to the atmosphere in pursuance of their domestic imperatives for luxurious and commodious living, inordinate life style and profligate consumption and production of wealth. And the millions of people unsettled from their land as a result of this will flee to the neighbouring countries for shelter and livelihood to find themselves enmeshed in-group identity conflict with the receiving countries' native inhabitants. Thus, the western and rich North people's life style and their concept of development has come in for a greater security threat to the people of Bangladesh, and in turn to India, when Bangladeshis will flee to neighbouring Indian states for shelter and livelihood. The northeastern states of India have turned into a burning cauldron of ethnic conflict due to the migration of Bangladesh induced by environmental degradation and scarcity of land. In the analysis of Deudney while denying environmental security the status of national security is found lacking reference to these case studies with a view not to diluting the strength of his arguments. Even if his arguments that "most environmental problems are not international", "because", the causes, sources, problems, consequences and victims of environmental degradation are confined within the borders of one nation state[35] are accepted, as studied by Homer Dixon, environmental scarcity and degradation of resources within a territory can lead to various social effects in terms of poverty, economic deprivations, decline in agricultural productivity, migration, and weakening of social and political institutions i.e. state which in turn contribute to intra state conflicts such as insurgencies, coup de tats, guerrilla warfare resulting in shifting of allegiance and legitimacy. These intrastate violent conflicts are having international impacts inviting intervention from external powers.[36]

Another distinguishing criteria Deudney applies to differentiate environmental security from national security is the intention involved. In the inter state wars or conflicts is clearly marked the intention of the parties involved, while mobilizing forces, procuring weapons with definite aims in mind. Since this is lacking in the case of environmental conflict, environmental security does not deserve the status of national security. Environment conflict that will arise out of degradation of resources between states through military means attest to the presence of intention involved in waging wars. That there is no explicit presence of intentional behaviour should not denude environmental security of its status being christened as national security. America's contribution to global warming is indisputably larger than other countries'. Its impact in terms of sea level rise resulting in submergence of low-lying states such as Bangladesh, change of precipitation pattern and climate change, is not the result of intentional behaviour of America to harm Bangladesh, India or others but certainly in the knowledge that its pattern of development, lifestyle and wealth amassing economy and limitless consumption contribute immensely to climate change. The rejection of Kyoto agreement by America, which was designed to reduce emission of CO_2 and the hazardous effects of global warming on other nations, clearly demonstrates its intention. The realist zero sum logic that "what is nuisance to others is gain to us", is applied. That America would reduce CO_2 on the plea that this will compromise the life style of its people shows that America is aware of its repercussions on other nations and people. In this case is clearly ingrained the implied intention of the industrialized North powers in not reviewing what so far they have defined as development, universalization of which in the name of globalization has been a threat to the nature as well to the people dependent solely on it for their livelihood. Assume that there is no direct or explicit intention involved in the causation of environmental problems, to downplay its threat however severe these are, is illogical. This kind of absurd logic applied in international conferences and conventions on climate change and other important environmental issues while apportioning the burden and responsibility on powers for what have wrecked to the environment, would set a bad precedent and provide a scapegoat to scuttle the issue and pass on the buckle to others who happen to be the victims.

Deudney is of the view that "military organizations" which are "sensitive extremely hierarchical, and centralized, and typically deploy expensive highly specialized, and advanced technologies" to give protection from violence and threats are not the same with environmental security." In contrast, responding to the environmental problems requires very different approaches and organizations".[37] Environmental degradation that rekindles intrastate or interstate violent conflict is not dissimilar with other causes triggering armed conflict. With the advent of nuclear weapons, chemical and other biological weapons, the type of organization, methods and approaches required in case of classical military operations gets changed. Similarly, in case of environmental security the types of organization, techniques and approaches are bound to be different. If changes in techniques and approaches required in case of nuclear weapons do not in any way denude it of its importance, how the different approaches, methods and organization to deal with various aspects of environmental degradation could disrobe the environmental security of its significance and meaning? That environmental security needs different kind of organizations, approaches, methods and techniques different from those of classical military warfare, according to Deudney creates "a conceptual muddle rather than the paradigm or world view shift".[38] Environmental security does include not all kinds of evils as threat but only those that are caused by environmental degradation or scarcity of resources along with its social effects, which in turn creates intrastate violence with implications on international security and stability. The concept of environmental security is not a narrative analysis of the conflicts that arise from environmental degradation, but is suggestive of a new paradigm that challenges the established dominant ethnocentric view of development, realist notion of security, and the divided hierarchical world and self vrs. other syndrome. It aims at a normative shift in this western worldview ubiquitously practiced as the Bible of development – the sole cause of the despoliation of the earth and the destitution of the world. Ingrained in such a western view, which is premised on Judeo-Christian tradition of anti nature, the critics of environmental security underrate the magnitude of the crisis, and challenges to the worldview are considered as "dedefinition rather than a redefinition of security".[39]

To say that environmental security is a motivational, psychological and rhetorical strategy to divert the social, political and economic wherewithal now expended on military towards alleviating the environmental conditions is too narrow a view and negative approach. In the United States on many social issues 'war on drops', war on poverty or war on crime' movements as "moral equivalent to war" [40] have been launched in the past without any success. But these movements are different from environmental security in that the latter aims at reinventing the established view of the world, its political and economic thinking on which hinges the concept of national security. No doubt Ken Conca and others are right when they are of the view that discourse of national security has a set of powerful associations that cannot simply be redirected.[41] Because the discourse in national security is based on an established and western dominant view of the world which is very difficult to change. This is what environmental security aims at. The end of the cold war raised an apocalyptic ushering in of a new world order based on justice, equity, democratization of international institutions with multilateralism to replace the bipolarism. Nothing of the sort happened. Because everything depended on America and western powers, the key and dominant players crowning the world political system. It was America's unwillingness to cast off its dominance pontificating to the world its political and economic script to be followed in letter and sprit that could belie what Fukuyama to declare end of cold war as an epoch making 'end of history'. That does not mean the new and alternative perspectives on national security that came up even before and after the end of cold war have lost their significance. This is what led United Nations Secretary General Kofi Annan to note in his Millennium Report that while security policy had traditionally focused on the defence of territory from external attack, it has now come to embrace "the protection of communities and individuals from internal violence". This focus on the protection of individuals rather than borders is the central element of what has become known as human security.[42]

Environmental security is more than a mere motivational or inspiring doctrine. It is based on a matter of fact understanding of the world phenomenon. It raises the basic question related to the established pattern of development, life style, the relationship between man and nature, the impact of the pursuance of such a type of development on future generation both living and non living, and the legitimacy based on ensuring inordinate life style, consumption and wealth production, which is taken for granted beyond space and time. It focuses on the security development – governance nexus. Prescriptively, while not discounting the military response to crisis created directly by the environmental degradation and scarcity of resources, it stresses on non-coercive prevention policies – from preventive diplomacy, conflict management and resolution strategies to security system reform and the promotion of good governance, sustainable and equitable development, and democratization.

Environmental security is not synonymous with a motivational strategy. It is a normative and ethical paradigm aiming at awakening the people to the dangers of environmental crisis, which is the result of persistence in the western pattern of development, industrialization, extravagant life style and inordinate consumption a synonym for heightened happiness and euphemism for being highly civilized. Are the people of America and North ready to come down to level of a poor man in South with the knowledge that this will not compromise the life style of their future generations? Accustomed to such an extravagant and commodious living, the people in North are not ready to awake themselves to such ethical imperatives required of them to ensure environmental security. That there will be reactions, discordant behaviour and opposition to such an awakening in spiritual terms, as a part of environmental security, does not divest environmental security of its meaning, and essence. Fundamental questions raised to review the inordinate life style and way of life for a sustainable world make environmental security a viable and alternative security concern to replace the traditional concept. If this be definition, scope and gamut of environmental security, then Jyrki Kakonen's fears of "militarized environment"[43] are ill founded, because environmental security never advocates military prowess necessary to protect the people against threats from environmental degradation. As nuclear weapons make nuclearisation of war, the environment makes security the environmentalisation or greening of security.

It is also argued that war, nation and state are intrinsically connected and reinforced by each other in realism's frame of security. As the historian

Michael Howard has observed: "self consciousness as a Nation implies, by definition, a sense of differentiation from other communities, and the most memorable incidents in the group memory usually are of conflict with, and triumph over, other communities. It is in fact very difficult to create national consciousness without a war".[44] Echoing the dominant perspective of national security strengthened by war, Charles Tilly observes that "states make war and war makes states". [45] These attributes of jingoism of war distinguishing nations, states and communities from other communities, nations and states, and uniting one against the other in a divided and hierarchical world, it is said, are found absent in the concept of environmental security. Hence the lack of the cementing force of jingoism in environmental security divests it of any qualifications to be called as environmental security. Environmental security argues for a redefinition of national security not in the sense of one vrs. the other or uniting one nationality against another but in the sense of transcending the Westphalia model of security tied to the sovereign state system on the basis of self help in a supposed anarchic international system. Since most of the sources and causes of environmental problems, which lay embedded in western pattern of development based on fossil fuel based industrialization, wasteful inordinate consumption, life style and production of wealth are global and transboundary, national security is to be defined with environment as a fundamental component not in a Westphalian, and European sectarian language turned global in scope during the last centuries but in terms of an interconnected, not only between and among nations but also between the nature and man, and between the present and future generations, and living and non living. It is not the jingoistic forces of war but the envision of a universal self different from the self help, tied symbiotically with others living and nonliving in a timelessness frame beyond territorial exclusivity and spatial distancing of traditional nation state, and new planetary interests, ethics and wisdom that will define the national security. The movements for global governance of the environment, the rise of non-state actors like NGOs transcending nationalities and territorial boundaries and environmental regimes point to the inadequacy of Westphalian sovereign state systems to ensure security to human beings. Nobody can refute the fact that to deal with environmental problems, their management and regulation entails the expansion of state capabilities but not on military terms. This requires coordinated efforts of science and technology, socio-political institutions, finance, various organizations and state machinery including the international community.

Jason Clay points out that in many parts of developing countries, and particularly its tropical rain forests, states are dispossessing and destroying indigenous people whose claim to distinct national identity is high but whose potential for statehood is very low or non-existent.[46] This is what the proponents of environmental security are going to address not in terms of enhanced military capabilities but in terms of relooking at the western pattern of development based on fossil fuel technologies and industrialization.

It is the imposed western liberal market economy in the name of globalization, the entry of multinational corporations into the developing countries that is mostly responsible for deterioration and depletion in their environment. Environmental scarcity of sources along with their social effects in terms of poverty, economic deprivation and weakening of state capabilities has led to in these countries insurgencies, group violence questioning the very basis of legitimacy. The cases of banditry in rural Sind in Pakistan, the guerrilla war waged by the Sendero Luminoso in Peru and the New People's Army (NPA) insurgency in the Philippines are good illustration of the links between environmental scarcities, grievance and violence.[47] What has led to coercive conservation[48] in many fragile and despotic regimes in African countries by dispossessing local inhabitants of their traditional natural resources, is not part of a design to fulfill the requirements of environmental security, it is to benefit state elites, multinational corporations and the western nations. The very argument that environmental security will lead to ecofascism seems preposterous and not in line with what environmental security is meant by. Environmental security and authoritarianism are antithetical to each other. The very stipulations of environmental security envisage the democratization of governance, participation of all people including the locals and indigenous, the non-state NGOs, in environmental conservation loosening of the Westphalia politico-military construct of security straitjacket, review of the western pattern of development, western life style, replacement of anthropocentric relation between man and nature and inculcation of new values, nuances, and new vision into the individuals' schema of life, and planetary interests to determine the national interest of state. On the contrary, the western democratic regimes especially the United States seem to be democratic within, but in their relation to other countries in South for procuring natural resources and raw materials as part of their politico-military construct of national security, they have exhibited the signs of authoritarianism symptomatic of military regimes. The recent Gulf wars stand witness to this kind of authoritarian behaviour. In all international conferences and conventions whether on climate, forest, biodiversity, intellectual property rights or WTO the definition of national interests of rich industrialized North in terms of domestic imperatives such as, inordinate consumption and exorbitant life style and production of wealth, remained dominant. If Kyoto protocol dealing with stabilizing of carbon dioxide in the atmosphere comes into effect, many developing countries will be carbon sinks for the developed world, resulting in many indigenous people being evacuated for creation of forests or trees cover as a part of climate trading system. Then what comes as a threat to the indigenous people is not the requirements of environmental security but the dominant developed world's definition of national security in terms of domestic imperatives such as production of wealth, ensuring exorbitant and inordinate life style and consumption, for which the large chunk of historic emission of CO_2 in the past and the present to the atmosphere of the developed countries can be accounted.[49]

Contemporary national security is closely connected to the institution of state sovereignty as defined in Westphalia convention. In the international realm, sovereignty has come to mean the existence in polity of a final and undivided authority over a particular territory, which only states can possess, and the reciprocal recognition of this authority, which states extend to one another.[50]

Claimants within state and outside the state to the prerogative of sovereignty are considered not legitimate but encroachments. Similarly it is said, responding to international and global pulls and pressures exercised upon state sovereignty on environmental issues and problems mean a diminished or dilution of the sovereign state's legitimates authority. Thus, the requirements of environmental security come in direct clash with the enhanced concern for its sovereign prerogatives. When nations clash over environmental scarcity of renewable resources such as river water as found in various parts of the globe, for example, India and Bangladesh over Ganges water, water conflict in Middle East and Africa they lay claims to water within the nonnegotiable prerogative of sovereignty. When intrastate conflicts in terms of group violence, insurgencies, and guerilla war fare occur in fragile and weak states presided over by authoritarian regimes and exacerbated by environmental scarcity of resources in combination with other factors like social, political, economic and cultural context, these conflicts occur over the issue of legitimacy to the sovereignty state system. The environmental issues, which are global, need global governance and management. In that case, traversing beyond the sovereignty is what is required of environmental security. Traversing beyond is not always an erosion of sovereignty rather an extension of its effectiveness and influence in dealing with environmental problems. Changes in international situation are taking place so fast and pervasively that to think solution in terms of the rigid logic of Westphalia sovereign state system in the changing scenario is an expression of European arrogance. Barry Buzan, who recognizing environmental degradation as a security threat keeps it at par with economic and political factors, is of the view that "the sources of threat are also diversifying away from the state. Many of the new threats seem to stem from complex systems both natural (the ecosystem) and the human made (the global economy), and the operation of these systems is often poorly understood." [51]

Two perspectives on sovereignty and environment linkage continue to be debated. The first perspective led by Deudney and others observe that there has been an erosion or weakening of sovereignty. Environmental concerns are said to be erecting new, and effectively global standards for state behaviour. These new global standards are said to manifest themselves in many ways: in formal dealings among states such as the creation of international environmental regimes, in rules of environmental conditionality attached to the actions of international organizations such as the World Bank[52], in the evolving norms of a growing body of international environmental law[53], and in the political pressures brought to bear on governments by increasingly transnational environmental movements, citizens' networks, and non-governmental organizations.[54] Ecosystems and environmental processes do not respect state borders, sovereignty itself becomes a key institution of global scale environmental destruction. It creates a scale for decision-making, adjudication, and authority that does not coincide with fundamental ecological realities, and thus frustrates ecologically responsive management.[55]

The second perspective is that the emergence of multilateral institutions for environmental protection, does not inevitably erode state soverignity and may even strengthen it. By placing states at the center of institutional responses and strengthening their capacity to act collectively, it is argued, the menu of choices available to state is being expanded not restricted.[56] Lhevy, Keohane and Haas have argued that, although environmental regimes may limit the scope of governments to act unilaterally, they also facilitate collective state based problem solving.[57] Ken Conca striking a balance between the two perspectives states that "sovereignty is in fact being transformed as a result of global ecological interdependence, but not in the manner sketched by either of the above claims, or even by the net effect of the two taken together."[58] A new universal norm of environmental responsibility is emerging in a highly segmented set of activities, including the lobbying of scientists, the pressure of public opinion, the calculation of governments, and the targeted political pressures of eco activists. Responding to international environmental pressures can create resources and purchase legitimacy, at the same time it may constrain the menu of policy choices. Sovereignty as conceptualized in Westphalia carries with a complex bundles of rights: equality among states, non-intervention, exclusive territorial jurisdiction, the presumption of state competence, restrictions on binding adjudication without consent, exclusive right to wield violence, and the embeddeness of international law in the free will of states.[59] This is not to argue that a particular set of international pressures affects these various components, norms of sovereignty equally or in parallel fashion. There is reason to expect that some normative pillars of sovereignty can be strengthened as others are undermined or eroded. For example, in the case of transboundary pollutant flows, "institutional mechanisms" and agreements "to control them could erode the sovereign right to exclusive territorial jurisdiction, but at the same time strengthen aspects of the principle of non-intervention, if the flows themselves are viewed as unjustified intervention".[60] The Westphalian concept sovereignty is based on the legal framework that it has exclusive jurisdiction over the territory. This constitutes the raison de tre to claim the status of the international standing. The claim of the enduring sovereignty in the face of environmental pressures stresses states as problem solvers. Deudney's views that "enhanced state concerns for its sovereign prerogatives could greatly impede international environmental cooperation[61], stand discredited. Hardly the ink on the major agreements signed at the 1992 UNCED conference at Rio dried than the Brazilian diplomat Marcos Azambuja offered the following analysis:

> **"Brazilian interests are reinforced in the majority of the documents. At no time did we face opposition to our basic interests ... We came out of the negotiations without the slightest scratch to our sovereignty" [62].**

While assuming that the concept of 'sovereignty' is based on the foundation of territorial exclusivity and spatial distancing, its internal capability to ensure that the legitimacy given to it by society and various sections of people on the basis of its performance continues, is lost sight of by those who want to confine environmental security to the Westphalia procrustean bed. Environmental scarcity and degradation of resources when coalesced with other economic, political and cultural factors accentuates economic deprivation, decline in agricultural productivity, and weakening of political institutions such as state. In this situation "if the state fails to meet the grievances of the disadvantaged people, then threat of violence, guerrilla warfare and other forms of conflict manifest challenging the legitimacy of those who are in power and their claim to sovereignty. This internal failure in terms of lack of capability and effectiveness to ensure environmental security is reflection of limitations of sovereignty. When Brazilian government was very much concerned that there are no scratches on the wall of its sovereignty, its inside surface shows signs of being slightly scratched. The following excerpt shows the irony:

> **Whenever one looks in the Amazonian economy, the state is in retreat; unable to finance tax breaks or build highways without the aid of multilateral banks, unable to include more than one per cent of the rural population in official colonization schemes, unable to control land tilting or land conflicts, unable to register or tax the greater part of the Amazonian economy, unable to enforce federal law on more than a sporadic basis [63].**

Efforts to scratch the wall by constructing a regime for the preservation of the world's remaining rainforests and of the Amazon in particular were defeated. Assessment of the limits of state capabilities comes at a time when the Brazilian state has been placed squarely at the center of most schemes for sustainable development in the region. Far from prohibiting state action, the net effect of international pressures has been to stimulate a more active, interventionist role in the region under the rubric of supporting sustainable development. Without eroding sovereignty, these pressures strengthened the presence of state in the region and in Brazilian society as a whole. A multifaceted character of sovereignty is emerging where "the freedom of state to undertake, promote or tolerate process of environmental degradation is being limited, and many of the limits emanate from sources external to state itself. At the same time there is little doubt that new international institutions have made some governments more effective problem solvers. That both effects could be happening at once is testimony to the multi faceted character of sovereignty." [64] What is lost sight of by the many critics of environmental security is that the internal forces questioning the capability of state to deal with environmental scarcity of resources are downplayed to magnify the international environmental agreements as constraints on external sovereignty. But as seen from the above analysis, rather the international environmental forces and pressures strengthen the role of the sovereign state system as problem solvers. The requirements of environmental security do not aim at the proselytization of sovereign state system or its erosion. It aims at a coordinated and cooperative effort of sovereign state systems in dealing with the management of environmental problems. Given the magnitude of the crisis and the threats to be very survival of humanity on the earth, the new planetary interests would constitute the national interests of sovereign states. The need is to reflect upon what this means for humanity as a whole, and for each nation state. It is time that the planetary interests became the principal political concept guiding decision-making on survival issues such as sustainability and environmental integrity. It is time that the sovereign nations pursue a legitimate national interest that is in each case, compatible with the greater good of us all. On the true global issues, a new approach for decision-making is required. Instead of negotiations being the consequences of competing claims of all national interests, the global objectives need to be identified first, and accepted as binding, with subsequent negotiation determining what national obligations must arise from this. The relationship between national and planetary interests has been the focus of environmental security. The impending environmental crisis global and transboundary in its nature and scope coming as greater threats to humanity, calls for the institutionalization of supranational loyalties to the planet and to humanity as a species. This means subordination of national sovereignty to the imperatives of environmental ethics and values.[65]

In 1995 a commission headed by former Swedish Prime Minister Innguar Carlsson and former Commonwealth Secretary General Shridath Ramphal declared: "the idea that people have common interests irrespective of their national or other identities, and that they are coming together in an organized way across borders is of increasing relevance to global governance".[66]

Alleviating the fears of eco fascism of the critics of environmental security, the very requirements of environmental security suggest a global governance of environmental crisis with involvement of all institutions including the state, non-state actors, regions and groups. Given the sources of many of the new threats stemming from complex systems both natural and human made, and diversifying away from the state into diverse, regional and local in character, the monolithic statist Westphalia approach quite familiar with realist paradigm seems to be inadequate to solve the environmental crisis "Global environmental governance emerges because the spatial scale of the state is inadequate in dealing with the scales of environmental change, and thus the practices of governance move towards regional and global levels and at the same time towards local levels in response." [67] The ecological project of governance envisions a world of small interacting communities, what Bookchin named as municipal confederalism[68] or what Karliner termed it as grass roots globalization, [69] which means a myriad locally organized, but transnationally networked, social movements and NGOs are becoming increasingly mobilized to resist the dominant practices of TNCs and states. To create alternative forms of the western dominated political economy the most common phrase used is the "common". It is defined as a site of ecologically sustainable and socially just, political economy. This means the construction of a myriad small-scale society organized around common regimes through resistance to the globalising practices of TNCs, state and international development agencies.[70] To quote Caldwell:

> **Rhetorical assertions of national sovereignty continue to be heard, but the imperatives of geophysical hazards to all nations are pushing their governments toward modification of their asserted freedom to act as they please in relation to their natural resources, industrial practices, and the environment. A rhetorical strategy to evade the sovereignty road block is the concept of 'merged sovereignty', which infact occurs when nations seek to realize there own national objectives through treaties with other nations having interests in common.[71]**

Deudney is of the view that "national identity and security collides directly with world views and identities supportive of sustainable environmental practices. The nation is not an empty vessel or blank slate waiting to be filled or scripted but is instead profoundly linked to 'us vrs. them' thinking". Further he states that "nationalism means a sense of 'us versus them', of the insider vs. the outsider, of the compatriot vs. the alien."[72] The "us vs. them" thinking comes in direct conflict with environmental political thought, which stresses on 'one world' and 'global village' sensibility of environmental awareness.

As Homer Dixon and his associates have shown in their studies, many conflicts that arise directly out of environmental scarcity of the renewable resources such as water, fish and others can be put into the "us vs. them" framework, where one nation knows that the causes of conflict lay directly with the environmental degradation of certain sources of the other countries. Where there is differential degree of contribution among nations to the degradation of the environment, lack of scientific precision to quantify the magnitude of each country's contribution, and scientific certainty about the imminence of environmental catastrophe and about its country and region wise impact, all argumentations against applying this "us vs. them" paradigm into international relation on environmental problems seem to be contextualization of national security within the Westphalian model. On environmental issues in international forums a clear line is drawn between North and South. The seemingly inapplicability of this "us vs them" thinking does not mean that environmental crisis is not a national security issue in the sense of a realist framework but in the sense that the environmental problems will affect the livelihood of its citizens whose security has traditionally been tied with territorial impregnability. How security defined in terms of this territorial, impregnability, exclusivity and spatial distancing stands in the face of flow of pollutants, climate change, change in precipitation patterns, global warming, acid rain, ozone hole impact? The scientifically arrived at findings can no longer be ignored in the name of adherence to classical model of sovereignty and Eurocentric realist understanding of the world, and on the other hand requires rethinking of security in terms of environment.

This reality of struggle among nations for survival and dominance resulting in elitism enforces local and domestic hierarchies and legitimizes the existence and use of military apparatus, while life is permanently threatened by the imperatives of military security. Military imperatives dictate that states develop and deploy the most effective military technology available. The effects on land and nature are little considered. No military technology could be more environmentally damaging than nuclear weapons. Thus, the environmental effects of producing, storing, developing, and dismantling them not to mention the effects they would have on the environment if ever used, are considered secondary. A similar argument could be adduced about the entire range of military technologies, from cluster bombs to napalon to defoliants to biological weapons.[73] Land has no morai or little worth except that it is a spiritless other that humans can rightfully exploit to serve their own ends. Just-war theory generally evaluates collateral damage's significance in the context of civilians killed or injured due to military operations. Yet collateral damage also kills and injures animals and destroys biotic nature that have even less stake and less say in the conflict than civilians. Where is their right to life? The realist ethic to disrupt or destroy the evolutionary process, which includes all its organic and non-organic components, reducing the diversity of life and stability and beauty of the natural system, is unethical.[74] Responding to power politics, the ecologists allege that if power politics is real, it is a constructed and deconstructable reality. "Reality is a social construction". It is "created and constructed by beliefs and behaviour. Structures do in fact shape beliefs and behaviour the way some positivists thought, but these structures are the product of human action".[75] To hold such logic of structural realist assumptions of power politics as permanent is the result of application of Thomas Hobbes and Issac Newtonian view of man" as particles of constant motions" to social relations.

From the realist axioms of structural and motivational conflictuality flow a series of corollaries with a devastating impact on life and freedom, of which hierarchy or elitism is the obvious problem. This gives rise to the emergence of a strong state always embarking on devising a system of accumulation and control from the top.

Realism is also criticized for its homogenizing worldview in its power politics framework. It reduces motives to a few universals, such as power quests and physical growth. "In the process, realism has also homogenized the political unit by emphasizing a statist ontology that not only ascribes a natural aura to such a form of association, but also minimizes its internal variance".[76] This is particularly characteristic of Waltz's third image.[77] By reducing all to a narrow groove of power motives, and holding these as immutable and permanent, realism imposes a structural straitjacket upon all cultural issues, diversities and anthropological insight. In the words of Eric Lafarriere, "From an ecological perspective, the power assumptions and political language of realism can only portray the world as a giant machine fixated on the goal of survival or victory; they can only trivialize culture and accultured individuals in the process of social creation".[78]

In its idioms of anti ecological dimension of power, realism depicts the world as basically materialistic, conflictual and elitist devoid of any social utopia and idealism.

By arraigning one individualized self in case of a group or class, or one super power nation, against the other to satisfy the elite's interests in terms of accumulations, consumption and control, realism super imposes an artificial, fictitious construct over and above a universalized or expanded self, typical of ecological portrayal of the natural world. "By limiting the definition of threat to the other's potential ambitions over the finite, zero sum game of the state system, and by turning this preeminent reality into the main engine of history, the call to arms by realism turns nature into raw materials, and legitimizes warfare as a vehicle of the good".[79]

Impelled by the objectifying bias of Newtonian science, the positivism and behaviouralism taking cue from the classical realism took the recurrent pattern of history as constants, quantified the power and state capabilities and replaced ethics with problem solving. Thus, realism as the ahistorical science of the state stunting human development and questioning its survival stood opposed to organicism, subjectivity and historicism characterizing the ecological thought. Critical Theory challenges this statist denomination of realism. "If states dominate the arena, this is a feat of power politics representing other dimensions of reality that could potentially replace the states if an emancipatory praxis could-with the help of Critical Theory-empower other subjectivities than those who dominate at present. The social world does not exhibit any iron laws, all regularities can be broken, and it is the task of Critical Theory to show this...".[80] Ecological approach can add to completion of emancipatory project in this direction by relying on what Bookchin said earlier about municipal confederalism. Critical Theory can take non-military environmental security threats as a part of its argumentation against established discourses of security, thereby relativising conventional wisdom.

Critique of Liberalism

Liberalism, which started as a doctrine of freedom was based on possessive individualism of Hobbes and Locke in search for accumulation of wealth, profligate and commodious lifestyle. At the individual level, he/she needs freedom to achieve the goals set by the materialistic world opened before him/her by the Newtonian age. At the state level, liberal democratic government legitimized by the individuals' criteria of wealth production, profligate and inordinate lifestyle and commodious living emerged as the guarantor of these goals to its individuals by introducing into the world, its market economy, liberal ideas, free exchange, trade, and protectionism.

The liberal tradition set by America and Western allies was to guarantee these objectives to the individuals at home by getting unimpeded access to resources available any where in the world even by the application of force. Like realism, it viewed the nature and other nations as the other to be exploited for satisfaction of individuals' material needs at home. The liberal institutionalism cannot escape its entanglement with and commitment to the capitalist market system. Its anthropocentric view of nature and universe, and consequent emphasis on economic growth leads to a relative lack of concern for the stability, integrity, and beauty of the earth. Obsessed with growth fetish the western liberal market economy destroyed both the nature and the poor. In other words, "If Judeo-Christian monotheism took nature out of religion, Anglo-American economists took nature out of economics." [81] Overconsumption and inordinate life style of the western people has proved to be a nuisance to nature. The liberal tradition combining individual consciousness with responsibility is eminently attractive to ecologists. Liberal literatures in International Relation articulate a normative commitment to freedom by favouring a cooperative utopia based on open exchange, material growth, positive law and specialized knowledge. These include the early advocates of free trade, [82] the functionalist and neo-functionalist arguments stressing the relationship between peace and elite co-operations, [83] the regime literature and its descriptive emphasis on 'mechanics of cooperation, [84] and part of the contemporary normative literature on global humanism.[85]

The liberal cosmopolitan project aims at the attainment of a global commonality with the gradual elimination of borders. But the overriding concern was unity. From an ecological perspective, the question pertains to the purpose of liberation in espousing unity. The ecologists are in favour of global concert but surely not at the cost of integrity, and diversity of member communities. The worst nightmare for the ecologists is the current spread of western liberal market economy throughout the world culminating in globalization. It involves the most fundamental centralized restructuring of socio-economic and political relations since the industrial revolution. It has created a new corporate colonialism in TNCs to which all individuals and nations must adjust. The new corporate colonialism is likely to dispossess, impoverish, and marginalize more people, destroy more cultures, and cause more environmental devastations than either the colonialism of old or the development of the last 50 years.[86] In the current context it means the homogenization of prices, products, wages, rates of interest and profits to become the same all over reinforcing the economic interests of North countries. The process of economic globalization advanced by the Bretton Woods institutions promoted the interests of the superrich so successfully that it also damaged their concern for and obligations to less fortunate inhabitants and their natural ecosystem in the developing world. In other words, it is nothing but another euphemism for the continuing exploitation of the underdeveloped by the developed, and redistribution of resources and wealth from the less to the more developed.[87] Globalization has not created a global village in transcendence of national boundaries, rather a highly divided, hierarchical elitist political structure. Thus, the ecologists' critique of liberal cosmopolitanism stands vindicated in that the homogenizing logic of liberalism is ruining ecosystems and decimating cultural specificity. The integration theory of the 1950s and

1960s for all its neutral tone, also assumed a basic link between global freedom and increasing communication.[88]

In contemporary liberalism, as held by James Rosenau, global culture based on 'reason' and 'analytical skills' can be disappointingly defended as an emancipatory tool for the individual.[89] Trade based globalization unfolding of western liberal market based economic-political order has been raised to a high moral level a synonym for development to which the developing world has been asked to dedicate themselves in slavish adulation of what the west terms it as good. Siphoning off the resources and materials from the developing world like an inverted blood transfusion from the sick to the healthy, the globalization has enabled the rich North to promote their domestic imperatives in terms of guaranteeing the profligate, inordinate consumption, life style, and production of wealth. Thus, the approach of liberals to global growth is based on total disregard of the imperatives of finiteness and diversity of nature, and the ever increasing hiatus between the rich and poor, freedom of the individuals and right to life of all other non human living and non-living.

The ecological critique should examine what David Mitrany and Harold Laski propounded their commitment to the materialist utopia in their defense of efficient servicing. For Mitrany, servicing formed a clear path to freedom.[90] Normative endorsement of growth is also found in Peace studies and within the Southern Perspectives on world order reform.[91] Ecologists can appreciate Mitrany's attempt at replacing a mere voting democracy with a working one.[92] But they are distrust of" the enlightened mission of experts". In their views, "technocratic depoliticisation rather is viewed as the embodiment of totalitarianism, the vehicle for a very distinct brand of politics".[93]

Ecologicalising Emancipatory Mission

An ecological approach to International Relation Theory and global governance rests on alternative ontologies, epistemologies, and ethical/ political prescription. The mechanical view of nature and attribution of the 'Other' needs to be reconsidered. Nature is finite, whole, an interdependent body connecting all living matter in a cyclical and non-hierarchical manner. It is more often a function of cooperation within and between species. Diversity and timelessness are the other attributes of nature. Diversity allows nature to withstand the demise of individual life forms while maintains its grandeur, beauty and bounty. Timelessness shows life is not imposed or spontaneously created but is undissociable from time. It is a long, slow and cumulative process. Recognition of longevity supports the assumption of mutual aid in nature. Thus it rejects the traditional utilitarianism, and mechanical view of nature, and ontologies of conflict. What Pope John Paul II said in the Conference of Roman Catholic bishops in the Philippines and Dominican Republic in 1988 deserves excerption: "... One cannot use with impunity the different categories of beings, whether living or inanimate – animals, plants and natural elements-simply as one wishes, according to one's economic needs. On the contrary, one must take into account the nature of each being and its mutual connection to an ordered systems, which is precisely the cosmos".[94] It advocates a harmonization with physical surroundings admonishing against imposition of structures of domination. The principle of classical theory of democracy, freedom, individual fulfillment and equal treatment are vindicated by ecological ethics. Instead of looking at the world of nature as the other, a more coordinated view of the world embracing both the world of nature and the world of humanity[95] is what the ecological approaches insist on." To deny moral value to ecosystem because they are not integrated in the same way as centralized individual organisms is to make a category mistake. In thinking about the value of social and biotic communities we should be concerned for a matrix of interconnections between centers, not for a single center".[96]

Thus, the mechanical view of the world and nature must be replaced by an organicistic one[97] which reads the world not as a soulless machine subjected to cause and effect, and repetitive patterns – sine qua non of scientific investigations, positivism and behaviouralism. To confine the study to the limitation of cause and effect syndrome means to fall short of understanding the complexity of nature, and its inextricable connections with the evolution of life in a timelessness frame. Not that these scientific investigations, assumptions and methods are not helpful, but should not constitute the principal means of understanding or attributing meaning without organicism being attached with mysticism.[98] The ecological project calls for a rejection of the detached object of study, objectivity and mechanism forming the core of the Cartesian – Newtonian dominance in social sciences in favour of subjectivity.

The ecological teleology points to the significance of historicity and dialecticism in understanding the current human conditions as the dynamic ebb and flow and product of synergistic forces through time. This means to get rid of Westphalian straightjacket [99]-the prevalence of ahistorical bias in formulating the concept of international system reinforced by the dominance of an economic, natural science based understanding of the social world.

"A silent acceptance of this cultural bias" —the imposed dominant economic and political thinking of western paradigm—"is virtually universal, not only within the context of a Western centred parochialism, but also among IR scholars who have tragically abandoned their own quite different historical and cultural traditions".[100] Seducing all cultural diversities, civilisational essences, regional specificities and bioregimes' particularities and their coordinated interconnections woven into the warf and woof of cosmos, into wearing the western straitjacket is to block communication of the mainstream International Relations with other disciplines, and snap man's eternal chord with the cosmos. It calls for a multi disciplinary and multidimensional approach that will travel beyond microeconomic analogies, handling forces that are much more elusive and much less amenable to behavioural manipulation than the heavily magnified state. Awakening it from the Westphalia Procrustean bed, it should be studied as an historical action and a social actor among many. Thus, the ecological vision includes a system cosmology, a theory of democracy of global structure of governance, a new scientific epistemology supplementing behaviourlism and Newtonian objectivity, a strategy for global peace and security on the basis of cooperation, and a recognition of intergenerational equity and accountability, and interspecies responsibility.

Revisiting Globalist Criticism

Deudney is impervious to the above changing views on the relationship between man and nature and its impact on the international relation. Critique of realism and liberalism from an environmental perspective challenges the very basis of Deudney's agruments denouncing the linkage between environmental degradation and conflict. To sum up, Deudney's globalist perspective sees environmental politics as subversive of the state, and the state as subversive of the emergent global environmental political sensibility. He makes three basic claims. First, he claims that it is 'analytically misleading' to characterize environmental degradation as a threat to national security, because "the traditional focus of national security has little in common with either environmental problems or solutions". Second, he argues that "the effort to harness the emotive power of nationalism to help mobilize environmental awareness and action may prove counter productive by undermining globalist political sensibility. Taking the position that the security notion is still primarily linked to the states system and national security, he argues that "environmental degradation is not a threat to national security. Rather environmentalism is a threat to 'national security' mindsets and institutions". He further buttresses that dressing the environmental program in the "blood soaked garments of the war system" will undermine environmental "core values" and create "confusion about the real task at hand". Third, he contests the thesis that environmental degradation will be significant cause of interstate wars.[101] Eric K. Stern disagreeing with Deudney is of the view that his "globalist orientation actually undermines the foundations of the domestic international decision. Recent history, most notably the tragic civil wars in Somalia and Rwanda, and the conflicts associated with the break up of the former Yogoslovakia indicate that this distinction is becoming less significant to the international community."[102] Buzan's conceptualization of security, which challenges the privileged status of national or state security, provides a more realist approach. He observes that" the concept of security binds together individuals, states, and the international system so closely that demands to be treated in a holistic perspective, and that "a full understanding of each can only be gained if it is related to the other too". Given this, "attempts to treat security, on any single level invite serious distortions of perspective".[103] While 'balancing enduring tensions between the several levels at once', Stern is of the view that, "an increasing sensibility to environmental threats by national communities and a resulting incorporation of environmental values into national security policy does not necessarily undermine more global efforts to protect the planetary environment".[104] He is of the further view that "the likely scenario for the next half century is one of a mixed system of governance characterized by an uneasy distribution of authority between autonomous sub national entities, national governments, and emergent supra national institutions, such as regional and global formal organizations, regimes, and a developing body of international law".[105] The post cold war period resembles to that of medieval Europe with its characteristic uneven process of integration and disintegration.[106] Stern also questions Deudney's characterization of common security as a marginal phenomenon and an unstable conceptual foundation for environmental security. 'By equating security exclusively with the national security from violence problematic, Deudney "tends to discount the significance of a broad range of parallels and interrelationship between environmental values and military security". He further states that Deudney's "approach prematurely dismisses the viability and persuasiveness of conceptual innovations building upon the notion of security and acknowledging the interdependence that actually characterize the problem of 'security from violence' to nearby the same extent as the problem of protecting the global environment".[107]

A Critique of Orthodox Realism

Rejection of treating environmental problems as security issues with a narrow definition of national or international security delimited to concern with threats originating in the military capabilities of the other states has been the main thrust of mainstream contemporary American realists. Reflecting the view held by mainstream American neo realism, Stephen Walt has recently defined the scope of security studies as "the study of the threat, use and control of military forces".[108] He argues that the security studies 'explore the conditions that make the use of force more likely, the ways the use of force affects individuals, states, and societies, and the specific policies state adopt in order to prepare for, prevent, or engage in war".[109] According to Walt, incorporating non-military phenomena expands the scope of security studies. In his words, "defining the field in his way would destroy its intellectual coherence, and make it mere difficult to devise solutions to any of these important problems". [110] "Walt's realist orientation is an orthodoxy seeking to protect a core of security studies focused on state and military security issues". [111]

Adherence to this conceptual exclusiveness-does not prevent Walt from incorporating "economics and security" in a peremptory place in his proposed "research agenda for security studies". [112] He justified his stand by pointing to the linkage between military spending and economic performance, posture resources, and the impact of the military industrial complex. But his exclusion of other non-military threats from his security agenda is less understandable. "Once the door is opened to non-military economic activities, it became difficult to justify exclusively other non-military issues from the security studies agenda".[113] A study of the links between environmental degradation and military issues in terms of environmental contamination from weapons development / production, pollution and influence attempts, the environmental consequences of warfare and environmental degradation as a cause of conflict, will show the unjustifiability of Walt's exclusion. The environmental consequences of production, storage and use of nuclear weapons, biological, and chemical weapons, and even the conventional weapons development, production, and storage[114] have led to discard the non-admission of the linkage between environment and security on the part of realists. Deliberate pollution has been a significant military and political device designed to influence the behaviour of other actors in world politics.[115] The intentionally taking of steps to produce environmentally catastrophic consequences in pursuit of political aims by the terrorist and non state actors being enraged at the injustice meted out to them in world system, cannot deny the linkage between environment and security. According to T.W. Hawley, the oil spills and oil fires of the Gulf war unleashed by Iraqi forces in 1990-1991 were "an environmental catastrophe on the order of the explosion at the Chernobyl plant or the lethal release of methyl isocyante at Union Carbide's chemical plants in Bhopal, India". [116]

"The threat and intentional inducement of environmental catastrophes bears a striking resemblance to the threat and use of economic sanctions as a diplomatic instrument, the importance of which Walt concedes".[117] Examples are not wanting to show the intentional inducement of environmental disasters, as a part of warfare. It is not a new phenomenon. It has already been pointed out by Dixon that environmental degradation along with its social effects causes simple scarcity conflicts, group identity conflicts, and relative deprivation conflict, which increase the probability of resort to inter and intra-state violence. Other analysts also similarly argued that the economic and social dislocations associated with climate change may result in civil and international wars.[118] Lodgaard's proposal for a regime of environmental confidence and security building measures (CSBMs) to mitigate the tendencies to violence identified by Homer Dixon further points to the untenability of a rigid separation between the environmental and traditional security concerns.

Another interface concerns opportunity costs, [119] multiple purpose capabilities and conversion. Opportunity costs are incurred when assets invested in military security projects become unavailable for the purpose, a phenomenon Buzan sees as a part of" defense dilemma".[120] Such tradeoffs occur between defence and education, health care and environmental clean up. Another interface is the multiple purpose capabilities, which the military through its capability is engaged in various rescue-and disaster relief missions, required of in natural cataclysms or technologies disasters having serious environmental consequences. Finally, conversion alludes to the possibilities of reallocating existing military assets and capabilities to other uses outside the military sector such as environmental clean up measures.[121]

Stern sums up saying the realist argumentations against incorporating the environmental phenomena into the security agenda are not well founded.[122]

Reformist Criticism of Environmental Security Revisited

Lhevy defines the term environmental as referring to "issues involving biological or physical systems characterized by significant ecological feedbacks or by their importance to the sustenance of human life".[123] He makes a commendable attempt to specify the central terms involved and to assess soberly the costs and benefits associated with integrating environment and security. Stern, on the other hand specifies the types of environmental values most likely to be perceived as security threats in the following, admittedly anthropocentric terms: "threats to human health (such as highly contagious bacterial or viral diseases), threats to essential resources which support life in human eco system (e.g. air, water supply, and food production), and threats to the integrity of valued non human ecosystem and local / global biological diversity".[124] Three arguments made by Lhevy deserve examination. First, Lhevy holds that "the assertion that many environmental problems constitute security risks is correct, and is of very little importance".[125] He argues that the two key threats – ozone depletion and climate change-do appear to constitute "environmental problems that currently pose a direct physical harm to US interests", but he questions whether anything is gained by labelling them security issue.[126] Second, Lhevy argues that taking these environmental issues out of the realm of "low politics" where significant progress has been made may actually be counter productive. Third, Lhevy recommends that the study of indirect threats produced by environmentally induced conflict be left to researchers studying more general processes of social conflict, instability and war. These researchers should incorporate environmental factors into their more general models of conflict escalation and de-escalation. Overall, Lhevy essentially defends continued compartmentalization and advocates more research within the traditionally defined sub fields of international relations and comparative environmental policy. Despite Lhevy's arguments giving a number of good observations on environment security his study is stymied by several serious limitations. First, walking on the same furrow left by Deudney, Lhevy deliberately puts a primacy on the issue of national security and was averse to considering the implications of tying the environmental issues with supranational security concepts. Furthermore, Lhevy seems to frame the more general types of conceptual issues on the basis of the specific configuration of US interests. That means his study of security and seriousness of the climate change threat is rated high and low on the basis of the magnitude of the disastrous effects it will have on US interests, natural resources and its capability to cope with these changes. The crucible is the US interests on which is to be tested the magnitude of the environmental crisis. On the basis of the impact on US interests, resources and capability, the qualifications required of environmental security to be incorporated into the mainstream of national security, are to be defined. If the scientists prediction about the immediacy of effects of climate change on the survival of human lifes, more specifically the submersion of small island states under sea come true due to even the modest rise of sea level, then there are obvious reasons to argue for associating environmental security with the fundamental national security goal of survival.

According to Stern, problematiq is with Lhevy's claim that it is counter productive to raise environmental issue to the status of "high politics". Lhevy challenges the assumption that assigning an issue to the realm of high politics automatically increases the likelihood that forceful action will be taken. But his argument hinges primarily on a single historical example – policy with regard to protecting the ozone layer. Lhevy claims that progress was made on this issue by "sub cabinet officials operating out of the limelight and with little Congressional meddling".[128] He claims that "it is hard to escape the conclusion that we probably saved more lives by treating the stratosphere as low politics than as high politics".[129] "Yet is it really possible to draw far reaching conclusions on the basis of a single case of alleged policy success? It may be the case that a 'high politics' route might well more effectively and rapidly address other issues, arising under other circumstances. Stern further says" issues requiring significant investment and research, and public sacrifice, might require high level and more public leadership."[130] Lhevy argues that climate change, in contrast to the relatively straight forward ozone problem is" much more like the problem of containing Soviet Union; it requires a ground strategy to guide actions in the face of distant, uncertain threats, and an overarching commitment from high levels of leadership to stay the course through the ebb and flows of popular sentiment."[131] Thus, for this important environmental issue; Lhevy calls for a high politics type solution. Third, most importantly and seriously, he delimits his concern to only" links from process of environmental degradation to deterioration in security positions and excludes from considerations "connections that run in the opposite direction (from use of force to deterioration of environmental quality)."[132] In the words of Stern, "Nor are links between preparations for the use of force and environmental degradation are considered. Thus, his overall conclusion is based upon an examination of only part of the case made by advocates of environmental security."[133]

Comprehensive Security

As seen from the above analysis, the security problematiq is caught between two extreme positions. The traditionalist position represented by

Deudney, Stephen Walt, and others envisages to keep environmental affairs off the security for variety of different reasons, none of which seems compelling. Stephen Walt giving probably the strongest statement of the traditionalist position is averse to widening the security agenda outside this strictly military domain. He argues that this tendency to widen the security domain

> **"runs the risk of expanding 'Security Studies' excessively; by this logic, issues such as pollution, diseases, child abuse, or economic recessions could all be viewed as threats to 'security'. Defining the field in this way would destroy its intellectual coherence and make it more difficult to devise solutions to any of these important problems." [134]**

Walt does import economics and security into his picture but only as they relate to military issues, and not as economic security per se. According to Barry Buzan, given the political function of the word security, it extends the call for state mobilization to a wide range of issues. Central among the arguments for the conceptualization of environmental security is the mobilization potential: the concept of national security

> **"has an enormous power as an instrument of social and political mobilization," and therefore" the obvious reason for putting environmental issues into the security agenda is the possible magnitude of threats posed, and the need to mobilize urgent and unprecedented responses to them. The security label is a useful way both of signaling danger and setting priority, and for this reason alone it is likely to persist in the environmental debates." [135]**

So the traditionalists' criticism of the wideners that they risk intellectual coherence can be a powerful point. Further he said that "the wider agenda tends, often unthinkingly, to elevate security into a kind of universal good thing-the desired conditions towards which all relations should be moved." [136] The debate over whether security label is worthwhile appending to environment remains dominant in the conception of 'comprehensive security'. It points to the emerging values of environmentalism establishing their own moral basis, which according to Buzan, are already emerging as a new norm of international society[137] Deudney in a similar vein talks about ecological awareness being linked to "a powerful set of values and symbols" that "draw upon basic human desires and aspirations", which should be mobilization basis and not the regressive logic.[138]

Given the nature and scope of environmental problems, which are global in character, the state centric paradigm of national security evades the solution. The concept of 'security' tends to carry with it the implications that the answer, the defence, is to be given by the state. This is what stated by Moss:

> **"The most serious consequences of thinking of global change and other environmental problems as threats to security are that the sorts of centralized governmental responses by powerful and autonomous state organizations that are appropriate for security threats are inappropriate for addressing most environmental problems. When one is reacting to the threat of organized external violence, military and intelligence institutions are empowered to take the measures required to repel the threat. By this same logic, when responding to environmental threat, response by centralized regulatory agencies would seem to be logical. Unfortunately, in most cases this sort of response is not the most efficient or effective way of addressing environmental problems, particularly those that have a global character."[139]**

As argued above, the concept of security includes the message that here is an issue where the state is or should be licensed to take appropriate steps, but "the instinct for centralized state response to security threats is highly inappropriate for responding effectively to global environmental problems".[140]

At the other extreme is found the concern for environment in a privileged position, in effect tumbling the threat of international violence from its traditionally privilege and hegemonic position at the core of the security discourse, and replacing it with a new environmental "king of mountain". [141] How to chart a course of policy action between these two extreme-one is a politico-military construct of state security, and the other is environmental security as national security? "A unifying conceptual" framework "is needed from which to overview the complex relationships and trade offs among domains of life and values held by political communities such as nation states". Instead of giving a primacy to either environmental security, military or any other threats, "we should attempt to level the playing field in order to better appreciate the side effects associated with particular choices, and has best to allocate scarce collective resources." [142] Psychological and organizational constraints stand in the way of achieving such a unifying overview. Alexander George identified the perennial problems of value complexity in policymaking. Policy problems "are laden with competing values and interest" and "the standard textbook model of rationality cannot be employed in such instance, because the multiple values embedded in the policy problems cannot be reduced to a single utility function that can then be used as criterion for choosing among options".[143] It so happens in the decision making process that sometimes the core values go unnoticed only to be identified with hindsight. "Even where a range of competing values are identified by a decision making process, there are strong organizational and cognitive pressures towards suppressing value conflict rather than confronting it".[144] A myriad of psychological theories and empirical research findings suggest that individuals betray a subconscious need for cognitive consistency.[145] Yugo Verzberger has argued that "people see the social environment as consistent and balanced". As a result, 'they believe that a policy that serves one value is also likely to contribute to other values, thus avoiding consideration of value trade offs', and "even salient internal contradictions are often ignored".[146] In order to deal with these problems Ralph Kenney propounded a radically different decision paradigm: "value focused thinking". In this paradigm: significant effort is devoted to articulating values, prior to other activities. Then, "the articulated values are explicitly used to identify decision opportunities and to create alternatives". [147] In his view, such a value-focused orientation will help "create better decision situation with better alternatives which should lead to better consequences." [148] According to Stern, the concept of comprehensive security formulated by Barry Buzan, Arthur Westing, and others promises to serve this important integrating function by explicitly recognizing the multiple and interrelated dimensions and core value clusters of domestic and international life".[149] Buzan's formulation is useful because it includes military, economic, environmental, societal, and political dimensions. In the first edition of Barry Buzan's People, States and Fear was evident that security at the three levels individual, state and international were central to the argument, but in some sense national security was still privileged. "Did Buzan want to make a three-decker out of the concept of security, or was it a conceptualization of national security" ?[150] It was clarified in the second edition (1991). The state level is privileged, and the argument about the levels is the absolutely correct one that national security cannot be comprehended at the state level alone: the dynamics of national security can only be grasped by seeing the interaction with processes at the societal / individual and the international level. Thus, the argument is no longer one for "the right balance between the three levels", but one for enlightened national security taking in dynamics at all levels.[151] "The security label is one solution", says Barry Buzan – but tends himself towards recommending the other path: to 'identify by environmental issues as part of the economic agenda, "which has the" advantage of sitting the issue at the heart of the action that is most relevant to it. There might, in the long run, be more advantages to making producers, consumers, tax men, and economists factor environmental costs into their accounting activities, than to arming the state with emergency powers derived from an analogy with war. It might be argued that process type threats are better met by the process type remedies of economics, than by the statist solution of security logic." [152] In Buzan's analysis is found dominant the economic content approach to environmental crisis, though the security label at the state seems to be privileged. His later writings after the end of the cold war seem to have shifted the security label down from the state, but the state "remains central but no longer dominates either as the exclusive referent object or as the principal embodiment of threat in the way it did previously". [153] A spurt of a new range of referent objects for security and sources of security is found above, below and alongside the state. What ascend above the state to the status of referent objects are new international regimes, rules, norms, and institutions on matters ranging from climate change, to economic liberation, and proliferation of weapons of mass destruction. If the predictions of scientists about the imminence of climate change, major changes in temperature and precipitation pattern due to global warming become certain and accurate within a few years, Buzan does not mind keeping environmental security at the top of the global agenda. A dilution of his earlier stand that attaches the privileged security label at the state takes place. In the environmental sector the range of possible referent objects is very large, ranging from relatively concrete things such as the survival of individual species (animals, human kind) or types of habitat (rain, forest, lakes) to the maintenance of the planetary climate and biosphere. The relationship between the human species and the rest of the biosphere not only within the present time frame but also beyond timelessness, and carried into the future remains central to whether that relationship can be sustained without risking either or both resulting in the collapse of the achieved levels of civilization or a whole sale disruption of the planet's biosphere. At either the macro or micro extremes "of interplay amongst all of these things" there are some pretty clear cases of existential threat (the survival of species, the survival of human civilization) that are be securitized." [154]

Critical Security Studies

It studies security in constructive terms. It challenges the traditionalists and wideners by applying post positivist perspective, such as critical theory and post structuralism[155]. Much of the work on this like Buzan's deals with social reconstruction of security. But the Critical Security Studies shows that change is possible because things are socially constructed. If states dominate the arena, this is a feat of power politics repressing other dimensions of reality that would potentially replace the states if an emancipatory praxis with the help of critical theory empowers other subjectivities than those dominate at present. The social world does not exhibit any inexorable iron laws, all regularities can be broken, and it is the task of Critical Theory to show this. On the issue of security, the Critical Security Studies is often less constructive." As part of the argumentation against established discourses of security, it will often try to mobilize other security problems-environmental problems, poverty and unemployment as more important, more threatening, and there by relativizing conventional wisdom. By this method they often end up reproducing the traditional and objectivist concept of security.[156] As observed by Waever, this approach will often contribute to the general securitization of ever-large spheres of social life.[157] But the critical theory remains half way emancipatory without taking into mainstream of its thinking ecological crisis or the environmental movement as sources of emancipatory change. They have not yet pursued the many insights offered by ecological thought.[158]

Treating nature as whole while observing its rich diversity, the Critical Theory would appreciate the patterns of mutual aid and the complexity of natural phenomena, and question arguments based on ontological stratification or linear thinking.[159] Holism would not associate with global control and homogenization but with an expanded self.[160] How the widening view of security proposed by Critical Theorists is possible for its emancipatory mission without the environment forming its mainstream thinking? In this chapter, the above discussion of the ecological critique of both realism and liberalism forming the mainstream of the dominant international prospective on security shows, the Critical Theorists need to make a review of the dominant hegemonic portrayal of human nature, its relationship with nature, and a dismantling of self help versus the other syndrome as a basis of redefining its security from a widening perspective.

The ecological approach gets it at the root of emancipation by revealing the relationship between the control of nature and control of man/woman. In this sense, ecology is the holistic approach par excellence. By definition, it cannot limit its defence of freedom to specific constituencies, for no long-term freedom may be gained for any group at the expense of nature; nature is nothing but the larger self of human kind.[161]

References

1. Kenneth W. Waltz, Theory of International Politics (Reading, Massachusetts: Addison-Wesley, 1979), p. 102.
2. Richard N. Lebow, "The Long Peace, the End of the Cold War, and the Failure of Realism", International Organization Vol. 48, no-2, 1994, pp. 249-77.
3. Michel Frederick, "A Realist's Conceptual Definition of Environmental Security", in Daniel H. Deudney and Richard A. Matthew ed., Contested Grounds: Security and Conflict in the New Environmental Politics (Albany: State University of New York Press, 1999), p. 92.
4. Charles Philippe David, "Strategic Studies in Crisis", Etudes Internationales Vol. 20, No. 3, 1989, pp. 513-15.
5. Barry Buzan, "Change and Insecurity: A Critique of Strategic Studies", in Barry Buzan and R.J Barry Jones, eds, Change and the Study of the International Relations: The Evaded Dimension (New York: St. Martin's Press, 1981), Lester Brown, "An Untraditional View of National Security", in John Reichart and Steven Sturm, eds, American Defence Policy, 5th edn (Baltimore, Md.: Johns Hopkins University Press, 1984).
6. Norman Myers, "Environmental Security" Foreign Policy Vol.-74, 1989, pp. 23-41.
7. Richard Ullman, "Redefining Security", International Security Vol-8, No. 1, 1983, pp. 129-53.
8. Michel Frederick, *op. cit.,* p. 94.
9. Michel Frederick, *op. cit.,* p. 96.
10. Sverre Lodgaard, "The Transformation of Europe and the Gulf War: Implication for the Research Agenda", UNIDIR Newsletter Vol. 4, No. I, 1991, pp. 7-9.
11. Arthur H.Westing, "Comprehensive Human Security and Ecological Realities" Guest Comment, Environmental Conservation Vol. 116, Winter 1989, p. 295.

12. Daniel B.Botkin, Discordant Harmonies: A New Ecology for the Twenty First Century (New York: Oxford University Press, 1990); Rice Odell, Environmental Awakening: The New Relation to Protect the Earth (Cambridge, Mass.: Ballinger, 1980).
13. Johan J. Holst, "Security and the Environment" : A Preliminary Exploration", Bulletin of Peace Proposals Vol. 20, no-2, 1989, pp. 123-28.
14. *Ibid.*, p. 123.
15. M.Frederick, *op. cit.,* p. 98.
16. Barry Buzan, "Environment as a Security Issue", Geopolitical Perspectives on Environmental Security, Paul Painchaud, ed. (Quebec: Laval University, GERPE, Occasional Paper, 92-05, 1992), p. 4
17. Raymond Aron, Peace and War: A Theory of International Politics (New York: Doubleday, 1966), pp. 72f and 598f.
18. Ole Waever, Securitization and Desecuritization, Working Papers, Centre for Peace and Conflict Research, Copenhagen, 5, 1993, p. 5.
19. Barry Buzan, "Environment as a Security Issue", *op. cit.,* p. 4.
20. Ole Waever, Securitization and Desecuritization, *op. cit.,* p. 5.
21. Barry Buzan, People, States and Fear: An Agenda for Security Studies in the Post-Cold War era (Hemel Hempstead: Wheatsheaf, 1991), p. 117.
22. Egbert Jahn, Pierre Lemaitre and Ole Waever, European Security: Problems of Research on Non-Military Aspects (Copenhagen: Copenhagen Papers of the Centre for Peace and Conflict Research 1987) p. 9.
23. Michel Frederick, *op. cit.,* p. 100.
24. Prue Taylor, "The Failure of International Environmental Law", Our Planet Vol. 4, No. 3, 1992, pp. 14-15.
25. Arthur H. Westing, ed; Comprehensive Security for the Baltic: An Environmental Approach (London: Sage, 1989) pp. 1-13.
26. L.H. Brown, "Regional Collaboration in Resolving Third World Conflicts", Survival, (London) Vol. 28, 1986, pp. 208-220. See also L.J. Cantori and S.L. Spiegel, ed., International Politics of Regions: A Comparative Approach (New Jersey: Prentice Hall, 1970), p. 432; B.M.Russett, International Regions and the International System: A Study in Political Ecology (Chicago: Rand –McNally, 1967), p. 252.

27. Michel Frederick, *op. cit.,* p. 101.
28. Daniel Deudney, "The case against Linking Environmental Degradation and National Security", Daniel Deudney," Environmental Security: Muddled Thinking", Bulletin of the Atomic Scientists Vol. 47, No. 3, 1991, pp. 22-28.
29. Clive Ponting, A Green History of the World: The Environment and the Collapse of Great Civilization (New York: St. Martin's, 1992).
30. SIPRI, Warfare in a Fragile World: Military Impact on the Human Environment (London: Taylor and Francis, 1980).
31. T.W. Hawley, Against the Fires of Hell: The Environmental Disaster of the Gulf War (New York: Harcourt Brace Jovanovich, 1992). Arthur H. Westing, "Environmental and Ecological Consequence of War", Sent on email to author on 15th August 2003, p. 4.
32. Paul R. Ehrlich, Carl Sagan, Donald Kennedy, and Walter Orr Roberts, The Cold and the Dark: The World After Nuclear War (New York: Norton, 1984).
33. Animesh Roul, Environmental Effects of the Production and Use of Weapons of Mass Destruction, Dissertation submitted to Jawaharlal Nehru University, for M.Phil, New Delhi, 1998. See also Michael Renner, "Assessing the Military's War on the Environment", in Lester Brown, ed., State of the World 1991 (New York: Norton, 1991), pp. 132-52.
34. Daniel H. Deudney "Environmental Security: A Critique", in Daniel H.Deudney and Richard A. Matthew ed., Contested Grounds (Albany: State University of New York Press, 1991), pp. 192-93.
35. Deudney, *Ibid.*, p. 193.
36. Thomas F.Homer Dixon, Environment, Scarcity and Violence (New Jersey/ Princeton: Princeton University Press, 1999), pp. 142-47.
37. Deudney, *op. cit.,* p. 194.
38. Deudney, *op. cit.,* p. 194.
39. Deudney, *op. cit.,* p. 194.
40. William James, "The Moral Equivalent of War", Memories and Studies (New York and London: Longmans, Green &Co, 1911).
41. Ken Conca, "In the Name of Sustainability: Peace Studies and Environmental Discourse", in Jyrki Kakonen, ed., Green

Security or Militarized Environment (Aldershot, U.K.: Dartmouth, 1994).

42. Kofi Annan, We the Peoples: the Role of the United Nations in the 21st Century March 2000, quoted by Andrew Mack "Human Security in the New Millennium", Work in Progress: A Review of Research Activities of the United Nations University Vol. 16, No. 3, Summer, 2002, p. 4.
43. Jyrki Kakonen, ed., Green Security or Militarized Environment, *op. cit.*
44. Michael Howard, "War and the Nation-State", Daedalus Vol. 108, No. 4, Fall 1979, pp. 101-10.
45. Charles Tilly, "War Making and State Making as Organized Crime" in Peter Evans, Dietrich Rueschemeyer and Theda Skocpal, eds., Bringing the State Back in (Cambridge, UK.: Cambridge University Press, 1985), pp. 169-91.
46. Jason Clay, "Resource Wars: Nation and State Conflicts of the Twentieth Century" in Barbara Rose Johnston ed, Who Pays the Price? The Sociocultural Context of Environmental Crisis (Washington D.C.: Island Press, 1994).
47. Nancy Peluso, Rich Forests, Poor People (Berkeley: University of California Press, 1993), and Charles S. Wood and Marianne Schmink, "The Military and the Environment in the Brazilian Amazon", Journal of Political and Military Sociology Vol. 21, Summer 1993, pp. 81-105.
48. See Thomas F. Homer Dixon, Environment, Scarcity and Violence, *op. cit.* p. 144.
49. Anil Agarwal, Sunita Narain, Anju Sharma and Achila Imchen, eds., Poles Apart: Global Environmental Negotiation 2, (New Delhi: Centre for Science and Environment, 2001)
50. Michael Ross Fowler and Julie Marie Bunck, Law, Power and the Sovereign State: The Evolution and Application of the Concept of Sovereignty (University Park: Pennsylvania State University Press, 1995).
51. Barry Buzan, "Rethinking Security after the Cold War", Nordic Journal of International Studies Vol. 32, No. 1, March 1997, p. 12.
52. On environmental conditionality, see Andrew Hurrell 'Green Conditionality', Overseas Development Council Policy Paper, March 1993.

53. See Patricia Birnie, "International Environmental Law: Its Adequacy for Present and Future Needs", in Hurrell and Kingsbury eds., The International Politics of the Environment (Oxford: UK: Clarendon Press, 1992), p. 84.
54. Kathryn Sikkink, "Human Rights, Principled Issue-networks, and Sovereignty in Latin America", International Organization Vol. 47, no, 3, Summer 1993, pp. 411-41, and Ronnie D.Lipschutz, "Reconstructing World Politics: The Emergence of Global Civil Society", Millennium Journal of International Studies Vol. 21, No. 3, Winter 1992, pp. 389-420.
55. See Hurrell and Kingsbury, "introduction" in Hurrell and Kingsbury, eds., *op. cit.,* pp. 6-8.
56. Mark A Lhevy, Robert O Keohane, and Peter M. Haas, "Imposing the Effectiveness of International Environmental Institutions" in Haas, Keohane and Lhevy, eds., Institutions for the Earth: Sources of Effective International Environmental Protection (Cambridge, MA: MIT Press, 1993), pp. 415-17.
57. Ken Conca, "Rethinking the Ecology Sovereignty Debate", Millennium: Journal of International Studies Vol. 23, No. 3, 1994, p. 702.
58. Ken Conca, *op. cit.,* p. 703.
59. Quoted from Ruth Lapidoth, "Sovereignty in Transition", Journal of International Affairs Vol. 45, No. 2, winter 1992, pp. 325-46.
60. Conca, *op. cit.,* p. 706.
61. Deudney, *op. cit.,* p. 198.
62. Summit Document Safeguard Brazilian Interests", Daily Report: Latin America, FBIS-LAT-92-114-5, 12 June 1992, p. 27.
63. David Cleary, "After the Frontier: Problems with Political Economy in the Modern Brazilian Amazon", Journal of Latin American Studies, Vol. 25, part. 2, May 1993, pp. 331-49.
64. Conca, *op. cit.,* p. 711.
65. *Ibid.*, p. 311.
66. Quoted Kennedy Graham, "Leadership ethics for the future: Tread lightly on the Planet", Point of view, UNU nexions, April 2002, p. 5.
67. Matthew Paterson, "Interpreting trends in global governance", International Affairs Vol. 25, No. 4, 1949, p. 795; and Lamont

Hempel, Environmental governance; the global challenger (Washington D.C: Island Press, 1996)

68. Murray Bookchin, The Ecology of Freedom: The Emergence and Dissolution of Hierarchly, Revised Edition, (Montreal and New York, Ny: Black Rose Books, 1991).
69. Joshua Karliner, The Corporate Planet Ecology and Politics in the Age of Globalization, (San Francisco: Sierra Club Books, 1997), Chapter-7.
70. Matthew Paterson, Understanding Global Environmental Politics: Domination, Accumulation, Resistance (London: Macmillan, 2000).
71. Lynton Keith Caldwell, International Environmental Policy: Emergence and Dimension (New Delhi: Affiliated East-West Press pvt. Ltd., 1991), p. 68.
72. Deudney, *op. cit.,* p. 199.
73. See William Thomas, Scorched Earth: The Military's Assault on the Environment (Philadelphia, PA, and Gabriola Island: New Society Publishers, 1995), See also Matthias Finger, "The Military, the Nation State and the Environment", The Ecologist Vol. 21, No. 5, 1991, pp. 220-25.
74. John Barkdull, "Why Environmental Ethics Matter to International Relations", Current History Vol. 99, No. 640, November-2000, p. 362.
75. John A.Vasquez, "The Post-positivist Debate: Reconstructing Scientific Enquiry and International Relations Theory After Enlightenment's Fall", in Ken Booth and Steve Smith ed., International Relations Theory Today (Cambridge, Polity Press, 1995), p. 221.
76. Eric Laferriere, *op. cit.,* p. 68.
77. Kenneth N. Waltz, Man, the State and War: A Theoretical Analysis (New York, NY: Columbia University Press. 1959).
78. Eric Laferriere, *op. cit.,* p. 68.
79. *Ibid.*
80. Barry Buzan, "Rethinking Security after the Cold War", Nordic Journal of International Studies Vol. 32, No. 1, March-1997, p. 19.
81. J.R.McNeill, "Ideas Matter: A Political History of the Twentieth-Century Environment", Current History Vol. 99, No. 640, November.2000, p. 374.

82. Richard Cobden, Political Writings Vol. 1 (London: T Fisher Unwin, 1903), Norman Angell, The Great Illusion (New York, NY: Knickerbocker Press, 1911).
83. David Mitrany, A Working Peace System (Chicago, IL: Quadrangle Books, 1966), Ernst B.Haas, Beyond the Nation-State: Functionalism and International Organization (Stanford, CA: Stanford University Press, 1969).
84. Robert O. Keohane, After Hegemony: Cooperation and Discord in the World Political Economy (Princeton, NJ; Princeton University Press, 1984) and Stephen D Krasner, ed., International Regimes (Ithaca, NY: Cornell University Press, 1983)
85. Robert C. Johansen, The National Interest and the Human Interest: An Analysis of US Foreign Policy (Princeton, NJ: Princeton University Press, 1980).
86. Edward Goldsmith, "Development as Colonialism", World Affairs Vol. 6, No. 2, April-June 2002, p. 36.
87. Ismail Shariff and David M.Littig, "Globalization old wine into new bottles", World Affairs Vol. 6, No. 2, April-June 2002, p. 42.
88. See Karl Deutsch et al., Political Community and the North Atlantic Area (Princeton, N. J.; Princeton University Press, 1957), and Amitai Etzioni, Political Unification: A Comparative Study of Leaders and Forces (New York, NY: Holt, Rinehart and Winston, 1965)
89. James N.Rosenau, Turbulence in World Politics: A Theory of Change and Continuity (Princeton, NJ: Princeton University Press, 1990), p. 289.
90. Mitrany, *op. cit.,* p. 96, Hoarold Laski, A Grammar of Politics (London: Allen and Unwin, 1967), p. 614 ; See also David Long, "International Functionalism and the Politics of Forgetting", International Journal Vol. 48, No. 2, 1993, pp. 356-79.
91. Bruce Russett, "Causes of Peace" in Carolyn M Stephenson ed., Alternative Methods of International Security (Washington, D.C.: University Press of America, 1982), pp. 188 & 191.
92. Mitrany, *op. cit.,* p. 36.
93. Eric Laferriere, *op. cit.,* p. 72.
94. Origins: NC Documentary Service 17, 3 March 1988, p. 645 ; Quoted in J.Ronald Engel," Introduction: The ethics of

sustainable development", in J.Ronald Engel and Joan Gibb Engel ed., Ethics of Environment and Development (London: Belhaven Press, 1990), p. 4.

95. Stephen Toulmin, The Return to Cosmology: Postmodern Science and the Theology of Nature (Berkeley: University of California Press, 1982), pp. 255-56.
96. Holmes Rolston, III, and Environmental Ethics: Duties to and Values in the Natural World (Philadelphia: Temple University Press, 1988), p. 174.
97. Carolyn Merchant, The Death of Nature: Women Ecology and the Scientific Revolution (New York, NY and Toronto: Harper and Row, 1980).
98. Janet Biehl, Finding Our Way: Rethinking of Ecofeminist Politics (Montreal and New York, NY: Black Rose Books, 1991), pp. 89-90.
99. Barry Buzan and Richard Little," Why International Relations has Failed as an Intellectual Project and What to do about it", Millennium Vol. 30, No. 1, 2001, pp. 25.
100. *Ibid.* p. 26.
101. Deudney, "The Case against Linking Environmental Degradation and National Security", Millennium vol 1990, pp. 461-76.
102. Eric K.Stern, "The Case for Comprehensive Security", in Daniel H.Deudney and Richard A. Matthew, eds., Contested Grounds, *op. cit.,* p. 139.
103. Barry Buzan, Peoples, States and Fear: The National Security Problem in International Relations (Chapel Hill: University of North Carolina Press, 1983), p. 245.
104. Eric K.Stern, *op. cit.,* p. 139.
105. *Ibid.*
106. Ken Booth, "Security in Anarchy: Utopian Realism in Theory and Practice," International Affairs Vol. 67, No. 3, 1991, pp. 527-45.
107. *Ibid,* p. 140.
108. Stephen Walt, "The Renaissance of Security Studies," International Studies Quarterly Vol. 35, No. 2, 1991, p. 212.
109. Joseph Nye and Sean Lynn Jones, "International Security Studies: A Report of a Conference on the State of the Field," International Security Vol. 12, No. 4, 1988, p. 6.
110. Walt, "The Renaissance of Security Studies," p. 213.

111. Stern, *op. cit.,* p. 135.
112. Walt, *op. cit.,* p. 135.
113. Stern, *op. cit.,* p. 135.
114. See M. D. Antonio, Atomic Harvest: Hanford and the Lethal Toll of America's Nuclear Arsenal (New York: Crown Publishers, 1993); and Murray Fesbach, Ecological Disaster: Cleaning up the Legacy of the Soviet Regime (New York; Twentieth Century Press, 1995).
115. See David Baldwin, Economic Statecraft (Princeton; NJ: Princeton University Press, 1985).
116. T.W Hawley, Against the Fires of Hell: the Environmental Disaster of the Gulf War (New York: Harcourt Brace Javonovich, 1992), p. 8.
117. Stern, *op. cit.,* p. 136.
118. N.Brown, "Climate, Ecology, and International Security", Survival Vol. 31, No. 6, 1989, pp. 519-32.
119. S. Lodgaard, "Environment, Confidence Building and Security", in Hjort af Ornas and Lodgaard, eds., The Environment and International Security (Uppsala: PRIO/ Uppsala University Program on Environment and International Security, 1992), pp. 11-22.
120. Barry Buzan, Peoples, States and Fear, 2nd edt, *op.cit.*
121. Stern, *op. cit.,* p. 138.
122. *Ibid.*
123. Marc A Lhevy, "Is the Environment a National Security Issue" ? International Security Vol. 20, No. 2, 1995, p. 39.
124. Eric K.Stern, "High Politics and Crisis: Military and Environmental Dimensions of Security", in Hjort af Ornas and Laggard, eds., The Environment and International Security, *op. cit.,* p. 90.
125. Lhevy, "Is the Environment a National Security issue" ? p. 60
126. *Ibid.,* p. 61.
127. See for details, Eric K.Stern, "The Case for Comprehensive Security", *op. cit.,* p. 141.
128. Lhevy, Is the Environment a National Security Issue" ?, *op. cit.,* p. 50.
129. *Ibid.*
130. Stern, "The Case for Comprehensive Security", *op. cit.,* p. 142.
131. Lhevy, "Is the Environment a National Security Issue?", *op. cit.,* p. 54.

132. *Ibid*, p. 36.
133. Stern, "The Case for Comprehensive Security", *op. cit.*, p. 142.
134. Stephen M. Walt, "The Renaissance of Security Studies", International Studies Quarterly Vol. 35, No. 2, 1991, pp. 212-13.
135. Barry Buzan, "Environment as a Security Issue" in Paul Painchaud ed. Geopolitical Perspectives on Environmental Security, Cahier du GERPE, No. 92-05, Universite Laval, Quebec, pp. 1and 24f.
136. Barry Buzan, "Rethinking Security after the Cold War", Nordic Journal of International Studies Vol. 32, No. 1, March 1997, p. 11.
137. Barry Buzan, n.135, p. 26.
138. Daniel Deudney, "The Case against Linking Environment Degradation and National Security" *op. cit.*, p. 469.
139. Richard H.Moss, "Environmental Security? The illogic of centralized state responses to environment threats", in Paul Painchaud, ed., Geopolitical Perspectives on Environment Security, *op. cit.*, p. 24.
140. Moss, *op. cit.*, p. 32.
141. Patricia M. Mische, "Ecological Security and the Need to Reconceptualize Sovereignty", Alternatives Vol. 14, 1989, pp. 389-427.
142. Stern," The Case for Comprehensive Security", *op. cit.*, p. 143.
143. Alexander L.George, Bridging the Gap: Theory and Practice in Foreign Policy (Washington, D.C.: US Institute of Peace Press, 1993), p. 27.
144. Stern, "The Case for Comprehensive Security", *op. cit.* p. 143.
145. Irving Janis and L.Mann, Decision Making: A Psychological Analysis of Conflict, Choice, and Commitment (New York; Free Press, 1977).
146. Y.Vertzberger, The World in Their Minds (Palo Alto, California: Stanford University Press, 1991), pp. 138-39.
147. R.Kenney, Value-Focused Thinking: A Path to Creative Decision Making (Cambridge, Mass: Harvard University Press, 1992).
148. *Ibid*, p. IX.
149. Stern, "The Case for Comprehensive Security", *op. cit.*, p. 144.
150. Ole Waever, Securitization and Desecuritization, *op. cit.*, p. 3.

151. Egbert Jahn, Pierre Lemaitre and Ole Waever, European Security: Problems of Research on Non-Military Aspects, *op. cit.,* pp. 51-53.
152. Buzan, "Environment as a Security issue" in Paul Painchaud ed., Geopolitical Perspectives on Environmental Security, *op. cit.,* p. 25.
153. Barry Buzan, "Rethinking Security after Cold War", *op. cit.,* p. 11.
154. Barry Buzan, "Rethinking Security after the Cold War", *op. cit.,* p. 18.
155. Keith Krause and Michael C.Williams, "From Strategy to Security: Foundation of Critical Security Studies" in Krause and Williams, Critical Security Studies (Boulder, CO: Lynne Rienner, 1996).
156. Barry Buzan, "Rethinking Security ..." *op. cit.,* p. 19.
157. Ole Waever, "Securitization and Desecuritization in Ronnie Lipschutz ed., On Security (New York: Columbia University Press, 1995), pp. 46-86.
158. Eric Laferriere, "Emancipatory International Relations Theory: An Ecological Perspective", Millennium: Journal of International Studies Vol. 25, No. 1, 1996.
159. Peter Kropotkin, Mutual Aid: A Factor of Evolution (Boston, M.A: Extending Horizon Books, 1955).
160. Warwick Fox, Towards a Transpersonal Ecology: Developing New Foundations for Environmentalism (Boston, MA: Shambhala, 1990).
161. Eric Laferriere, *op. cit.* p. 74.

4

Critical Theory: Half Way Emancipatory Sans Environmental Ethics

Disenchanted with, and in reaction to the socio-political inertia of mainstream theory, which was a mere apologist of the prevailing dominant and hegemonic world order, and unable to generate the necessary normative reflection and political action to improve the lot of human kind, the Critical Theory emerged on a crusading spirit to provide a picture of a particular kind of society, one in which individuals would lead free, unconstrained lives equal and totally open in their communications and relations with one another, through an ideal speech situation. Habermas, an exponent of Critical Theory believes that the fully emancipated human society, which Critical Theory envisages to fashion, is actually built into the very nature of human speech.

What is centrality to Critical Theory is the very notion it harbours that knowledge is for human liberation and emancipation, and is very crucial in unearthing lies, repression, false consciousness, self-deception, and exploitation. Its ultimate aim is to change the world for better.[1] Discontent with the positivist belief that the laws, which govern society, operate in much the same way as the laws of natural science. Habermas identified three knowledge constitutive interests. The empirical analytical science meets the predictions and control aspect, the historical hermeneutics sciences enable one to understand the meaning, and the Critical Theory satisfies the human quest for freedom from domination, emancipation and the achievement of rational autonomy.[2]

Robert Lox, Hoffman and Linklater are the few scholars who applied explicitly Haberman's emancipatory project to International Relations.

According to Robert Cox, if theories are expressions of diverse perspectives linked to certain social and political projects, then the central task of the Critical Theory is to achieve a 'perspective on perspectives'[3], which involves a distinction between two distinct, rival and incommensurable paradigms. The first termed as 'problem solving' by Cox "takes the world as it finds it, with the prevailing social and power relationships, and the institutions into which they are organized, as the given framework for action. The general aim of problem solving is to make these relationship and institutions work smoothly by dealing effectively with particular sources of trouble".[4]

The Critical Theory is distinguished from the problem solving thinking in that it "stands apart from the prevailing order of the world and asks how that order came about". It "does not take institutions and social and power relations for granted but calls them into question by concerning itself with their origins and how and whether they might be in the process of changing". Not that the Critical Theory lacks "problem-solving theories within itself, but contains them in the form of identifiable ideologies, thereby pointing to their conservative consequences". Pointing to "the range of possible alternative" as a "principal objective", Critical Theory "allows for a normative choice in favour of a social and political order different from the prevailing order".[5]

Jettisoning the deification of state by the hegemonic mainstay of International Relation, Critical Theory purposes instead to focus on individual, society, community, continuing integrity of ethnic or cultural groups, and global society. Critical Theorists like Linklater advocate critical or new social movements such as those engaged in peace activism, the struggle for human rights and the survival of minority cultures, and so on.[6] In his view, the Critical Theory stands opposed to empirical claims about the social world, which assume that existing structures are immutable. It examines the prospects for new forms of community in which individuals and groups can achieve higher levels of freedom. Mark Hoffman, another proponent of Critical Theory argues that this theory "seeks not simply to reproduce society via description, but to understand society and change it. It is both descriptive and constructive in its theoretical intent: it is both an intellectual and a social act".[7] Post Marxists create more complex historical sociology, which is based on the idea of social learning and envisaging the democratization of politics, domestic and international. The production paradigm of conventional Marxism should be replaced by the discourse ethics. Discourse ethics reflect a particular stage in moral development in which human beings question inherited systems of inclusion and exclusion, and ask whether the boundaries between insiders and outsiders can be justified by principles which agreeable to all. It invites the questioning of traditional notions of sovereignty and reconsideration of citizenship. Notions of cosmopolitan democracy imagine communities in which insiders and outsiders participate on equal terms. It is at this point that post Marxism merges with cosmopolitan/normative school all the more that the same people Linklater represent the two currents.

- Ecological thought's project widening the term 'other' to include the living and non-living nature, and democratic reconstruction of society beyond state centric denomination, will add more to the purpose of Critical Theory.

As to epistemological dimension of gender in International Relation (IR), a central claim of feminism is that this discipline has a deafness to women. IR discourse excludes women by giving primacy to certain roles, rules and events and excluding others. Its dominant paradigm is based on positivism, and the knowledge claims of positivism reflect a particularly masculine and western set of experiences.[8] A major debate within IR pertaining to gender is that of relationship between women, nature, war and peace. Their proposition is that women by nature and nurture are more peaceable than men. Identifying with nature, the women have put the blame on masculine aggregate of power that has damaged both nature and women. Feminists are fascinated with some post modernist writings, which argue that the discourse that is used to secure the identity of those on the inside, through the association of danger with these on the outside, is frequently framed in gendered terms.[9]

Feminists join other post modern schools in their criticism of realism to argue that the state as presently constituted is not adequate security provider for all its citizens. The unitary state actor model favoured by realists conceals the extent to which individuals' insecurities are dependent on race, class and gender, categories that also cross-state and regional boundaries.[10]

If Critical Theory is the most serious intellectual challenge to realism and even more significant than idealism or post modernism, and, considers "extending community beyond the nation-state as its most important problem", [11] then it is inconceivable how reconstruction of society or carrying the nation-state beyond border, and recognizing community or group as new referents alternative to state, could take place without paying sufficient attention to ecology or the impending environmental crisis, which challenges the dominant established frame of mind about security, social way of life, economic and political thinking and state. It is not that the

Critical Theorists have failed to mention the ecological crisis or the environmental movement as sources of emancipatory change, they have not yet incorporated the many insights offered by ecological thought into their theory.

Environmental Dimension in International Relation

An entrenched notion runs in the realm of International Relation that ecological thought is not progressive and cannot as such provide an impetus for a new theoretical paradigm different from the established ones. It thus presents a myriad of choices and dilemmas to the political and International Relation theorist. If ecology or environment has ever been brought into focus by the IR theorist, it was with the intention to buttress and legitimize the epistemological undercurrent of the dominant mainstream of International Relation. For instance, Harold and Margaret Sprout in their celebrated efforts at devising an ecological approach to IR, used concepts of 'ecology', environment and 'milieu' interchangeably without mentioning the ecological crisis merely to stress the point that the political actors indeed react to external factors.[12] That ecological crisis is an independent variable and needs an attention traditionally given to political, economic or social factors, has never been taken note of. In a later book they had discussed the ecological crisis, and there only as a policy field and not in epistemological terms.[13] In their words, "We conceive of the ecological approach as a system of concepts and theory that is useful to the student of international politics, not as a substitute for, but as a compliment to the behavioural and other approaches to the study of foreign policy and the international capabilities of state". [14]

The Sprouts' work reveals how the concept of ecology has been stripped of its radical meaning, and reduced to a subordinate, external factor impeding human achievement, or to meet the crisis, the case for a new contractual ingenuity is argued without asking for a restructuring of the dominant paradigm on the basis of ecological epistemology. It is held that the current literatures on 'environmental security', 'environmental conflict' and 'environmental regimes' are to been seen in this light; not as tangible theoretical innovations, but as interesting case studies for liberal and realist approaches.[15]

Environmental Security in International Relation

Among the emergent problems replacing the threat of East-West ideological divide, military aggression and struggle for global preponderance is the global environmental crisis. It looms large in terms of global warming, sea level rise, acid rain, greenhouse effect, diminishing capacity of the agricultural system, depletion of earth's finite resources, punching holes in the ozone layer, and biodiversity loss. Simply put, the global agenda has expanded since the demise of cold war as has the need for urgent attention to these problems for solution. It is thus seen that "welfare not warfare, will shape the rules and global threats like ozone holes and pollution will dictate the agenda." It is within this context that the environmental question has gained worldwide significance as a security issue. In fact, environmental security stands out as perhaps the most widely debated issue, especially due to its all-pervasive nature, cross national scope and inter generational implications.[16]

While many of the past, present and future causes of conflict and war may seem to have little or no direct connection with the environment or with resources, a strong argument can be made for linking certain resource and environmental problems with the prospects for political frictions and tensions, or even war and peace. At the centre of ongoing debate is the assertion that resource scarcity and certain forms of environmental degradation are important factors contributing to political instability or violent conflict at local, regional and interstate levels. There is a growing perception that local, regional and global environmental deficiencies or resource scarcities will increasingly produce conditions that may lead to conflict.[17]

It was in this backdrop of future non-military threats that a number of studies and research institutions undertook works to determine if and how environmental factors were related to the intra and inter state conflicts or violence that appeared to be surfacing around the globe[18]. These studies varied in their approach, their terminology, and their specific findings, and consistent in their explanations suggested that environmental stress, operating through a set of intervening variables, could contribute to violent conflicts, and thus constituted a threat to national and international security. Lodgaard feels that "the concept of environmental security challenges established frames of mind and political conflicts. It conveys a message that environmental problems have a legitimate claim for status as military problems have." [19]

Though a plethora of studies have spawned up recently demonstrating the linkage between environmental stress and conflict, there has been some criticisms. With the end of cold war and collapse of Soviet Union, the exposure of secretive nuclear installation to international scrutiny, and security being associated not with state, but with the individuals or people, the language of security is no more couched in terms of militarism, competition and secretiveness, rather in terms of demilitarization, nuclear free world and public democratic governance. The dominant geopolitical paradigm of national interest was based on realist parlance of US and its allies' interests overwhelming the entire globe since the Second World War. When environmental security because of environmental catastrophic consequences threatening the existence of human beings leapfrogs to the center stage of national security concern, it as assumed, is not to be based on same dominant geopolitical paradigm of North's interests to acquire the status of national security. Rather it calls for a redefining of the very foundation of traditional outlook of national security based on geopolitical interests of the dominant players in the international realm. If it is to be just an appendage to the geopolitical interests of the dominant players defining the world order since the Second World War, then environmental security is not in any way different from conventional security based on secrecy, militarization and competition for dominance. It has climbed up to the top of the national security agenda not on the basis of realist paradigm, but on a different paradigm. That what cannot be described in old traditional languages, lacks the raison detre to be called national security, stands discredited in the face of new kinds of threats that are stemming from unprecedented environmental crisis. Advocacy of hesitancy to term environmental security as national security means advising to navigate the uncharted seas of environmental crisis with a warped, discredited and conventional realist cartography. If in the words of old ideas of security, environmental security is tried to be defined, the very dilution of what it stands for, takes place, and the perpetuation of the geopolitical interests of the dominant North led by US continues to the perils of the people in the developing South. When the discourse of environmental security is defined in terms of old conventional idioms i.e. the unhindered right of dominant players to resource supply sources in the South, it merely 'extends the explicitly geopolitical understanding of security that were widespread during the cold war to maintain the current global division of wealth." [20]

Fissures within Ecological Thought

The portrait of individuals as predatory and self-aggrandizing in realist parlance when related to nature results in a basic distrust of humankind and its way of political and economic life. This has led to serious divisions within the ecological thought. Whenever questions over solution to the impending environmental degradation come up, some professed democrats did not hesitate to prefer a centralized and elitist solution. The famous defense of 'lifeboat ethics', [21] the proposed approach to nature's carrying capacity, or stressing on meaningful participation or putting environmental restriction on poor South at GATT or WTO from the perspective of the poor, suggestive of denying access to the poor to resources, and enunciating the" survival of the fittest" thesis at best and reinforcing the interest of the healthy rich. Lifeboat ethics orders the strong to deny the weak access to a lifeboat that cannot support every one. Initially, William Ophuls and Robert Hilbroner exuded confidence in elite wisdom.[22] But later on Ophuls changed position is that the ultimate goal is one of local democracies, where leaders are fully acceptable to public, and where only sustainable patterns of production and consumption are favoured.[23] Any authoritarian approach to the solution of the crisis is bound either to collapse under the morass of bureaucracy and corruption or for legitimizing in the long run a rigid social hierarchy. Radical ecology is comprised of two parts, deep and social ecology.

Deep Ecology: Aura of Holism Strewn Around Nature

Deep ecology is preservationist and concerned with defense of wilderness, ecosystems, and biospecies. It is perceived as a social being solely concerned with the health of plants and animals. A product of nineteenth century preservationist battles, deep ecology failed to cast the ecological crisis within a wider social context and to reflect on the specificity of humankind. Its ecological holism describes, humanness as a mere biological component of the interdependent biospheres has no necessary purpose but to serve the cycle of life, as they are at the top of the food chain, humans do not appear very important to the long-term sustainability of life.

In other words, "deep ecologists can be accused of dissolving humanness, either through biological reductionism or through the doctrine of the larger self".[24] In case of the larger self, a declared empathy for other life forms has been interpreted as a negation of diversity and an assertion of human/male/white superiority.[25] Indian philosophy expresses in the heightened stage of God realization, the individualized self is transcended into the Universal or larger self in which he/she perceives both the living, and non-living as the living power of God, and in all his/her Universal self. Here the Universal or larger self is not an extension of Hobbes or Morgenthau's man. It is a transcendental or enlightened one encompassing within it the entire universe and in the universe his or her own self. The emancipatory mission of Critical Theorists should aim at the transformation of human beings as its main objective while reconstructing the societies from an ecological perspective. The doctrine of larger self does not mean only that it gives an attribute of sacredness to the non-human living and non-living, but it elevates human beings to higher plane of feelings towards the living and non-living beings as manifestation of the Universal Self. Rather, the concern for the protection of the natural world and attribution of divinity to it, as found in various religious scriptures of the world, gives rise to a transcendental being thinking always in terms of larger self over and above the realist portrait of self aggrandizing and predatory human beings. This may have dissolved the atomistic, avarice and self-aggrandizing human beings, but not the enlightened human beings.

Social Ecology: Self-empowerment of Community

On the other hand, social ecology and its ecoanarchist branch under Murray Bookchin unlike the deep ecologists stressing on unicellular earth and its ecological holism put emphasis on political and economic aspect of the ecological crisis and construction of an ecologically proper ethic/polis theory for human kind.[26] Inspired by Peter Kropotkin's rejection of the facile interpretation of Darwinism as a theory of struggle in nature, and his advocacy of self-empowered commune.[27] Bookchin argued for ecology of freedom, which is a defense of both the individual and community. The liberty of one is ensured by egalitarian and democratic relationship within the other. Solution to the ecological crisis is quite dependent on the democratic reconstruction of society with a sensibility of sociality to freedom, peace and ecology extending to a municipal confederalism, which will bind the sovereign communities through non-representational democratic rules. The respect for life, human and non-human is based on his advocacy of equality of unequals and recognition of differences not indiscriminate attribution of rights in the name of justice.[28] Thus, ecoanarchism's main concern is with attribution of equal rights to all life forms, human and non-human to live on this earth with freedom subjected to domination by none. An ecocentric political thought weaved into Critical Theory can be emancipatory.

Male dominated and masculine interpretation of power structure has resulted in despoliation of nature and exploitation of women. Ecofeminism, a branch of social ecology drawing impetus from the coincidence between women's subjugation and the control of the nature, in both cases by men, aims at disabusing the political theorists of a world view of both women and nature as useful and expendable matter to be controlled, exploited and discarded to satisfy the male needs. As social theory, ecofeminism defends a particular constituency by reflecting on the modern killing of nature, on the deadly cumulative impact of science, monopoly capitalism, and the global state system. Though the mindset of male domination predates the Enlightenment, it finds in it means to similar ends. As advocated by ecofreminists, the empowerment of women could enable them to discharge their historically vital function in the global primary economy, recapture their decaying space and restore the nature.[29] The relationship between ecofeminism and ecoanarchism is apparently expressive of the same ontological foundation of ecocentric radical ecopolitical thought that aims at the diffusion of power, empowerment of both community and women and nature eliminating forever the male domination. Attributing an ontological significance to nature with a critique of social domination, and envision of a self-empowered community can be key to emancipatory framework of critical theorists.

Ecosocialism a fine example of social ecological thought does not give priority to nature, though keeps it in the backdrop for human activity. It emphasizes human needs as ontologically superior to nature. It joins the general criticism levelled against capitalism, one important ecological demon. The healing power of state is advocated as an instrument for the attainment of basic needs, social justice, and environmental protection.[30]

Reconciliation: End and Means

To sum up, it can be said that deep ecology casts a halo of sacredness around nature, and social ecology, on the other hand puts emphasis on self-empowerment of community and promotion of non-hierarchical ethical values. If the former is the end, the latter provides the means. The reconciliation between the two can be found in the attainment of the end through the means provided by the social ecology. In the words of Bookchin, "one of my goals is to foster the development of a non-hierarchical ethics of complimentarity among humans and between humanity and non-human life. This should be the fundamental starting point...of the radical ecology movement".[31] In concurrent with the mainstream of this thinking Arne Naess who coined the term "deep ecology" has stated that "supporters of deep ecology movement seem to move more and more in the direction of non-violent anarchism".[32] Conversing the two arguments put forth by deep and social ecologists, Michael Zimmerman argues that deep and social ecology both value nature intrinsically, reject a facile human-nature dichotomy, insist on nature's complexity and the need for wilderness preservation, and are very critical of the hierarchical, centralized, and plundering character of the modern project.[33] Obligations to fulfill the requirements of future generation's right to life can be redeemed only in recognition of the holistic, intrinsic and an appropriate husbandry of nature.[34]

Realist and Liberal Framework: An Ecological Critique

The dominant realist framework to understand the current realities created by the impending environmental crisis seemed to be inadequate to secure the traditional objectives of politics, those being security, liberty, peace, and happiness. The questions realism used to ask, and the answers it provides in this changing scenario may become increasingly less relevant.[35] Many scholars had rejected it as incomplete, misdirected, non-rigorous, unscientific and incapable of accounting for the catastrophic changes wrought to nature and environment. They often referred to the poverty of realism, poverty of neorealism[36] and the dangers of real politick based policies.[37] Situation has changed to give rise to reconstruction of realist paradigm of security.[38]

In the realist framework, everyone is the self-atomized individual and considers the rest—the other individuals and nature as either a potential threat or source of material aggrandizement. If power is the means to achieve this material ambition project, then it becomes the monopoly of elites to the exclusion of the other. Politics thus, becomes through the exercise of this power "a technique of value extraction: in an ontology of competition, everyone is an other to be feared or to be used".[39]

Thus, the politics of realism and liberalism with the extractive individualized self arrainged against the nature and other human beings as the other, and identified with elite group, class or nations' global control and homogenization as the sole objective can never be the realm of the expanded or universal self. An ecological approach to International Relation will stress on alternative ontologies, epistemologies and ethical / political prescriptions making an overhaul of its established mainstream thinking which is based on the defense of the virtue of force, materialism, elitism, homogenization and inordinate and profligate consumption. The positivist epistemology in International Relations encourages objectification, and control, and obviously is averse to normative goal prescribed by ecology. The self-aggrandizing individual, its inordinate life style and pattern of development based on fossil fuel industrialization is at the root of the ecological crisis and consequences in terms of global warming, sea level rise, ozone hole and climate change. These devastating effects of climate change, in turn challenge the sovereign state system's legitimacy and security system built around it to give protection to its people against these threats in statist military terms. Thus, an ecological approach requires International Relation Theory to reconsider its understanding of reality, study of man's nature, mechanical worldview and conception of security, peace and freedom. In other words, it means

International Relation Theory needs to make a leap of faith. It must be convinced that the radical ecological ideal better embodies its social objectives. To subscribe to the mainstream International Relation theory that it is ahistorical and social mechanics, cannot open the doors to such a possibility. It is not Hobbesian or realist's concept of right that what is conducive to one's self interest is morally worth doing, but what constitutes the basic assumption of ecological approach is Aldo Leopold's land ethic: "a thing is right when it tends to preserve the integrity, stability, and beauty of the biotic community.[40]

The realistic theory a synonym for power politics is antithetical to ecological worldview. The first problem with realism is its ontology of conflict and aggression. The structural argument of realism assumes that the main impulse of human kind for survival is associational. From this it deduces that political associations are finite, exclusionary and spatial, and finite bodies must collide in their struggle for power and control of the resources. So precautions against collision mean use of force or resort to war. Another strand of realism specifically endows political conflict with purpose and cognition: domination appears to be a human need, a universal construct: "the drives to live, to propagate and to dominate are common to all men".[41] Realism qua romanticism what Raymond Aron has correctly described as 'realist idealism' overtly relies upon the ethic of force, the impact of which is much more to enslave and to kill than to free. Political association must be ordered, seemingly from above; those who instill order and dominate the political system will exert their domination wherever it is possible and sustainable. The struggle for survival and dominance as the endless game becomes a part and parcel of realism.

This reality of struggle among nations for survival and dominance resulting in elitism enforces local and domestic hierarchies and legitimizes the existence and use of military apparatus, while life is permanently threatened by the imperatives of military security. Military imperatives dictate that states develop and deploy the most effective military technology available. The effects on land and nature are little considered. No military technology could be more environmentally damaging than nuclear weapons. Thus, the environmental effects of producing, storing, developing, and dismantling them not to mention the effects they would have on the environment if ever used, are considered secondary. A similar argument could be adduced about the entire range of military technologies, from cluster bombs to napalon to defoliants to biological weapons.[42] Land has no moral or little worth except that it is a spiritless other that humans can rightfully exploit to serve their own ends. Just-war theory generally evaluates collateral damage's significance in the context of civilians killed or injured due to military operations. Yet collateral damage also kills and injures animals and destroys biotic nature that have even less stake and less say in the conflict than civilians. Where is their right to life? The realist ethic to disrupt or destroy the evolutionary process, which includes all its organic and non-organic components, reducing the diversity of life and stability and beauty of the natural system is unethical.[43] Responding to power politics, the ecologists allege that if power politics is real, it is a constructed and deconstructable reality. "Reality is a social construction". It is "created and constructed by beliefs and behaviour. Structures do in fact shape beliefs and behaviour the way some positivists thought, but these structures are the product of human action".[44] To hold such logic of structural realist assumptions of power politics as permanent is the result of application of Thomas Hobbes and Issac Newtonian view of man "as particles of constant motions" to social relations.

From the realist axioms of structural and motivational conflictuality flow a series of corollaries with a devastating impact on life and freedom, of which hierarchy or elitism is the obvious problem. This gives rise to the emergence of a strong state always embarking on devising a system of accumulation and control from the top.

Realism is also criticized for its homogenizing worldview in its power politics framework. It reduces motives to a few universals, such as power quests and physical growth. "In the process, realism has also homogenized the political unit by emphasizing a statist ontology that not only ascribes a natural aura to such a form of association, but also minimizes its internal variance".[45] This is particularly characteristic of Waltz's third image.[46] By reducing all to a narrow groove of power motives, and holding these as immutable-and permanent, realism imposes a structural straitjacket upon all cultural issues, diversities and anthropological insight. In the words of Eric Lafarriere, "From an ecological perspective, the power assumptions and political language of realism can only portray the world as a giant machine fixated on the goal of survival or victory; they can only trivialize culture and accultured individuals in the process of social creation".[47]

In its idioms of anti ecological dimension of power, realism depicts the world as basically materialistic, conflictual and elitist devoid of any social utopia and idealism.

By arraigning one individualized self in case of a group or class, or one super power nation, against the other to satisfy the elite's interests in terms of accumulations, consumption and control realism super imposes an artificial, fictitious construct over and above a universalized or expanded self, typical of ecological portrayal of the natural world. "By limiting the definition of threat to the other's potential ambitions over the finite, zero sum game of the state system, and by turning this preeminent reality into the main engine of history, the call to arms by realism turns nature into raw materials and legitimizes warfare as a vehicle of the good".[48]

Impelled by the objectifying bias of Newtonian science, the positivism and behaviouralism taking cue from the classical realism took the recurrent pattern of history as constants, quantified the power and state capabilities and replaced ethics with problem solving. Thus, realism as the ahistorical science of the state stunting human development and questioning its survival stood opposed to organicism, subjectivity and historicism characterizing the ecological thought. Critical Theory challenges this statist denomination of realism. "If states dominate the arena, this is a feat of power politics representing other dimensions of reality that could potentially replace the states if an emancipatory praxis could with the help of Critical Theory empower other subjectivities than those who dominate at present. The social world does not exhibit any iron laws, all regularities can be broken, and it is the task of Critical Theory to show this..." [49] Ecological approach can add to completion of emancipatory project in this direction by relying on what Bookchin said earlier about municipal confederalism. Critical Theory can take non-military environmental security threats as a part of its argumentation against established discourses of security, thereby relativising conventional wisdom.

Critique of Liberalism

Liberalism, which started as a doctrine of freedom was based on possessive individualism of Hobbes and Locke in search for accumulation of wealth, profligate and commodious lifestyle. At the individual level, he/she needs freedom to achieve the goals set by the materialistic world opened before him/her by the Newtonian age. At the state level, liberal democratic government legitimized by the individuals' criteria of wealth production, profligate and inordinate lifestyle and commodious living emerged as the guarantor of these goals to its individuals by introducing into the world, its market economy, liberal ideas, free exchange, trade, and protectionism.

The liberal tradition set by America and Western allies was to guarantee these objectives to the individuals at home by getting unimpeded access to resources available any where in the world even by the application of force. Like realism, it viewed the nature and other nations as the other to be exploited for satisfaction of individuals' material needs at home. The liberal institutionalism cannot escape its entanglement with and commitment to the capitalist market system. Its anthropocentric view of nature and universe and consequent emphasis on economic growth leads to a relative lack of concern for the stability, integrity, and beauty of the earth. Obsessed with growth fetish the western liberal market economy destroyed both the nature and the poor. In other words, "If Judeo-Christian monotheism took nature out of religion, Anglo-American economists took nature out of economics" [50].Overconsumption and inordinate life style of the western people has proved to be a nuisance to nature. The liberal tradition combining individual consciousness with responsibility is eminently attractive to ecologists. Liberal literatures in International Relation articulate a normative commitment to freedom by favouring a cooperative utopia based on open exchange, material growth, positive law and specialized knowledge. These include the early advocates of free trade, [51] the functionalist and neo-functionalist arguments stressing the relationship between peace and elite co-operations[52] the regime literature and its descriptive emphasis on 'mechanics of cooperation, [53] and part of the contemporary normative literature on global humanism.[54]

The liberal cosmopolitan project aims at the attainment of a global commonality with the gradual eliminations of borders. But the overriding concern was unity. From an ecological perspective, the question pertains to the purpose of liberation in espousing unity. The ecologists are in favour of global concert but surely not at the cost of integrity, and diversity of member communities. The worst nightmare for the ecologists is the current spread of western liberal market economy throughout the world culminating in globalization. It involves the most fundamental centralized restructuring of socio-economic and political relations since the industrial revolution. It has created a new corporate colonialism in TNCs to which all individuals and nations must adjust. The new corporate colonialism is likely to dispossess, impoverish, and marginalize more people, destroy more cultures, and cause more environmental devastations than either the colonialism of old or the development of the last 50 years.[55] In the current context it means the homogenization of prices, products, wages, rates of interest and profits to become the same all over reinforcing the economic interests of North countries. The process of economic globalization advanced by the Bretton Woods institutions promoted the interests of the superrich so successfully that it also damaged their concern for and obligations to less fortunate inhabitants and their natural ecosystem in the developing world. In other words, it is nothing but another euphemism for the continuing exploitation of the underdeveloped by the developed, and redistribution of resources and wealth from the less to the more developed.[56] Globalization has not created a global village in transcendence of national boundaries, rather a highly divided, hierarchical elitist political structure. Thus, the ecologists' critique of liberal cosmopolitanism stands vindicated in that the homogenizing logic of liberalism is ruining ecosystems and decimating cultural specificity. The integration theory of the 1950s and 1960s for all its neutral tone, also assumed a basic link between global freedom and increasing communication.[57]

In contemporary liberalism, as held by James Rosenau, global culture based on 'reason' and 'analytical skills' can be disappointingly defended as an emancipatory tool for the individual.[58] Trade based globalization unfolding of western liberal market based economic-political order has been raised to a high moral level a synonym for development to which the developing world has been asked to dedicate themselves in slavish adulation of what the west terms it as good. Siphoning off the resources and materials from the developing world the globalization has enabled the rich North to promote their domestic imperatives in terms of guaranteeing the profligate, inordinate consumption, life style, and production of wealth. Thus, the approach of liberals to global growth is based on total disregard of the imperatives of finiteness and diversity of nature, and the ever increasing hiatus between the rich and poor, freedom of the individuals and right to life of all other non human living and non-living.

The ecological critique should examine what David Mitrany and Harold Laski propounded their commitment to the materialist utopia in their defense of efficient servicing. For Mitrany, servicing formed a clear path to freedom.[59] Normative endorsement of growth is also found in peace studies and within the Southern perspectives on world order reform.[60] Ecologists can appreciate Mitrany's attempt at replacing a mere voting democracy with a working one.[61] But they are distrust of "the enlightened mission of experts". In their views, "technocratic depoliticisation, rather is viewed as the embodiment of totalitarianism, the vehicle for a very distinct brand of politics".[62]

Ecologicalising Emancipatory Mission

An ecological approach to International Relation Theory and global governance rests on alternative ontologies, epistemologies, and ethical/ political prescription. The mechanical view of nature and attribution of the 'other' needs to be reconsidered. Nature is finite, whole, an interdependent body connecting all living matter in a cyclical and non-hierarchical manner. It is more often a function of cooperation within and between species. Diversity and timelessness are the other attributes of nature. Diversity allows nature to withstand the demise of individual life forms while maintains its grandeur, beauty and bounty. Timelessness shows life is not imposed or spontaneously created but is undissociable from time. It is a long, slow and cumulative process. Recognition of longevity supports the assumption of mutual aid in nature. Thus, it rejects the traditional utilitarianism, and mechanical view of nature, and ontologies of conflict. What Pope John Paul II said in the Conference of Roman Catholic bishops in the Philippines and Dominican Republic in 1988 deserves excerption: "... One cannot use with impunity the different categories of beings, whether living or inanimate – animals, plants and natural elements-simply as one wishes, according to one's economic needs. On the contrary, one must take into account the nature of each being and its mutual connection to an ordered systems, which is precisely the cosmos".[63] It advocates a harmonization with physical surroundings admonishing against imposition of structures of domination. The principle of classical theory of democracy, freedom, individual fulfillment and equal treatment are vindicated by ecological ethics. Instead of looking at the world of nature as the other, a more coordinated view of the world embracing both the world of nature and the world of humanity[64] is what the ecological approaches insist on." To deny moral value to ecosystem because they are not integrated in the same way as centralized individual organisms, is to make a category mistake. In thinking about the value of social and biotic communities we should be concerned for a matrix of interconnections between centers, not for a single center".[65]

Thus, the mechanical view of the world and nature must be replaced by an organicistic one[66] which reads the world not as a soulless machine subjected to cause and effect, and repetitive patterns – sine qua non of scientific investigations, positivism and behaviouralism. To confine the study to the limitation of cause and effect syndrome means to fall short of understanding the complexity of nature and its inextricable connections with the evolution of life in a timelessness frame. Not that these scientific investigations, assumptions and methods are not helpful, but should not constitute the principal means of understanding or attributing meaning without organicism being attached with mysticism.[67] The ecological project calls for a rejection of the detached object of study, objectivity and mechanism forming the core of the Cartesian – Newtonian dominance in social sciences in favour of subjectivity.

The ecological teleology points to the significance of historicity and dialecticism in understanding the current human conditions as the dynamic ebb and flow and product of synergistic forces through time. This means to get rid of Westphalian straightjacket[68] the prevalence of ahistorical bias in formulating the concept of international system reinforced by the dominance of an economy, natural science based understanding of the social world.

"A silent acceptance of this cultural bias "the imposed dominant economic and political thinking of western paradigm" is virtually universal, not only within the context of a Western centred parochialism, but also among IR scholars who have tragically abandoned their own quite different historical and cultural traditions".[69] Seducing all cultural diversities, civilisational essences, regional specificities and bioregimes' particularities and their coordinated interconnections woven into the warf and woof of cosmos, into wearing the western straitjacket is to block communication of the mainstream International Relations with other disciplines, and snap man's eternal chord with the cosmos. It calls for a multi disciplinary and multidimensional approach that will travel beyond microeconomic analogies, handling forces that are much more elusive and much less amenable to behavioural manipulation than the heavily magnified state. Awakening it from the Westphalia Procrustean bed, it should be studied as an historical action and a social actor among many. Thus, the ecological vision includes a system cosmology, a theory of democracy of global structure of governance, a new scientific epistemology supplementing behaviourlism and Newtonian objectivity, a strategy for global peace and security on the basis of cooperation and a recognition of intergenerational equity and accountability, and interspecies responsibility.

Given the sources of many of the new threats stemming from complex systems both natural and human made, and diversifying away from the state into diverse, regional and local in character, the monolithic statist westphalian approach quite familiar with realist paradigm seems to outstrip the solution. "Global environmental governance emerges because the spatial scale of the state is inadequate in dealing with the scales of environmental change, and thus, the practices of governance move towards regional and global levels and at the same time towards local levels in response".[70]

The ecological project of governance envisions a world of small interacting communities, what, as mentional earlier, Bookchin named it municipal confederalism or what Karliner termed it as 'grassroots globalization'[71] which means a myriad locally organized, but transnationally networked, social movements and NGOs are becoming increasingly mobilized to resist the dominant practices of TNCs and states. To create alternative forms of the western dominated political economy the most common phrase used is the 'commons'. It is defined as a site of ecologically sustainable and socially just politically economy. This means the construction of myriad small-scale societies organized around commons regimes through resistance to the globalizing practices of TNCs, states and international development agencies.[72]

The western picture of human beings as selfish, atomistic, individualistic, acquisitive, profligate, aggressive and conflictual always in quest for a commodious living, inordinate life pattern needs to be redefined. "The excessive use of nature and its resources in the North is a principal block to greater justice in the world... A retreat of the rich from the over consumption is thus, a necessary first step towards allowing space for improvement of the lives of an increasing number of people.[73] To reorient society and its economy towards a more sustainable path is necessary recognizing the future generations' right to life and without severing the organic bond between the present and future generation and the living and non-living. As mentioned earlier, about the speech situation by the critical theorist, the ecological ethics emphasizes engaging the sectorised 'other' in democratic dialogue, which requires "abandoning the notion that nature and social are distinct. The social and natural are inextricable. We constitute nature through our practices at the same time we constitute the social world. Thus an ecologically informed political discourse will be one that recognizes the environmental ethics embedded in all political worldviews".[74] What will define the individual is not acquisitive individualism and consumerism. Springing from the limitless and profligate acquisitiveness of market political economy driven way of life-contribution of both science and the liberal possessive individualism of Hobbes and Locke-the concomitant decline in human beings' sensibility to other humans, living and non-living beings, the human beings have been on a rapacious rampage that cuts at the very root of the common organic bond with the whole of creation and the very survival of all. Acceptance of ecological ethics and enlargement of self that includes all will certainly usher in an atavistic change in human approach, vision and way of life. As Aldo Leopold has pointed out, ethics is the recognition of constraints put on an individual as a member of the community, and the ecological ethic simply enlarges the boundaries of the community to include soils, waters, plants and animals or collectively the land.[75]

The Critical Theorist should take note of the need for an overhaul of the western pattern of development, way of life and social philosophy based on acquisitive individualism and consumerism-a wrong notion of providing happiness. So for as restructure of a society remains uppermost to the Critical Theorist, different from the dominant western universalized one, the question is not just about a technocratic, or expertise response because these technocratic or expertise knowledge emanate from some rich North powers." Ecologists along with Critical Theorists cannot escape the fact that law and knowledge, rules and technicity, are mere expression of power over nature, power over men and women".[76] Critical Theorists while emphasising the significance of studying historicity, should not be oblivious of the fact that science and liberal political theory share the same ontological foundation.

References

1. M.Horkheimer, Critical Theory (New York: Seabury, 1972).
2. Jurgen Habermas, Knowledge and Human Interests (London: Heinemann, 1972).
3. Robert Cox, "Social Forces, States and World Orders", in Richard Little and Michael Smith eds., Perspectives on World Politics, 2nd edition, (London and New York: Routledge, 1991), pp. 444-456.
4. Cox, "Social Forces, States and World Orders", *op. cit.,* p. 445.
5. *Ibid*, p. 447.
6. Andrew Linklater, "The Achievements of Critical Theory", in Steve Smith, Ken Booth, and Marysia Zalewski eds., International Theory: Positivism and Beyond (Cambridge: Cambridge University Press, 1996), pp. 288-89, 294-95.
7. Mark Hoffmann, "Critical Theory and the Inter-Paradigm Debate", Millennium: Journal of International Studies Vol. 16, No. 2, Summer 1987, p. 233.
8. Christine Sylvester, Feminist Theory and International Relations in a Postmodern Era (Cambridge: Cambridge University Press, 1994), p. 167.
9. David Campbell, Writing Security: United States Foreign Policy and the Politics of Identity (Minneapolis: University of Minnesota Press, 1992) p. 238.
10. Ann Tickner, "Revising Security" in Ken Booth and Steve Smith ed., International Relations Theory Today (Cambridge: Polity Press, 1995), p. 192.

11. A. Linklater, Beyond Realism and Marxism: Critical Theory and International Relations (London: Macmillan, 1990), p. 171.
12. Harold and Margaret Sprout, The Ecological Perspective on Human Affairs, with Special Reference to International Politics (Princeton, NJ: Princeton University Press, 1965).
13. Harold and Margaret Sprout, Towards a Politics of the Planet Earth (New York, NY: Van Nostrand Reinhold, 1971).
14. Harold and Margaret Sprout, "Environmental Factors in the Study of International Politics", in James N.Rosenau ed., International Politics and Foreign Policy: a reader in research and theory (New York: The Free Press, 1969), p. 56.
15. Eric Laferriere, "Emancipating International Relation Theory: An Ecological perspective", Millennium Vol. 25, No. 1, 1996, p. 54.
16. M.Shamsul Haque, "Non-Traditional Security and the Environment in North east Asia", Work in Progress Vol. 16, No. 3, Summer 2002, p. 24.
17. Peter H.Gleick, World's Water: The Biennial Report on Fresh Water Resources (Washington D.C.: California: Island Press, 1998), pp. 105-106.
18. Ted Gurr, Minorities at Risk: A Global view of Ethnopolitical Conflicts (Washington DC: US Institute of Peace Press, 1993).
19. Sverre Lodgaard, "Environmental Conflict Resolution," paper presented at the UNEP meeting on Environmental Conflict Resolution, Nairobi, 30 March 1990, p. 18
20. Simon Dalby, Threats from the South?", *op. cit.,* p. 160
21. Garrett Hardin, "Living on a lifeboat", Bioscience Vol. 24, 1974, pp. 561-68.
22. William Ophuls, Ecology and the Politics of Scarcity (San Franciscs, CA: Freeman and Co, 1977), and Robert Heilbroner, An Inquiry into the Human Prospect (New York, NY: W.W. Norton, 1974).
23. William Ophuls and A. Stephen Boyan Jr., Ecology and the Politics of Scarcity Revisited: The Unraveling of the American Dream (New York, NY: W.H. Freeman and Company, 1992), introduction.
24. Eric Laferriere, Emancipating International Relation, *op. cit.,* p. 58.
25. See Val Plunwood's rebuttal of Warwick Fox in Feminism and the Mastery of Nature (London and New York, NY: Routledge, 1993), Chapter-7.

26. Murray Bookchin, The Ecology of Freedom: The Emergence and Dissolution of Hierarchy, Revised Edition (Montreal and New York, NY: Black Rose Books, 1991), The Philosophy of Social Ecology: Essays on Dialectical Naturalism (Montreal and New York, NY: Black Rose Books, 1995), Toward an Ecological Society (Montreal and New York, NY: Black Rose Books, 1991)
27. Peter Kropotkin, Evolution and Environment, ed., George Woodcock (Montreal and New York, NY: Black Rose Books, 1995), pp. 71-74, p. 117.
28. Bookchin, The Ecology of Freedom, *op. cit.,* Chapter-6.
29. Vandana Shiva, Staying Alive: Women, Ecology and Development in India (New Delhi: Kali for Women, 1988)
30. David Pepper, Eco-Socialism: From Deep Sociology to Social Justice (London and New York, NY: Routledge, 1993), p. 233.
31. Murray Bookchin and Dave Foreman, Defending the Earth (Montreal and New York, NY: Black Rose Books, 1991), p. 133
32. Arne Naess, Ecology, Community and Lifestyle trans and ed., D.Rothenberg (Cambridge: Cambridge University Press, 1989), p. 156.
33. Michael E.Zimmerman, Contesting Earth's Future: Radical Ecology and Post-Modernity (Berkeley and Los Angels, CA: University of California Press, 1994), p. 151.
34. Bill Devall and George Sessions, Deep Ecology: Living as if Nature Mattered (Layton, UT: Gibbs Smith, 1985), p. 69.
35. Charles W. Kegley, Jr., "The Neoidealist Moment in International Studies? Realist Myths and New International Realities," ISA Presidential Address, 27 March 1993, Acapulco Mexico, International Studies Quarterly Vol. 37, 1993, p. 34.
36. C. Krauthmmer, "The Poverty of Realism," The New Republic Vol. 194, 1986, pp. 14-22, R.K. Ashley, "The Poverty of Neo-Realism", International Organization Vol. 38, 1984, pp. 255-86.
37. C. Hitchens, "Why We are Struck in the Sand: Real Politik in the Gulf: A Game Gone Tilt", Harper's Vol. 282, 1991, pp. 70-74, 78.
38. P. Diehl and F.Wayman, ed., Reconstructing Realpolitik (Ann Arbor: University of Michigan Press, 1993).
39. Eric Laferriere, *op. cit.,* p. 62.

40. Aldo Leopold, A Sand Country Almanac (New York, NY: Ballantine Books, 1966), p. 262.
41. Hans J.Morgenthau, Politics Among Nations, Abridged Edition (New York, NY: Mc Graw-Hill, 1993), p. 37.
42. See William Thomas, Scorched Earth: The Military's Assault on the Environment (Philadelphia, PA, and Gabrisla Island: New Soviet Publishers, 1995), See also Matthias Finger, "The Military, the Nation State and the Environment", The Ecologist Vol. 21, No. 5, 1991, pp. 220-25.
43. John Barkdull, "Why Environmental Ethics Matters to International Relations", Current History Vol. 99, No. 640, November-2000, p. 362.
44. John A.Vasquez, "The Post-positivist Debate: Reconstructing Scientific Enquiry and International Relations Theory After Enlightenment's Fall", in Ken Booth and Steve Smith ed., International Relations Theory Today (Cambridge, Polity Press, 1995), p. 221.
45. Eric Laferriere, *op. cit.,* p. 68.
46. Kenneth N. Waltz, Man, the State and War: A Theoretical Analysis (New York, NY: Columbia University Press. 1959).
47. Eric Laferriere, *op. cit.,* p. 68.
48. *Ibid.*
49. Barry Buzan, "Rethinking Security after the Cold War", Nordic Journal of International Studies Vol. 32, No. 1, March-1997, p. 19.
50. J.R.McNeill, "Ideas Matter: A Political History of the Twentieth-Century Environment", Current History Vol. 99, No. 640, November 2000, p. 374.
51. Richard Cobden, Political Writing Vol. 1 (London: T Fisher Unwin, 1903), Norman Angell, The Great Illusion (New York, NY: Knickerbocker Press, 1911).
52. David Mitrany, A Working Peace System (Chicago, IL: Quadrangle Books, 1966), Ernst B. Haas, Beyond the Nation-State: Functionalism and International Organisation (Stanford, CA: Stanford University Press, 1969).
53. Robert O. Keohane, After Hegemony: Cooperation and Discord in the World Political Economy (Princeton, NJ; Princeton University Press, 1984) and Stephen D Krasner, ed., International Regimes (Ithaca, NY: Cornell University Press, 1983).

54. Robert C. Johansen, The National Interest and the Human Interest: An Analysis of US Foreign Policy (Princeton, NJ: Princeton University Press, 1980).
55. Edward Goldsmith, "Development as Colonialism", World Affairs Vol. 6, No. 2, April-June 2002, p. 36.
56. Ismail Shariff and David M.Littig, "Globalisation old wine into new bottles", World Affairs Vol. 6, No. 2, April-June 2002, p. 42.
57. See Karl Deutsch et al., Political Community and the North Atlantic Area (Princeton, NJ ; Princeton University Press, 1957), and Amitai Etzioni, Political Unification: A Comparative Study of Leaders and Forces (New York, NY: Holt, Rinehart and Winston, 1965).
58. James N.Rosenau, Turbulence in World Politics: A Theory of Change and Continuity (Princeton, NJ: Princeton University Press, 1990), p. 289.
59. Mitrany, *op. cit.,* p. 96, Hoarold Laski, A Grammer of Politics (London: Allen and Unwin, 1967), p. 614 ; See also David Long," International Functionalism and the Politics of Forgetting", International Journal Vol. 48, No. 2, 1993, pp. 356-79.
60. Bruce Russett, "Causes of Peace" in Carolyn M Stephenson ed., Alternative Methods of International Security (Washington, D.C.: University Press of America, 1982), pp. 188 & 191.
61. Mitrany, *op. cit.,* p. 36.
62. Eric Laferriere, *op. cit.,* p. 72.
63. Origins: NC Documentary Service 17, 3 March 1988, p. 645; Quoted in J.Ronald Engel, "Introduction: The ethics of sustainable development", in J. Ronald Engel and Joan Gibb Engel ed., Ethics of Environment and Development (London: Belhaven Press, 1990), p. 4.
64. Stephen Toulmin, The Return to Cosmology: Postmodern Science and the Theology of Nature (Berkeley: University of California Press, 1982), pp. 255-56.
65. Holmes Rolston, III, and Environmental Ethics: Duties to and Values in the Natural World (Philadelphia: Temple University Press, 1988), p. 174.
66. Carolyn Merchant, The Death of Nature: Women Ecology and the Scientific Revolution (New York, NY and Toronto: Harper and Row, 1980).

67. Janet Biehl, Finding Our Way: Rethinking of Ecofeminist Politics (Montreal and New York, NY: Black Rose Books, 1991), pp. 89-90.
68. Barry Buzan and Richard Little, "Why International Relations has Failed as an Intellectual Project and What to do about it", Millennium; Vol. 30, No. 1, 2001, p. 25.
69. *Ibid.*, p. 26.
70. Matthew Paterson, "Interpreting trends in global environmental governance", International Affairs Vol. 75, No. 4, 1999, p. 795; Lamont Hempel, Environmental governance: the global challenge(Washington D.C.: Island Press, 1996).
71. Joshua Karliner, The Corporate Planet: ecology and politics in the age of globalisation (San Francisco: Sierra Club Books, 1997), Chapter-7.
72. Matthew Paterson, Understanding global environmental politics: domination, accumulation, resistance (London: Macmillan, 2000).
73. Report of the Wuppertal Institute for Climate, Environment, and Energy, quoted in Ramachandra Guha, "The Paradox of Global Environmentalism", Current History Vol. 99, No. 640, November-2000, p. 370.
74. John Barkdull, *op. cit.,* p. 366.
75. Aldo. Leopard, *op. cit.*
76. Eric Laferriere, p. 72.

5

Liberal Democracy, Faith in the Market and Mode of Legitimation: Rethinking Towards Sustainable Development

The rediscovery of man as a self atomized individual in terms of a bundle of human brute needs, desires, and rights an a quest for required power for their fulfillment was what led to the foundation of a democratic edifice in 15th and 16th century Europe. Hobbes and Lockean picture of a man as a self atomized self centered, self-moving, self-directing and self-fulfilling resembling a matter was shaped by Newton's discovery of matter as particles of motion. It was the guiding metaphor in the emerging liberal conception of possessive individualism.[1] Since the fruits of earthly city which were supposed to be materialistic fulfillment, aggrandizement, appeasement to sense derived pleasures pandering to outside or external object and sense interactive impulses and not idealization of the 'other worldly' were to be made available to individuals within the political space which was left vacated by a monistic, and absolute view of state in favour of individuals, not forming then exactly what is today called 'civil society' but no doubt constituted identifiably a broadened base of political structure.

Politics and Science Sharing the Same Ontological Foundation

Thus, the understanding of man as a mechanical structure built by desires and senses not surprisingly, coincided with rediscovery of matter in place of spirit as the only reality by the scientists of Newtonian age. Scientific discoveries, inventions and their methods of study could be able to inform the human beings about the possibilities and vast avenues for materialistic attainment. It was science, which could bring the so called religious bound and apocalyptic Heavenly city down to Earth. No wonder, the view of political scientists then about the man, state and society were really very much determined by the scientists' portrayal of the earth or planet as a heap of objects to be harnessed for the materialistic fulfillment of human beings. Thus, science and political science shared the same ontological foundation so far as the political space occupied by the self atomized individuals accepted goals or objectives as manifested by science and became a democratic structure because they wanted freedom to move as directed by their own self interest without any trammels from authority.

Liberal Democratic Foundation: Wealth Production and Inordinate Consumption

From the seventeenth century onward and from left to right across the political spectrum, Western thought has been characterized by an overarching faith in science. The belief in science to improve human life is perhaps the quintessential hallmark of modern state, a belief that is reinforced by the material achievements of industrialization.[2] During the second half of twentieth century that belief spread across the globe. The application of scientific discoveries and inventions by these self atomized individuals usurping the political space from the absolute and monistic authority in society, resulted in what is most widely known as industrialization as one of the dominant aspects of development which brought a dramatic change in the field of transport, communications, agriculture or in life pattern in the entire socio-economic field. The already liberal democratic edifice of the political space occupied by the self atomized possessive individuals founded on Newtonian science got combined with the glittering materialistic achievements of industrial revolution to form its economic metaphysics. It was these economic interests in terms of materialistic aggrandizement, say, wealth production, and what Hobbes called commodious living and inordinate consumption to satiate the desire and needs encumbered self, to which self atomized individuals occupying the political space moved, and accepted these as sonnum bonnum of a liberal democratic state. This is what led to Adam Smith's Wealth of Nations constituting a capitalist political and economic order.

Political and Economic Space: Usurpation by the Dominant Class

It is these self-atomized individuals occupying the political space because they overshadowed others in terms of power and capability formed the dominant class to corner the whole of economic abundance. This is what led Marx to call it the capitalist class or bourgeoisie who usurped the entire political space for the aggrandizement of this dominant class's economic interests at the cost of others. Marx was right when he said that it was the economic dominant class that scripted the liberal democratic capitalist political order. The legitimation of this political order hinged on what industrial revolution and science put before the individuals, the abundance of wealth production, economic growth, glittering life style and inordinate consumption. Thus, the economic dominant class defined development in these terms of economic growth, production of wealth, inordinate consumption and extravagant life style.

The vast diverse civil societal space, thus was usurped by the dominant economic class to the negligence of other aspects. Economy dominated the society and entire divergent societal functions were reduced to an economic activity. Society instead of determining the economy became a part of economic activity.

Economic Space Colonized the Societal Space

Adam Smith using the term market helped the transformation of community-based subsistence into a national political economy covering the entire society and space. The economy as chiselled by the economic dominant tended to overshadow every other reality. Society, which is a multiverse using the phrase of Willam James, was understood in terms of nothing else than its functional achievements leaving aside the rest as just folklore, or flittering nothingness. To use the words of Wolfgang Sachs, the laws of economy tried to dominate the society and not the rules of the society, the economy. The term market economy reduces all the societies to mere an economy making the proponents of liberal democratic and market order oblivious of the very basic thing that every society has an economy.[3] The market economy as promoted by the west, edged its way into all the development thinking of the entire world and assumed a deterministic character imprinting its rules and rhythms upon the society, and even dictating the drama and role in it of individuals. The entire global space including all the nations not even barring communist states like China, have been reduced to an economy controlled by the rich industrialized North. Thus, according to the architects of this liberal democratic market economic order, development which is held synonymous with the national sovereignty to define in its own way quite independent of what it means to others, was identified as economic growth, inordinate consumption, increasing commodity based wants and accumulation of wealth and its production. The atomized individuals grouped to be called dominant economic class for political convenience, legitimized the political order on these terms. The criterian was simply what the self atomized individuals bred in such a market society characteristic of an industrial society built by science, consider as conducive to their own interests. C.B. Macpherson's theorizing this initial period of liberal political order as protective democracy was based on keeping the entire political machinery of the state at the disposal of the dominant class for the protection of its interest. The state never acts or judges, it is reification [4] of what the economic dominant class determining the political structure in the forms of a government, decides to do for its own interests.

Subduing the Earth: Testaments of Development

Wealth production, inordinate consumption and profligate life style defined, as inalienable human rights to pursue were so paramount to the liberal democratic market based political order that Locke did not forget to drive out the propertied less class as irrational from the political purview. He grounds his understanding of individual property rights in Biblical injunction. He commanded man to "subdue the Earth", God gave the world to the use of the Industrious and Rational". Land that is left to nature is wasted.[5] Likewise, those who are not industrious and rational are not truely human and can therefore be justifiably treated as animals. Given that, communal ownership of land was the norm throughout most of the world at the dawn of modernity, this liberal theory of possessive individualism represented a major change as said above, into world wide national economy. Locke offered the required rhetorical justification. Thus, the political authority is premised upon the state's ability to guarantee property rights and thereby facilitate market relations. What was considered ethical and moral action was not other worldly' not just to go beyond the world of interests, the economic dominant class thinks its domain – the exploitation of nature and pursuit of sense pandering pleasures.

The economic negligent class-the poor section of society not finding a place in the 'protective democraty' was proletarianised by Marx in a revolutionary way in order to bring it to power center. Rousseau devised General will to include within it the interests of all – the community. J.S. Mill distinguished between a dissatisfied Socrates and a satisfied pig to make a gradation of happiness and pleasure. The concern for the negligent class shaped his concept of development democracy, which brought a drastic change in the liberal democratic political order. Of course, the militancy of working class and Marx's prediction about the inevitability of proletariat revolution could signal the direction in which the evolution of democracy was moving then. The liberal democratic political order took into account the interests of the working class to counter revolutionary Marxism. In the beginning of twentieth century the world witnessed a revolutionary political restructuring of Soviet Union and Eastern Europe and also China not on liberal democratic nuances.

Market Economy: Chinks in Armoury of Communism

From a close hindsight it would seem that Marxists propounding such a revolutionary doctrine exposed their weaknesses, as happened in Soviet Union in 1990 and is taking place in China at present where in its armoury of communism, the liberal democratic market nuances have already appeared as chinks. The revolutionaries aimed at capturing power of the state and replacement of the economic dominant class by a monolithic party and bureaucracy permeated with a Marxist ideology. It was not, as envisaged, a community based economy, but all-powerful party controlled state based economy. The very basic paradigm of liberal democratic order built on industrialization, economic growth, production of wealth, profligate life style, and application of science and technology to the enjoyment of human sense derived pleasures, could not be considered as nuisances to environment. It is the western pattern of development, based on fossil fuel technology and industrialization, the inordinate consumption and life style, production and a massing of wealth-the root causes of poverty, inequality and injustice – were imitated by all as ideal models of development. In stead of wiping out the basic fundamentals of liberal democratic order for ushering in of a community based economy or as conceived by Marx, a classless and stateless society or by Gandhi, a sarvodaya state, the power structure revolving around the state which Marx's philosophy advocated to be withered away, was touched upon and handed over to the revolutionary political party. The very basic metaphysics that gave rise to such a power structure stayed where it was, though denounced in a modified and rhetorical sense. Private means of production were to be replaced by public ownership. Whether the means of production are privately owned or controlled by the state, the fact remains that both the rivers Missouri Mississippi and Volga are polluted. Here public meant to Communists and Socialists a party controlled state not the civil society. A bourguisie state was replaced by a party dictatorial state in the name of proletariats.

Mechanistic Worldview: Nuisance to Nature

As seen from the above analysis, the liberal democratic market based political order is based on a mechanistic worldview in sharp contrast to the organistic worldview, which linked the individual to God in a great chain of being.[6]

Such a view held both nature and man as 'the other' to be exploited for the benefit of the economic dominant class. Acting upon these premises, as said above in a world of finite resources inevitably produced dire ecological consequences. Ubiquitous acceptance of and dedication to the western liberal democratic market based political order as the Bible of development and hallmark of modern civilized life, has resulted in what is adorned as globalization, making western pattern of development as ethnocentric. The poor people remained at the periphery of state concern and pattern of development.

Rightfulness of Liberal Democracy: Questioning Legitimacy

What promotes production of wealth, inordinate consumption and profligate life style is the rightfulness of action on the part of state-worth drawing legitimacy from the people. What constitutes rightfulness? Increasingly in the modern era from perspective of democratic rules and norms, that question has been answered in terms of the consent of the governed and institutionalized through democratic elections. Legitimacy requires a reflective subject capable of judging whether an action, rule, or proposal is in accordance with either its interests or else with established rules, principles or standards.[7]

The economic dominant class thus finds in the legitimacy the proliferation and invigoration of its interests. There were no other criteria of morality or ethical consideration. The rightfulness of state action was judged in terms of its capability to provide all these goods or so to say, a commodious living to these people. The rightfulness of action deriving legitimacy from the people was not based on universal, cosmocentric or eternal principles. While putting a theory of legitimacy and political obligation on this criteria, Hobbes and Locke did not conceive or foresee then, that for the pursuit of pleasure, amassing wealth, inordinate consumption, and extravagant life style by exploiting nature, would one day result in an environmental catastrophe with dire consequences upon the very survival of mankind on earth. Persistence of such a kind of belief in the rightfulness of action on the part of liberal democratic order which redounded to the economic interests of the rich and which could not be a panacea for social ills even in all ages and times is the unfolding of this mechanistic view of the universe resulting in western ethnocentric pattern of development. Since the economic dominant class holds the reins of power not only in industrialized rich North, but in all countries including the South, it is not surprising to find this class remaining persistent in such kind of belief in the rightfulness of liberal democratic political order as the only road leading to Mecca of development.

Liberal Democracy defines Development: Towards Unsustainability

The mechanistic view of the universe and anthropocentric view of liberal democratic political order while defining development tends to portray the universe and nature as "the other" or objective world to be exploited for the benefit of the economic dominant class. To sustain its economic interests, it continued to frame its economic development on the unsustainability of nature or the environment, as a result of which the planet earth has been robbed of its beauty and bounteous growth. The economic deprived, famished poor remains at the fringe of concern and continues to be exploited. By holding its inalienable right to exploit the nature as the thesis of development, it serves the dependence of the poor people on the nature for their survival. The entire civil societal space is usurped by the economic space – the servant turns out to be master. The multiverse in many and divergent aspects was regimented into looking like putting on a western economic strait jacket. The whole man appears to be "a consumer man" only to be fed into the political schema of liberal democratic market based order for the fulfillment of its functional utility.

The criteria of judgement, legitimacy and rightfulness of action are temporal, onesided, not universal, and confined to time and space, as such stop short of being called eternal, moral or ethical. The wealth production, luxurious living and life style are mere confined to the economic dominant class, leaving the civil societal space uncared for. What about the future generations' right to live on this earth? What about the right of the non-human living being' right to nature?

Taking for Granted the Future Generations' Consent: An Ethical Usurpation

The concept of liberty, equality and human rights are not only intra generational problems to be dealt with in democracy. The established democratic political order has not taken into consideration the future generations' right to life on this earth. Given the finite resources of the earth, the question of intergenerational equity crops up while considering criteria for giving legitimacy to the state, or tendering belief in the rightfulness of action of a liberal democratic state. Not finding its due place in the legitimacy of the democratic system, intergenerational equity challenges its very foundation and finds it narrow and shortsighted.

Happiness and liberty are subjective pursuits. It is not Benthamite equalizing of pleasures rather more of a Mill's dissatisfied socrates or Rousseau's identification with one's real will. Liberty and happiness must answer to the intergenerational principle. Put another way, the question is more difficult: Are Americans prepared to overconsume in the knowledge that life for their children will be at a lower level? Probably not, if they just think about it. Thus playing global roulette with future generations as the stake, while judging the rightfulness of action or giving legitimacy to the state on wealth production, inordinate consumption, and life style, is a moral inequity of historic proportion.[8]

Economic Growth and Happiness: Illusive Link

Besides keeping the consumptive and possessive aspects of individuals in materialistic terms at the base of liberal democratic order is to gloss over other equally important aspects of human needs. The illusive link between happiness and economic growth is debatable. Runaway consumerism puts the individual onto a never ending ever accelerating treadmill aptly summarized by David Myer's wry comment, "The Victor belongs to the spoils". Such a wealth driven happiness is ethically vacuous – and not anchored in concepts of rights and responsibilities. To persist in such consumerist happiness by the rich and affluent means to condemn permanently the poor and future generations to constant penury. Maslow's hierarchy of needs starting from deficiency needs to self actualization needs or Galtung's basic human needs' approach can constitute new criteria while giving legitimacy to the democratic liberal market based political economic state as the guarantor of wealth and promoter of life style. What Maslow's hierarchy of needs suggests is that while liberal market based political economy giving importance to the consumer wants of the economic dominant class, and meeting the demands of this class fulfilled to the basket, ignores the basic human needs of others, and also the self actualization needs. In his words, "If we define growth as the various processes which bring the person towards ultimate self actualization, then this conforms better with the observed fact that it is going on all the time in the life history ...Growth is seen here not only as progressive gratification of basic needs to the point where they disappear, but also in the form of specific growth motivations over and above these basic needs".[9]

Similarly, to humanize the mainstream economic thinking based on inordinate consumerism of those who want to fulfill their demands to the brim, Galtung propounds a basic human needs approach, "It is an effort to cut through rhetoric, focusing on what is essential and basic, and to provide individuals and societies with a measuring rod that lowers the focus of social attention downwards 'unto this last', saying this: tell me how much material and spiritual misery there is at the bottom of society, and I will tell you what kind of society you have ... Human suffering deprivation shall count more and serve to set our priorities straight".[10]

To overstretch the consumptive self to found the basis of market based political order is to ride rough shod over all other selves. According to Lutz and Lux, "the human enrichment of economics involves the recognition that we have a dual self. The lower self seeks its own advantage regardless of the interests of others, while the higher self seeks the well being of common humanity. The recognition of the existence of the higher self as well as lower is necessary for an economics that is responsive to human needs and not merely human fancy driven by dollars. This is an economics that promotes the well being of all, rather than just a commercialization of human activity which by itself eats away at the moral, social and ecological fibre of society".[11]

Rethinking Criteria of Legitimacy

So in order to have a review of the nexus between liberal democratic market based political order and the criteria of judgement on which it seeks legitimacy from the people, what needs to define the individuals is certainly not mindless consumerism, acquisitive individualism, unbridled avarice for wealth production and a particular economic and technological way of life characteristic of the liberal democratic system that has spelt a dooms day for the present and future generations. Amitai Etzion in his "The Moral Dimension" is of the view that apart from rationality, which should not be confined to a mere benefit-cost calculus of maximum self-interest, altruism and moral duty are equal motivators of human behaviour in the economic realm. Adam Smith, the father of classical economics in his "The Theory of Moral Sentiments" assumed that a higher providence ordains that the working of market economy remains within moral and ethical bounds not resulting in total selfishness.

Leap of Faith

Intergenerational and interspecies criteria of accountability based on intergenerational equity is to redefine the established criteria – production of wealth, promotion of economic growth and profligate life style—of giving legitimacy to the liberal democratic order. It means a leap of faith by the people. The established faith in the criteria of the people while legitimizing rightfulness of economic thinking of a liberal democratic order, has to be shifted to a different criteria in which is to be found the interests of future generations – both human beings and living non human beings. This is what led Oren Lyons two decades ago to admonish the present generations:

> **Take care how you place your moccasins upon the earth, step with care, for the faces of the future generations are looking up from earth waiting their turn for life.**[12]

To assume or take for granted the future generations' yet to be born interests while giving legitimacy to the liberal democratic order based on exploitation and ravage of nature, is simply an usurpation of the very right of the future generations to carve out their destiny. The crucial question is how can the future generations give their consent to the present political authority's jurisdiction over the exploitation of natural resources?

Relooking at the Ontological Foundation

The ontological foundation shared by both science and liberal democratic political authority comes in for a very critical look. The authority of science that emerged as a solution in the form a magic wand to provide a luxurious life during industrial revolution has now turned out to be a blemish due to the effects of industrialization and western life pattern on the environment. The future generation's acceptance of liberal democratic market based political authority as rightful can be ensured only when the science comes out with much certainty, consensus and finality providing alternatives to the basis of individuals' consent to the state in the broader context of the organistic bond that exists between nature and the present and future generations, both living and non living.

Globalization: Promoting the Domestic Criteria of Legitimacy to Western Liberal Democracy

The domestic imperatives of wealth production, exorbitant consumption and faith in the market as superior to all other views of life in the west, have been extended to the international world as globalization or configured into domesticisation of the universe. The dominant class in the domestic realm was represented by the dominant state, for example the countries in North promote the domestic imperatives-the basis on which the people considers the rightfulness of liberal democracy.

The western model of economics based on an intensive non-renewable fossil fuel industrialization that measures progress and growth in wasteful material consumption at the cost of nature and man, tends to view both nature and economics as poles apart. Thus, world economy, trading system and the concomitant institutional and structural management shaped at Brettonwoods on the indices of neo-classical economics legitimize and reinforce the monopoly of the rich industrialized North to have continued extraction of resources from the South and sell out production at a price solely determined by their own economic intents. The result of which is the developing countries' natural resource base continues deteriorating sinking them in deep poverty. This kind of economy shaped by the western liberal market based democratic order, and universalizing it, has made the poor South countries so much dependent on North for financial help, which they are virtually in a debt trap. "Once they are in debt, rather than cut down on expenditure, it can be predicted in advance that they will do exactly the opposite and indeed be encouraged to do so until such a time as they become hooked on to further borrowing, and eventually fall under the power of the lending countries".[13] The amounts paid off as debt servicing by the South which have already been many more times than the principal amount they received from the North, debunk the generally western held view that resources flow from North to South, and keep on going like what Willy Brandt once said, "the blood transfusion takes place from sick to healthy".[14] This has been a major contributing factor to the continued poverty and environmental degradation in poor South, where economic and natural resources have to be exploited quickly, simply to pay off debt.

The IMF and World Bank and other financial institutions spreading the western message of liberal market based democratic order, have been structured in a manner keeping in view the perpetuation of colonial economic interests of the rich industrialized North. These institutions' insistence on structural adjustment programmes, export oriented economy, devaluation to boost exports, cut in deficit budgeting, and subsidy measures, and other severe austerity measures have impelled the developing South to earn more foreign exchange by exploiting their environment. These institutions perpetuating the economic interests of the dominant North have turned out to be potent states reducing the South states to mere client or colonial stooges. The international arrangements to ensure that resources flow are maintained, and their prices kept low, reinforce the current economic discrepancies allowing continued destruction of the environment of resource producing areas and continued pollution where the products of these resources are disposed.[15] Coupled to international financial arrangements and the problems of debt crisis, the perpetuation of the existing international arrangements are likely to render many of the poorest of the planet even more insecure not only at present but also in the future.[16] The concept of development based on western market economy is not ecologically sustainable, nor is in the interests of the poor. Through non-sustainability of both the nature and the South, the economy of the North continues to be sustained. If sustainable development is couched in a Western verbiage as perpetuating the economic interests of the wealthier and wasteful North, it is not only an apotheosis of ecological imperialism but spells an environmental catastrophe on the South. The TNC and MNCs globalising the economic interests of the rich North are likely to dispossess, impoverish, and marginalize more people, destroy more cultures, and cause more environmental devastation than either the colonialism of the old or the development of the last fifty years.

Even the South's vast rich and resourceful biodiversity has not remained impervious to the colonial haunt of the rich North. The total contribution of wild germplasm to the American economy has been to the tune of more than US $ 60 million during the nintees.[17] While the genetic dependence of the North on South is accelerating, the former has not been so concerned with the latter's socio-economic development. By ascribing concepts like "free access to biodiversity" and 'common heritage of mankind', to the genetic weath pool of the South, the rich North perpetuates and legitimizes the exploitation of the poor South for their own economic interests. In GATT, WTO or FAO the rich North headed by US while skirting questions on due compensation, and legal protection against exploitation of their biodiversity, has kept always insisting on South to concede to the demands of the North.

Liberal Democratic Market Based Development: A Synonym to Envelopment

The very definition of sovereign state system suggests independence and autonomy. Liberal market based political order provides freedom and opportunity to the people of a state to define and chisel their own way of life. Liberal democracy based on inordinate consumption and production of wealth has been accepted as a role model for the other countries, especially after the eclipse of communism. Considering the fact that there are many cultures in the world, even civilizations spanning vast regions of space and time, so the roads to development are many, varied and multifold. If one civilization imposes its definition of development on another, a clear case of cultural violence occurs. Such a case of grafting another cultural code on to another results in culturocide, gross alienation and killing of culture.[18] The western liberal market based political order has been shaped by its Judeo-Christian tradition, and in the context of its scientific development. There is no reason why all other nations should be fitted into that western procrustean bed overlooking their own specific cultural context and civilizational values. If the very definition of development is the unfolding of a culture, realizing the code or cosmology of that culture, like the unfolding of flower preprogrammed in the seeds, the world should have been a beautiful garden of varieties of flowers wilting according to their own genetic code preprogrammed in their respective seeds. When a particular flower is allowed to blossom according to its own cultural code at the expense of all other varieties, superimposition of one culture on many cultures and civilizations takes place reducing all to fit into western straitjacket. Then, this is very antithesis of development and has become a synonym to envelopment.

Poverty of Philosophy

The very concept of liberal democracy advocates freedom of thinking not alike but divergent and pluralistic. But the very faith in the market as the universal and only model of development is a monistic way of thinking cutting at the very root of liberal democracy. It exposes a great distrust in one's own capability or ingenuity to devise one's own model of development, and an inclination to walk on other's crutches. It also marks a poverty of philosophy in one while blindly dedicating to the faith in the market as the only way to defining one's development. This is like leading credence to the doctrine of the double mandate, once formulated by Lord Lugard, the British imperial administrator, economic profit coupled with the responsibility to elevate the colored races to a higher level of civilization.[19] To persist in this kind of belief in the other as the cause of development of another, and belief in the logic of western market society as the base of liberal democracy, helps the reinforcement of an imperialistic design in the name of globalization blocking all other roads to development.

Thus, it can be said that to make development sustainable what is required is to bring about a transfiguration of mechanistic and Hobbesian outlook and view of the world. The atomized and individualist self is to be replaced by an enlarged self. The basic foundation of western liberal market economy and globalization based on wealth production and profligate life-style comes in for a review. To take for granted the future generations' consent and legitimacy to the government is highly misplaced, because in the legitimacy is found absent their right to life. Inter generational equity and inter species accountability constitute the new criteria of judging the rightfulness of liberal democratic order. Liberal democracy cannot survive on the unsustainability of both nature and the poor people in South. Liberal Democracy is to be redefined not in terms of only forming and unmaking a government or putting emphasis on human rights or promoting economic growth, wealth production and commodious living of the industrialized rich. It is to move beyond the mechanistic unto the cosmocentric world where all living and non-living are symbiotically interrelated. The hegemonic cultural bias of the west and its superimposition on the developing world needs to be revisited in order to make globalisation not a western cultural regimentation but a pluralistic and multicultural one where all cultures, societies, civilizations and people live together without the feeling of being tramped upon. It resembles a garden where varieties of flowers of different size, colour and fragrance blossom together freely to the beauty of the garden.

References

1. C. B. Macpherson, The Political Theory of Possessive Individualism: Hobbes to Locke (Oxford: Clarendon Press, 1962).
2. Yaron Ezrahi, the Descent of Icarus: Science and the Transformation of Contemporary Democracy (Cambridge, M. A.: Harvard University Press, 1990). Robert Heineman, Authority and the Liberal Tradition: from Hobbes to Rorty (New Bruswick: Transaction Publisher, 1994).
3. Wolfgang Sachs, "Development: a guide to the ruins", New Internationalist, June 1992, p. 5.
4. Karen T.Litfin, "Environment, Wealth, and Authority: Global Climate Change and Emerging Modes of Legitimation" International Studies Review Vol. 2, summer, 2000.
5. John Locke, Two Treaties of Government (New York: New American Library, 1965), p. 333.
6. Carol YN. Merchant, Death of Nature: Women, Ecology and Scientific Revolution (San Francisco: Harper Collins, 1990).
7. Thomas M. Frank, The Power of Legitimacy Among Nations (Oxford: Oxford University Press, 1990).
8. Kennedy Graham, "Leadership ethics for the future: Tread lightly on the planet", UNU Nexions, April 2002, p. 6.
9. Abraham H. Maslow, Toward a Psychology of Being (New York: Van Nostrand Reinhold, 1968).
10. Johan Galtung, "International Development" in Roger A Coate and Jerel A.Rosati, Ed., The Power of Human Needs in World Society (Boulder and London: Lynne Rienner Publishers, 1988) p. 151.
11. Mark A Lutz and Kenneth Lux, Humanistic Economics: The New Challenge (New York: Bootstrap Press, 1988) p. 29.
12. Oren Lyons, "An Iroquois Perspective" in Christopher Vecsey and Robert W.Venables, ed., American Indian Environments: Ecological issues in Native American History (New York: Syracuse University Press, 1980).
13. Edward Goldsmith, "Development as Colonialism", World Affairs Vol. 6, No. 2, April –June 2002, p. 30.

14. Roger D. Stone and Eve Hamilton, Global Economics and the Environment (New York: Council of Foreign Relations Press, 1991) p. 20.
15. J.B.Opschoor, "North-South Trade, Resource Degradation and Economic Security", Bulletin of Peace Proposals Vol. 20, No. 2, 1989, pp. 135-142.
16. Samir Amin, Mal development: Anatomy of Global Failure (London: Zed, 1990), Susan George, A Fate Worse than Debt (Harmondsworth: Penguin, 1988).
17. Shiva Vandana, "Biotechnology and Profit", Ecoforum, Nairobi, December 1990.
18. Johan Galtung, Development and Alternative Economics, presented to the participants in EPU, fall 1993, Standtschlaining, Austria.
19. Sachs, *op. cit.*

6

Politics of Combating Global Climate Change

The atmosphere surrounding the earth constitutes a dynamic and integral component of the global ecosystem on which all life depends. But to the perils of the well being of the biota, the atmosphere has been used to be a waste disposal site in terms of accumulation of green house gases like carbon dioxide, methane and nitrous oxide resulting in enhanced temperature of the earth, otherwise known as global warming. The concentration of these gases has been occurring in the atmosphere since the industrial revolution which is based on the combustion of fossil fuels with the hazardous environmental consequences of such global air pollution-second only to those of a global nuclear war.[1]

A green house acts as a heat trap when a portion of the sun's heat coming in through its glass wall is prevented from escaping outside and results in temperature inside the glass house to be higher than what is outside. The 'green house effect' gets its name because of a similar phenomenon occurring on a global scale. A number of gases in the earth's atmosphere, like the glass in green house, let solar radiation pass to the surface of the earth. The trapping of the infrared radiation that would have otherwise escaped to space results in increasing global temperature, and is referred to as the greenhouse effect. The best illustration of the green house effect on this scale is the fact that the earth would have been 33° C cooler than it is but for the naturally occurring greenhouse effect resulting from these gases injected into the atmosphere. What is the issue at present however is not this naturally occurring greenhouse effect but the enhanced greenhouse effect in recent times. The Intergovernmental

Panel on Climate Change (IPCC) concluded in 1995 that the observed warming trend is unlikely to be entirely natural in origin, and that there is a discernible human influence on global climate.[2] That means, due to anthropogenic reasons when the level of such waste disposal in terms of these gases exceeds the rate of disappearance, the atmospheric injections begin to threaten the very survival of life on this earth.

Much of the global carbon dioxide emission today emanates from the industrialized North. That is to say, from only 27 of all the sovereign states, accounting for 43% of global land area and 20% of global population. On the contrary, comparatively little of the carbon dioxide emissions today flows from the remaining nations accounting for 57% of global land area and 80% of the global population. Since the western pattern of development based on combustion of fossil fuel technology is being ubiquitously imitated by the developing countries, their contribution to carbon dioxide emission into the atmosphere will also be dangerously aggravating the situation.

According to the United Nations Environment Programme (UNEP), the global surface temperature has on average, increased by about 0.6°C during the past 100 years. The World Energy Council (WEC) reported that global carbon dioxide emissions increased by 12 per cent between 1990 and 1995. As the United Nations predicts, even if all OECD countries reduce emissions, the amount of CO_2 in the atmosphere would be only four per cent less than 1990 levels by 2000.

The Intergovernmental Panel on Climate Change (IPCC) set up in 1988 by UNEP and World Meteorological Organization to study the impact of human activities on climate change, in association with the United Nations Framework Convention on Climate Change (UNFCCC) while reviewing the situation in October 1997 pointed out that even if industrialized countries reduce emissions by 90%, global emissions would still be two to three times of 1990 levels by 2010. This, according to Bert Bolin, the chair emeritus of IPCC, would result in global warming of 1-35°C in a hundred years-probably the fastest rise in temperature in the past 9, 000 years.[3]

To sum up, it can be said that firstly, the atmosphere is being used on a continuing basis as a waste disposal site for CO_2 emissions, secondly, the rich industrialized North, more particularly the United States are primarily responsible for this. Thirdly, the quantities of gases emitted into the atmosphere exceed the ability of the atmosphere to absorb them and finally, this relentless and continuing carbon dioxide emission destroys the entire global ecosystem with diabolic environmental implications coming as greater threats to the very survival of living human and non-human beings.

Table 6.1 A Summary of Key Green House Affected by Human Activities

	CO_2	CH_4	N_2O	CFC-12	HCFC-22 (a CFCsubstte)	CF_4 (a Perfluro carbon)
Preindustrial Concentration	280ppmv[(a)]	700ppbv[(b)]	275ppbv	0	0	0
Concentration	355ppmv	1714ppbv	311ppbv	503 pptv[(c)]	105pptv	70pptv
Recent rate of conc. Change per year (Over 1980)	1.5 ppmv/yr	13 ppbv/yr	0.75 ppbv/yr	18-20 pptv/yr	7-8 pptv/yr	1.1-1.3 pptv/yr
	0.4% /yr	0.8%/yr	0.25% /yr	4%/yr	7% /yr	2% /yr
Atmospheric Life time (years)	(50-200)[(d)]	(12-17)[(e)]	120	102	13.3	5000

Note (a) Part per million by volume

(b) Part per billion by volume

(c) Part per trillion by volume

(d) No single lifetime for carbon dioxide can be defined because of the different rates of uptake by different sink processes.

(e) This has been defined as an adjustment time that takes into account the indirect effect of methane on its own lifetime.

Source : Climate change 1994: Radioactive Forcing of Climate Change and an Evaluation of the IPCC Emission Scenarios, (Cambridge: Cambridge University Press, 1994), p. 25

Thus, the global warming is not a myth. While it may be difficult to predict the long-term impacts of global warming, they are likely to be serious. Although the theory of the "green house effect" caused by the radiation trapping properties of certain gases, is one of the oldest and most widely accepted theories in the atmospheric sciences, global warming has only recently become an international policy problem.[4] As early as 1896, the Swedish scientist Svante Arrhenius calculated that a doubling of carbon dioxide would increase average global temperatures by 6°C, an estimate that was remarkably close to those of today's computer models.[5] Until 1957 it was the belief among the scientists that the oceans would absorb virtually all anthropogenic CO_2. In that year two scientists concluded that only half of the CO_2 produced by humans was being absorbed by the oceans with the declaration that "mankind is conducting a great one-time geophysical experiment".[6] This dire warning, however attracted neither policy attention nor research funding until the emergence of environmentalism in the 1970s. Concern was amplified in the 1980s by the discovery that other trace gases, including methane, chloroflurocarbon (CFCS) and nitrous oxides, would nearly double the warming trend expected from CO_2 alone.[7] CO_2 has made the largest individual contribution to the increased radioactive forcing.

The table 6.1 shows the estimates made by the IPCC in 1994 and indicates that more than half of the increased radioactive forcing was from CO_2. Subsequent work has revised these figures slightly, but did not change the finding that CO_2 has made the largest contribution to the increased radioactive forcing, while CH_4 and CFCs have contributed roughly equal but smaller amounts.

Since the beginning of the 1970s the concern received increasing attention in national and international institutions. Starting in 1958 in Mauna Loa, Hawaii, Charles Keeling of the Scripps Institute of Oceanography at LC Jolla, California kept accurate observation of the atmospheric concentration of CO_2. By the mid 1970s almost 20 years' worth of data were available to show that the concentration was steadily increasing.[8] At the same time atmospheric scientists intensified their efforts to estimate the impact that an increasing CO_2 concentration would have on global climate. At first with relatively simple models, but by the end of the 1970s, also with general circulation models of the atmosphere, estimates were made of the responses to a doubling of the CO_2 concentration from its pre-industrial value. The figure 6.2 shows the evolution of climate change science and politics.

This suggests that the scientific work began to increase its efforts in the mid-1950s with the creation of the first major international programme, the International Geophysical Year. It also heralded the era of global circulation models, spurred on by the US Department of Defense. The 1972 Stockholm Conference on the Human Environment created the political impetus for national responsibility towards transboundary environmental deterioration. The evidence was sufficient for the World Meteorological Organization, the UN Environment Programme and the

International Council of Scientific Unions to hold the first World Climate Conference in Geneva in 1979. Unlike its successor in the same city 11 years later, this was primarily attended by scientists, and, at the time commanded little political attention.

Table 6.2

History of Climate Change Science and Politics

International Geophysical Year (1957-1958)

↓

Early general circulation models (1960-1995)

↓

UN Conference on the Human Environment (1972)

Ozone depletion research	First World Climate Conference 1979	energy economics modelling

Villach Conference

(World meteorological Organisation; UN Environment Programme International Council of Scientific Unions) 1980, 1983, 1985

↓

Advisory Group on Greenhouse Gases Villach 1987, Bellagio 1987

↓

World Conference on Changing Atmosphere Toronto, 1988

↓

Intergovernmental panel on Climate Change 1988-Present

↓

Working Group-1	**Working group-2**	**Working group-3**

↓

Second World Climate Conference, 1990

↓

Intergovernmental Negotiating Committee, 1991-1994

↓

Framework Convention on Climate Change, 1992

Subsidiary Body for scientific and Technological Advice	Conference of Parties since date	Subsidiary on Financing Instrument

Source : Jill Jagar and Tim O' Riordan, "The History of Climate Change Science and Politics", in their ed., Politics of Climate Change: A European Perspective (London / New York: Rout ledge, 1996), p. 13.

This was followed by a series of conferences and workshops held in Villach in Austria, In 1979, the US National Academy of Science published a report in which they concluded that the doubling of the CO_2 concentration would lead to an increase of the average temperature of the earth's surface of between 1.5 and 4.5°C. In the following years up until and including the 1994 IPCC assessment, the scientific consensus was that there was no reason to widen or narrow this range. In 1985, a major international review of the issue formed the basis of the third Villach conference organized by the World Meteorological Organization (WMD), the United Nations Environment Programme (UNEP) and the International Council of Scientific Unions (ICSU). Scenarios for future emission of all of the significant green house gases, not just CO_2 were considered and an international scientific consensus about the potential seriousness of the problem was achieved.[9] The problem of anthropogenic climate change was moved at this point onto the political agenda.

A culmination of scientific development in climate change analysis is the work of the Intergovernmental Panel on Climate Change (IPCC). Established in 1988, the IPCC had three working groups. The first was asked to access available scientific evidence on climate change, the second to assess environmental and socio-economic impacts of climate change and the third to formulate response strategies. The report of the Working Group1 (WG1) had the most impact.[10] With accuracy it stated that there is a natural green house effect and that human activities are increasing the atmospheric concentrations of green house gases. Further more, it calculated that CO_2 was responsible for over half of the enhanced green house effect in the past and is likely to remain so in the future. On the basis of the strong statements made by IPCC waking Group1, the issue of climate change was given even more priority on the political agenda, and negotiations for the climate convention began.

The success of WG1 was partly because it was regarded as scientific and hence detached from political bias, and in part because the late 1980s witnessed a series of much publicized abnormal climate events across the globe. Notably was the very hot and dry summer of 1988 in the US, an event that led to Congressional hearings and much political attention to scientific predictions.[11] It was because it operated on the basis of consensus, it was therefore inherently conservative scientifically speaking, and it sought to detach itself from the negotiations taking place in all important Intergovernmental Negotiating Committees that led to the Rio convention. As Lanchberry and Victor observe, "although non controversial conservation may be good feature in a body designed to reflect the balance of scientific thought, it is not necessarily a good feature in a body called on to inform a negotiating process."[12]

The other working groups were far less successful, partly because it is considerable to separate adjustment from impacts, and also to isolate analysis from policy prescriptions. The fact that the Russians chaired WG2 and the Americans chaired WG3 was also politically dictated, and virtually guaranteed that both groups would be ineffective in informing the all important negotiation process. As Jill Jager and Tim 'O' Riordan observe:" It is also a sad reflection on the state of the social science at present, that their practitioners cannot produce a coherent view of what causes climate change in terms of human needs and wants and associated economic and technological drivers, what should be done about these, and what would be the social, political and economic consequences."[13]

The work of IPCC has been criticized for representing rich world agenda and interests and for limiting the extent to which the industrialized world needs critically to re-examine and reconstruct its own deep commitments in order adequately to address the contemporary debate. What is needed to save the earth from catastrophic climate change is to reduce emissions by 50-70 per cent below 1990 levels by reducing, or even altogether abandoning the use of carbon based fuels. The use of these fuels and hence carbon emissions are closely linked to economic growth and life style. Every human being contributes to the carbon dioxide concentration in the atmosphere, though the person's lifestyle decides the amount that is emitted. The more prosperous a country's economy, and the higher its per capita income, the higher its fossil fuel consumption for power generation and transport, and the higher its green house gas emissions.

Historical Responsibility

Since the inception of industrial revolution the accumulation of green house gases in the atmosphere emitted by the industrialized countries, has led to their current prosperity and high rate of emission. On the other hand, the developing countries, which have just started stalking on the path of industrialization, have comparatively a very low level of per capita emissions. According to Center for Science and Environment (CSE), "the GHG emissions of one US citizen, for instance, were equal to 19 Indians, 30 Pakistanis, 17 Maldivians, 19 Sri Lankans, 107 Bangladeshis, 134 Bhutanese and 269 Nepalis in 1996".[14] What has happened to climate change is due to the historical emission of GHG by the industrialized countries of the North. The industrialized countries have always tried to scuttle their responsibility for this. From the very beginning of international negotiation on climate change they have been trying to share their responsibility with the developing countries despite their negligible contribution to the problem. The World Resources Report of 1990-1991 prepared by the World Resources Institute (WRI) was demonstrative of the manipulation of science, an attempt to implicate the developing countries. It demonstrated that the annual green house gas emissions of the South countries are equal to those of the industrial North and the South's emission would overtake the North in the near future. The Centre for Science and Environment a NGO in New Delhi challenged this in its 1991 publication, Global Warming in an Unequal World.

The following table shows the differential emission of GHGs, by both the industrialized world and the developing countries as studied by CSE and WRI.

Percentage of Distribution of Net Emissions of GHGs by Industrialized and Developing Countries

Country	*WRI Formula*	*CSEFormula*
United States	17.0	27.4
Soviet Union and Eastern Europe	16.0	17.6
Western Europe	14.3	11.9
Japan	3.9	2.5
Other industrialized Countries	1.4	7.5
India and China	10.3	0.6
Brazil	10.3	18.2
Other developing Countries	26.7	14.3

Source : Anil Agarwal and Sunita Narain, Global Warming in an Unequal World: A Case of Environmental Colonialism (New Delhi: Centre for Science and Environment, 1991), p. 12.

According the CSE, the WRI's methodology was faulty and it allocated unfairly earth's ability to clean up carbon dioxide and methane to different countries. On the other hand, the CSE has allocated natural sinks for carbon dioxide and methane to each nation on the basis of population, hence calculating the permissible levels of emissions for each country. The result showed that industrialized countries together exceeded their permissible quotas of carbon dioxide by 2839 million tonnes of carbon equivalent (mtc)-the amount that would remain in the atmosphere. Developing countries, on the other hand actually provided space for 1459 mt of carbon equivalent to be released in the form of carbon dioxide by industrialized countries. The following table shows this discrepancy.

Comparative Figures of Total Emissions of GHGs of WRIs Top 10 Emitting Nations as Calculated by CSE (Million Tons of Carbon Equivalent)

Country	*Accumulation in the atmosphere*		*Absorbed by natural sinks*	
	WRI	*CSE*	*WRI*	*CSE*
United States	1000	1532	1368	836
Soviet Union	690	730	882	842
West Germany	160	155	144	149
United Kingdom	150	132	160	178
Japan	220	140	202	281
France	120	69	121	173
Brazil	610	1017	826	418
China	380	32	793	1141
India	230	0.7	643	871
Indonesia	140	9.5	240	370

Source : Anil Agarwal and Sunita Narain, Global Warming in an Unequal World, *op. cit.*, p10

The first deficiency with WRI calculation is that by taking into account the current emissions, it exhibited a bias that would work to the advantage of the industrialized rich countries more particularly the US. As Susan Subak of the Stockholm Environment Institute put it, "Any green house index that ranks countries by current emissions, rather than cumulative emissions which take the past into account, will find developing countries to be more accountable for global warming than would an index that includes historical emissions which continue to trap heat in the atmosphere decades after their release. For example, the WRI index lists Indonesia as the seventh greatest emitter. Its high ranking is due largely to carbon dioxide emissions from land use changes, especially deforestation. The country's relative ranking would decline, however, if its emissions from earlier decades preceding the accelerated deforestation were included in the calculation and compared with historical emission from an industrialized country that no longer depletes its forest stock. Such an analysis of green house gas emissions by country would yield very different rankings for a broad range of countries." [15]

Secondly, by giving primacy to the immediate heating effect as the WRI proposes, the atmospheric residence time of the different green house gases currently emitted and their long term warming effected is ignored. As a result, the countries that produce greater quantities longer lived gases such as carbon dioxide are less accountable, again an advantage that goes to US. The result is to hook the countries that produce more of the shorter lived green house gases namely methane. The developing countries that are engaged in activities like rice and livestock production come within the purview and figure more prominently than the industrialized countries.[16]

Methane emissions have more than doubled in concentration since pre-industrial times. Anthropogenic sources of methane include coal mining, natural gas and petroleum, landfills, domesticated livestock, paddy cultivation, natural gas and oil production, coal mining and biomass burning. But recent measures indicate that although methane continues to increase, the rate of increases has slowed. Measurements made during the 1984-1996 period suggest that methane emissions have been constant during the time period. If global emissions remain constant, globally averaged methane will increase from 1730 parts per billion (ppb) to a maximum of about 1800 ppb over the next few decades, with little change in the contribution of methane to the green house effect.[17]

According to John Lanchbery of the Verification Technology Centre, London, methane emissions are known only to within 25 per cent in industrialized countries, because they are produced in unpredicted organic processes in fields, landfills and other places.[18]

This inability to pinpoint the amount of methane produced led to controversy during early climate negotiations, when industrialized countries blamed livestock and paddy cultivation in the South for a larger share of the world's methane emissions. In a 1990 report, the World Resources Institute (WRI) said 40 per cent of the world's methane emissions came from leakages during hard coal mining and natural gas exploration and transportation as well as from urban landfills and sewage plants. The rest come from anaerobic fermentation in irrigated fields and from the enteric fermentation, or stomach gas, of livestock.[19] WRI held livestock in developing countries responsible for 60 per cent of the total animal methane generated in the world. But another study conducted by the International Project for Sustainable Energy Paths (IPSEP) came up with different conclusions, despite the fact that both WRI and IPSEP depended on the same paper, published by P J Crutzen of the Tellus Institute, for their methane calculations.

Crutzen had estimated that each head of cattle emits 45kg of methane every year on an average. But because this figure depends on the quality and quantity of feed, methane production of cattle in industrialized countries is higher-about 55kg per head of cattle-compared to cattle from developing countries, which is about 35kg per head of cattle. This difference is because the big eaters are daily cows, which are fed three times their maintenance feed level in industrialized countries, while a large portion of the developing country cattle are draught animals. On this basis, Crutzen calculated that the total animal methane production was about equal from developed and industrialized countries, even though the number of cattle in developing countries was double the amount of cattle in industrialized countries.

According to Crutzen, almost 75 per cent of all animal related methane comes from the world's 1300 heads of cattle. The IPSEP study advocated a reduction of cattle herd and beef consumption.[20] But it pointed out that most of the action lies in industrialized countries, not developing countries, since the per capita meat consumption in the former was six times higher (78 kg/year) than in the latter (14 kg/year). This was a realistic solution, according to IPSEP, because people in these countries consume several times more meat than the 30 gm per day recommended for a balanced non-vegetarian diet. A 50 per cent decrease in per capita consumption of beef would still allow ample supplies of dairy products while reducing the methane production by 40 per cent. Developing countries on the other hand, cannot afford to reduce their cattle populations, since they have a broader role than supplying milk and meat. They are used as draught animals, replacing tractors, and provide dung to fertilize fields and burn for cooking in addition to providing meat, milk and hide.

Estimating methane production from irrigated rice fields is equally tricky. In 1990, the Intergovernmental Panel on Climate Change (IPCC) had estimated methane production from the world's paddy fields as 110 million tonnes (mt), but had revised this figure to 60 mt in 1992, and then to 37 mt in 1994. But these figures were challenged by the former director of the Indian Agricultural Research Institute, SK Sinha, who contended the IPCC figures were based on extrapolations from a few studies done in temperature regions. According to his experiments, methane emissions from paddy fields could be as low as 7.8mt [21]

Further, methane has such a short lifetime (about 10 years) compared to carbon dioxide (over 100 years), its relative importance decreases quickly. After 20 years, the methane released at the beginning of the period has become less than 10 per cent as important as the carbon dioxide. After 100 years, less than one in ten thousand of the methane molecules is left, while about half the carbon dioxide remains. From most perspectives, the relative impact of the current atmospheric methane concentration is much less than the 40 per cent indicated by an instantaneous index.[22]

Thirdly, the problem with WRI index is that carbon dioxide emissions from fossil fuel consumption have been lumped together with carbon dioxide emissions from deforestation and methane emissions from irrigated paddies and cattle populations, which have an extremely high order of uncertainties. Again the bias is made against the developing countries. The WRI index, which is based on bad science, bad mathematics and bad data, is also based on bad politics. It is also anti third world.

The WRI index quite like the IPCC index does not differentiate between survival emissions of the poor and the luxury emissions of the rich. If most human activities – from industry and transport to cattle rearing and agriculture-generate green house gas emissions that are generated by the poor for survival from those that emitted as a result of luxurious and inordinate life style of the rich.[23]

According to Centre for Science and Environment, a composite index of all green house gases has to be used. This would mean disaggregating total emissions into survival and luxury emissions. Further pointing to the unfairness of WRI index, it alleges that the WRI index of net emissions is based on an assumption that the national collection of net emissions should follow the national distribution of total emissions. This method implicitly allocates the natural sinks among different nations according to the national distribution of total emissions. Since the natural sinks are largely a global common property, there can be both ethical and practical objection to such an allocation of natural sinks. The WRI methodology allocates the largest share of the natural sinks to the largest polluter, and thus provides a pervasive impetus to pollute.[24]

The industrialized countries blow up disproportionately the role of methane in global warming emitted from the paddy fields in developing countries with a view to putting the burden of the management of the atmosphere on the shoulder of the developing countries. Paddy fields are said to be a major source of methane emissions. But is the human impact of reducing 20 per cent cars in London the same as reducing 20 per cent land under paddy in Bangladesh or Thailand? As reinterpreted by CSE of WRI's own biased data and methodology, the developing countries as a group contributed to only 33 per cent of the net emissions in 1987. This was when the unused emissions of developing countries were traded with all countries including industrialized countries on an equal per capita basis. But when the unused emissions of developing countries were traded only with other developing countries which were emitting in excess, the industrialized countries share increased to 91 per cent while that of the developing countries dwindled to just nine per cent. This can be seen from the following table

Contribution of Industrialized and Developing Countries to Global Warming According to Different Indices

Index	*Time horizon Years*	*% contribution Industrialized countries*	*Developing countries*
IPCC (global	20	49.3	50.7
Warming potential	100	52.3	47.7
	500	55	45.0
WRI (global forcing contribution)		54	46
CSE (modified WRI)		67.0 (1)	33
		91.0 (2)	9.0

Note: (1) On the basis of unused emissions of developing countries also being traded with industrialized countries.

(2) On the basis of unused emissions of developing countries being traded only with other developing countries.

Source : Allen Hammond, Eric Rodenburg and William R. Moomaw, The Green house Index in Environment, March 1991; and Anil Agarwal and Sunita Narain, Global Warming in an Unequal World (New Delhi: Centre for Science and Environment 1991)

Kirk Smith adopting a different index, which is called the integrated forming contribution (IFC) has generated an approximation of different nations' contributions by summing up the total emissions of the most important green house gas, carbon dioxide, from the most important source, burning of fossil fuels, and over the most important period, 1900 to the present. This measure shows that the total carbon released into, and mostly still present in the atmosphere as carbon dioxide is about 260 tons per living US resident compared to about six tons for the average resident of India. This amount played into the atmosphere since 1900 by a US citizen, as part of the US industrialized process through the burning of fossil fuels, is more than 40 times that of an average Indian.[25]

In an analogy to national financial debt, Smith calls these cumulative emissions, the natural debt of a nation. Just as the nations take on a financial debt over years in order to grow faster, they also take on a natural debt for the same reason. In the latter case, economics borrow the assimilative capacity of the environment by releasing waste gases faster than they can be removed naturally. Just as there can be economic disruptions if the financial debt becomes too large. So too can there be ecological disruptions if the natural debt grows too large. Smith's calculations show that developed countries are the holders of the largest natural debts 260 t/capita for the US compared to six t/capita for India in 1990. The average US citizen's share of this natural carbon debt today is more than ten times that of the average person in the rest of the world. During the 35 years between 1990 and 2024, the per capita Indian natural debt would have quadrupled (six to 24 tons/ capita in India) while an American's per capita natural debt would have only increased by 70 per cent (from 260 to 440 tonnes / capita).[26]

Impacts of GHGs

The Intergovernmental Panel on Climate Change's (IPCC) first working group released its input for the Third Assessment Report on the current state of understanding of the climate system in January 2001. The main findings are listed below.

Temperature

- The 20th century saw unusual warming as temperature increased by about 0.6°C. Globally, 1990s was the warmest decade and 1998 the warmest year since 1861.
- Human activities have contributed most to global warming in the past 50 years.
- Global surface temperature will rise by 1.4-5.8°C by 2100 with the warming rate being significantly greater than the last century's. The second assessment report of IPCC had estimated a lower increase of about 1.0-3.5°C.
- Extreme low temperatures have reduced in frequency while extremely high temperatures have become more frequent since 1950.
- Warming in northern and central Asia will be about 40 per cent more than the global average rate.
- The lower the stabilization levels of greenhouse gases (GHGs) in the atmosphere, the smaller the temperature change. On stabilization, temperature will rise at a rate of only a few tenths of a degree per century as against several degrees per century otherwise.

Sea-level

- Global sea level rose by 10-20 centimeter (cm) in the 20th century.
- Sea level may rise between 9-88cm by 2100. Thermal expansion and loss of ice from glacier and ice caps will cause the rise.

- Temperature and sea level will continue to rise for hundreds of years even after GHG-levels have stabilized at present levels.

Snow cover

- Snow cover has decreased by about 10 per cent since 1960s. Annual duration of ice cover on lakes and rivers in the Northern Hemisphere's mid-and high altitude regions reduced by about two weeks over the 20th century.
- Glaciers and ice caps in non-polar region will continue to retreat in the 21st century. The Northern Hemisphere snow cover and ice extent will decrease further.
- The Antarctic ice sheet will gain mass due to greater precipitation, while the Greenland ice sheet will lose mass because increase in runoff will exceed precipitation increase.
- Ice sheet will contribute to sea level rise for thousands of years after GHG levels have stabilized. Models show that local warming over Greenland is likely to be 1 to 3 times the global average. A local warming of more than 3°C, if sustained for millennia, can cause complete melting of the Greenland ice sheet raising sea level by about 7 meters.

Precipitation

- Precipitation over mid-and high-latitudes in Northern Hemisphere has increased by about 0.5-1 per cent per decade in the 20th century. Heavy precipitation events became more frequent by 2-4 per cent in the later half of the century.
- Over the 20th century, rainfall in tropical areas increased by 0.2-0.3 per cent per decade, while it decreased by about 0.3 per cent in subtropical regions of the Northern Hemisphere.
- Warming will increase Asian summer monsoon precipitation variability. Global average water vapour concentration and precipitation are projected to increase during this century.

Other aspects of climate

- The EI Nino southern oscillation (ENSO) phenomenon has become more frequent, persistent and intense since the mid – 1970s as compared to the previous 100 years.
- In parts of Asia and Africa, droughts have increased in frequency and intensity in recent decades. Extreme events like drought and floods will become more frequent in the future.

Greenhouse gases

- Atmosphere concentrations of carbon dioxide, methane and nitrous oxide have increased since 1750 by 31 per cent, 151 per cent and 17 per cent, respectively. During the last two decades, about three-quarters of anthropogenic emissions of carbon dioxide were due to fossil fuel burning.
- Carbon dioxide levels increased at an unprecedented rate about 1.5 parts per million (ppm) per year in the past two decades. During the 1990s, this rate varied from 0.9-2.8 ppm.
- For IPCC emissions scenarios, carbon dioxide levels will reach 540-970 ppm by 2100, an increase of 90-250 per cent from 280ppm in 1750.
- Global anthropogenic emissions of carbon dioxide will have to be reduced below 1990 levels within a few decades to stabilize at 450 ppm. If reduced over a century, they can be stabilized at 650 ppm.
- Currently, the ocean and land absorb about half the carbon dioxide emissions from human activities.
- Hypothetically, if all of the carbon released by historical land use changes could be restored over this century, carbon dioxide levels would be reduced by 40-70 ppm.[27]

The Intergovernmental Panel on Climate Change's (IPCC) second working group released its input for the Third Assessment Report on the potential consequences of climate change in February 2001. The main findings are listed below.

- More people will be harmed than benefited by climate change. The greatest impact will be on developing countries in terms of loss of life, effect on investment and economy. Least-developed regions are especially vulnerable.
- In many developing countries, net economic losses will increase with temperature rise. Industrialized countries will experience a mix of economic gains and losses for few °C increase in temperature.
- These losses will widen the economic gap between developing and industrialized countries. This disparity will grow as warming increases.
- Regional changes in temperature due to global warming have already begun to affect various physical and biological systems in many parts of the world. Glaciers are shrinking, frozen subsurface soil, known as permafrost, is thawing, freeze-free

season for ice on rivers and lakes is lengthening, population of some plants and animals is declining, and trees are flowering earlier than usual.

- Climatic changes over the 21st century may significantly slow down ocean circulation transporting warm water to the North Atlantic. This will affect deep-water oxygen levels and carbon uptake by oceans and marine ecosystems, and will also decrease warming over parts of Europe.
- Warming may cause large reductions in the Greenland and west Antarctic Ice Sheets.
- Terrestrial carbon from permafrost regions and methane from hydrates in coastal sediments may be released as temperatures increase over 21st century.

Water

- Water availability will decrease in many water scarce regions, particularly in the sub-tropics. However, in some water-scarce regions of Southeast Asia, it will increase.
- Climate change will decrease streamflow and groundwater recharge in many water-stresses countries in central Asia, South Africa and around the Mediterranean Sea.
- Annual mean streamflow will increase in high latitudes and south Asia.
- In seasonal low flow periods, streamflow will decrease in many areas due to increased evaporation.
- Where winter snowfall significantly contributes to water balance rain will replace it to a large extent causing an intense streaming.
- Runoff will increase in many areas as floods increase in intensity and frequency due to increase in heavy precipitation events. But in some floodplains, this can lead to groundwater recharge.
- Water quality will deteriorate as increased runoff brings more pollutants and wastes with it. Heavy streamflow will dilute these pollutants and improve the quality while less streamflow will further degradation.

Agriculture and food security

- Benefits of increased carbon dioxide concentration in term of greater crop yield will not always overcome adverse effect of excessive heat and drought.

- In tropical regions, crop yields will decrease with even minimal temperature increases.
- In mid-latitudes, crop yields will increase if warming is less than a few °C and decrease for more than few °C warming.
- Being largely dependent on rainfall, tropical crop yield will be even more adversely affected in regions where there is large decrease in rain. Crops will require more irrigation as higher temperature increases evaporation
- Models show that impacts on crop yield will result small decline or increase in income in developing regions. More industrialized regions will experience larger increases in incomes.
- Temperature rise will cause food prices to increase because food demand will grow at a faster rate than supply.
- Climate change will lower incomes of the vulnerable population like small producers and poor urban consumers. It will also increase the number of people at risk of hunger.
- Climate change will worsen food security in Africa.

Human health

- Vulnerable lower income populations, predominantly within tropical or subtropical countries, will experience the greatest adverse health impacts.
- Geographic range of vector-borne diseases like malaria and dengue will increase, as also their incidence and seasonality.
- Number of people exposed to these diseases and water-born aliments like cholera will increase.
- Heat waves will increase with rising temperatures, and high humidity and urban air pollution will exacerbate them.
- Illnesses and deaths related to heat stress are projected to increase
- In temperate countries, reduced mortality during winters may out number increased summer deaths.
- Risk of diarrhea, respiratory disease and drowning will increase with increase in flooding.
- In developing countries, flooding will aggravate hunger and malnutrition. Reduced crop yield and food production in tropics will lead to malnutrition in populations that are already food insecure. This will impair child development and decrease adult activity.

Terrestrial and Freshwater Ecosystem

- Changes in climate will alter species composition and dominance in a given ecosystem, but migration of these systems as discrete units may not happen. Such alternations will lag behind climatic changes by years to decades to centuries.
- Distribution, population size and density, and behaviour of wildlife will be affected by regional or global changes, and by changes in vegetation.
- With a one metre rise in sea-level, the Sundarbans – the largest mangrove ecosystems-of Bangladesh will completely disappear
- Temperature rise will move freshwater fish distributions.
- Species already at high risk will be placed at a greater risk as changes in climate render some part of current habitat unsuitable. The risk will compound in cases where land-use change has fragmented habitats causing problems in migration of species.
- Such pressures will lead to the extinction of critically endangered species while pushing endangered ones to extinction in the 21st century.

Costal Zones and Marine Ecosystems

- Sea surface temperature and global sea level, sea ice cover, salinity, wave conditions, and ocean circulation will be affected by climate change.
- Many coastal areas will experience increased flooding, accelerated erosion, loss of wetlands and mangroves. And intrusion of seawater into fresh water sources.
- Due to sea-level rise and climate change, the extent and severity of impacts of storms will increase. Storms surge floods and shore erosion will also increase.
- Coasts in high-latitude regions will suffer additional impacts related in greater wave energy and permafrost degradation.
- Adverse effects on mangroves, coral reefs, atolls and reef islands, and salt marshes will depend on the rate of sea-level rise, scope for horizontal migration, changes in climatic-ocean environment and stress from human activities.
- Stress on coral reefs and coral bleaching will increase with sea surface warming. Marine diseases will also become more frequent with increasing temperatures.

- Climate variability will strongly affect fish abundance and population, with strong impacts on fish-dependent societies.

Human Settlements, Energy and Industry

- The most widespread direct risk to human settlements due to climate change is from increase in rainfall leading to flooding and landslides, and sea-level rise. Industrial, transport and commercial infrastructure is vulnerable to the same hazards as settlement infrastructure.
- Riverine and costal settlements are particularly at risk.
- Flooding will severely affect urban settlements with inadequate drainage, water supply and waste management.
- In such settlements, areas with population density, poor shelter, and little or no access to safe water and public health services are highly vulnerable.
- Existing environmental problems will be exacerbated due to higher temperature and increased precipitation.
- As low-lying costal areas rapidly urbanize in both developing and industrialized countries, population and assets exposed to climatic extremes like cyclones are greatly increasing.
- The number of people annually flooded by coastal storm surges will increase by 75-200 million by the 2080s for a 40-centimeter sea-level rise relative to the scenario of no rise.
- Potential damage to infrastructure like Egypt, Poland and Vietnam is projected to be tens of billions of dollars.
- Settlements economically dependent on climate-sensitive sectors like agriculture; forestry and fisheries are more vulnerable than those with higher economic diversification.
- In Arctic settlements, thawing of permafrost will severely damage buildings and transport infrastructure.
- Higher summer temperatures will increase energy demand for space cooling. Alternatively, demand for spacing heating will reduce during winters due to higher winter temperatures.

Insurance and Other Financial Services

- Expansion of financial services into developing countries will slow down, insurance costs will rise, insurance may not be available for certain risks and demand for government-funded compensation following natural disasters will rise.
- Annual global economic losses from catastrophic events increased about ten times from US $3.9 billion (in 1999 US $) in the 1950s to US $40 billion in the 1990s.

- About 25 per cent of these losses occurred in developing countries.
- The insured part of these losses increased from a negligible level to 23 per cent over the same period.
- A part of this increases in losses is linked to climatic factors like changes in precipitations and flooding events while the rest is linked to socio-economic factors such as population growth, increased wealth and urbanization in vulnerable areas.

Climate Change Negotiations: From Toronto to Kyoto

Toronto Conference

In response to the recommendations of the Brundtland Commission, a conference on the Changing Atmosphere: Implication for Global Security took place in Toronto in 1985 which was attended by a host of scientists, environmentalists, industrial representatives including the Prime Ministers of Canada and Norway along with 340 people from 46 countries. It heralded the beginning of a high level political debate on climate change.[28] It set a target of 20 per cent reduction of carbon dioxide emissions over 1990 by 2005. The Toronto meeting was not a formal intergovernmental meeting, but the presence of senior policy makers in Toronto marked the entry of government into the climate debates.[29]

Noordwijk Conference

A ministerial conference on atmospheric pollution and climate change attended by representatives of 67 countries was held in November 1989 in Noordwijk, the Netherlands. It urged all countries to take steps to control green house gas emissions. Developing countries were called upon to meet future targets on emissions. It was urged upon the industrialized countries to facilitate the transfer of technology to developing nations to limit climate change. Further, it came out with recommendations for a framework convention on climate change committing parties to addressing the needs of developing nations in gaining access to technology, and suggested that the Intergovernmental Panel on Climate Change (IPCC) explore ways of relating the effects of other GHGs to those of carbon dioxide, and consider the feasibility of a net growth of 12 million hectares of forest per year by the start of the next century.[30]

What pushed the issue of climate change to the global agenda in 1988 and onwards were some unexpected and alarming events that took place then. A drought worst since 1930s affecting half the countries in US,[31] and a tropical storm hitting Southeast England and London in late 1987, Northern France, Belgium[32] and Netherlands and drought in Soviet

Union and both floods and drought in Africa, India, China, Brazil and Bangladesh and cyclone in New Zealand, Philippines, and hurricanes in Caribbean[33] were some of the events that raised the concern of policy makers for global negotiation on climate change.

Divagating from his traditional 'wait and see' approach James Hansen, chief climate scientist at National Aeronautics and Space Administration's (NASA) Goddard Institute for Space Studies told the US Senate's Energy and Natural Resources Committee that it was "time to stop waffling so much...the evidence is pretty strong that the green house effect is here."[34]

Climate Change on UN Agenda

As a part of the 'common heritage of mankind' initiated by Malta and supported by 19 countries along with many developing countries, the climate issue surfaced at the UN General Assembly in December 1988. It was raised to the status of a common concern of mankind in 1988 UN resolution.[35] In the late 1980s, a UN General Assembly noted that "the largest part of the current emission of pollutants into the environment including toxic and hazardous wastes, originates in developed countries... those countries have the main responsibility for combating such pollution."[36] Further, it affirmed that "the responsibility for containing, reducing and eliminating global environmental damage... must be in relation to the damage caused, and must be in accordance with (the country's) respective capabilities and responsibilities."[37]

North –South Differences Emerged on Climate Change Negotiation

At a preparatory meeting organized by UNEP and WMO to discuss negotiation on climate convention in September 1990, developing countries pressed for a forum established by the UN General Assembly to conduct negotiations, instead of UNEP and WMO. It resolved that the General Assembly recommend ways, means and modalities for further pursuing negotiations. It also stressed that the negotiation process should be organized and conducted in such a manner that it ensures openness, transparency, universality and legitimacy, and reflects the commitment of all nations to the negotiations.[38]

Differences between North and South appeared at the fourth Plenary session of IPCC held in Sundsvall, Sweden in 1990, when it was said in its first report of the common responsibilities of industrialized and developing nations to combat climate change. The developing countries wanted it to be the main responsibility of the industrialized nations, but not without strong opposition from UK and US. A compromise statement finally reached: industrialized and developing countries have a common but differentiated responsibility in dealing with the problem of climate change and its adverse effects.[39]

Second World Climate Conference

It was held in Geneva in November 1990, attended by 137 countries. The debate mostly rested on the report of World Resources Institute (WRI), which showed that the annual GHG emission of developing countries almost equaled those of the industrialized world. It claimed that the South's emissions were growing and would overtake the North in the near future.[40] Here the South failed to get the North accept the main responsibility for climate change mitigation, or the polluter pays principle, as it held that the developed countries are responsible for about three fourths of all emission of GHGs.[41] Weaving a chord of compromise between North and South around the convention, the declaration finally said:

"Recognizing... that the principle of equity and the common but differentiated responsibilities of countries should be the basis of any global response to climate change, industrialized countries must take the lead. They must all commit themselves to action to reduce their major contribution to the global net emissions and enter into and strengthen cooperation with developing countries to enable them to adequately address climate change without hindering their national development goals and objectives".[42]

This conference witnessed the thaw of differences between developing countries on the climate issue. The OPEC countries did not like to accept the arguments of developing countries that carbon dioxide emissions from fossil fuels account for more than half of global warming. The small island states fearing their vulnerability to sea level rise due to global warming clashed with OPEC countries over the issue of climate change.

Before the earth summit took place at Rio in 1992, the intergovernmental negotiating committee (INC) held five sittings at different places viz. Washington, Geneva, Nairobi, New York. These sittings only demonstrated the difference between the North and South countries. North-South differences persisted over the questions of technology transfer and a financial mechanism. Developing nations reiterated their demand for a separate financial mechanism under the convention, while industrialized nations stuck to their stand of using the Global Environment Facility (GEF).[43]

Earth Summit at Rio

The industrialized countries did not agree to owe any liability for past emissions or damage done to climate, non-even the per capita concept that gave equal rights to the atmosphere to all human beings. They only accepted the common but 'differentiated responsibility' principle in complete disregard of the polluter pays principle. According to the North, the acceptance of differentiated responsibilities does not mean the acceptance of their past liability. The US delegation remarked, "we all argue that industrialized countries should take the lead, but we do not agree why". In spite of its insistence the South was unable to get the convention say that unsustainable consumption patterns lead to global warming.[44]

The NGOs described the summit as true trash. US environmentalists called it a neutral convention. Gurmit Singh, president of the Environmental Protection Society, Malaysia, commented that the lame duck convention was worse than not having a convention, because it would give the impression that the global warming problem was being addressed.[45] "At best this convention provides a procedure that could lead to commitments in the future", pointed out Michael Oppenheimer, senior scientist at Environmental Defense Fund.[46]

In the negotiation leading up to FCCC (Framework Convention on Climate Change), the principles of permanent sovereignty over natural resources, common but differential responsibilities, justice and equity, right to development, duty to cooperate, and the precautionary principle, served as the basis for proposals from developing countries.[47]

All these principles were included in a modified form. But through the framework convention, industrialized countries got away with not having to account for their historical emissions. Moreover, the 1990 IPCC report had made it clear that to stabilize GHGs to existing levels, an immediate reduction of over 60 per cent in 1990 emissions was required.[48]

Conference of Parties (COP)

Berlin Summit

At the first Conference of Parties (COP-1) held in Berlin from 26 March-April 1995, the alliance of small island states (AOSIS) urged industrialized countries to cut their carbon dioxide emissions by 20 per cent by the 2000, where as the industrialized countries continued to argue about the stringency of targets. A restructured Global Environmental Facility (GEF) was given another four-year term as the interior financial mechanism. However the Berlin mandate recognized for the first time the need to tie the industrialized countries to binding targets, highlighting the fact that the existing community for industrialized countries under FCCC was inadequate.[49]

Geneva Summit

The second conference of Parties held in Geneva from July 8-19, 1996 marked a change in the attitude of US. US in the summit strongly supported the IPCC Second Assessment Report's call to take urgent action and stressed on the need for intensified negotiation on a binding medium term emission target and a longer-term goal for atmospheric concentration of GHGs.[50] Progress was hindered in this summit by OPEC members who were unwilling to allow urgent action. The main problems were posited by the US. First, the US called for a realistic, verifiable and achievable target without indicating any number or base years, second, it included a caveat that the proposed target should be reached through activities implemented jointly (AIJ) and emissions trading on a global scale, which included developing countries. Third, the statement emphasized that industrialized and developing countries have to take measures in the context of the Berlin Mandate.[51]

The United States which had in COP-2 meeting seemingly been convinced by the scientific evidence again turned volta face and stressed on long term rather than short term targets to reduce GHG emissions at the 1997 United Nations General Assembly Special Session.[52] President Bill Clinton's hand appeared to be tied by opposition to commitment from the US Congress. In July 1997, two senators Republic Chuck Hagel and Democrat Robert Byrd called on the US Senate to pass a resolution refusing to ratify any climate treaty that would "mandate new commitments to limit or reduce GHG emission for the annex I parties, unless [it] also mandates new specific scheduled commitments... for Developing Country Parties within the same compliance period".[53]

The Byrd. Hagel resolution was passed unanimously by the US Senate. The months prior to COP-3 summit at Kyoto witnesses a concerted attempt by the US to include the issue of developing countries on it agenda. In particular it called for the involvement of the growing economic competitors of the US, such as China, South Korea and India in any agreement on climate change.[54]

Kyoto Protocol

The Kyoto Protocol took shape at COP-3 in Kyoto, Japan. Heated exchanges, and much wrangling marked the conference, which ended abruptly to hastily patch up a lukewarm agreement. After much debate, industrialized countries collectively agreed to reduce emission by 5.2 per cent below 1990 levels during 2008-2012.

Weakness of the Protocol

The strategy outlined in Kyoto protocol enjoins upon the Annex I parties to meet their commitments without shouldering the responsibility of reducing greenhouse gases at home. It may therefore, not lead to stabilization of greenhouse gas concentration at a level that would prevent dangerous anthropogenic interference with the climate system.

Except through Clean Development Mechanism and Emissions Trading introduced into the strategy outlined in the protocol, it does not insist on the participation of developing countries. It means, it does not recognize the atmosphere rights of the current and future generation by the developing countries while bestowing the same on the current generation by industrialized countries of green house gas, not based on equity but on the basis of current emissions.

The world is stressing on the percentage of reduction being targeted by a country. In the Kyoto Protocol number game, anything that helps increase the emission in the base year, especially because of activities that have since ceased or reduced, immediately gives the country a head start. Emissions trading, joint implementation and clean development mechanism, further provide opportunities to borrow emission reduction from other countries where 'emission reduction' is already taking place because of a slowing down of the economy. Countries, which promise a higher percentage reduction, are seen as good players and those arguing for a lower percentage are seen as difficult ones. For example, if a developing country were to achieve energy efficiency in a big way, then it would already have an energy efficient economy by the time its base year is set and then high percentage reductions on that base year would be not only difficult to achieve but also too expensive. On the contrary, if that country were to persist in the use of high emission technologies and fossil fuels, then by the time its base year is set, it could easily agree to stick to high percentage reduction and look good in front of the world. Where as those who have already taken advance action and contributed proportionately less to the atmospheric greenhouse gas concentration would look bad. Thus, the strategy spelt out in the protocol provides non-Annex I countries with a perverse incentive to perpetuate their current rate greenhouse gas emissions and make it even worse, if possible.

Art 12 defines the Clean Development Mechanism (CDM) which has been identified as mechanism for North-South cooperation in combating climate change. The Kyoto Protocol says that the purpose of CDM is to allow developing countries to assist parties in Annex I in achieving compliance with their quantified emission limitation and reduction commitments. There has been no other role left for the developing countries expect helping the Annex I countries in combating climate change. The only rationale for joint implementation is the one that was outlined by the Government of Norway in the early 1990s. The argument by the Norwegian government was that cutting future carbon dioxide emissions in developing countries is less expensive and cheaper than cutting those in industrialized countries. This means the industrialized countries need not be bound by any kind of commitment to reduction of greenhouse gas emission at their home front, and yet meet their carbon dioxide emission reduction targets by investing in joint implementation projects in developing countries.

Many experts and countries are of the view that it is not really very expensive to reduce emission in developed countries. What is at stake is the political cost, as people may not relish higher energy prices and also a change in their life pattern and style. Democratic governments will not risk the discontentment of people, by recourse to such unpalatable measures. Once the developing countries attain high levels of energy efficiency with the investment and assistance from developed countries, the latter will no longer feel any economic incentive to continue investment in the developing countries. Since the developed countries have not taken any step to reduce emissions on their domestic front, the threats of global warming will loom large thrusting pressures on the developing countries to cut down emissions on their own. This will prove very expensive for these developing countries. The CDM does not answer the question: what will be the form of North-South cooperation then? In other words, it allows the current generation of the developing countries to sell off cheaper emission-control options today leaving the future generation gripped with high-cost options.

The worst aspect of the Kyoto protocol is that barring the small amounts that the industrialized and heaviest emitters of green house gases are expected to reduce as a percentage of their current emission, these countries are bestowed with full entitlement to their heavy current emission without taking into account their past emissions and differential responsibilities. The final level of emissions that industrialized countries are expected to reach in their first commitment period from 2008 to 2012 is described as their assigned amount. But in the Kyoto protocol this assigned amount has gone well beyond being a mere target to be reached. It has been turned into a right by giving developed countries several property rights over these assigned amount, the right of a nation to trade any part of the assigned amount it is not going to use in the first commitment period for use in future commitment periods.

This provision of rights over the assigned amounts of industrialized countries, which takes them well beyond being mere targets to be reached, has not only opened up opportunities for hot air to be traded but also left developing countries without any entitlements of their own. Even though their per capita emissions are both currently and have historically been low, they cannot back any emissions for use by their future generations. Measures to combat climate change must be based on two key elements as identified in Art. 3 of the Framework Convention on Climate Change (FCCC)-These should bring benefits to both the current and future generations, and they should be built on the basis of equity. Pathetically there is nothing in the Kyoto protocol that comes as a testament to these two key elements being adhered to. Entitlements built around current emissions have been created on the basis of a most unjust principle, and there is spectacular absence of protection given to the rights of the future generations living in the developing countries.[55]

Going beyond Kyoto to Stabilize CO_2

The cutdown in the emission of carbon dioxide to the atmosphere as agreed to by the industrialized rich in the Kyoto treaty are like a drop in the ocean. It shows their lukewarm response to the magnitude of the crisis and the threats that global warming will pose to humanity in future. They seem to have ignored the wake up warning given by IPCC. Even if global annual emission of carbon dioxide and fossil fuel burning air stabilized at present levels, a near doubling of pre-industrial atmospheric concentrations would still occur by 2100, which would probably result in the onset of climate change. To avert this threat, it further suggested that global emissions be reduced by 60% by 2050 and stabilized thereafter. But the current government policies and business practices are driving emissions in exactly opposite direction. It also predicted a 70% increase in global emissions by 2025. This increase will likely trigger climate catastrophe for millions of people in low-lying coastal regions around the world.[56]

In order to have a safe atmosphere permitting a fair share of access to the global atmosphere as a waste dump to all the nations, Westing suggested a more radical step. According to him, "to achieve the goal of safe atmospheric carbon dioxide levels will require overall reductions of the order of 50% present world wide emission levels, that is, to the levels of about the year 1965.[57]

The level of CO_2 emissions to which the rich industrialized countries agreed to climb down, is far below the suggested levels and appear to be too inadequate to combat the spectre of global warming.

US opposition: Exploiting Scientific Uncertainties

The United States all along opposed the idea of a strong climate treaty setting a very high target, on the ground that it would impact its economy.[58] But studies show that with a very minimal impact on the economy, green house gases can be reduced through sensible policies and international cooperation. On the best case scenario they predict stimulated economic growth.[59]

Such a goal, though expensive is achievable without insurmountable social disruptions.[60] The kind of response and address needed to combat the crisis, the Kyoto meet failed to winnow from the rich industrialized North, who are, being the biggest polluters, expected to set the target.

This means, to achieve the goal, a gradual though not immediate overhaul of its pattern of economy and development has to take place simultaneously with digging out alternatives to cope with the situation. The core position peremptorily occupied by the US and its allies in the world economic structure with the developing world plummeting to the periphery coupled with its paradigm of development based on combustion of fossil fuel technology and industrialization, being accepted as a universal model of development, hence increasingly redounded to the economic bonanza of the North. The predominant role that the US and its allies play in the world economy may remain fundamentally central to the success of any climate treaty in future a very high target for these countries for reduction of CO_2 emissions. This remains the million-dollar question whether the US and its allies are in a position to overcome this kind of limitation and impact that the treaty will be having on their economy.

A study by Electric Power Research Institute, an industry R & D organization, estimates that after discounting to present value, the cost to US economy of cutting CO_2 emissions by 20% would be US $800 billion to US $3.6 million.[61] Attainment of a higher target than this would add much more to this. The industrial lobby often used to rely on those scientific predictions, which say that global warming is uncertain.

This is the kind of pressure tactics put on the government, to which as it is alleged, the US government caves in. Industry supporters of the US policy point out that if the uncertainties are great, so too are the consequences of misjudgement. If it transpires that the planet is not experiencing a significant climate change, they argue, the money wasted will run into billions of dollars. The US-based Global Climate Coalition (GCC), founded in 1989 with American Petroleum Institute, Shell Oil, Exxon, General Motors and more than 40 other corporations as members, is the biggest, and most powerful of these corporate think tanks. Since 1994, it has spent more than US $1 million annually to downplay the threat of global warming and climate change. The Information Council for the Environment (ICE), another US-based corporate coalition, was formed in 1991. Comprising the National Coal Associations, the Western Fuels Association and Edison Electrical Institute, ICE launched a US $500, 000 advertising campaign roping in Patrick Michaels a leading scientist from the University of Virginia's department of environmental services propagating global warming as a myth not a fact. To create public opinion in their favour, in September 1997 US automobile manufacturers and oil companies launched a US $13 million advertisement blitz convincing the public that a strong climate treaty would result in spiralling price rise and would benefit the poor in the South and the US consumers were to foot the bill.[62] In short, politics intervenes in interpretations of science and in policy to address climate change.

Putting a price tag on green house gas (GHG) emissions and putting them on the market will not work. Nor will allowing countries to reach their emission targets by planting trees or using other biological carbon traps like wetlands, farmlands and pasturelands. The reason ignored by the architects of the Kyoto Protocol, is simply the overwhelming uncertainly involved in these methods. With poor data and a poor understanding of how GHGs move between the air, soil, plants, animals and water, it will be impossible to police whether countries have actually reduced their emissions. A study released in August 2000 by the International Institute for Applied Systems Analysis(IIASA), Austria, titled *Full Carbon Account for Russia*, reveals how the protocol is an open invitation to cheat by reporting unreal success in reducing GHGs.

Article 3.3 of the protocol allows industrialized countries to use sinks to meet their emissions reduction commitments through afforestation, reforestation and deforestation (ARD) activities. Article 3.4 provides for the possibility of meeting reduction commitments through activities 'additional' to ARD, such as sustainable forest management or adopting farming methods that increase uptake of carbon dioxide by agricultural soils. But these two articles make the Kyoto Protocol impossible to verify, says IIASA. Scientists' understanding of carbon movements even on a gross level is fraught with large uncertainly which makes fine calculation such as those needed to verify the protocol virtually impossible. For instance, on the global level, as much as 25 per cent of atmospheric carbon dioxide remains unaccounted for in the known terrestrial and oceanic sinks.[63]

Yet, uncertainly in reporting carbon movements is an issue that has been largely ignored by the Intergovernmental Panel on Climate Change (IPCC), which actually advocates 'partial accounting' IPCC argues that in order to implement the protocol, countries need not account for all source and traps of carbon, but can restrict themselves to carbon stock changes since 1990 in lands designated as sinks under the protocol. Partial carbon accounting is restricted to emission from fossil fuel combustion and cement production, as opposed to a more comprehensive exercise of full carbon accounting.

A May 2000 report of IPCC, on 'land use, change and forestry' (LULUCF) mentions various sources of uncertainty but does not define uncertainty and does not provide a way to verify results in the face of this uncertainty. It suggests that countries should learn to eliminate uncertainty over time through a process of trial and error in practice; countries would construct a tool to tell them which direction their emissions changes go but not whether the goal is verifiable.

IIASA carried out a full carbon accounting for Russia to see whether the accounts add up by the end of the day. A full carbon accounting was done for 1990, the base year of the protocol and for 2010, based on three alternative economic growth paths, generating different carbon emissions. IIASA monitored even those changes in the biosphere, which are not taken into consideration under the protocol. Their study includes all stages of carbon cycle including carbon trapped or released by soils, flora, decomposing organic matter even considering carbon carried by river waters which becomes sediment in the sea.

The study goes into great detail to identify interactions between carbon and land, water, air, animals and plants. For instance, IIASA identified 15 different types of soil with different carbon respiration profiles, and calculated mean temperatures that precipitates or decrease respiration. The study found that the emission intensity varies to a great extent depending on soil type and area temperatures, with emissions increasing as temperature and humidity increases.

For instance, the steppe zone emits the most carbon in Russia-it occupies 9 per cent of the total soil area in the country, but accounts for almost 17 per cent of carbon emissions from soil. The tundra zone, on the other hand, has a lower number of biologically active days due to colder weather. Though it occupies 16 per cent of Russia's soil surface, it generates only 11 per cent of carbon through soil respiration.[64] There is also a large variation in the rate at which carbon accumulates in the soil, depending on the productivity of vegetation, physical and biological conditions in the soil and past history of disturbances. Some scientists go far as to say that no country can present a convincing estimate of carbon content in soils, whereas milder views are that the uncertainty range for carbon content in US agricultural soils, for instance, is plus or minus 40 per cent.[65]

Calculating the exact carbon content of forests presents its own hurdles. An area for potential mistakes is in converting volume of forest into mass of wood and then converting mass of wood into carbon content. Or simply defining a forest and its boundaries, or insufficient remote sensing data to decide forest densities, or telling 'like' plots from 'unlike' plots. A forest's carbon balance is a delicate equilibrium between the activities of respiration and photosynthesis, and small changes can turn a forest from carbon sink to a source. For instance, a study of 15 European mountain ecosystems found vast differences between their forest carbon balance.[66] High latitude forests show more volatile carbon balances than low latitude forests. Old high latitude forests tend to change from absorbing carbon to releasing carbon during mild winters. In total, forests varied from being net sources to being net sinks. For its study, IIASA classified forests by climatic zones, tree species and age of trees. Forest growth was classified into crown wood, foliage, roots and shrubs. Disturbances such as fires or pests were also taken into account.

Assessing fossil fuel emissions is also fraught with crippling amounts of uncertainty. One of the major sources of uncertainty is related to unmonitored losses during extraction, transportation and storage. For instance, long and aging pipelines may have caused one-half to two-third of annual methane emissions from the gas industry in early 1990s. The total figure of uncertainty in Russian fugitive methane emissions from oil and gas activity is as high as plus or minus 30-40 per cent.[67]

IIASA found that in Russia, soil respiration is the largest source of carbon, followed by emissions from the energy sector, animal respiration, and disturbances such as fires, harvests and pests. Meanwhile, primarily forests, followed by grasslands and shrubs, agriculture and wetlands absorb carbon. This full carbon account is complemented by expert assessments of uncertainty for all categories of sinks and sources identified by the study. It was found that Russia emitted 527 million tons of Carbon (mtC) into the atmosphere in 1990. But once uncertainty industrialization added to this number, emissions for 1990 are anywhere within the range of 155 and 1209 mtC.[68]

With such a large range of uncertainty in emissions, a small decrease such as the 5 per cent called for by the protocol is practically invisible. It is impossible to know whether Russia carries out a decrease of 100 million tons when the calculation has an error margin of 682 mtC. The stifling uncertainty seems to occur for all nations-for example, another project that developed full carbon accounting for Austria showed the same problems of verification of carbon movements. The findings are not better for Norway, where uncertainty of GHG emissions is as high as plus or minus 20 per cent.

The uncertainty of whether a ton of reduced emission claimed by a country trying to meet its Kyoto target is really a ton or just 700 kg can bring the Kyoto Protocol to its knees. Cheating can range from doing nothing to prevent losses in mining, transportation and storage of fossil fuel to falsifying reports of forestry projects claiming to absorb carbon dioxide, relying on poor measurements, ignoring leakage from biological sinks and many other cases which will be impossible to monitor. If the architects of Kyoto ignore the risks of uncertainty and allow land management, forestry and other biological sink projects to claim credits; cheating or suspicions of cheating will gain ground and will kill the momentum for an effective global policy to arrest climate change.

Any system that removes carbon dioxide from the atmosphere is a 'carbon sink'. The oceans and terrestrial ecosystems like vegetation and soils are the two known 'natural' sinks. The processes of photosynthesis, respiration and decomposition control their role in the carbon cycle. Over the past 150 years, oceans and terrestrial ecosystems have absorbed about 60 per cent of carbon dioxide emissions caused by human activities.[69]

Plant remove carbon dioxide from the atmosphere via photosynthesis, a process where sunlight facilitates conversion of carbon dioxide and water into glucose and oxygen. Trees rapidly absorb carbon dioxide during growth and as they reach maturity, the rate of absorption stabilizes. A mature oak can contain about 3 tons of carbon and a hectare of plantation forest can hold around 200 tons of carbon.[70] The complementary process of respiration, which helps plants to derive energy by breaking down organic compounds, releases carbon dioxide back into atmosphere. Carbon dioxide is also returned to the atmosphere when plants decay, burn or are cut. Soils get their carbon content from plants and store vast amounts of it as compared to plants and forests.

In the ocean, phytoplanktons, which are microscopic plants, convert carbon dioxide into organic carbon through photosynthesis. This carbon is stored in the deep ocean when micro-organism and other higher life forms that consume them die and settle down at the bottom. However, the uptake by oceanic sinks is limited by the quantity of carbon dioxide present in sea water and the slow rate of mixing between water from the surface and deep water. The transfer of carbon deep down into the oceans is important as it is stored for relatively longer periods.

What is LULUCF?

Human activities of 'land use land use change and forestry' (LULUCF) increase or decrease the amount of carbon dioxide absorbed by terrestrial sinks. 'Land use' refers to the sum total of activities undertaken on a certain land area including grazing and timber extraction, which release carbon trapped in terrestrial sinks, and conservation efforts, which lead to increased carbon dioxide sequestration.

Clearing forests for agricultural use, conversion of grassland to cropland and abandoning cropland or pastureland qualify as 'land use' change activities. From 1850 to 1998, land use change led to an emission of about 134 billion tonnes of Carbon (gtC) into the atmosphere. This represents a share of 33 per cent of the total emissions in this period due to fossil fuel burning and cement production, and land use change.[71] 'Forestry', meanwhile, includes wide range of activities like planting, and tending of growing trees, pest control, fire management, wildlife protection and production of non-time-products.

How does the Kyoto Protocol deal with LULUCF?

Kyoto Protocol has two articles relating to land use, land use change and forestry activities. Article 3.3 of the protocol allows countries to get credits for reducing carbon dioxide concentrations through land use change and forestry activities that are a result of direct actions. Only afforestation, reforestation and deforestation (ARD) activities undertaken since 1990 are eligible under this article. Consequent changes produced in the quantity of carbon present in a system should be measured in each commitment period and should be verifiable.

Article 3.4 discusses changes in content of carbon in terrestrial sinks caused by human induced land-use change and forestry activities, and activities in agricultural soil. Possible examples in this category are forests management, grazing land and crop management. The activities considered here should be additional to those mentioned in the article 3.3. This article does not have a list of eligible activities and advises countries to take a decision on this. A consensus on which activities are to be considered and how they should be included is yet to emerge. This decision in the second and subsequent commitment periods. A country can claim credit for such an activity in the first commitment period (2008-2012) provided the activity has taken place since 1990.

In addition, a decision on the eligibility of LULUCF projects under article12, on the Clean Development Mechanism (CDM), and article 6, Investment (JI) is yet to be taken. The issue of allowing industrialized countries to buy credits for LULUCF activities under CDM is likely to be particularly contentious.

What are the Problems with LULUCF?

A report released by Intergovernmental Panel on Climate Change (IPCC) at the twelfth meeting of subsidiary bodies highlighted several scientific uncertainties surrounding the definition of terms related to the LULUCF activities.

What is a Forest?

Article 3.3 of the Kyoto Protocol can be implemented only after consensus is reached among countries on the exact definition of a forest. Most forest definitions are based on a minimum 'canopy cover', but the IPCC report on LULUCF says a common figure for canopy cover for forest in various regions is insufficient. If a forest was defined as a mass of trees with a canopy cover of say, 70 per cent then areas with sparse vegetation would not be considered forests. They could be cleared without any accounting for the resulting carbon dioxide emissions. Similarly, a very low threshold of, say, 10 per cent, allows dense forests to be heavily degraded without the particular activity qualifying as deforestation. Alternatively, the forests may be enhanced without the actions being considered as reforestation. The IPCC report suggests that biome-specific definitions be adopted, like a low canopy covers for savannas and high canopy cover for moist forests.

Reforestation, meanwhile, is commonly defined as planting of trees on land that has just been harvested. Here too, controversy arises if the definition for deforestation does not include harvesting. Then countries will be able to use the amount of carbon dioxide sequestered due to regeneration towards fulfilling Kyoto commitments. However, in such conditions corresponding emissions due to harvesting will go unaccounted for.

The implementation of article 3.4 requires accurate definitions for 'additional' (to ARD activities) land use change and forestry (LUCF) activities and activities that improve sequestration by agricultural soils. When an additional LUCF activity is interpreted broadly, the net effect of all practices such as reduced tillage and irrigation in cropland management, in a specific area is considered to measure carbon content. A narrow definition, on the other hand, means various practices undertaken on an area of land are taken individually to calculate the net change in the quantity of stored carbon. The way an activity is defined has implications in terms of separating naturally occurring changes from those due to human actions. A narrow definition can help in identifying the causes of decrease or increase in carbon content.

Direct or Indirect

A difficult condition attached to ARD activities is that these should be 'direct' in nature. IPCC explains this by saying that the closer in time and space the activity is to impact, the more direct it is. The reasons for engaging in a particular activity would also help in determining how direct it is. 'Indirect' effects would include climate change phenomenon like EI Nino cycles, and carbon dioxide 'fertilization' (where higher concentration of carbon dioxide in the atmosphere leads to plants absorbing more of it through photosynthesis). Such effects would significantly affect carbon dioxide sequestration during the commitment period of five years as prescribed by the protocol. Terrestrial ecosystems sequester an average of 2.2 gtC per year through natural regeneration and such indirect effects. IPCC warns that if countries are allowed to receive credits for even 50 per cent of sinks from these factors, they will be able to meet their Kyoto commitments without lifting a finger.[72]

However, given the present availability of scientific tools, separating direct effects from indirect ones will be very difficult, if not impossible. Existing methods cannot precisely determine either the total or incremental amounts of carbon dioxide absorbed due to indirect effects like carbon dioxide fertilization. At a project level, this may only be possible when sequestration in a land area under the LULUCF project is compared with an area where no project is carried out.

Human Induced

LULUCF activities must also qualify as 'human induced', calling for yet another precise definition that distinguishes 'human induced' effects from natural effects. Factors such as natural cycles of disturbance and recovery from fires, pests and diseases could lead to significant changes over the five-year commitment period of the Kyoto Protocol. Sometimes these natural incidents may drive human decisions to undertake a LULUCF activity. When a forest devastated by floods, with no scope for regeneration, is converted into a cropland, the activity cannot necessarily be called human induced – more so when emissions from these natural disturbances are not counted but the subsequent sequestration is considered. Equally confounding is the fact that human actions may contribute towards natural occurrences, like fires and pest infestations. Management practices may specify that certain fires be allowed to burn for ecological reasons.

Techniques are available to measure the changes in carbon content, but attributing a given change to a particular cause is difficult. Even the most direct measurements on small areas cannot distinguish between intentional and natural causes for this change. Narrow definitions facilitate this separation of human induced activities from natural activities. Comparison between managed and unmanaged lands may help in quantifying changes occurring due to factors that are not natural, but even this technique may be expensive when applied over large areas.

No permanent fix: Another problem with including LULUCF activities is that they tend not to be permanent. While reducing fossil fuel consumption provides a long-term solution to the problem of global warming, sequestered carbon dioxide can easily be released back to the atmosphere by fires, pests, encroachments, or even climatic variations like drought or storms.

The IPCC report suggests that establishing projects in different areas may reduce damages, as geographical separation will prevent fires, pests, and diseases from spreading from one project area to another. Ensuring accounting of reductions even if it happened due to natural reasons, will help in fixing liability on a country in case the project is disrupted. Projects may be assigned a minimum lifetime or limited credits may be issued in view of the risks, However, such measures help only to a limited extent as the stored carbon may eventually be emitted.[73]

Leakfproof: A LULUCF project may indirectly lead to carbon dioxide emissions outside the project's geographical limits. Since these emissions may not be taken into account, such spillover effects are called leaks. For instance, a forest management activity that restricts the amount of land available for agriculture purposes or logging may compel local communities to clear forest elsewhere leading to carbon dioxide emissions. It is necessary to include such emissions, which do not fall within the confines of project area, in calculations of changes in carbon dioxide levels.

However, it is a daunting and often impossible task to anticipate these impacts and attribute them to a particular project.

Cost versus uncertainty: Measuring changes in the quantity of carbon in plants and soils involves a compromise between precision and investment. Sample land areas are considered to assess variations in stored carbon. The greater the number of samples, the more precise the estimate. However, the more the number of samples, the greater is the cost incurred by countries undertaking the project.

Countries need to make substantial investment in human resources, technology and infrastructure to implement measurement methods. Additionally, carrying out such measurements on a regular basis, as required by the protocol, will entail high operational expenses. Most industrialized countries have, at least, a part of the infrastructure, like well-equipped laboratories, accurate maps for the types and vegetation, and trained personnel, in place. Even then the incremental cost to perform these measurements regularly on a national scale may be substantial and particularly taxing for developing countries. For instance, Australia is investing US $5 million annually upgrade its existing system. Developing countries, with less resources, will be expected to establish similar systems when it is their turn to undertake emission reductions.[74]

Moreover, the report points out that the effect of climate change on the sequestration potential of sinks is also uncertain. Forests could behave very differently with increasing concentrations of carbon dioxide in the atmosphere. Scientists feel that with rising temperature sinks may absorb lesser amounts of carbon dioxide.

The rising concentrations of carbon dioxide in the atmosphere and the rise in temperature may eventually turn sinks into sources in a few decades. As concentration increases, plants soak more carbon dioxide through photosynthesis; this process is called carbon dioxide fertilization. Respiration process, on the other hand, releases carbon dioxide. Scientists project that fertilization may start to diminish at higher concentrations while respiration increases with rising temperature. Therefore, the overall capacity to fix carbon sink become a source. The IPCC report mentions that the global sink is likely to decline from its current level of approximately 2gtC per year and become a source within a few decades.[75]

A parallel hypothesis suggests that the present sink itself may be a temporary consequence of carbon dioxide fertilization. Respiratory losses may eventually overtake removal by fertilization converting sinks into sources.[76]

Should Developing Countries Support LULUCF Activities under CDM?

According to the IPCC, there is a large potential for LULUCF activities in developing countries, particularly for additional activities (like forest and cropland management). In fact, the entire industrialized country reduction commitment of around 700 million tonnes of carbon by 2010 can be met from a additional activities in developing countries alone. LULUCF activities under sinks would provide some of the cost-effective mitigation opportunities.

On the one hand the annual deforestation rate in developing countries of around 15million hectares (mha) since 1980 is likely to increase, at least for the next 10-30 years. To stop this trend by slowing deforestation as well as enhancing afforestation in the already degraded lands, developing countries need technological developments and transfer, appropriate policies, programmes and funding. Therefore, some scientists are of the view that the developing world should use every opportunity for forest conservation, sustainable forestry and reforestation, including CDM.[77]

Including LULUCF projects under CDM is also one way of ensuring that CDM funds reach the indigenous communities and do not just go into the pockets of the industry. Agro forestry based agricultural development is a traditional practice in many developing countries, offering opportunities to provide benefits to rural societies. In India, for instance, more than 70 per cent people live in rural areas and rely mostly on forest for their basic biomass needs, such as cattle feed, fuelwood food and shelter. Establishment and management of village woodlots for fuel wood and fibre, intercropping systems (mixture of tree, agronomic and horticulture crops), and shelter belts or windbreaks are ways to combine improved food production, harvestable wood by the local poor, and carbon sequestration through the forestry component, all within the same system. There are suggestions that establishment of one hectare of agro forestry in the tropics could offset deforestation of 5-10 hectares (ha), for meeting local needs. Such systems may store up to 50 tonnes of carbon per hectare (tC/ha).[78]

In addition, sustainable bioenergy plantations could offer an alternative to fossil fuels. Plantations on 40 mega hectares (Mha) of degraded land in India could produce 160 million tonnes (mt) of biomass per year after 8 successive years of plantation as replacement for fossil fuels. They thus have the potential to reduce total carbon emission of about 1.75 billion tonnes (gt), 3.86 gt and 8.07 gt in the next 25 years, 50 years and 100 years respectively.[79]

But, on the other hand, there is the fear that the race for credits will overpower the immediate concerns of developing countries of improving the quality of life of the rural poor. Many indigenous groups in the developing world have opposed the inclusion of sinks in CDM out of fear that industries will start viewing forests as gigantic carbon sponges, rather than the source of livelihood for the poor. Fast-growing monoculture plantation could replace bio-diverse forests, which provide a wide range of services to poor communities. Old-growth forests could be cut to make way for these plantations.

This is indeed a genuine fear, which is already coming true as industry starts grabbing land for carbon sequestration. India has already seen several attempts on part of the paper and pulp industry to grab so called 'degraded' land, which nevertheless provides a range of services to the poor. The industry has tried to buy this land from the government for commercial plantations that the communities will not be allowed to access.

Short Term Focus

The Kyoto Protocol had a short-term focus. But any reasonable trajectory of emissions in the future ought to show a rise for same decades and a rapid decline late in the century. There are several reasons as outlined by Thomas C. Schelling[79] First, the technologies needed to drastically reduce fossil fuel consumption through alternative energy sources, greater energy efficiency, and sequestration of carbon dioxide or its removal from fuel are not developed.

Second, it is economical to use durable equipment until it is due for replacement; early scrapping is wasteful. Thirdly, the richer countries will almost certainly have higher incomes in the future and be better able to afford drastic changes in energy use. Finally, the economic trajectory for emission over the coming century will differ substantially among the developed countries. Any reasonable rationing scheme should contemplate a time line of at least a century not a few decades. But no possible consensus exists on how much total emission should be allowed for the coming century. In short, the Kyoto Protocol's exclusive focus on the short term neglected the crucial importance of expanding worldwide research and development of technologies to make severe reduction feasible later in the century.

The provision of emission trading is perfectionist and impractical. The problem with trading regimes is that initial quotas are negotiated to reflect what each nation can reasonably be expected to reduce. Any country that is tempted to sell part of an emission quota will realize that the regime is continually subject to renegotiation, so selling any excess is tantamount to admitting it got a generous allotment the last time around. It then sets itself up for stiffer negotiation most time. The proper approach is not a trading system but a financial contribution from the rich countries to an institution that would help finance energy efficient and decarbonized technologies in the developing world.[80]

In contrast with other regimes, what is found in the case of Kyoto Protocol is that commitments were made not to action but to result that were to be measured after a decade or more. This approach has disadvantages. An obvious one is that no one can tell, until close to the target date, which nations are on course to meet their goals.

Uncertainty remains embedded to the Kyoto Protocol about how much carbon dioxide can be absorbed into various natural sinks-oceans and forests – or sequestered underground or deep in the ocean. IPCC has never proposed what concentration of green house gases would constitute unacceptable damage.[81]

Future of the Treaty Shrouded in Uncertainty

The Kyoto climate treaty seems to be shrouded in uncertainty, as the US could not ratify the treaty on the pretext that India, China and other developing nations did not participate meaningfully in the quantitative emission-reduction commitment programmes which are so far exempt from such commitments under the treaty. To keep up anti-treaty rumbling alive in the US Denver-based Western Fuels Association has been financing papers by some scientists who propose that "having more carbon dioxide in the atmosphere will be good not bad". This attitude has been reflected in the American Congress.[82]

The US Senators signed the Byrd-Hagel Resolution which stated that the Senate would not ratify any treaty to reduce emissions until there was meaningful participation from key developing countries. This is a major stumbling block to the ongoing negotiation, on climate change. The International Conference on climate change in Buenos Aires saw the developing countries ranged against the US, which was trying to impose greenhouse gas reduction targets on them. The US also managed to win over developing countries such as Argentina to its clean development mechanism programmes. The developing countries accused the developed countries of non-performance and the developed countries accused the developing countries of non-participation. A shift was perceptible in the position of the EU away from the US. An emerging alliance between EU and G-77 was marked when Dominique Voynet, French Minister for environmental affairs took up cudgels for the G-77 position against voluntary commitment and for a principle of convergence. Given that, under US law an unratified treaty can remain pending indefinitely, the fate of the treaty hangs in uncertainty. Only strong world public opinion and pressures both from the South, the EU and other countries may bind the US to its commitments agreed to in Kyoto.

The North's advocating of an equity principle on the issue of management of the atmosphere is very much opposed by the South. This will be major stumbling block to future negotiation, unless and until the North provides leadership to the whole world by unilaterally reducing emission of carbon dioxide, which encourage other nations to follow suit. According to a US study, if equity was adopted as the guiding principle for managing the atmosphere, the industrialized countries had exhausted their quota of carbon dioxide by 1986. Morally, they ought to stop all carbon dioxide emissions right away.[83]

To achieve the goal of equity in controlling carbon dioxide emissions will require the apportionment to each of the 169 nations of a permissible maximum release. Such apportionment will have to be based on national area not on population, wealth or past national arrogation. Total land area on earth within national boundaries excluding Antarctica is 133 million square kilometers. One carbon dioxide release chit for each of these square kilometers will have to be created, each one permitting the discharge of 133 millionth of the total permissible amount. Each nation will then be awarded the number of such one-square-kilometer chits corresponding to the size of its national territory. Since many developing nations would not yet be making use of their chits, they may lease temporarily their unused chits to the developed nations who have already gone beyond their permissible chits while building up their industrial and transportation bases.[84] The money earned this way can be harnessed for exploring alternative models of development by the South countries.

Kyoto Alternative Strategy of the United States

US new climate policy in total rejection of Kyoto Protocol and the need for capping total GHG emissions, calls for a cut in GHG intensity by 17.5 per cent over the next 10 years. The policy announced by President George W. Bush at National Oceanic and Atmospheric Administration on 14 February 2002 will actually cause emissions to increase by about 30 per cent over 1990 levels in 2010 contrary to the Kyoto commitments that it had to bring down its emissions to seven per cent below 1990 emission levels. Between 1990 and 2000 though GHG intensity fell by about 17 per cent, the emissions increased by 14.7 per cent. With GDP increase projected to be almost the same as in the 1990s, the emissions will increase by about 14 per cent even as GHG intensity declines by 17.5 per cent. Among other measures power plant emissions of sulphur dioxide, nitrogen oxides and mercury will be cut by about 70 per cent. However no such reductions are proposed for carbon dioxide. The US policy and actions are being guided more by the politics of fuel economy than the wider issue of CO_2 regulation. The US Kyoto alternative strategy has become worthless as far as its effectiveness in reducing total GHG emissions or even slowering their growth are concerned.[85]

Equal Per Capita Entitlements

In order to maintain equity, the Centre for Science and Environment (CSE) has devised 'equal per capita entitlements' which could be built on the following premises:[86] The emissions absorbed annually by the global atmospheric sinks could be distributed equally amongst all the people of the world thus providing each person with an equal entitlement. A long long-term per emission convergence target could be identified and each person could be given that as an entitlement. On the basis of the latest scientific data about the imminence of threats of global warming this target could go up and down.

Future atmospheric concentration targets for different greenhouse gases could be agreed upon keeping in mind that the targeted concentration does not threaten to seriously destabilize the global climate, and then the global emissions budget that would allow humanity to reach that concentration target could be equally distributed among all nations on the basis of equal per capita entitlements. Once such a concentration and convergence strategy is accepted the national entitlements can be phased in towards a convergence point of equal per capita entitlements over successive commitment periods. At the same time the targeted atmospheric concentration could be kept subject to review based on latest scientific information available.[87]

According to them, the convergence principle towards a just, equitable and sustainable norm can be the only rational principle. Those who have higher emission can come down to the norm and those who have lower emission can climb up to the norm. On the grounds of economic efficiency that the developing countries provide the opportunity to reduce emissions more cheaply than the industrialized countries, international cooperation sought from developing countries to combat climate change cannot be said as based on just and equitable principles.

US withdrawal from Kyoto Protocol

Soon after assumption office, US President George W. Bush reneged on a campaign pledge to curb emissions from coal-powered generating plants. He then unveiled his administration's energy plan which is basically a short cut to climate hell. As seen recently in the Hague and Bonn Conference of Parties to the climate change convention, the US withdrew from the rest of the world community working desperately to begin to address the climate crisis. Stabilizing the climate requires global emissions reduction of 60 to 80 per cent. This will require a far more radical approach than is embodied in the current draft protocol. A recent study published in the journal *Nature* found that unless the world gets half its energy from non-carbon sources by 2018, the planet will experience an inevitable quadrupling of heat trapping atmospheric carbon concentrations near the end of the century. Against this backdrop, the Kyoto Protocol falls far short of its goal of climate stabilization.[87] According to Prof. Adil Nazam, the net result arrived at the Hague and Bonn conferences with the US shadow falling entrenchedly large on Japan and EU, who acted as its proxies, is that the Kyoto Protocol is now even more (or rather less) of a paper victory than earlier. But more than that, it represents a wasted opportunity. Given that the largest polluter is no longer part of the signatories, and the provision of more loopholes for use of sinks and hot air trades, the Protocol will now do even less than it was originally going to do in terms of reducing actual emissions or concentrations.[88]

Per Capita the Only Way

Support from unexpected quarters came as a welcome surprise for developing countries such as India, which have demanded that international climate change negotiations be based on the principle of equity. A report released by the UK's Royal Commissions on Environmental Pollution (RCEP) in June 2000 said that an effective, enduring and equitable climate agreement will require greenhouse gas (GHG) emission quotas to be allocated to nations on a simple and equal per capita basis.

The UK government is expected to respond in writing in the form of a commentary on the report, an explanation of how existing policies and programmes can be reconciled with it and what new policies-if any-the government is considering in light of the report. So far, the UK has held a position of indifference towards the South's demand to calculate GHG emissions on a per capita basis as each human being has an equal entitlement to the atmosphere.

As a system of per capita entitlements cannot enter into force immediately, the report proposes 'contraction and convergence'. "Initially shares are 'as is', that is, approximately proportional to each country's income", explains Aubrey Meyer from the London-based Global Commons Institute, a leading advocate of this approach. "Over an agreed future period of years however, all countries will converge on the same allocation per head of their population in a base year to be agreed.[89]

This means the quotas of industrialized countries fall year by year, while those of developing countries rise until all nations emit equal amounts of GHG per head (convergence). The RCEP report proposes 2050 as the year for convergence. It will also be cut-off date for national populations, that is, further changes in a country's population will not affect its emissions quota.

From then on, after convergence has been achieved, the quotas of all nations would decline together at the same rate (contraction). According to the report, commentators on climate diplomacy have identified contraction and convergence as the leading contender among the various proposals for allocating emissions quotas to nations in the long run. To make an agreement based on per capita allocation quotas more feasible, the report supports emission trading between nations. Countries that wish to emit GHG in excess of their respective quotas would be able to purchase unused quotas at prices that incline other countries to emit less than their quotas.

There are other similarities between the conclusions of the RECP report and the Indian position. The commission also recommends that the international community adopt an upper limit for carbon dioxide concentration in the atmosphere of 550 parts per million (ppm). Current global concentration levels stand at 368 ppm. A target of 550 ppm is not entirely safe because, according to international scientific community, even stabilization at 450 ppm would result in a temperature rise of 0.7^{0}C and a corresponding 10-65 centimeter rise in sea level.

If the contraction and convergence approach and the target of 550 ppm are adopted, the UK's carbon dioxide emissions will have to be reduced by almost 60 per cent from their current level by mid-century, and by almost 80 per cent by 2100. Though carbon dioxide emissions are falling at the moment in the UK, they are expected to rise again as all but one of its existing nuclear power stations will close by 2025. Nuclear power is the main source of carbon-free energy in the country at present.

To achieve the 60 per cent reduction target, RECP recommends reductions in energy demand and a large deployment of renewable energy sources, both of which can be achieved partly through the introduction of a carbon tax. Revenues from this tax could be used to fund other measures of cutting down emissions, such as subsidies and tax relief for energy efficiency improvements and research and development of renewable technologies. Future sources of renewable energy for the UK, says the report, could include energy harnessed from waves, undersea turbines powered by the tidal waves, wind energy and even solar energy.[90]

The Third Proposal

In June 2001, Jan Pronk, president of the failed sixth Conference of parties (COP-6) to the United Nations Framework Convention on Climate Change (UNFCCC), came out with a third compromise proposal in an attempt to resolve 'crunch' issues plaguing the negotiations. He had first come out with a compromise proposal on November 23, 2000 at Cop-6, and had revised it again in April 2001. The third proposal, described below, formed the basis of negotiation at the resumed session of CoP-6 in July 2001.[91]

Funding and Technology Transfer

Pronk suggested setting up an adaptation fund, financed by taking two per cent off the credits generated from projects under the clean development mechanism (CDM). Proceeds from other flexibility mechanism, which involve only industrialized countries, are exempt from such a contribution. He also suggested a special climate change fund to finance technology transfer, capacity building and economic diversification.

Pronk proposed that total annual contributions towards climate change activities should rise to US $1 billion by 2005. Over a certain number of years, the amount to be used towards adaptation programmes should increase to about half of this billion. The commitment is not binding, and unlike the earlier proposal of November 23, 2000 failure to contribute does not result in a levy being imposed on Joint Implementation (JI) projects and emission trading.

Trading Cheap

The third proposal said climate change policies and measure should seek to reduce inequalities in per capita emissions of developing and industrialized countries. Therefore, industrialized countries must meet their emissions reduction targets chiefly through domestic action undertaken since 1990. No quantitative limit was suggested.

The proposal reiterated the Kyoto Protocol provision allows industrialized countries to bank surplus credits from the first commitment period to meet reduction commitments in the second commitment period. Industrialized countries can therefore can buy emissions reduction credits at throwaway prices from developing countries and bank them for future use. Developing countries, having sold the cheap options, will be forced to adopt expensive methods when it is their turn to take on emission reductions in the future.

The proposal did not put forward a 'positive list' of projects allowed under CDM. Host developing countries were left to decide what projects were in line with their sustainable development objectives and national priorities. However, the proposal called on countries to refrain from using nuclear projects under JI and CDM Simplified procedures would apply to specific small-scale projects to facilitate equitable regional distribution of CDM projects. The proposal emphasized that use of public funding in CDM projects should not result in diversion of official development assistance (ODA).

Pronk's proposal directed each industrialized country to keep at least 90 percent of its assigned amount, or five times its greenhouse gas (GHG) emissions in the most recently reviewed inventory, whichever is lower, as reserve. The earlier proposal did not give a choice and asked countries to keep a fixed amount of 70 per cent of their assigned amount as reserve.

The North's Trash Cans

The compromise proposal gave a complex formula to calculate credits from land use, land use change and forestry activities under article 3.3 and 3.4. The Kyoto Protocol, had included under article 3.3 the use of afforestation, reforestation and deforestation activities to absorb carbon dioxide and gain credits, whereas activities under article 3.4 were still open for future agreements. The proposal considered forest, cropland and grazing land management and vegetation as eligible activities under article 3.4. It offers a three tier method to calculate credits arising from these activities in the commitment period (2008-2012).

In the first tier, countries could fully count carbon dioxide removed from the atmosphere through forest management, up to the level of net carbon dioxide emissions (if more carbon dioxide is released due to deforestation, than is absorbed by afforestation and reforestation) reported under article 3.3. But annual credits in this tier were capped at 8.2 million tomes of carbon (mtC). The limit could be extended to 13 mtC, if the country met certain criteria for energy efficiency, forest cover and population density.

Beyond the credits obtained under the first tier, countries could get only 15 percent credits for forest management-A discount factor of 85 per cent was applied to exclude carbon dioxide absorbed due to natural reasons, or due to effects of practices employed before 1990. This was done as article 3.4 calls for separating carbon dioxide absorbed due to human induced activities from absorption occurring naturally. For example, only forest regeneration done intentionally could be considered, and not regeneration without human assistance.

Similarly, carbon dioxide absorption is attributed to activities undertaken before 1990 was not considered, for credits in the first commitment period. It is extremely difficult to attribute muses to the change observed in carbon content and separate human induced effects from natural; and pre1990 from post 1990 emissions. In order to overcome this problem, the proposal took refuge in an arbitrary discount factor Strangely, no discounting was applied to the first tier, even though those credits were no less riddled with such problems. In the third tier, full credits were given for agricultural management (cropland, grazing land management and revegetation). The proposal further imposed an overall limit on the sum total of LULUCF credits gained from the second and third tier, CDM projects, and JI projects. For a country required to reduce its GHG emissions below base year levels, the total should not be more than 50 percent of the country's Kyoto target. For a country allowed to maintain its base year emissions level, or increase its emissions over the base year level, the total should not be more than 2.5 per cent of the country's emissions in the base year. These limits did not apply to credits and debits under article 3.3. The proposal allowed afforestation and reforestation projects under CDM, while forest, grazing and cropland management were excluded.

Ensuing Compliance

The proposal put forward a compliance committee with enforcement and facilitative branches. The facilitative branch would provide advice to countries and assist them in implementing the protocol.

The enforcement branch, which could prescribe legally binding consequences, was to assess industrialized countries' compliance with their commitments and their obligation to put in place a national accounting system to estimate GHG emissions and their absorption by sinks at least by 2007. It would decide a country's eligibility to participate in the flexibility mechanisms. If an industrialized country failed to meet these commitments, the enforcement branch could deduct a certain number of tonnes from the defaulting country's assigned amount in the next commitment period. The number of tonnes deducted would depend on the value by which the country exceeds its assigned amount. As the value increases, the deduction becomes higher.

It asks the defaulting country to submit an action plan detailing measures it proposes to take to meet its commitments. The enforcement branch would review and assess the feasibility of this plan, and suspend the defaulting country's ability to sell assigned amount units under the emissions trading mechanism.

Pronk proposed that emissions reduction targets of industrialized countries in the second commitment period must be decided before 2008 and discussion on the issue should start by 2006

Constraints

Quite not awake to the danger emanating from global warming, the industrialized rich countries have not attested the goal of global equity in controlling carbon dioxide emission as suggested above. Nor have they suo motu reduced carbon dioxide by 50% to the 1965 level. The pressures from NGOs, South countries and above all, the public opinion of the world, may be said as being not enough to bind the North to a target as envisaged above. In spite of the treaty and conventions signed among countries, the fundamental problems remain unsolved. Firstly, the inordinate life style and unrestricted consumption pattern of the North is symbiotically related to carbon dioxide emission and pattern of development. Are the western people ready to have a cut in their standard of living by asking their governments to reduce CO_2 emission to the atmosphere?

Secondly, the very cause of this nuisance to the environment is the ethnocentrism of western paradigm of development based on extraction of fossil fuels and industrialization. The problem of climate change puts a challenge to the prevailing pattern of development. To what extent alternative paradigms conducive to the environment, the life pattern and style and future generation's right to exist, are explored, will determine the nature of the future course of action on the part of the nations of the world to combat the crisis

Modern civilization based on oil is prepared to go to war to secure oil supplies, but is it prepared to face the situation, if the world's oil wells suddenly dry up? Are multinational corporations and energy sectors dominating the modern state in a position to change their structure, power and style of functioning?

According to Pad Green, the solution to climate change requires a revolution to the way society produces and uses energy and in the way people's needs for mobility are met. However, fighting climate change is not just a question of replacing fossil fuels with wind power, biomass, solar or other technologies. As he said, energy renewable technology had environmental impacts, particularly land use (wind power and biomass) and mineral extraction and toxic chemicals.[95]

Thirdly, the question who pollutes the atmosphere needs to be axed, and remains central to the solution of the crisis. Whether the rich North shoulders the responsibility to unilaterally reduce CO_2 to an exemplary extent and accept equity in the share of the access to the atmosphere, always remains in the centre stage. The treaties fail to answer the key question about equity, rights of access to resources and the role of multinational corporations in energy sector with the government lacking the political will to tame them. The developing countries always tried to put equity on the global climate change agenda but failed to find to it US and its allies' acceptability. Recently, the US came out with its own version of equity fashioned by none other than the Pew Centre on Global Climate Change, established in 1998 by the Pew Foundation, which in turn was set up by an oil company called Sun. The Pew Report is called Equity and Global Climate Change: The Complex Elements of Global Fairness.[96] This report has little in the common with what the South demands. According to the report, in line with the 'polluter pays principle' responsibility would include not only who emitted in the past, but also who will emit in the future. That means meaningful participation from South is stressed on. Secondly, if one country can more cheaply reduce emissions than another, and then perhaps it should be asked to do so. Thirdly, all nations should work to the best of their abilities-or with the help of other countries to reduce emissions. So, the report pushes the US argument that developed countries should be allowed to meet their entire commitments under the Kyoto protocol through emission trading without any action at home. This report rejects per capita argument claiming that it creates perverse incentives for population growth.

Fourthly, the countries of the South always trying to oppose any move by the North to bring them within the ambit of climate change treaty, also contribute to the emission of CO_2 to the atmosphere though much less than the North countries do. In their aspiration to attain the level of development the Western countries have reached, the South may add significantly to the emission. Their argument that since they are far behind the western level of industrial development, they should be exonerated from the responsibility to reduce CO_2 emission at their home front sounds logical. Rather than imitating the western pattern of development, the South countries should develop and define development in their own civilizational context. The South countries cannot keep pace with the level of development the North has reached unless and until the people in the North change their luxurious and inordinate life style. So the success of the climate change treaty is very much contingent on the kind of revolution needed in ethnocentrism of western consumption pattern, life style, and economic thinking.

Fifthly, another stumbling block to rich industrialized countries like the US not agreeing to a major or required reduction of carbon dioxide emission to the atmosphere is the great uncertainty associated with climate science. Being a horizon science not a core science[97] global climate change is certainly inter-disciplinary. Since the world's climate involves a continually changing and highly complex set of relations, climate research faces severe obstacles in linking theory and empirical evidence. Climate science relies heavily on elaborate computer models. The most sophisticated of these models are General Circulation Models (GCMs) whose accuracy is tested by comparing their predictions of past global climate with historical data. Modelled predictions of future climate change are based upon incorporating current and projected greenhouse gas emissions into GCMs. "Because of gaps in the data (e.g. cloud behaviour, methane and emissions are to agricultural practices and ability of oceans to absorb CO_2) GCMs should be viewed as heuristic devices rather than reality maps." [98] Since uncertainty is greatest for horizon science like climate change, its perceived legitimacy in policy making should be especially low.[99] That's why this uncertainty is taken advantage of by the rich industrialized North being influenced by their respective industrial lobby to back out from their required commitments to reduction of CO_2. Commitments to reduce green house gas emissions to atmosphere to the level as required for the rich industrialized North, can be binding on these countries only when climate science becomes more certain and accurate.

Lastly, in terms of local pollution and climate effects, the exponential increase in the consumption of fossil fuels contributed to a worldwide quadrupling of green house gas emissions between 1950 and 1995. This corresponds to a quadrupling of Gross World Products during the same period.[100] So this link between economic growth and prosperity, and emissions would be harder to break. If the industrial countries subscribe to the belief that prosperity can be decoupled from green house gas emissions, then governments' willingness to reduce their emissions represents a kind of leap of faith.[101] The only apparent reason for taking that leap is a strong scientific consensus, accuracy and certainty that burning fossil fuels will cause global climate change. Then prosperity will be defined not in terms of fossil fuel-based economic growth, but in terms of what constitutes good for society and recognizes the rights of the future generation's right to atmosphere.

References

1. H.L. Ferguson, ed., Changing Atmosphere: Implications for Global Security (Conference statement, Toronto, 27-30 June 1988), New York: UN General Assembly documents No. A/C2/43/2, 3 October 1988, p. 122.
2. James Mackenzie, Climate, Protection and the National Interest: The Links Among climate change, Air pollution, and energy Sensitivity, WRI, October 1997.
3. Quoted in Anil Agarwal and Anju Sharma, "A farce of a face off", Down to Earth Vol. 6, No. 15, 31 December 1997, p. 29.
4. H.R. Charlson Rodhe and E. Crawford, Svante Arrhenius and the Greenhouse Effect", Ambio, 26, 1997, pp. 2-5.
5. Aant. Elzinga, "From Arrhenius to Megascience: Interplay Between Science and Policy making", Ambio, 26, 1997, pp. 72-80.
6. R.Revelle and H.E. Suess, "Carbon Dioxide Exchange between Atmosphere and Ocean and the Question of an Increase of Atmospheric CO_2 during the Past Decades", Tellus Vol. 9, 1957, pp. 18-27.
7. William W. Kellogg, "Mankind's Impact on Climate: The Evolution of Awareness", Climate Change Vol. 10, 1987, pp. 110-21.
8. W.C. Wang, Y.L. Yung, A.A. Lacis, T.Mo, and J.E. Hansen, "Greenhouse effect due to man made perturbations of trace gases", Science, 194, 1976, pp. 685-690.
9. B.Bolin, B.R. Doors, and R.A. Warrick, The Greenhouse Effect, Climate Change and Ecosystems, SCOPE 29, (Chichester: Wiley 1986)
10. J.T. Houghton, G.J. Jenkins, and J.J. Ephraums, Climate Change, The IPCC Scientific Assessment (Cambridge: Cambridge University Press, 1990).
11. Jill Jager and Tim O' Riordan, *op. cit.,* p. 16.
12. J. Lanchberry and D.Victor, "The role of science in the global climate negotiations", in H. Bergeson ed. Green Globe Yearbook, (Oxford: Oxford University Press, 1995), pp. 29-39.

13. Jill Jager and Tim O' Riordan, *op. cit.,* p. 16.
14. Anil Agarwal, Sunita Narain and Anju Sharma, ed., Global Environmental Negotiations 1, Green, (New Delhi: Centre for Science and Environment, 1999), p. 18.
15. Susan Subak, "The greenhouse index', Environment, March 1991.
16. Anil Agarwal and Sunita Narain, Towards a Green World (New Delhi: Centre for Science and Environment, 1992), p. 29.
17. E.J. Dlugokencky et al., Continuing Decline in the Growth Rate of the Atmospheric Methane Burden, abbreviated draft on climate uniforming and Diagnostic Laboratory website http:// www.cmdl.noaa.gov.ccg/news.html
18. All you Ever Wanted to Know about the Politics of Global Warming, New Scientific Planet Science website, 1999, http:/ / www.cmdl.noaa.gov.ccg/news.html
19. World Resources Institute 1990, World Resources 1990-91: A Guide to the Global Environment (New York: Oxford University Press).
20. Florentine Krause, Energy Policy in the greenhouse, International Project for Sustainable Energy Paths (IPSEP), EL Cerrito Vol. 1, 1989.
21. "A lot of gas" in Down to Earth Vol. 3, No. 19, February 28, 1995, p. 37.
22. *Ibid.*
23. Anil Agarwal and Sunita Narain, Global Warming in an Unequal World (New Delhi: Centre for Science and Environment, 1991).
24. Anil Agarwal and Sunita Narain, Towards a Green World, *op. cit.,* pp. 31-32.
25. Krik Smith, "Developing countries and Climate Change: Implications for Risk Management" in D.G. Streets and T.A. Siddiqui(eds), Responding to the Threat of Global Warming ; Options for the Pacific and Asia, Proceedings of a workshop sponsored by Argonne National Laboratory and East-West Centre, Honolulu, June 21-27, 1989.
26. Anil Agarwal and Sunita Narain, Towards a Green World, *op. cit.,* p. 35.
27. Intergovernmental Panel on Climate Change 2001, Climate Change 2001: The Scientific Basis, Third Assessment Report, Summary for Policy makers 2001, Bonn.

28. John Lanchbery and David Victor, The Role of Science in the Global Climate Negotiations, in Helge Ole Bergesen and Georg Parmann ed., Green Globe Year Book of International Cooperation on Environment and Development (Oxford: Oxford University Press, 1995), p. 32.
29. Anil Agarwal et al., Global Environment Negotiation I, *op. cit.,* p. 27; see also Mukund Govind Ranjan, Global Environment Politics; India and the North South Politics of Global Environment Issue (Delhi: Oxford University Press, 1997), pp. 94-95.
30. The Noordwijk Declaration on Climate Change, Ministerial Conference on Atmospheric Pollution and Climate Change, Ministry of Housing, Physical Planning and Environment, the Netherlands 1989, Para 7.
31. Fred Pearce, Turning Up the Heat (London: Paladin, 1989), p. 1.
32. John Houghton, Global Warming: The Complete Briefing, (Cambridge: Cambridge University Press, 1994), p. 3.
33. Stewart Boyle and John Ardill, The Greenhouse Effect: A Practical Guide to the World's Changing Climate (London: Hodder and Stoughton, 1989), pp. 47-48.
34. Quoted in Fred Pearce, Turning Up the Heat, *op. cit.*, p. 1.
35. General Assembly Resolution 43/53, United Nations, New York, 6 December 1988.
36. General Assembly Resolution 44/228, United Nations, New York 22 December 1989.
37. *Ibid.*
38. AdHoc Working Group of Government Representatives to prepare for Negotiations on a Framework Convention on Climate Change, WMO/UNEP Geneva, September 24-26, 1990.
39. IPCC First Assessment Report: Overview, WMO/UNEP, Geneva, August 31, 1990, p. 10.
40. World Resource 1990-1991 (Oxford: Oxford University Press, 1990).
41. Anil Agarwal et al., Global Environmental Negotiations, 1, *op. cit.*, p. 31.
42. Second World Climate Conference Ministerial Declaration in Environmental Policy and Law (North Holland: Elsevier Science Publishers) Vol. 20, No. 6, 1990, p. 220, paragraph 5.

43. See for details, Anil Agarwal et al., Global Environmental Negotiations I, *op. cit.*, pp. 31-39.
44. "For a Fistful of Dollars", in Down to Earth, (CSE, New Delhi) Vol. 1, No. 2, June 15, 1992, p. 4.
45. Anil Agarwal et al., Global Environmental Negotiation I, *op. cit.*, p. 42.
46. Anjani Khanna, "Climate Negotiations Conclude: US Rules the Clouds", in Down to Earth, May 15, 1992, p. 12.
47. Tariq Osman Hyder, "Looking back to see Forward", in Irving M Mintzer and J Amber Leonard eds., Negotiating Climate Change: The Inside Story of the Rio Convention (Cambridge: Cambridge University Press, 1994), p. 215.
48. IPCC First Assessment Report: Overview, WMO/UNEP, Geneva 1990, August 31, p. 2.
49. Climate Change Convention: COP-I Follow up to the Berlin Mandate, in Environmental Policy and Law, North Holland; Elsevier Science Publishers, 1995) Vol. 25, No. 6, 1995, pp. 297-298. Vinayak Rao, "The Climate for a change" in Down to Earth Vol. 5, No. 4, 15 July 1990, p. 34.
50. Sebastian Oberthur, The Second Conference of the Parties in Environmental Policy and Law, op cit. Vol. 26, No. 5, 1996, p. 196.
51. Anil Agarwal et al., Global Environmental Negotiations I, *op. cit.*, p. 47.
52. Sabri Zain, Earth Summit II Signals a Bumby Road to Kyoto, in SEANEWS, Climate Action Network, South East Asia, Malaysia, July 1997, p. 3.
53. Backgrounder: US Cities Strong Proposals to Deal with Global Warming, United States Information Service, 3 December 1997, p. 2.
54. "Rubbing Sleep from their Eyes", in the Economists (London), December 13, 1997, p. 42.
55. Anil Agarwal, Down to Earth Vol. 6, No. 15, 31 December 1997.
56. Pad Green, "Where Climate Change Meets Sustainable Societies", Third World Resurgence, No. 87/88, November/ December 1997, p. 6.
57. Arthur H. Westing, "The atmosphere as a common heritage of humankind: its role in environmental security", scientific World (London), 34(4): 5-6, 1990, p. 207.

58. Robert Repetto and D. Austin, The Costs of Climate Protection: A Guide for the Perplexed, WRI, June 1997.
59. Devra Davis, "Worldwide Deaths Ralated to Fossil Fuel Consumption", The Lancet, 8November 1997; James Mackenzie, Climate protection and the National Interest: The Links Among Climate Change, Air Pollution and Energy Security, WRI, October, 1997.
60. A.B. Lovins and L.H. Lovins, F.Krause and W.Bach, Least-cost energy: Solving the CO_2 Problem (Andover, Mass: Brick House, 1981), pp. 184.
61. Peter Nulty, "Global Warming that We Know", Fortune, April 1990. Anil Agarwal and Sunita Narain, Towards a Green World (New Delhi, Centre for Science and Environment, 1992), p. 39.
62. Anil Agarwal, et al in Down to Earth, *op. cit.,* pp. 31-32. see also David L. Lhevy and Daniel Egan, "Capital Contests:National and Transnational Channels of Corporate Influence on the Climate Change Negotiations", politics and society Vol. 26, No. 3, September 1998, pp. 337-361.
63. Sten Nilson et al, Full Carbon Account Russia, Interim Report, "International Institute Applied Systems Analysis, Luxemburg, http://www.iiasa.ac.at/Admin/Pub/Document/ir-oo-021.pdf, as viewed on August 18, 2001.
64. *Ibid.*
65. *Ibid.*
66. *Ibid.*
67. *Ibid.*
68. *Ibid.*
69. Intergovernmental Panel on Climate Change, Land use, Land Use Change and Forestry, Summary for Policy Makers, 2000, Bonn, p. 25.
70. Janet N Abramouitz, Taking A Stand: Cultivating A New Relationship With The World's Forests, World watch paper 140, World watch Institute, Washington DC, April 1998, p. 14.
71. Intergovernmental Panel on Climate Change, Land Use Change and Forestry, 2000, *op. cit.,* p. 25.
72. *Ibid.*
73. *Ibid.*
74. *Ibid.*

75. *Ibid.*
76. N.H. Ravindranath, Sinking Feeling, India Institute of Science, Bangalore, 2000, mimeo.
77. P.S. Ramakrishnan, Reaction to Intergovernmental Panel on Climate Change's Land Use, Land Use Change and Forestry, JNU, New Delhi, mimeo.
78. Murari Lal, Forests As Carbon Sinks in India, Indian Institute of Technology, Delhi, mimeo.
79. Thomas C. Schelling, What Makes Greenhouse Sense? Foreign Affairs Vol. 8, No. 3, May/June 2002, p. 4.
80. *Ibid*, p. 8.
81. *Ibid*, p. 4.
82. Nikhat Jamel Qaiyum, Climate Change, Meddling Albright, Global environmental Governance, Supplement to Down to Earth, May 31, 1998, pp. 63-64.
83. Kirk Smith, *op. cit.*
84. Arthur H. Westing, *op. cit.*
85. Benito Muller, Creative Accounting, Down to Earth Vol. 10, No. 31, 31 March 2002, pp. 52-53.
86. Anil Agarwal and Sunita Narain, Sharing the Air, Centre for Science and Environment, Down to Earth Vol. 17, No. 8, August 15, 1998, pp. 37-42.
87. *Ibid.*
88. *Ibid.*
89. Aubrey Meyer, Director, Global Commons Institute, London, July 20, quoted in Anil Agarwal et al, Global Environmental Negotiations 2, *op. cit.*, p. 237.
90. Energy The Changing Climate, Royal Commission on Environmental pollution, Stationery Office Limited, London, pp. 1-9.
91. Quoted in Anil Agarwal et al., Global Environmental Negotiation 2, *op. cit.*, p. 260.
92. Down to Earth Vol. 10, No. 11, October 31, 2001, p. 52.
93. Quoted in *Ibid.*, p. 51.
94. Down to Earth Vol. 9, No. 15, 31 December 2000, pp. 27-29.
95. Pad Green, *op. cit.*
96. Anju Sharma, 'Shades of Equity' Down to Earth Vol. 7, No. 19, February 28, 1997, pp. 56-57.
97. Eugune A. Rose and Thomas Dietz, "climate Change and Society: Speculation, Construction and Scientific

Investigation", International Studies Review Vol. 2, No. 2, summer 2000, p. 131.

98. Aant Elzinga, "From Arrhenius to Megascience", Ambio Vol. 26, 1997, p. 99.
99. Karen T. Liffin, "Environment, Wealth and Authority: Global Climate Change and Emerging Modes of Legitimation", International Studies Review Vol. 2, No. 2, summer 2000, p. 131.
100. Lester Brown, Nicholas Lessen and Hal Kane, Vital Signs 1995 (New York: Norton 1995).
101. Karen Liffin, *op. cit.*, p. 142.

7

Environment, Development and Human Rights: A South's Perspective

Nowhere the clamour for ethical consideration in human, organization or state conduct or activity regarding human rights is heard more intensely than in the field of international affairs. The long conventional debate on 'the sense of detachment' of political scientists to the issues of morality and ethics seems to be a low key affairs bordering on noncommittal among the actors and participants in the international field. Whenever there is war, military *coupd'etat*, external intervention, terrorists' massacre, bombardment of innocent civil persons, hijacking, earthquake or any natural calamity killing human beings, the reactions, responses and spate of activities from among the nations have always been couched in high sounding humanitarian, moral and ethical tones, though sometimes their real intent may be up their sleeves. Even, while giving economic aids to poor countries, refugees, women and children and championing nuclear disarmament, peace and security in the world and bringing an end to terrorism or civil war in a nation, countries always used to speak from a moralistic and ethical rostrum and act in considerable solidarity. Since the prevalence of liberal and democratic political systems in Western Europe, the attachment of much ethical value to the issues of human rights has become a centerpiece in international realm.

Two very unusual but significant phenomena before the twentieth century rolls back, namely, the end of cold war, burial of communism and systemic changes in Eastern Europe and Soviet Union; and ravage of the planet Earth with its horrendous consequences upon the very survival of mankind and living beings, bring into sharp focus the basic issues and problems hovering round human rights in two fundamental aspects.

(i) Issues of human rights have gone beyond their cold war narrow political grooves and no longer remained in the global strategic shafts of super powers as a potent weapon to reap their political and partisan dividends. Basic human rights involved in the environmental debate between the North and South hold it as half-truth that the Western nations along with the United States are the true torch bearers of human rights superseding the alleged dichotomy between morality and real politik.

(ii) The very ethical, moral and human content of human rights has been brought to the centrestage contesting North's political, social and economic metaphysics in which these continue to be interpreted.

The present chapter studies these two aspects from an environmental perspective and holds that an agenda for human rights, which would be shaped on the basis of moral tradition and ethical values, ingrained in human civilization since time immemorial, must incorporate rights to environment, survival and development as its foremost items.

The ideological debates during the cold war which confined political rights to western democracies and economic rights to socialistic countries, have already become sterile and the scope of human rights has not only covered both but also gone far beyond religious, ethnic groups and communities to mould their own systems of government according to their own way of thinking, and to have rights to access to the resources of the earth and environment equitably, and to have the very right to live and survive on this earth. The western ethnocentrism of liberal and democratic political system is marked on its uncontested representative and electoral politics, enjoyment of inalienable individual rights, wider participation in the decision making structure of the political system, a stronger belief in the prevalent capitalist market economy culture and some innovative structural and institutional arrangements. It seems to have provided an ideal type as a system of government and a way of life, to which all countries of the world would conform. With the advent of communism, as an anti-thesis of liberal political system and alternative model of political and economy restructuring and a host of South countries mostly during the post Second World war falling prey to its revolutionary ethos in order to provide a hearth and haven to the growing aspirations of the working class and poor people, the issues of human rights were configurated into the strategic realm of United States and her Western allies to contain communism and punish those who are against it by using a policy of carrot and stick. Nothing short of a conformity or degree of approximation to the Western ideal type remained no longer with the United States a measuring rod of human rights in those countries. Rather, the United States and its allies to further their global strategy of containment of communism and increase their spheres of influence in the South used issues of human rights as a diplomatic sleight of hand. To show concern for the moral content of human rights in the United States ran subsidiary to its global strategy.

As there is evidence, many tyrants and authoritarian regimes are either installed or allowed to stay in power in various part of the globe by the United States because of their anti communism credentials. It is due to America's direct or indirect, material, moral and military abetment, the Mujahidden guerrillas in Afghanistan, UNITA forces under Savimbi in Angola and K'hmer Rougue in Cambodia not only survived by sticking to heartless brutalities of mass murder, and violence but made an utter mockery of the Unites States' concern for human rights. According to a M.I.T. Professor in the United States, it is ironic that the state which has sponsored and supported the Somoza family, the Shah, Macros, Park, Pinochet, Suharto, and Mobutu, the Brazilian generals and their many confederates, in repression and violence, can announce a campaign for human rights thoughout the world and be taken with the utmost seriousness".[1]

The recent systemic transformations in the former Soviet Union and Eastern Europe, and eclipse of communism have rendered a great service to humanity in the front of rights by releasing them from their cold war political internment.

Notwithstanding the cataclysmic changes in the international scene as discussed above, which have succeeded in at least releasing the issues of human rights from their narrow cold war furrow into which they have been thrown by the so called champions of human rights, the United States and her Western allies have never been absolved of the charges that they are the main culprits in violating exorbitantly basic human rights in various part of the globe from any environmental perspective much ignored during the cold war. The fundamental issues in the environmental front confined mainly to climate, atmosphere, biodiversity and forest, exacerbating the difference between North and South, involve a wide spectrum of human rights. The following analysis would show how the rich North has been constantly depriving the South of their basic human rights.

Ecological Dishonesty of North and Basic Issues of Human Rights

It is a fact that there have been cataclysmic changes in the physical condition of the earth. Forests are dwindling at an alarming proportion.

Deserts are expanding and croplands are losing topsoils. Every year some six million hectares of land are so severely degraded that they lose their productive capability and become wasteland. The stratospheric ozone layer is depleting with the accumulation of greenhouse gases and deposition of CO_2 emission. As far as global warming, greenhouse effect and punching a hole in the ozone layer are concerned, it can be said in refutation of what the World Resources Institute (WRI) and the Inter Governmental Panel on Climate Change (IPCC) did, by juggling with the data to pass on the buck to the developing countries with a view to promote US interests, that a major contribution to this stems from the rich industrialized North. The Centre for Science and Environment (CSE) index, which has contested and modified the above two indices has not been so far challenged. [2]

Environmental Debate Favours North

The environmental debate has been so conducted, as evidenced at the Rio Earth Summit, as if not to punish the culprit but share his misdeeds. Instead of dealing with the systemic causes of environmental degradation, such as the unsustainable life-styles of their own population at the cost of the South, the rich North is very keen on relating the rights of the South to exploit their own resources to the fixing of limits of emission of CO_2 and the other gases which adversely affect the atmosphere, and of land and forest use with the ostensible purpose of gaining access to the abundant genetic material available in the South for reinforcing their patents on intellectual rights and dominance in trade. It speaks of the sinister double standards of the North that it proposes a sectoral approach to the environment without being concerned about the demands of the South for the inclusion of poverty, development and trade in the debates besides Western selective concern with South's assertion of sovereign rights over the atmosphere and other resources on the basis of equity and the local people's right to be compensated equitably for parting with their unique knowledge of genetic materials to the North. At the Rio UNCEP conference, the rich nations have taken a position that essentially gets them off the hook for their past production and inordinate consumption patterns and treat the past as past and now seek to ram an inequitable system for future global environmental management down the throats of the poor Third World countries.

The climate change convention, signed by a record number of 160 nations, prescribed the limits for carbon emission so as to offset the effects of climate change on the atmosphere caused by greenhouse gases and global warming. It contains much of North's contentions about sharing the management of the burden on an equitable basis, which has been denied to the developing countries in the sharing of the management of the resources of the atmosphere. The differential responsibility in causing damage to the environment was lost sight of at Rio.

North's Quota Already Exhausted

A study by the California based International Project on Sustainable Energy Paths (IPSEP) shows that if the historical inequity in terms of carbon emission is taken stock of, and the permissible global carbon emission budget of 428 btc from 1950 till 2100 instead of 300 btc between1986 and 2100, is distributed between the industrialized and developing countries then the latter can claim to continue emission of CO_2 till 2241 AD at their 1986 rate. But the industrialized North should have had exhausted their entire quota by 1986, if equity is assumed as the parameter. They ought to stop emission right away [3].

North Treats South's Forest as Carbon Sinks Destroying their Very Right to Existence

Another area over which the industrialized North has always been insisting on asserting its right to find as escape route for their emission of CO_2, as Kamal Nath, India's former Minister for Environment, told in the Earth Summit is forestry. In the face of the assertion and determined efforts of India and Malaysia, the developed countries led by the United States failed to bring all developing countries into an agreement to a convention on forestry which prohibited them from cutting down trees on the pretext that they are rainforests and needed as carbon sinks to absorb pollution. The White House document 'Forest for the Future Initiative', which seeks forests more as carbon sinks and reservoirs and not as the habitat and components of the food systems of the South's poor and indigenous people, was denounced as asking the South to pay the price for what the lavish North has done to the atmosphere in terms of CO_2 emission and deforestation of large tracts of forest and massive consumption of inordinate amounts of fossil fuels.

As one western environmentalist pointed out "creating carbon sinks in developing countries through forestry programmes without reducing carbon dioxide emissions in their own countries at the same time, is the wrong signal from G-7 countries meeting at Houston to discuss US government document on Forest Convention. This means the G-7 are not willing to make their own economies environmentally sustainable".[4] While disproportionately focussing attention on issues of forest management and conservation, the global agencies such as FAO, World Bank, UNCTAD or ITTO are giving short shrifts to South's demand for equity and fair trade in order to make forest use sustainable. As India's Minister for Environment contended in no uncertain terms: "our strongest objection is to the attempt to use forests as parts of the global carbon cycle. If it is such s resource, we should be paid for it not only now but also the opportunity cost (of leaving forest intact) for the past and future. The position, otherwise, is our forests are your dumps. They should stabilize their carbon emissions. We cannot supply them as an escape route".[5]

Montreal protocol

The Montreal Protocol, which India and other countries acceded to, on phasing out by 2010 CFCS (Chlorofluro carbons) and halogens that punch holes in the protective ozone layer allowing harmful ultraviolet radiation (UV-B) causing such diseases like skin cancers, cataracts and depression of the immune system and also greenhouse warming. Anti-South provisions safeguarding countries' share in the depletion of the ozone layer remains at 12.4 per cent, the developed countries 'share is alarmingly 87.6 per cent.[6] To expose its inequity and discrimination it can be said that fixing quotas for further consumption is unfair and highly erroneous.

A major constraint that affects the South is the financial and technological crunch for seeking alternatives to CFCS, which remains in the hands of the North. As Z.R Ansari, former Indian Minister for Environment apprehended at the 1989 London Conference: "The technology of substitutes, conservation, recycling and equipment modification will be the monopoly of a few countries in the developed world... the question that haunts us is the extent of resources required to get the technology as well as the products from the companies in the developed World".[7] Alternatives to CFCS, though claimed to be friendly to the environment, are emerging like new villains. Even when alternatives, friendly to the ozone layer are found, they will be under the control and the monopoly of the developed world, perpetuating their role in their trade to protect their economy in the scintillating words of an environmentalist:

"Instead of the treaty setting out a system in which a global common resource is shared and managed equitably, with equal rights for any citizen, the treaty operates within the context of existing inequities, creating a legal framework to institutionalize and perpetuate the gap between the poor and rich... It does not assign any entitlements to people nor any penalties for the overuse or abuse of the common resources of the earth. Any discussion of corrective action thus remains a mere charity from the penalized.[8]

Undue Claims on South's Biodiversity and Sovereign Rights

Another contentious issue, which marks the North-South divide in South's vast biodiversity widely used in world's agricultural system and west's biotechnological industries. The value of South's germ plasm for western pharmaceutical industries stands at US $ 4.7 billion now. It will reach US $47 billion by 2000.[9] While the genetic dependence of the North on the South is accelerating, the former has not been generous towards the latter's socio economic development.

All attempts at ascribing such concepts as 'free access to biodiversity' and 'common heritage of mankind' by the developed nations to the genetic wealth of the developing countries, appear to perpetuate and legitimize their exploitation of the South for expanding the North's economic interests. The developing countries convincingly contend why they should forgo their own development in order to guarantee conservation for the economic benefit of the North. They have sovereign rights over these biological resources and should control and restrict access that has been feeding the commercial interests of the North. Though there has been great deal of discussion and resolutions in international fora, such as, about farmer's rights, these have not yet been backed up with hard cash, compensation or legal protection against the exploitation of their traditional knowledge and South's genes.

The industrialized countries are vehemently opposing the inclusion of biotechnology within the convention. As found at Riode Janero, India led the South in persuading the United States to sign the convention, which sought to preserve the flora and fauna of the planet as part of the worldwide conservation strategy to minimize the ravages of pollution. The United States declined to sign the biodiversity convention on grounds that it would hit its two billion-biotechnology industry back home. The issue of Intellectual Property Rights (IPR) coming under the aegis of GATT negotiations also remained unresolved.

Thus, the industrialized countries are pressing hard in the GATT forum and elsewhere for greater protection and enforceability of corporate and private intellectual property rights including patents over genetic materials and declining to make commitment to developing countries on access to biotechnology and other associated technologies on the plea that there is no way that they can interfere with private sector interests.

Dubious Logic and Dubious Standard Redounding To North's Intellectual Property Rights over South's Genetic Knowledge

The North's habit of using dubious logic and double standards is revealed when they advise governments of the South to concede to the demands of the developed countries for free access to resources without the consent of or ignoring the farmers or indigenous people-the real owners of genetic diversity and its knowledge. Mostafa Tolba, executive director of UNEP at the second session of the adhoc-working group of legal and technical experts on biological diversity, highlighting this insidious double standard, said:

There is a continuous argument in international fora that because technology patents are held by private firms, governments cannot, in view of current international treaties, dictate to private sector policies regarding transfer of patent technologies... By the same token, areas rich in biodiversity are mostly in private hands. If Governments of developing countries are expected to convince landowners to participate in the implementation of provisions of the convention that requires access to biological resources, then it is certainly not asking the impossible of industrialized countries to persuade their private sector to act in a similar way. [10]

South's Staggering Debt Service

A relevant component of an industrial culture which resulted in the evolution of a frontier model of economics based on an intensive nonrenewable fossil fuel industrialization that measures progress and growth in wasteful material consumption at the expense of nature and the environment tends to view both nature and economics as poles apart. Thus, the world economy, trading system and the concomitant institutional and structural managements shaped at Bretton Woods on the indices of neo-classical economics were designed to legitimize and reinforce the monopoly of the industrialized countries of continued access to resources from the South at a cheaper price and to sell the products at a price solely determined by the former to contribute to their economic plenitude. The result is that the developing countries' natural resources base continues to deteriorate throwing them into deep poverty and uncontrollable pollution making it wellnigh impossible for them to purchase processed goods and technology or invest in environmental protection.[11]

As studies show, there has been an unprecedented growth in the global economy during the eighties. It is much more than that during the several thousand years from the beginning of civilization until 1950.[12] According to a British environmentalist, with world's population increasing more than three times since 1900, the Gross World Product has increased

21 times, the consumption of fossil fuels 30 times, industrial production 50 times and the average income of the richest one billion people is 20 times larger than that of the poorest one billion.[13] It seems that the enormous increase in the wealth of the world has not resulted in the equitable distribution of benefits; rather it has widened the gap between the North and the South.

A study shows that one billion live in unprecedented luxury and another one billion in destitution. Even American children have more pocket money $ 230 a year than the half a billion poorest people alive.[14] The environmental deterioration and decline of the economy have fed on one another through the operation of the world market system which has exacerbated this trend and consistently depressed prices of the commodities produced and exported by the developing countries, and aggravated the debt crisis faced by them. Ironically, the fate of the poor and the fate of the planet have become inextricably intertwined. As economist Herman Dely put it, "There is something fundamentally wrong in treating the earth as if it were a business in liquidation" [15].

The debt crisis has not only impoverished the South and deteriorated the environment but also made it the sole benefactor of the North. According to an estimate, by 1989, South's external debt stood at $1.2 trillion, 44 per cent of its collective gross national product (GNP). It is 140 per cent in Egypt and Zaire and in Mozambique 400 per cent. The annual interest obligations on this debt are mounting to about US $ 100 billion and the annual total debt service bill is a staggering $ 200 billion.[16]

Thus, the accepted view that resource flows from the North to the South stands discredited.[17] Resources flows from the South to the North have now reached $ 50 billion a year. This reverse resource flow is not only immoral, but it is a major contributing factor to the continued poverty and environmental degradation in poor countries where economic resources have to be exploited quickly, simply to pay off debt.[18]

To draw attention away from their exploitative role, the North accuses the countries of South of corruption, poor economic management, faulty investment and wrong priorities. The reality is that even if all the money were spent honestly, the South would still be in a debt trap.[19]

Perpetuation of Colonial Economic Interests of the North

The international financial institutions, such as the IMF, and World Bank have been so structured as to perpetuate the colonial economic interests of the rich nations. IMF's insistence on an export oriented economy, devaluation to boost exports, cut in deficit budgeting and severe austerity measures have impelled the South, in their bid to earn more foreign exchange, to exploit their environment and adopt economic policies with only short-term gains in mind. The World Bank continues its traditional lending policies to the South for the large capital-intensive projects without considering their impact on the local and regional environment and without taking into account the rural poor's resentment and opposition. This is despite the recent opening of a new environmental department in the World Bank.

The real question is how the South could be released from the debt trap. Will the rich North write off totally the debts the South owes? Though the Governments of Canada, Germany, the United Kingdom and the United States have between them already forgiven over $5 billion worth of public loans to Sub-Saharan African countries, [20] a successful debt reduction strategy is one that brings the South's debt down to a level that ensures environmentally sound development. It may mean a debt reduction to the order of 60 per cent, a cut from $1.2 trillion to $500 billion.[21] Though the Dutch Government has applied US biologist Thomas Livejoy's debt theory for nature swaps [22] by purchasing $33 million worth of Costa Rica's debt in exchange for $10 million of local investments in aforestation, watershed management and soil conservation, it is not a real solution to the debt problem.

The major stumbling block is the growing perception of the environmental crisis as being mainly a failure of technology and management. What is more horrendous is that UNCED paved the way for the transfer of control of the World's resources to a global technocratic elite by transforming an issue of changing life-styles and consumption levels of the lavish rich into one of population growth and inadequate managerial capacity of the poor. Kerstin Kiessling of the Royal Swedish Academy and Nathan Keyfitz of the International Institute of Applied Systems Analysis in Austria are of the view that the environmental problems lay more with the high consumption levels in the developed countries than with the supposed population growth in the South.[23]

From the above analysis, it can be said that in the South, environmental degradation is inextricably related to the global processes of trade and pattern of economic relations. But the irony is that the most profligate in environmental pollution are demanding that the most frugal and sparing abide by the most stringent rules and ethics of environmental protection. According to analysis, if economic progress in the North can be said to be sustainable, it is by "importing" it through non sustainability in other nations.[24] If sustainable development is understood and couched in the verbiage of western terminology as perpetuating the current system of economic activity, entrenched industrial structures, institutionalizing the economic interests of the wealthier nations of the world, it will not only be the apotheosis of "ecological imperialism" but will foreshadow an environmental catastrophe.[25]

Environment, Rights to Security and Equity of People

As seen, as a result of western paradigm of industrial development based on fossil fuel intensive technology, the planet Earth has been ravaged with many disastrous fallouts like greenhouse gases, ozone depletion, soil erosion, deforestation, rising sea level, acid precipitation and so on. The evidence is clear that poor people especially in the South are becoming more vulnerable to threats from natural hazards. Their poverty leads them to live in dangerous places on marginal lands where their lives and livelihoods are vulnerable. The poor are those who starve when climate changes cause famine. Another severe problem of global ecological interdependence looms large over the world food market. A more densely populated planet has led to a market that is increasingly influenced by production on marginal land. Very small changes in temperature could destroy this marginal agricultural production. A volcanic eruption on the scale of Krakotoa event could trigger a two or three years global cooling that could lead to the deaths of hundreds of millions in the countries least able to purchase food. A dangerous consequence of climate change caused by mostly North's emission of CO_2 will be unprecedented sea level rise, which would drown completely vast areas and a great populace of countries in South like Bangladesh, Egypt and Maldives.[26] A pertinent question arises. Have the poor, facing such environmental hazards no right to security of life against all such calamities? Are the North countries, largely responsible for these hazards conscious about the right to security of life of people of the South?

Intergenerational Equity

It denotes a standing commitment to social justice. Thus, equity is not only between North and South but also between and among all human beings inhabiting the earth. In other words, it is not only intragenerational but also intergenerational [27] which does not deprive the future generations and the yet to be born, of their rights to the resources of the planet earth and finally security of life and survival against all ecological hazards. To use the phraseology of one authority, "the metropolitan centres of power and today's men have no legitimacy to colonize the future. How is one to assure that the interests of the younger generation and the yet to be born generations of the future are somehow represented in the present" ? [29]

The above analysis suggests the necessity of looking at the situation of the most vulnerable sectors of a population of the South in trying to formulate a positive post cold war code of human rights in terms of equity and security of life into the foreseeable future, and the right to development in sustainability with the environment, of all individuals, groups, villages and local communities in their ways not in the supposed mimetic western model of development.

Ethical and Humanitarian content of human rights: No Anti thesis between Rights to Development and Environment

The Western ethnocentrism of capitalist development is based on the recognition of a selfish and atomic individual's right to infinitely exploit the resources of the planet earth at the cost of other individuals and the nature. As a result, the present civilization has turned out to be a civilization of inequity, injustice and exploitation. Coming to the second aspect of our analysis, the very ethical base i.e. the humanistic and moral content of human rights has been totally ignored. As seen from the analysis of the first aspect, the very right to survival, environment and development with dignity as due to a human person and security of all, whether children, women, refugees, homeless, community, and even future generations against ecological hazards constitute the humane base of the agenda of human rights. As will be seen, the very political and economic metaphysics of North's interpretation of human rights is too narrow to envelop what has been denied so far to the South.

Need for change in Basic Western Values

What is challenged is "the most basic political values of contemporary western capitalism: the assumptions of resources in nature as available for exploitation, ever enlarging consumption, and that affluence is intrinsically superior to any other forms of society, as well as faith in the market".[30]

Man has become so acquisitive that there has developed a dichotomy and essentially an antithesis between the planet earth and the human freedom to ravage it. A contradiction between anthropocentric and cosmocentric views of the universe seems to constitute the substructure of the present day concept of economic development. This has led to the question in the title of a book published some years ago, 'Man in Nature: Guest or Engineer'[31] and prompted another authority to write: "Springing from the unending acquisitiveness of our technological way of life and a concomitant decline in our sensibility to other humans we have been on a rampage that threatens our common organic bond with the whole of creation – and thus both our own survival and that of other species".[32]

North's Inordinate Consumption Rights: Antithetical to South's Right to Development

There is a growing tendency to define development just as the sole right to amass wealth or the conquest of extraordinary technological power and skill, which is the sole cause of persistent poverty and of human rapacity to despoil nature. Philosopher Hans Jonas, in his 'The Imperative Responsibility'[33] puts forward arguments to combat this very technological and economic thinking, for an ethic of responsibility for the cosmos. The crux of the debate is that the ethnocentrism of the dominant western economic thinking and pattern of development does not take into consideration the natural threshold, the carrying capacity of the planet earth and the ecological costs of production. It has also resulted in a western masculine metaphysical understanding of power in terms of dominance over nature, control over economic activities and territorial states. Can such an economic development be called successful if it has effected a terrible despoliation of nature and environment and destitution of the people in the South? This is what led many to denounce it as anti thesis of authentic development or antidevelopment.[34]

Many world organizations, such as the World Bank, CECD and UNCTAD have been ranking nations on the indices of aggregate economic growth measured in terms of gross national product (GNP). The authors of the first annual report of the United Nations Development Programme (UNDP) on human development in 1990, addressing the need to transcend the narrow economic vision of development, have challenged this.[35] Blind faith in the free market determined price mechanism to measure economic costs of resources is highly imperfect. The predominant stress of most neo-classical economists is only goods or services, which are either inputs or product or economic activities. This is what has led one authority to opine: "What is the cost of a tree which cleans air, regulates water flows, fixes nitrogen, absorbs pollutants, produces biomass and provides habitat to other flora and fauna? At best, economists can complete 'replacement costs' of those of these functions that are replaceable... But what happens to the irreplaceable".[36]

Premises of Development: Unfolding of a Culture Like a Flower Precoded in the Seed

Considering the fact that there are many cultures in the world, even civilizations spanning vast regions of space and time, so a consequence of choosing a definition would be that there are many roads to developments. If one civilization imposes its definition of development on another, a clear case of cultural violence occurs. Such a case of grafting another cultural code on to another people's culture results in culturocide [37], gross alienation and killing of their own culture. If the first definition of development is the unfolding of a culture, realizing the code or cosmology of that culture, like the unfolding of flower preprogrammed in the seeds, the world have been a beautiful garden of varieties of flowers wilting according to their own genetic code preprogrammed in their respective seeds. When flowers blossom according to the cultural code of the gardener, super imposition of one culture on many cultures and civilizations takes place dragging all to a uniformity killing varieties and pluralities, and forcing many to be shepherded by the Western master. If today, this is meant, the world is moving towards globalization and one world, then this is very antithesis of development, and has become a synonym to envelopment.

In other words, clamping its cultural code on all others and many, the Western civilization has squeezed and regimented them into its political economic thinking. So what was illegitimate and a blatant example of cultural imperialism and the very antithesis of development was legitimized and universalized, bringing ruin to sublime values of many great civilizations. One world is set against many worlds, making a dwarf of them. The concept of development is a pluralistic one suggesting as many roads to development as many societies and civilizations.

Economic Rethinking: a Basic Foundation of Human Rights

This definition of development aims at scaling economy down to its place in the societies. Adam Smith using the term market helped the transformation of community based subsistence economy into a nationwide political economy covering the entire society and reality. Society was understood in terms of nothing else than its functional achievements leaving aside the rest as just folklore or private affairs. The laws of the economy try to dominate the society and not the rules of the society.[38] The term 'market economy' reduces all the societies to mere an 'economy' making the developmentalists oblivious of the very basic thing that every society has an economy. The market economy as promoted by the West edged its way into all the developmental thinking of the entire world, and assumed a deterministic character imprinting its rules and rhythms upon the society and even dictating the drama and the role in it of individuals. The entire globe including all the nations have been reduced to an economy controlled by the West.

Thus, according to the nuances of market economy, development has been identified as economic growth, inordinate consumption and increasing commodity based wants and accumulation of wealth. Poverty is understood in terms of what other people lack or do not have in relation to the West. Destitution and imitating the profligate consumption style of the West, has been the price, the South pays for having ruined its multifarious culture of frugality, austerity and sacrifice.

Transforming the Consumer Man: North's Inordinate Consumption Rights Antithesis to South's Right to Development

The Western economic thinking has reduced a 'whole man' to an economic or insatiated consumer man ever inclining to satisfy his desires in terms of consumption or utility. It has reduced all hierarchy of human needs to a mere inventory of wants, which are measurable or commensurable quantitatively and translated into consumption items in terms of utility and entered as inputs into the market mechanisms. On the other hand, needs are incommensurable and as such cannot be simply added. Thus, the economics of utility comes out of a worldview or an image of society where all needs are purported to have been met. The shocking thing about this market economy, which relies on this unrealistic picture, is that it begins at a place where fundamental economic problems remain grotesque and are assumed to have been solved.[39]

Thus, the economic thinking involves the recognition of the existence of a higher self-repository of all good qualities like frugality, austerity, sacrifice, selflessness, materialistic detachment and humanistic concern for community. Over and above, the ordinary lower self is concerned with selfish materialistic consumption giving a free ride to its bodily-derived pleasures. Thus, an economy, which reduces all human activity and even existence and values to a sheer commercialization and utilizable commodities in a market place, has ruined the moral, social and ecological foundation of the society, sealing off permanently the mine of alternatives to this kind of market economy. The intrinsic human values, viz., altruism, selflessness, sacrifice and community life inherent in many great civilizations and cultures can be well cultivated giving a humanistic face to the current consumeristic market economy. For example, in a traditional Mexican village, the private accumulation of wealth results in social ostracism. Gandhian concept of Sarvodaya and trusteeship and village republic envisage an economy of self-sufficiency and common good, free from the frenzy of inordinate accumulation and extravagant consumerism found in the richest few at the cost of majority poor and the nature. John Keynes, father of neo-classical economics and the chief architect of the post-world war II financial institutions shaped at Brettonwoods, proposed a toast to economics and economists saying you are not the trustees of civilizations but one of the possibilities of civilization. Adam Smith, the father of classical economics in his 'The theory of Moral Sentiments' assumed that a higher providence ordains that the working of market economy remains within certain moral and ethical values inherent in many cultures and restoring these to a central place in the discipline of economics provide a substructure on which the foundations of economic rethinking can be laid.

The Other Cannot be the Cause of Development of Another

Glued to the view that the other is the cause of the development of another, the South demonstrates a great distrust in their own capacity and ingenuity to devise indigenous models of development, inclining them to walk on Western crutches. This is like lending credence to the doctrine of the 'double mandate' once formulated by Lord Lugard, the British imperial administrator: economic profit coupled with the responsibility to elevate the coloured races to a higher level of civilization.[40] To persist in this kind of belief that the another is the cause of development of another, helps the reinforcement of an imperialistic design blocking all the roads to initiatives to stand on one's leg. Thus, while the South countries remain acerbic against imperialistic powers in rhetorics, in reality imperialistic code has been programmed in all their systems. With a religious surrender to the Western paradigms of development, the South has provided the logic to the Western powers to continue the British colonial policy of 'white man's burden'.

Homo/Nature Balanced Development: No Anti Thesis between Right to Development and Environment

This premise of rethinking development aims at replacing the Western anthropocentric development by a cosmocentric view of development. The primary thrust of Judeo-Christian tradition of Western civilization has been, if any thing, anti-nature. A dichotomy and essentially an anti thesis between the planet earth and human freedom to ravage it for the material enrichment of the very few at the expense of both the majority many and environment, is the quintessential of Western economic and political metaphysics. Thus, the Western paradigm of development has been anthropocentric and homocentric development whereby human needs are given priority to exclusion of nature's needs. This has led S.J. Samartha and Lynn de Silva to question in the title of a book published some years ago, 'Man in Nature: Guest or Engineer'.[41] The ethnocentrism of the dominant and mimetic Western economic thinking and pattern of development does take into consideration rather vehemently ignores, the natural threshold, the carrying capacity of the planet earth, the ecological costs of production and destruction of environmental functions. It has also resulted in a Western masculine metaphysical understanding of power in terms of dominance over, and human capacity to exploit the nature and making economy ride rough shod over the society. Can such an economic development be called successful if it has effected a terrible despoliation of nature and environment and destruction of people in the South?

What needs a reexamining of anti-nature development whereby a compromise is struck between nature and man resulting in homo/nature balanced development or cosmocentric development. This envisages recognition of a coordinated and organic bond, man has with the whole of the creation. This kind of development is in conformity with the sustainability of nature so that the present and future generations are not deprived of their right to a healthy environment, access to the resources of the earth, as well as the nature itself not stripped of its right to existence. Thus, the rights to development and sustainable development are closely inter-related and to be understood not in terms of intra-generational or intergenerational equity but in terms of equity between man and nature. The very recognition that both human beings and non human nature along with its flora and fauna are equal partners in the cosmos to make it meaningful and worth living in, provides a basis for reexamining the Western pattern of development. The kind of development needed is one that relativizes economic growth, exorbitant consumerism and technological progress as values superior to other intrinsic human values inherent in many civilizations and disarms economics of its paramountcy with which it has so far reduced the society to a mere economic activity.

New Indices of Development

Measurement of economic growth in terms of GNP has become the classical indicator of development according to the mainstream economics. This is challenged on various grounds. Firstly, economic growth and development are not equivalent concepts, though conventionally used. National income accounts with data on aggregate production growth tell nothing about the meaning of development, but also how income is distributed either socially or territorially. Secondly, national income accounts are not merely imperfect but also misleading indicator of economic growth. Policy decisions based on them are more likely to exacerbate than alleviate social problems. Each year vast sums of money are spent on repairing or atleast controlling the damage of an advanced industrial civilization. In other words, the real social damages of economic growth go up, so does the national income. In the US Alaskan oil spill incident, the US government spent $2 billion to repair the damage, which showed an increase in GNP at the cost of human life and ecology. This happens in all societies when their conditions collectively become worse off as the years go by, even as GNP continues climbing up. Thirdly, the cost of environmental destruction or the 'destruction of environmental functions' is not added into national income accounts. As economist Robert Repetto, points out, this failure to distinguish between natural asset destruction and income generation makes the GNP "a false beacon, and can draw those who steer by it into the rocks".[42]

Growing realization of the GNP as a faulty measurement of progress, has led to the exploration of alternatives. There has already been burgeoning of new indicators of progress demonstrating mounting dis-enchantment with the customary habit of equating progress with economic growth. Herman Daly, a World Bank economist, and theologian John Lobb of the Claremout School of Theology, have developed an "Index of sustainable economic welfare" (ISEW). The UN has devised the Human Development Index (HDI). The third index is the grain consumption per person, a very sensitive measure of changes in well-being in low-income countries.[43]

Resurgence of ethical values and restoring them to a central place in the discipline of economics has already been noticed in the works of eminent writers namely, Amartya Sen's "On Ethics and Economics" and Herman Daly's "For the Common Good". Sociologist, Amital Etzinni, in his "The Moral Dimension" [44] is of the view that apart from rationality, which should not be confined to a mere benefit-cost calculus of maximum self-interest, altruism and moral duty are equal motivators of human behaviour in the economic realm. Paul Ekins and his colleagues have launched, The Living Economy Movement, which stresses the exploration of economic requirements of the common good and community building.

This ethical revolution in economics is still in a nascent stage. Unless and until the prevalent trends and tendencies of current economic development are reversed on suggested ethical lines, the continued antithesis between development and environmental cannot be replaced by new ethics of sustainable development. In the brilliant words of an authority: "It may well be that the kind of development needed is one that is open to transcendence in order to relativize economic growth and technological progress as values, as well as to de-absolutize the claims made by managerial absolutism and the modern nation-state".[45]

In the economic substructure, what is needed is an ethical resurgence, which would release policy planners and economists from a growth obsession, finding essentially a dichotomy between good and goods. It insists on developing alternative measures of progress based on equity and sustainability. What an authority addressed to Latin American some years ago deserves to be quoted:

Does man live by GNP alone? Should we not take advantage of our longer-term vision and ask what kind of person Latin America may wish to evolve by the end of this century? What are the transcendental values-cultural, ethical, artistic, religious, morals that extend beyond the current working of the purely economic and social system? How to appeal to the youth, who so often seeks nourishment in dreams, as well as in bread?[46]

To show a beacon light to man who is already in an environmental cul de sac, the need is not to trivialize the basic issues and concerns by putting emphasis on mere transfer of technology or funds. It necessitates, as discussed above, a rethinking of and a revolution in dominant western ethnocentric paradigms of development, which would be based on recognition of the moral contents of basic human rights.

References

1. Noam Chomsky, quoted in Sham Lal, "The International Scene: How the past lingers on", *Times of India*, May 23, 1993, p. 8.
2. See for details Allen Hammond, Eric Rodenburg and William R Moomaw, "The Greenhouse Index", *Environment*, March 1991, and Anil Agarwal and Sunita Narain, *Global Warming in an Unequal World*, Centre for Science and Environment, New Delhi, 1991.
3. Florentin Krause, Wilfrid Bach and Jon Moomey, Energy Policy in the Greenhouse Vol. I, *International Project for Sustainable Energy Paths* (IPSEP), EI Cerrito, 1989.
4. Khor Kok Peng, G-7 leaders fail to agree to combat global warming in *Third World Economics: Trends and Analysis*, Third World Network, 15 September, 1990, Penang.
5. *Times of India*, 12 June 1992.
6. Friends of the Earth, Ozone Protection Campaign: Materials for Montreal Protocol Review, London, 1990.
7. Anon, China attacks unfair Ozone Protocol in New Scientist 11 March 1989 London: Usha Rai, "India's terms for signing Montreal Protocol", *Times of India*, 17 March 1989, New Delhi.
8. Anil Agarwal and Sunita Narain, *Towards a Green World* (Centre for Science and Environment, New Delhi 1992), pp. 11-13.
9. Vandana Shiva, "Biotechnology and Profit", *Ecoforum*, Nairobi, December 1990.
10. Mostafa K. Tolba, Make haste slowly: Statement to the second session of the adhoc working group of legal and technical experts on biological diversity, UNEP, Nairobi, 1991, memeo.
11. J.B. Opschoor, "North-South Trade, Resource Degradation and Economic Security, *Bulletin of Peace Proposals*, 20:2, 1989 pp. 135-42. Also Samir Amin, Maldevelopment; Anatomy of a Global Failure (London: Zed, 1990).
12. See State of the World 1991, *A World Watch Institute Report on Progress Toward a Sustainable Society* (New York, 1991) p. 6.
13. Norman Myres, *The Gaia Atlas of Future Worlds* (Anchor Books/ Double Day, New York, 1990).

14. *The World Economy in the 20th Century* (Paris: OECD, 1989) Alan B. During, Poverty and the Environment: Reversing the Downward Spiral, World Watch Paper 92 (Washington D.C.: World Watch Institute, November, 1989).
15. Herman E. Daly, "Sustainable Development: From Concept and Theory towards Operational Principles," Population and Development Review (Proceedings of Hoover Institution Conference on Population and Development).
16. World Bank, *World Debt Tables 1989-1990: External Debt of Developing countries* Vols. I and II (Washington, D.C.: 1989).
17. Martin Khor, "The Drain from the South", *Third World Resurgence*, No. 46, June 1994, p. 20.
18. Roger D. Stone and Eve Hamilton, *Global Economics and the Environment* (New York: Council of Foreign Relations Press, 1991), p. 20.
19. Ben Jackson, *Poverty and the Planet: A Question of Survival* (Penguin Books, London, 1990).
20. Jane Perlez, "U.S. Forgives Loans to 12 African Countries", New York Times, 10 January 1990.
21. See David Bigman, "A Plan to End IDC Debt and Save the Environment Too," *Challenge* July/August 1990.
22. Diana Page, Debt for Nature Swaps: Experience Gained, Lessons Learned", *International Environmental Affairs*, January, 1990.
23. Kerstin Kiessling and Nathan Keyfitz, "The Population Debate: Urgency of the Problem", a paper presented at the Population Summit of the World's Scientific Academies held in New Delhi from October 24-27, quoted in *Down to Earth* Vol. 2, No. 13, November 30, 1993, p. 15.
24. David Pearce, Anil Markandya and Edward B. Barbier, *Blueprint for a Green Economy*, Earthscan Publications, London, 1989.
25. A.W. Corsby, Ecological Imperialism: The Biological Expansion of Europe 900-1900 (Cambridge University Press, 1986) M.Redelift, "The Multiple Dimensions of Sustainable Development", Geography 76:1 1990, pp. 36-42; D. Pearce, "Economics and the Global Environmental Challenge," Millennium 19:3 1990, pp. 365-87; Robert Paehlk and Douglas

Torgerson Managing Leviathan: *Environmental Politics and the Administrative State* (Peterborough Ont: Broadview, 1990; and Michael Jacobs, The Green Economy: *Environment, Sustainable Development and Politics of the Future* London: Pluto, 1991).

26. John D. Milliman, et al., *Environmental and Economic Impact of Rising Sea level and Subsiding Deltas: The Nile and Bengal Examples*, Woods Hole Ocenographics Institution, Woods Hole, Massachusetts, 1988.
27. Edith B. Weiss, *In Fairness to Future Generations: International Law, Common Patrimony and Intergenerational Equity* (New York: Transnational, 1989).
28. Rajni Kothari, "Environment, Techonology and Ethics", in J.Ronald Engel and Joan Gibb Engel, Ed., *Ethics of Environment and Development* (London: Belhaven Press: a Division of Printer Publishers 1990), p. 30.
29. Simon Dalby, "Security, Modernity, Ecology: The Dilemmas of Post Cold War Security Discourse", *Alternatives* Vol. 17, Number I, winter 1992, p. 114.
30. S.J. Samartha and Lynn de Silva, eds., *Man in Nature, Guest or Engineer* ? (Columbo: The Ecumenical Institute for Study and Dialogue, 1979).
31. Rajni Kothari, n.28, p. 31.
32. Hans Jona, The *Imperative* of Responsibility (Chicago: The University of Chicago press, 1989).
33. Denis Goulet, *The Cruel Choice: A New Concept in the Theory of Development* (New York: Atheneum, 1971), pp. 215-35.
34. Mahbub Ul Hag and Paul Streeten, *Human Development Report 1990 UNDP* (New York: Oxford University Press, 1990).
35. Sekhar Singh, "The Global Environmental Debate", *The Indian Journal Of Public Administration* Vol. XXXV, No. 3, July-September 1989, p. 371.
36. Quoted in Lester R.Brown, Christopher Flavin and Sandra Postel, *Saving the Planet* (New York/London: Norton & Company, 1991), p. 122.
37. Johan Galtung, Development and Alternative Economics, presented to the participants in EPU, fall 1993, Programee, Stadtschlaining, Austria where the author was a participant.

38. Wolfgang Sachs, "The Economist's blind eye's, New Internationalist, June 1992, pp. 15-16.
39. Mark A. Lutz and Kenneth Lux, Humanistic Economics: The New Challenges (New York: The Bootstrap Press, 1988), p. 29.
40. Wolfgang Sachs, "Development: a guide to the ruins", New Internationalist, June 1992, p. 5.
41. S.J. Samartha and De Silva Lynn, ed., Man in Nature, Guest or Engineer? (Colombo: The Ecumenical Institute for Study and Dialogue, 1979)
42. Herman E.Daly and John B.Cobb, Jr., For the Common Good: Redirecting the Economy Toward Community, The Environment, and a Sustainable Future (Boston: Beacon Press, 1989); U.N. Development Programme (UNDP), Human Development report 1990, *op. cit.,* see also Robert Costanza and Lisa Waigner, "No Accounting for Nature: How Conventional Economics Distorts the Real Value of Things, *Washington Post*, 2 September 1990, p. B3.
43. Amitai Etzioni, *The Moral Dimension* (New York: The Free Press / Mac Millan, 1988).
44. Denis Goulet, International Ethics and Human Rights", *Alternatives* Vol. 17, Number 2, Spring 1992, p. 241.
45. David H. Pollock, "A Latin American Strategy to the year 2000: Can the Past Serve as a guide to the future" ? In David H. Pollock and A.R.M. Ritter, ed., Latin American Prospectus for the 80's: What kinds of Development: Development, Reformation or Transformation? (Ottowa: Norman Patterson School of International Affairs, Carletion University Conference Proceedings, November 1980), pp. 1-37.
46. Denis Goulet, n. 44, p. 242.

8

Matter and Spirit, Unity or Split: Secularism, Sovereignty and Ecological Crisis Toward a Cosmic Whole Perspective on World Politics

Culture is one way of expressing the understanding of the subtle meaning attached to the traditionally ingrained beliefs and views about the inexorably operation of eternal cosmic laws unraveling the place of human beings in the cosmos in relation to other non human beings and nature itself. The mode of living out on a timeless span of generations not of weeks and years strewn with a value pattern derived and reproduced from that meaning based on certain metaphysical underpinnings in various forms such as language, art, worship, rituals even political and economic relationship is nothing but expression of the culture's portrayal of the cosmological order in which all the inanimate and animate are placed not in their exclusionary separatedness but in their universal inclusiveness. Universal acceptability, credibility and legitimacy of the cosmological order are due to people's indomitable faith in the immutability of the cosmic laws.

The developments in the field of science considering everything both animate and inanimate as objective unconnected particles, faith in instrumentality of reason, centrality of technology and progress replacing what is sacred and premium on matter over divine—all these came as a threat to the culture's entire world view. Thus, the traditionally established cosmic worldview came in clash with a secular modernist worldview resulting in a crisis situation. The secular worldview having its roots in

Renaissance and science became the dominant western worldview represented by the US and other European countries from a global perspective. The western definition of development from this perspective involves procuring a good, commodious and inordinate life style, to the people and wealth production at the expense of environment. It is not cosmic laws but mechanical laws as discovered and subject to control and manipulation by the scientists as well human beings that became the guiding metaphor for human progress and modernization. Viewing the entire planet as an external mechanical object to be exploited, and measuring progress in terms of inordinate and luxurious life style, exultant consumption, industrialization based on fossil fuel technology, and holding wealth production and richness as synonym for happiness, have become universally accepted norms of a secularist view of progress. Science played a key role in the emergence of a secularist world view which shifts human faith in the Ultimate Reality to matter, scripts the triumph of human reason over the vagaries of nature and usurps the space and time not in a timelessness but linearity frame for material progress. The secular is concerned with the worldly as opposed to the sacred. Its Latin root 'saecularis' refers to the temporal and material as opposed to the eternal and spiritual[1]. Secularism replaces intuition with senses, wisdom with knowledge, spiritualism with science, realization with facts and observation, and metaphysical with physical, and detachment and dispassion with brute desires, and spirit with physical body.

Secularism views the entire world as the lifeless other to be exploited for the fulfillment of desires of human beings. The secular portrayal of the world resulted in the spread of western democracy, market economy and globalization to all parts of the globe as standard of development and modernity. Secularist vision of duality –self vs. the other has been denied in Indian philosophy and religion. The Hindu scriptures point out that belief in the non-existence of matter and oneness of spirit should not be founded on dogmatic, illogical, unintelligible or inexplicable theories but on scientific inner investigation and exact understanding. The Upanishads have taught the same lesson of the subject and object fusing into a unified undifferentiated whole:

> **"Where there is duality, as it were, there one sees another; there one smells another; there one tastes another...But where everything has become just one's own self, then whereby and whom would one see? Then whereby and whom would one smell? Then whereby and whom would one taste" ?[2]**

In recognition of what Indian sages and seers experienced about basic oneness of the universe, eminent scientists like John Wheeler point out that in modern science the distinction between the observers and the observed breaks down completely. The Indian philosophy finds no distinction between matter and spirit. In the animate and inanimate both, it experiences the all ness of spirit making the entire cosmos as living and dynamic with the power of God. The division of nature into separate objects is not fundamental and any such objects have a fluid and ever changing character. The Eastern worldview is therefore intrinsically dynamic and contains time and change as essential features. The cosmos is seen as one inseparable reality-for ever in motion, alive, organic; spiritual and material at the same time. The Eastern image of the Divine is not that of a ruler who directs the world from above, but of a principle that controls everything from within:

He who, dwelling in all things,
Yet is other than all things,
Whom all things do not know,
Whose body all things are,
Who controls all things from within-
He is your soul, the inner Controller,
The Immortal [3]

In accord with this insightful ethos of Indian philosophy, a great scientist Pere Teilhard de Chardin points out:

> **"It is impossible to deny that, deep within ourselves an interior appears at the heart of beings, as it were seen through a rent. This is enough to ensure that, in one degree or another, this interior should obtrude itself as existing everywhere in nature from all time. Since the stuff of the universe has an inner aspect at one point of itself, there is necessarily a double aspect to its structure, that is to say, in every region of space and time-in the same way, for instance, as it is granular: coextensive with their without, there is a within to things" [4]**

The scientists as glimpsed by the secularist modern view have challenged even the mechanical picture of the universe. Sir James Jeans summed up in a memorable passage in his Rede Lectures:

> "Today there is a wide measure of agreement, which on the physical side of science approaches almost to unanimity, that the stream of knowledge is heading towards a non mechanical

reality; the universe begins to look more like a great thought than like a great machine." [5]

The ever expanding universal self heading towards that incomprehensible ultimate reality has been reduced by the secularist world view to an individualized self, thinking the entire universe as a mechanical lifeless other to be expended for satisfaction of its brute desires. The western view of the universe as framed by science has been able to sustain secularism as a globally viable culture dismantling what ancient sages and saints, and the present scientists have notioned about the universe. Not transcending beyond the cocoons of body, mind, intellect based reason and rationality, to get comprehension of the ultimate reality, and to enlarge one's atomized self into the universal self, the humans learnt from the western dominant secularist paradigm to apply the instrumentality of reason in the service of their desires. The ever growing consumption, inordinate life style and wealth production facilitated by secularist world view created a world of ever deepening contrast between conspicuous consumption in the North and gruelling poverty in the South. Myriad forms of pollutions threatening air, land, water, seas, and oceans have plagued the entire universe plunging the entire living system into the abyss of insecurity. Whereas, from a conventional international relation perspective these general problems are taken as distinct fields of study within the existing realist paradigms, they may also be understood more systematically as interrelated symptoms and causal connections of the global problematique. Ernst Haas conceptualizes the global problematique as "the problem of all the problems not merely the sum of the problems of pollution, war, famine, alienation, resource depletion, urban crowding, and exploitation of the Third world by the first. It is a systemic construct that assumes causal connections among these problems, connections that amplify the disturbance of the metasystem" [6]

From a cosmological perspective, the roots of the global problematique lie embedded in the mode of consciousness that is born out of the secular materialistic worldview. But the consciousness that is born out of the enlarged universal self is what the global ecology envisions to put humanity in the larger cosmos. Since the western secular world view has been irreversibly global, the danger it poses by destroying the environmental functions has also become global." For the first time in history, humanity has become a geophysical force capable of undermining Earth's life support systems." [7] The contemporary ecological crisis poses a serious challenge to the secular worldview. Nobody disagrees with radical political ecologists who castigate modernity as a source of ecological crisis.

The concept of expanded self does not mean return to undifferentiated oneness of humanity with nature or pre rational modes of consciousness. It means realization of the oneness of spirit in both nature and human beings. It means ascension to a higher stage of consciousness, which enables human beings to perceive spirit or sacredness in both animate and inanimate. It is enunciated in the Bhagvad Gita:

> Without and within all beings; the unmoving and also the moving; because of His subtlety He is incomprehensible; He is far and near.[8]

International Relations theories built around sovereign state system's legitimacy to procure material progress to its citizens through mastery over nature in the larger context of modern secular world view comes in for greater challenges from the global ecological crisis. The quest for material progress in terms of inordinate life style, commodious living and amassing wealth has resulted in instrumentalisation and valorization of human reason and autonomy not in Hegelian Absolute Reason or Eastern Universal Self. Matter is born from Divine Mind and is perceptible to mortal mind in itself and of itself matter has no reality, no intrinsic existence. "Man has discovered through theoretical investigation, through logic and through certain laboratory experiments (such as converting a visible piece of ice into invisible forces) that a permanent and unalterable creative power must underlie all the transitory and illusive forms of the phenomenal world."[9]

The most important characteristic of the Eastern worldview and its essence is the awareness of the unity and mutual interrelation of all things and events, the experience of all phenomena in the world as manifestations of a basic oneness. All things are seen as interdependent and inseparable parts of the cosmic whole; as different manifestations of the same ultimate reality. Despite several counter proposals and the philosophical problems involved in the interpretation of quantum theory, the universal interconnectedness of things and events, however seems to be a fundamental feature of the atomic reality. The following passage from David Bohm confirms this fact most eloquently:

> "One is led to a new notion of unbroken wholeness which denies the classical idea of analyzability of the world into separately and independently existing parts... We have reversed the usual classical notion that the independent elementary parts of the world are the fundamental reality, and that the various systems are merely particular contingent forms and arrangements of these parts. Rather, we say that inseparable quantum

> interconnectedness of the whole universe is the fundamental reality, and that relatively independently behaving parts are merely particular and contingent forms within this whole."[10]

Quantum theory views the universe not as a collection of physical objects, but rather as a complicated web of relations between the various parts of a unified whole. This, however, is the way in which Eastern mystics have experienced the world and their words of experience are almost identical with those used by atomic physicists:

> "The material object becomes... something different from what we now see, not a separate object on the background or in the environment of the rest of nature but an indivisible part and a subtle way even in an expression of unity of all that we see."[11]

The following statements from atomic physicists could, in turn, be read as a description of the mystical experience nature:

"An elementary particle is not an independently existing unanalyzble entity. It is, in essence, a set of relationships that reach outward to other things."[12] Another physicist in the same vein opines: The world thus appears as a complicated tissue of events, in which connections of different kinds alternate or overlap or combine and thereby determine the texture of the whole."[13]

The picture of an interconnected cosmic web, which emerges from modern atomic physics, has been used extensively in the East to convey the mystical experience of nature. For the Hindus, Brahman is the unifying thread in the cosmic web, the ultimate ground of all being:

> "He on whom the sky, the earth, and the atmosphere are woven, and the wind, together with all life-breaths, Him alone know as the one Soul."[14]

Similarly W. Heisenberg points to the nearly non-existence of matter in his autobiography that "atoms are not things. The electrons which form an atom's shells are no longer things in the sense of classical physics, things which would be unambiguously described by concepts like location, velocity, energy, size. When we get down to the atomic level, the objective world in space and time no longer exists, and the mathematical symbols of theoretical physics refer merely to possibilities not to facts."[15] Non acceptance of the oneness of spirit and of non-existence of matter has been the bedrock of secular worldview. Premised on this view the sovereign state system went on ravaging the nature to meet the requirements of profligate and inordinate life style of the people—the criteria of attributing legitimacy to the state. International system is the result of the sovereign state system's rightness of actions in this direction in a world of competitiveness for the scarce resources. International Relation theories bred in such a secular worldview have never been able to account for the changes in the environment, let alone show any beacon of hope. The constructive International Relation theorists tend to understand sovereignty as a historically variable set of norms and practices that are capable of mutating in response to new social conditions. Sovereignty being a social construct can be reconstructed into new forms with real material consequences. The deconstructive post-modernism advocates reducing sovereignty to mere discourse.

Having shared the same ontological foundation with science that human beings are mere particles of motion in quest for material welfare, the International Relation theories are becoming one-sided and inadequate to meet the impending challenges from the environment, since the ultimate truth or reality is not matter. There have been changes in the findings of scientists in recent years coming in proximity to the Eastern mysticism that from Atma have come forth all physical, biophysical and psychophysical energies, all worlds, all gods, and all beings.[16]

The world view emerging from atomic physics seems to be perfectly apropos with the words of a Tantric Buddhist, Lama Anagarika Govinda:

> "The Buddhist does not believe in an independent or separately existing external world, into whose dynamic forces he could inert himself. The external world and his inner world are for him only two sides of the same fabric, in which the threads of all forces and of all events, of all forms of consciousness and of their objects, are woven into an inseparable net of endless, mutually conditioned relations" [17]

Modern Physics has acknowledged this:

> "The field theories of modern physics force us to abandon the classical distinction between material particles and the void...in quantum field theory, this field is seen as the basis of all particles and of their mutual interaction....

The vacuum is far from empty. On the contrary, it contains an unlimited number of particles, which come into being and vanish without end. Here, then is the closest parallel to the void of Eastern mysticism in modern physics. Like the Eastern void, the physical vacuum—as it is called in field theory-is not a state of mere nothingness, but contains the potentiality for all forms of the particle world. These forms in turn are not independent physical entities but merely transient manifestations of the underlying void...The discovery of the dynamic quality of the vacuum is seen by many physicist as one of the most important findings of modern physics" [18]

Thus, based upon the neglected understanding of the oneness of spirit the international relation theories need to be reinvented from a rather different perspective: a cosmic view of the world as the unfolding of spirit. This view integrates all the disparate and divergent and synthesizes them into the web of larger universal self. Constructism, sovereignty, secularism, and post modernism have been interpreted and weaved into the cosmic whole as a foundation of international relation theories to countervail the excesses of materialism and move humanity towards a higher plane of consciousness. While describing sovereignty as a historical construct and secularism as a discourse it understands constructism, which is an important moment of truth in its recognition of, inter subjective dimensions of reality. Secular materialism has reduced the world to a mere instrumentality and observable objectivity, and undermined for centuries together the internal subjective aspects of reality. A deeper, vaster, and more meaningful dimension of reality exists above the sensate and material level. As stated by H. Schipperges:

> "Scarcely have we discovered the cosmos and are behind the moon, when there awaits us a new universe, namely the full inside of nature, the kingdom of the soul as it was previously called, the dimension of depth, that in the inside there is also a universe as Goethe said, actually a multiverse, the perspective of our modern world which nowhere shows the world but worlds, situations, anthropologies, fragments, aspects in upheaval. Everything in this grandiose, hectic, and also moving panorama of the ending second millennium points to the conclusion that we are in the middle of a second enlightenment." [19]

Premised upon such metaphysics of unfoldment of mundane self into super consciousness, this cosmic whole perspective never entails any specific evolutionary mechanism like natural selection, or idealism in terms of utopian quest or the unimportance of the material world. The cosmic whole view comprehends the universe as a manifested aspect of universal self or cosmic consciousness. It recognizes no duality or dichotomy between matter and spirit, nature and humanity, objectivity and subjectivity, only the oneness of spirit pervades them all. Mind and matter are not two dimensions but represent the manifestation of omnipresent universal self. It is the imperishable non dual self that pervades all.The opening verse of the Isa Upanishad proclaims the sublime truth: All this universe in all its changing forms is enveloped by the Lord, the Universal Self or Spirit.[20] Adi Sankaracharya in his commentary on Katha Upanishad says:

> He is the swan dwelling in the heaven in the form of the sun, the air filling the atmosphere, the fire dwelling on the altar, the holy guest in the house; he is in man, in gods, in the sacrifice, in the immensity of space, he is born in water as the aquatic creatures, on the earth as insects, reptiles and mammals, born as fruit of sacrifice, born of the mountains, as rivers, flowing from the mountains to the ocean; He is the True, The infinite.[21]

From the perspective of cosmic world, the humans who are endowed with the capacity to realize the universal divine self are "that being in whom the universe celebrates itself and its numinous origins in a special mode of conscious self awareness".[22] The cosmic worldview displaces secularism's description of humans as appropriator of the world with a new vision of humans as the expanded universal self-perceiving all as its own self. This finds expression in mysticism, philosophy and theology,[23] Gaia theory[24] and constructive postmodernism. The secular worldview in view of former's ecologically descriptive and unsustainable functions. An alternative cosmic world perspective in place of secular worldview is premised on Eastern mysticism and science. Drawing upon Gita, and works of Eastern scientists like Eddington, Copra, Bohr and Eastern philosophy, Upanishads and saints like Aurobionda, Yoganada Pramahansa and Vivekananda, in case for alternative cosmic world theory is put forth on two grounds: firstly,

The secular worldview with its materialistic socio political metaphysics represents a deficient human consciousness confined to materialism, which has been destructive of the environment. Secondly, this old view has been proved to be inadequate and not in synchronisation with the changing world. The metaphysical foundation of cosmic worldview is based on the very understanding that the universe is a manifestation of super consciousness i.e. the universal self. This perspective synchronizes the Eastern mysticism advocating every human of becoming and ultimately being one and in unity with the universal self, with developments in contemporary science.

Advantages of Cosmic View over Secularism

The cosmic worldview dissolves all divisions between nature and humans, matter and spirit, and self and the other. It ensures a rendezvous between science and religion. Science at present without being obsessed with matter, grips with void and nothingness which religion says spirit with common thread that binds together both the animate and inanimate and weaves into cosmic tapestry. Being at odds with reductionism of secular science, this cosmic view seems to be consistent with recent depiction of nature in physics, cosmology and biology. Eastern seers from time immemorial have experienced what modern science reveals today through its scientific rigour and observation. Referring to the basic unity of the universe, as upheld in Eastern mysticism and modern physics Capra says:

> **The Eastern traditions constantly refer to this ultimate indivisible reality, which manifests itself in all things, and of which all things are parts. It is called Brahman in Hinduism, Dharmakaya in Buddhism, Tao in Taoism...The basic oneness of the universe is not only the central characteristic of the mystical experience, but is also one of the most important revelations of modern physics. It becomes apparent at the atomic level, and manifests itself more and more as one penetrates deeper into matter, down into the realm of sub atomic particles. The unity of all things and events will be a recurring theme throughout our comparison of modern physics with Eastern philosophy[25].**

Since environmental degradation is a crisis of consciousness born of materialistic worldview, the cosmic worldview acknowledges humanity's special position and unique responsibility in the cosmos to redress the environment. Political and international relation theories always put primacy on institutions and structures, which they believe, can be manipulated to redound to the materialistic needs of the individuals. In these theories little importance is accorded to ethical and moral build up of individuals in owning responsibility for what they have done to the environment. But the environmental insights and ethics require individual responsibility and an ethical resurgence in human beings. The cosmic worldview can bridge the hiatus between these two approaches. The global environmental crisis urgents a heightened consciousness born of the realization of unity and oneness of spirit in both animates and inanimate. The onus is on individuals to evolve consciously into the realm of expanded self. The theories and practices in international relations and world politics have been determined by the secular materialistic worldview represented by the western powers led by the United States. The destructive consequences of such a view have already been writ large on the human life. In the context of western culture the hegemonic representation of such a materialistic view, the orientation has been so strongly towards creative physical activity to change, action, acquisition and expansion of power, and whose basic understanding of the world therefore involves conceiving of reality as tangible and object like, in order to be able to manipulate and get a grasp on it for our own benefit in this materialized form. The fundamental responsibility lies in awakening the humans to the devastating implications of the exterior and fragmented view of the reality of the materialistic view, and to the desideratum of being spiritually motivated to comprehend the ultimate reality.The main theme of the theories and practices of world politics has been to legitimize and reinforce the matter centric view deeply penetrated into western culture and civilization, and clamped its hegemony over all nations, people, societies, and nature.

Secularism and Sovereignty: Primacy on Matter

The separation of religious authority from political authority evolved gradually in modern Europe as the doctrine of secularism, was a specific historical development found expression in the works of Italian philosopher, Machiavelli. The treaty of Westphalia signed at the end of thirty years of religious war was epochal in that it dawned the birth of nation state and nuanced the territorial exclusivity as the basis of sovereign state system. Though it fused the political and religious authority of monarchs within their jurisdiction, religiously motivated foreign intervention was delegitimized and gradually the norm of religious tolerance within the domestic domain took root and later on expanded into a comprehensive ontological and epistemological secular worldview. Its acceptance and legitimization among nations as their political and economic build up has become almost universal. It signals the triumph of human reason over dogma, superstition and myth, knowledge as power; the mastery of nature through science and technology, describes history as a progressive march towards the material liberation of humanity. the individual citizen as the receptacle of political authority; and the sovereign state as the collective expression of the ideals of reason, progress and liberty[26]. The fundamental basis of secularism is "that man and not God must be the central focus of all development; his earthly freedom, well-being, progress and perfection of his body, life and mind and not some Heavenly post mortem salvation of his soul must be the aim of life." [27]

Roots in Western Culture

The Hebrew espoused of a transcendent monotheistic God removed from the cosmos.[28] It is rooted in the Judeo Christian notion of linear time, its teleology of progress, and its associated conception of nature as given to the service of a God like humanity.[29] The Sophists, similarly contend that "man is the measure of all things" [30] Thus, having roots in western religious heritage, secularism was further strengthened by the scientific conception of evolution leading to the popular belief that humans stand at the summit of biological evolution, and are free to keep nature at their disposal.

Overarching Faith in Science: Hallmark of Secularism

The credit of being the architects of secular modernity goes to Descartes, Newton and John Locke who while upholding the validity of the transcendental and the other world, promoted the secular values of reason, liberty and material progress. In modern thought the secular substitutes for God were reason, the sovereign state, the sovereign individual, and history.[31] Faith in the God is replaced by faith in the reason and nation state[32] A mechanistic world view substituted the organistic view, understanding the universe as a great machine to be discovered and exploited by human reason. According to secular materialism, all levels of reality, all dimensions of experience are reduced to matter alone. Thus, the modern western civilization became the first major civilization to deny reality to the oneness of spirit. To quote a well known nuclear physicist and philosopher:

> **"In the history of the west, the two differing fundamental attitudes, the exterior view and the interior one, have been in fertile interaction. They are reflected in the splitting up of knowledge and belief. Rationalism, and later the Enlightenment, deepened this split and declared the two valued exterior view to be the only true view, that is, one appropriate to the structure of reality. It is the basis of our triumphant science. It has taught us to manipulate the world around us for our own benefit, and to develop knowledge systematically as an instrument of power for ruling over people and nature."** [33]

The machine as an object of adoration and worship has become the diabolism of modern secularism. In the mediaeval period salvation was solicited through experience with God, where as modern secularism sought it through material progress. Liberated from religious dogma and superstition by help of reason and science, the humans paid obeisance to the Baconian injunction "to bind nature to your service and make her your slave." [34] The quest for truth shifted from knowledge of and experience with God to knowledge of the physical universe. The Heavenly city was replaced as the Earthly city in which not God but humans became the master and measure of all things. The progress of mankind was judged not in terms of their experience with and approximation to eternal truth or God but in terms of progress through linear times in terms of commodious living and greater liberty. Technology became an object of adoration exacting an unfailing adherence, and modernity's relationship with it assumes a religious faith.[35] Modernity founded on human beings' faith in the ability of science, reason and technology to improve their conditions of life sheet anchored secularist world view.[36]

Sovereignty: From Divine Status to Prudent Calculation

Historically, the institutions of sovereignty originated in mediaeval Europe as an attribute of God devolved first to monarchs and subsequently, to bureaucratic, territorial and more or less democratic states associated with modernity." The carving of Europe, and eventually the entire planet, into a patchwork of mutually exclusive territorial states is modernity's rendering of nature." [37] The grant ideals of the Enlightenment—reason, progress and liberty found their expression in notions of popular sovereignty and self-determination. Secularist notion of progress finds its expression in the modern democratic state elected by prudent and rational individuals. Sovereignty originally related to God shifted to the reason of calculated individuals. The basis of political authority was explicated in terms of consent of the governed. Faith in the rightfulness of the Divine was shifted to faith in the rightfulness of the sovereign state. The basis of the consent of the governed rested on rightfulness of action of the sovereign state to provide them a commodious living and guarantee wealth production, property rights and security. Radical individualism like atomistic particles implicit in foundation of domestic political authority resembles to mutually exclusive sovereign states comprising the international system. Sovereign state in its secular dimension founded on atomistic and calculative individuals' faith in its rightfulness of action to fulfill their materialistic needs thus, becomes a primary instrumentality in their hands to get salvation through material progress.

Liberal Political Theory and Science

Implicit in the liberal political authority as a part of a larger secular worldview is the radical individualism, promotion of which in terms of unhindered material progress constituted the criteria to provide legitimacy to the authority. The modern liberal political theory coincided with the rise of modern science. "The Newtonian image of particles in motion was the guiding metaphor in the secular formulation of possessive individualism, an image that characterized both the modern citizen and modern state."[38] The liberal political theory of possessive individualism founded by Thomas Hobbes and John Locke was shaped by the mechanistic worldview and Newtonian view of motion. Springing from the limitless and profligate acquisitiveness of market political economy driven way of life-the contribution of both science and the liberal possessive individualism of Hobbes and Locke-the concomitant decline in human beings' sensibility to other humans, living and non living beings; the human beings have been on a rapacious rampage that cuts at the very root of the common organic bond with the whole of creation and the very survival of all. Like realism, it viewed the nature and other nations as the lifeless other to be exploited for satisfaction of individuals' material needs at home. Its anthropocentric view of nature and universe and consequent emphasis on economic growth leads to a relative lack of concern for the stability, integrity, and beauty of the earth. Obsessed with growth fetish, the western liberal market economy destroyed both the nature and the poor. In other words, "if Judeo-Christian monotheism took nature out of religion, Anglo-American economists took nature out of economics".[39] In a liberal political tradition as the individuals are free, autonomous, and atomistic to purse their material progress unimpeded, the sovereign states, their collective counterparts in the international system, are free and have jurisdiction over citizens and resources within their borders.

Secularism: Single Point or One sided Perspective

The secular worldview born of a specific structure of consciousness associated with the discovery of matter by science has become a single point or one-sided perspective of carrying out a political or economic life. Thus, the sovereign state system and its liberal political dimensions are the expressions of single point perspective of the autonomous individuals with authority over him. At the individual level, the single point perspective is represented by the insatiable and inordinate consumption and exorbitant life style prompted by secularism, which holds that the universe is a receptacle of objects to be exploited. Though there are other non-material perspectives of living out, the single point perspective resting on matter has dominated the other perspectives disseminating that affluence, production of wealth, wanton consumption and technological mastery are the primary objects to be achieved in human life. The single point perspective is so deeply ingrained in the collective and individual consciousness that the devastating consequences of humans' penchant for material progress received scant attention and little concern. The imperious consequences of pursuing such a materialistic way of life through science and technology on the environment and society put a challenge to the single point perspective of individuals and sovereign state built on a materialistic secular world view. At issue is whether a materialistic secular world can survive its own created implications. The horrendous consequences of materialistic secular worldview have been universal degradation of soil, mass extinction of species, deforestation, depleted aquifers, pollution of water, climate change, sea level rise and global warming. A finite planet of six billion plus possessive individuals seeking inordinate life style, affluence and consumption is simply unsustainable.

The growing interdependence among nations, a host of international institutions and transnational social movements suggests that the old individualistic atomistic secular view is on the decline. These developments are symptomatic of "a contagion of reperception".[40] But the consciousness confined to matter has not yet been transcended into cosmic consciousness while individuals pursuing their atomistic life style are showing short shrifts to the very fact of growing interdependence. In the face of the impending ecological, political, social and economic upheavals, the redundancy of one-sided perspective of secular modernity looms large.

Cosmic Whole View

The secular worldview born of a historically specific stage of human development represents a similar mental structure of consciousness. The secular worldview is one sided or single point perspective of the individual subject. The cosmic whole view is a transcendental one, it expands the mundane self into a universal self where all animate and inanimate seem as nothing but the manifested universal self. It comes to the perception of all those shining in the glaze of the spirit that all are strung to the cosmic whole like rows of gems on a string. It is not a multi verse perspectival approach as post modernists adduce, it is a cosmic whole perspective of consciousness that moves beyond the materialism informed rationality. While in form and structures all retain their individualities, and multi perspectival dimensions in essence and interior, they are the manifestations of cosmic consciousness.The oneness of spirit is reintroduced into an alienated secular ontology. The supposed dichotomy between matter and spirit is dissipated. What exists only spirit and energy. The oneness and unity between subject and object is postulated as fundamental to cosmic view. The cosmic perspective is profoundly challenging, since it enjoins upon all human beings and collectivities to evolve their material and bodily consciousness into cosmic consciousness.

Unity and Universality of Spirit: Taking on the Challenges

The notion of spirit appears problematique, either because it is inherently incomprehensible and meaningless within a secular worldview or because it represents divergent views to different people. But many idealists pre modern western thought, and Eastern philosophy have accepted spirit as fundamental reality. In reality, the essence of matter is invisible electrons or forms of energy. Modern science shows that matter is composed of vibratory forces. In scientific experiments and analysis all matters can be reduced to electronic vibratory forces. In other words, that which can be dissolved into invisibility cannot be said to have valid existence. In this sense, matter can be considered as not existing, but matter does have relative existence. Matter exists in relation to our mind, and as an expression of invisible electronic forces that do exist, being unchangeable and immortal. For example, ice, water or vapour is manifestations of invisible gases, and have only formal, transitory existence. Similarly, mortal mind and matter are fleeting manifestations of divine consciousness and possess merely formal existence, in reality only cosmic mind exists.[41] The Latin root spiritus, is breath, suggesting a living dynamic self animating universe, as opposed to the lifeless world of secularism. In Hinduism, it is said, people generally identify themselves with the body, but they fail to realize that the basic source of bodily existence is prana (life energy), which is the link between human's material body and their immaterial mind. "The blind or unintellectual electronic forces of creation are nevertheless creative teleological agents because they contain within themselves the vibrations of the universal conscious of itself life force or prana which is in turn issued from the fiat of Divinity."[42]

Thus, the cosmic whole world view purports that the entire universe is the projected manifestation of the Divine thought and will in the form of vibratory energy, the flowing forth of life current and electrons which further vibrate more strongly and became diverse subtle or unseen forces of nature, which in turn externalized themselves as the various elements of matter constituting the universe. That means, there is a permanent and unalterable creative and intelligent power that is underlying all the transitory and illusive forms of the phenomenal world, from stones, stars and galaxies to human forms.

The traditional metaphysics of idealism going back to Plato was dualistic. It created a wedge between matter and spirit by putting primacy on trans-physical ideas or consciousness. The cosmic view finds all phenomenal world, matter and mind as the manifestation of the same divine spirit or universal self. The Eastern mysticism recognizes the all perfectedness and 'conscious of itself' of the spirit and asks the imperfect humans seeking liberation from the shackles that binds them to the transitory non-existent material and phenomenal world, and union with the spirit, the western evolutionary idealism represented by Hegel finds spirit in the making towards perfection. In his Phenomenology of Spirit, Hegel said:

> "Everything that from eternity has happened in heaven and earth, the life of God and all the deeds of time simply are the struggles for spirit to know itself, to make itself objective to itself, to find itself, be for itself, and finally unite itself to itself; it is alienated and divided, but only so as to be able thus to find itself and return to itself. Only in this manner does Spirit attain its freedom." [43]

In a secular world view freedom means moving away from oneness with the all pervasiveness of spirit to association with and subjugation to materialistic affluence. It is a bounded concept fettering humans to the limits and relativism of time, space, and causality. It is an external movement from material deficiency to unending cause and effect process of material fulfillment. From cosmic perspective in Eastern philosophy freedom implies liberation from the material bondage and sensory attachment, and union with all Infinite Divine self. It is a strife to be won, as Hegel said, against the distorted, fragmented, and immature self-identified with the material and temporal world. To Sri Aurobindo, freedom is the transformation of mundane man into a universal divine self-superhuman hood, a conscious identity with all pervasive whole. In his words:

> "Man is a transitional being; he is not final. For in man high beyond him ascend the radiant degrees that climb to a divine superman hood. There lies our destiny and the liberating key to our aspiring but troubled and limited mundane existence.... Superhuman hood is not man climbed to his natural zenith...super mind is something beyond mental man and his limits; it is a greater consciousness than the highest consciousness proper to human nature." [44].

In a secular worldview freedom identified with a distorted individualistic ego implies domination over others and nature. From the cosmic whole perspective freedom heals the subject-object dichotomy when the individualized self comes to know itself as universal and free. As Hegel said, self transcendence is a struggle that necessarily entails the passing away of previous forms of existence; a dialectical movement from fragmentation to integration, from alienation to integration of an omnipresent spirit. This dialectic is not applied to inert matter from some external force or intelligence, "but is matter's very soul putting forth its branches and fruits organically." [45] Thus, the transcendence of the individualized self as conceived of in Eastern philosophy or the dialectic movement of the spirit in Hegel's philosophy, are applicable to contemporary ecological thought and realities.

Inadequacy of Marxist Approach

Since there is close relationship between economic justice and domination over nature the materialistic approach led by Marxism seems plausibly preferable to the cosmic whole approach. But this is not so. Because Marx's dialectical materialism is internally inconsistent and contradictory, and impliedly adduces those principles on which Hegel's idealism is based. Materialism understands matter as inert, animated by mechanical means rather than by any inherent consciousness or intelligence. According to Marx, it is not mechanical manipulation but dialectical movement of internal forces within matter that propels human history towards socialism. It raises the metaphysical question, how the inert material universe move in a purposive direction unless it is constituted by some innate animating intelligence what Hegel and Eastern philosophy call spirit. According to scientific materialism, matter being inert and passive cannot possess self-conscious free will and purpose. Marxism failed to explain about what the movement of internal forces within matter means. Since dialectical movement proceeds by a struggle between opposites, "Marx's dialectical materialism does not provide any means for change unless there is some principle within matter that somehow oppose it." [46] Dialectic materialism in fact asserts that matter is matter, but that it develops as ideas do. Only, while we can see why ideas develop as they do, there is no conceivable reason why material things should develop in the same way. Eastman maintains, however, that Marx was by no means as successful in getting rid of Hegel as he had supposed, and that having declared the world to be made up of unconscious matter, he then found himself obliged to read into matter the very essence of Hegel's Absolute.[47] Despite its self association with Marxism, the post modern Marxism represents a distinct departure from its original. In epistemology, postmodern Marxism is critical of the subject /object distinction in traditional Marxism. The works of Gramsci and Althusser marked a turn in Marxist theory towards the ideological or discursive levels of the state, initiating theoretical discussions in the left circle as to the relationship between base and superstructure, between the material relations of production and the cultural or ideological expressions that win social consent to those relations. Post modern Marxism develops the so called discourse ethics following Habermas to resolve the moral differences through the force of better argument, and it remains half way as their arguments envisaging an alternative political and social order did not rest on self evolving conscious efforts of the individual human beings to rise to the super conscious stage, though it has shifted its analysis away from primacy to Marx's economic determinism towards questions of consciousness. Social ecologist Murray Bookchin, for instance disavows the traditional Marxist faith in material progress and embraces the Frankfurt school' critique of instrumental rationality[48]. Critical theory grows out of the fertility of the decomposition of the internal contradictions of the secular worldview. In contrast to Marxism, the evolutionary idealism represented by Hegel harps on dialectical movement: the infinite, absolute and universal spirit remains immanent within the finite, diverse and various forms of nature. Though Marxism made a vitriolic attack and humanizing influence upon capitalism, it is still embedded in the same secular worldview.

Where there is concept of division, duality and dichotomy, exclusion and inclusion, and self vs. the other, the question of acceptance or rejection of one at the expense of the other comes in. But where there is no division, and matter is itself spirit, from a cosmic whole perspective the question of repudiation of modernity never arises to the latter. Rather it redefines the modernity's secular notion of freedom, rights of the individuals, and doctrine of equality not on the basis of atomism but on the basis of an expanded universal self.The modernity's secular world view portrays humans as mere mundane pandering to the temptations of egotism, senses and intellect, and holds progress as mere material development not progress of humans from rationality to divinity. Therefore, the secular worldview is inwardly not satisfying and outwardly unsustainable in view of the disastrous consequences, the pursuit of which has had on nature. The very recognition that what secular worldview holds as real is unreal, and holds what unreal, is real opens the door to the cosmic whole approach. It never repudiates matter rather divines it. What are profane and sacrilegious are made sacred, by perceiving the spirit immanent in matter. The insightful truth perceived in Eastern mysticism concurrent with present day development in physics makes the cosmic approach attractive in the context of increasing awareness of globally ecological degradation to augur a new vision.

Kinship between Ancient Vedanta and Modern Science

Religion as developed in India in her Vedanta, and modern science are close to each other in spirit, temper and objectives. Both are spiritual disciplines. Even in the cosmology of the physical universe, in the theory of the unity of cause and effect, in the unity and conservation of matter and energy, and in the concept of evolution, cosmic and organic, the two reveal many points of contact. Unlike as in the super-naturalistic theologies of the west, the fundamental position in the cosmology of both Vedanta and modern science is the postulate of a self-evolving cause. To the modern scientist, that self-evolving cause is a material reality, the background material or cosmic dust as astrophysicist Fred Hoyle terms it.[49] Referring to this kinship, Swami Vivekananda reiterated in his speech at the Parliament of Religions held at Chicago in 1893:

> "Manifestation, and not creation is the word of science today, and the Hindu is only glad that what he has been cherishing in his bosom for ages is going to be taught in more forcible language, and with further light from the latest conclusion of science." [50]

Although modern scientific thought does not yet have, like Vedanta, a recognized place for any spiritual reality or principle, several scientists of the twentieth century, including biologists like Teilherd de Chardin and Julian Huxley have endeavoured to soften the materialism of physical science and to find a place for spiritual experience in the scientific world picture. Even Thomas Huxley had termed materialism as intruder. Capra reiterated this:

> **"the basic elements of the Eastern world view are also those of the world view emerging from modern and of becoming divine., whereas science remains confined to theory building about and explanations of nature of the universe, though Brahman or spirit pervades all in the form of consciousness. Atomic physics is confronted with the problem of consciousness."** [51]

Religion is not a doctrinaire formulation of theories away from realization of the reality but a question of being one with the spirit. According to Capra, "in modern physics, the question of consciousness has arisen in connection with the observation of atomic phenomena. Quantum theory has made it clear that these phenomena can only be understood as links in a chain of processes, the end of which lies in the consciousness of the human observer." [52] In the same vein Eugene Wigner points out," it was not possible to formulate the laws (of quantum theory) in a fully consistent way without reference to consciousness." [53] What Wigner and other physicists argued that the explicit inclusion of hunıan consciousness might be an essential aspect of future theories of matter, such as development would open exciting possibilities for a direct interaction between physics and Eastern mysticism. The understanding of one's consciousness and its relation to the rest of the universe is the starting point of the cosmic approach replacing the secular worldview. If physicists really want to include the nature of human super consciousness in their realm of research, a study of Eastern ideas and insights may well arm them with stimulating new viewpoints and philosophical background to the theories of contemporary science.

In Eastern mysticism it is held that the spirit is embedded pervasively in all and all parts of the universe animate or inanimate, lie embedded in spirit. There is no part of the universe, which is without God or spirit. Each represents a reflection of the Universal Spirit or Self. Even the smallest particle of the atom contains within itself the entire cosmos.In modern physics, the situation is quite similar as its hadron bootstrap philosophy buttresses that all particles are dynamically composed of one another in a self consistent way, and in that sense can be said to contain one another. In Mahayana Buddhism, a very similar notion is applied to the whole universe. This cosmic network of interpenetrating things and events is illustrated in the Avatamsaka Sutra by the metaphor of Indra's net, a vast network of precious gems hanging over the palace of the god Indra. In the words of Sir Charles Eliot:

"In the heaven of Indra, there is said to be a network of pearls, so arranged that if you look at one you see all the others reflected in it. In the same way each object in the world is not merely itself but involves every other object and in fact is everything else. In every particle of dust, there are present Buddhas without number." [54] In the Isa Upanishad, it is said, That (Self) moves, that does not move; that is far off, that is inside all this, and that is also outside all this.[55]

The cosmic approach endorses the radical ecologists' allegation that the secular world view has caused unprecedented wreck of the planet.It also recognizes that this devastation of nature stems from the rapacious possessive individualism that arrogates to itself all power and instrumentality of reason to dominate and plunder the desacralized nature. This unidimensional portrayal of human consciousness embedded in secular world view is considered as lopsided and one-sided view of progress that needs to be redefined in the light of the understanding of the cosmos as an unfoldment of spirit. One of the positive dimensions of secularism is that it provides human beings religious freedom disavowing interference of state and its related institutions into it. Its negative aspect is that it remains glued to the matter and superimposes its one sided unreal view of matter on its all aspects of relation and development-political, social, and economic-with human beings and nature. The cosmic view rejects the lopsidedness of secularism and not its positive aspect. Whereas secularism advocates an anti spirit stance, the cosmic perspective has never been anti matter, because matter is spirit. It recognizes the role of matter in progress of society in economic terms. It only jettisons the secularist view of matter as devoid of spirit. The scientists' recent perception of matter as nothing but consciousness in the line of Eastern philosophy has never factored into modernity's secular state building.

Through the saga of freedom secularism while ushering in a materialistic world in terms of socio-economic development, commodious living and unsustainable life style also beckoned the possibilities of ascension to super consciousness. The primacy is on quest for infinity in its unbounded pursuit of economic growth and technological progress not in the attainment of Godhood. Thus, secularism represents a distorted view of the matter while outwardly disowning the presence of infinitude of spirit in matter. The very notion that humans are on last rug of evolution resulted in self arrogance and mastery over the supposedly inert and lifeless world of land, water, air, and other life forms. Objectively, the world affects the humans in the form of ecological devastation. Subjectively, happiness consisted in material progress eludes humanity with every new advance in technological development simmering them in perpetual state of dissatisfaction. Desire is like phoenix, which on its fulfillment used to give birth to new desires. In this sense the secular vision of the world universalizes what is distorted, fragmented, unscientific and unreal as the basis of human pursuit, state policy and action, and individualizes and finitizes what is infinite and cosmic immanent in all living and non living. "Thus, the impulse towards mastery of the environment should not be dismissed as a historical blunder, but grasped more broadly as an immature expression of a yearning towards inner mastery and self transcendence."[56]

Anthropocentric utilitarianism has been the preponderant value orientation under secular worldview, which finds no difference between goods and what is good. What is conducive to the commodious living and profligacy in life style is considered as good. There is no intrinsic value inherent in anything except that it is a rational instrumentality to be utilized for the achievement of materialistic goals. The sovereign state is based on these criteria to promote greatest good of the greatest number. Ecological devastation and global inequality-the twin disasters of modernity due to relentless pursuit of materialistic aggrandizement thus, question secularism's anthropocentric value orientation. On the other, under the cosmic whole perspective the intrinsic value of human beings lies in their realization of the universality of spirit in all both animates and inanimate. Unlike the secular worldview, it measures individuals not in terms of material goods they possess or consume, but in terms of spiritual ascendancy, unity and identity with the universal self. Perceiving the spirit in all the human beings can delimit their needs and consumption "as little complexity and depth of consciousness." [57] In the context of ecological disaster the imperative is to correct their distorted identity with matter, being the intelligent parts of God's creation. The Indian view of evolution and of human's uniqueness finds expression in its text in the Srimad Bhagavatam:

> **"The divine one, having projected with His own inherent power, various forms such as trees, reptiles, cattle, birds, insects and fish, was not satisfied at heart with forms such as these; He then projected the human form endowed with the capacity to realize Brahman (the universal divine self of all), and became extremely pleased."** [58]

Development in the field of matter, technology, and living conditions of human beings, and their related institutions is given primacy under secular worldview over the required transformation of human beings from rationality to pure consciousness. All approaches, and theories within a secular view are bound to fail in their apocalypse of a better world without the idea of transforming human beings into divinity. The human beings have a historic role to play. Unlike Hegelian man remaining a passive spectator to the denouement of spirit in the evolution, the cosmic man gets involved, and participates consciously and actively in the process of evolution towards attainment of Godhood. Unity and identity with universal self eternally and constantly as subjectivities in all without cleaving the world into subject and object. In the Shvetashvatara Upanishad the message of the ancient sages to humanity is, "Ye children of immortality know thyself as the Infinite. Become the All".[59] The cosmic view never agrees with what Hegel says: "The owl of Minerva begins its flight in the shadows of the dusk." [60] It is completely a stage of merge or stabilization with spirit. This is a stage to arrive at where the distinction between observer and observed melts down and where subject and object fuse into a unified whole. This is the experience as described in the words of Chuang Tzu:

"My connection with the body and its parts is dissolved. My perceptive organs are discarded. Thus, leaving my material form and bidding farewell to my knowledge, I become one with the Great Pervader. This I call sitting and forgetting all things".[61] Hegel likens this reality to2 "a Bacchic dance in which there is not one of the constituents that is not drunk." [62]

In Hinduism, the meditator withdraws his mind from the senses by interiorisation, and remains fixed in God. His consciousness merges in the Cosmic Spirit. In the higher spiritual state he communes with God without bodily fixation; and in his ordinary waking consciousness, even in the midst of exacting worldly duties. Both states are characterized by oneness with the ever-new bliss of spirit. [63] In atomic physics, the distinction between a detached objective observer and the observed objects is blurred. John Wheeler sees this involvement of the observer as the most important feature of quantum theory and he has therefore suggested replacing the word' observer 'by the word 'participator'. In his words.

"Nothing is more important about the quantum principle than this, that it destroys the concept of the world as sitting out there, with the observer safely separated from it by a 20 centimeter slab of plate glass; even to observe so miniscule an object as an electron, he must shatter the glass. He must reach in. He must install his chosen measuring equipment. It is up to him to decide whether he shall measure position or momentum. To install the equipment to measure the one prevents and excludes his installing the equipment to measure the other. Moreover, the measurement changes the state of the electron. The universe will never afterwards be the same. To describe what has happened, one has to cross out that old word observer and put in its place the new word participator. In some strange sense the universe is a participatory universe".[64]

The Eastern seers are not satisfied with a situation analogous to atomic physics, where the observer and the observed cannot be separated, but can still be distinguished. Going further, they in deep meditation arrive at a point where the distinction dissolves completely, where subject and object mingle into a unified undifferentiated whole. Modern physics, which works in a different framework, cannot go that far in the experience of the unity of all things. But it has made certainly a great stride towards the worldview of the Eastern mystics in atomic theory.

New Paradigm Thinking in Science: Similarities with Eastern Philosophy

In recent years, the developments in the realm of scientific research have witnessed a shift from the mechanistic, classical scientific paradigm to a new paradigm thinking in science. It was believed that from the study of the properties of the parts, the dynamics of the whole could be understood. The rule was in order to understand any complex system; it must be broken up into smaller pieces. The pieces themselves cannot be explained further, except by splitting them into smaller pieces. The process of splitting into smallest pieces continues till it ends up with fundamental building blocks: elements, substances, and particles, and so on-with properties that cannot be explained. From these fundamental building blocks with their fundamental laws of interaction the larger whole can be explained in its dynamics in terms of the properties of the parts. Started with Democritus in ancient Greece this process formalized by Descartes and Newton, continued until the twentieth century. In the new paradigm, the whole is primary. On the basis of understanding the dynamics of the whole the properties and patterns of interactions of the parts can be explained. The scientists began to realize that the universe is no longer composed of fundamental building blocks but rather as a network of relations, and that ultimately, there are no parts at all in this interconnected cosmic web. The awareness of the unity and mutual interrelation of all things and events, the experience of all phenomena as manifestations of the basic oneness, is also the most important common characteristic of Eastern worldviews.

In the classical physics the basis was fundamental structure or material substance. With Einstein's theory of relativity the shift from structure to process became the basis of new paradigm thinking in science in which it was recognized that mass or subatomic particles are not made of any material stuff; they are patterns of energy which are by nature dynamic, bristled with activity and processes. On observation they are found as not consisting of any substance or fundamental structure. They are ever changing, dynamic patterns and continually transforming into one another-a continuous dance of energy. In Eastern philosophy the universe is nothing but a flow, a movement and a change. Derived from Sanskrit root, what does not exist for tomorrow is known as universe. Behind the changing, ever flowing phenomenal world lays the changeless and imperishable spirit.

In the classical paradigm, scientific descriptions were believed to be objective, independent of human observer and process of knowledge.

In the new paradigm, unlike the classical image of the universe as a machine, the universe is held as an interconnected, dynamic whole weaved into an interconnected web of relationships. When these relationships are presented to the world, the observers present these in different ways by using different techniques. Accordingly, for example, the electron may appear as a particle or wave or a shadow depending on the understanding of the process of knowledge of the observers. Thus, in the new paradigm the shift is from objective science to epistemic science. In eastern philosophy, as aforementioned, the ultimate truth or reality appears differently to the spiritual practitioners depending on the depth, magnitude of quest for perception of the ultimate truth. With participation of the seekers' whole being, mind and soul, in the highest stage of realization the distinction between observer and the observed breaks down completely, where the subject and object fuse and merge. The duality by the meditation-born consciousness of Unity, in the realization of thus, how all-dual manifestations of nature arise from and dissolve into oneness of Spirit, melts away. Water may manifest as small or big waves in the ocean; or as surf foam or bubbles; or as rain drops or icebergs-but in these various forms it is water the same. In the Bhagavad Gita it is said: in whatever way people are devoted to Me, in that measure I manifest to them.All people, in every manner purse a path to Me[65]. (Chapter 4, verse 11)

The classical Cartesian paradigm was based on the belief that whatever the scientists have found out is a finality and certainty of truth. In the new paradigm it is recognized that all scientific concepts and theories are limited and approximate. Their description of the reality is limited and approximate. On the other hand the Eastern philosophy is concerned with absolute knowledge involving an understanding of the totality of existence. The Eastern seers being aware of the essential interrelationship of all aspects of the universe, realize that to explain something means, ultimately, to show how it is connected to everything else. They are generally not interested in explaining things but rather in the direct, nonintellectual perception of the unity of all things.

The reduction of nature to fundamentals, foundations or building blocks is basically the classical approach. The metaphor of knowledge as a building with solid foundation has been the main plank of western science. In the new paradigm, the foundations of science are moving. Einstein admitted to this fleeting foundations in his autobiography while putting his comments on the developments of the quantum physics: It was as if the ground had been pulled out from under one, with no firm foundation to be seen anywhere, upon which one could have built.[66] In Eastern philosophy, the seers are concerned with the ultimate Reality – the only constant changeless and imperishable existence-that underlies the ephemeral and fleeting universe.

Consciousness in Matter

In Eastern mystical tradition consciousness is regarded as an integral part of the universe. Human beings, like all other life forms, are considered parts of an inseparable organic whole. Human beings are seen as the living proof of cosmic intelligence; in us, the universe repeats over and over again its ability to produce forms through which it becomes consciously aware of itself. In modern physics, the question of consciousness has arisen in connection with the observation of atomic phenomena. Quantum theory has made it clear that these phenomena can only be understood as links in a chain of processes, the end of which lies in the consciousness of the human observer. In Eastern philosophy, the perception of the universal spirit depends on the level and depth of consciousness of the individuals in transcendence of their mundane confinement. In the words of Eugene Wigner, "It was not possible to formulate the laws of (quantum theory) in a fully consistent way without reference to consciousness."[67]

In the same vein Werner Heisenberg, one of the giants of quantum physics emphasizes in his autobiography "atoms are not things. The electrons which form an atom's shells are no longer things in the sense of classical physics, things which would be unambiguously described by concepts like location, velocity, energy, size. When we get down to the atomic level, the objective world in space and time no longer exists, and the mathematical symbols of theoretical physics refer merely to possibilities, not to facts."[68] Similarly, Arthur Eddington said in his The Nature of the Physical World:

"In the world of physics we watch a shadow graph performance of familiar life. The shadow of my elbow rests on the shadow table as the shadow ink flows over the shadow paper.... The frank realization that physical science is concerned with a world of shadows is one of the most significant of recent advances."[69] But this perception of modern physicists has never factored into modernity's secular view. Wigner and other physicists have argued, however, that the explicit inclusion of human consciousness may be an essential aspect of future theories of matter. A study of Eastern ideas may well provide them with stimulating new ideas. Such a development would open exciting possibilities for a direct interaction between physics and Eastern mysticism. Thus the future enlargement of the hadron bootstrap, with the bootstrapping of space-time and of human consciousness it may require, opens up unprecedented possibilities, which may well go beyond the conventional framework of science:

"Such a future step would be immensely more profound than anything comprising the hadron bootstrap; we would be obliged to confront the elusive concept of observation and, possibly, even that of consciousness. Our current struggle with the hadron bootstrap may thus, be only a foretaste of a completely new form of human intellectual endeavour, one that will not only lie outside of physics but also will not even be describable as scientific."[70] That spirit is not subject to observation and observation is an illusive concept has been echoed in Indian philosophy since centuries back: His form does not exist within the range of vision; nobody sees Him with the eye.The eye does not go there, nor speech, nor mind.[71] The secular view proposes a random world in which the manifold order of the cosmos emerged by happenstance. Rather than proceeding by random combinations of brute matter, nature in the cosmic view is understood as suffused with divinity. Such a cosmic view would more likely be ecologically friendly than one that reduces nature to a mere object for human consumption. If environmental degradation is symptomatic of a deficient worldview, then it is imperative that human beings review their distorted worldview. A person who lives in a greater sense of oneness and unity with spirit, is likely to be less acquisitive, less driven by the frenzy of insatiate desires, and the quest for material aggrandizement. Matter in humans gives way to divine in humans. The person having arisen to the super consciousness stage restrains all the senses, even minded everywhere, and engage in the welfare of all beings. It is further argued by the secularists that the ascension to super consciousness can be attributed to individuals not to the level of nation state or other collectivities. This misses the fundamental premise of cosmic view that in all the ephemeral phenomenal existence remains immortal, the imperishable noumena. If all of the phenomenal existence is the unfoldment of spirit, then all forms of creation-galaxies, rocks, plants, people and nation state is also the manifestation of supreme self.

Sovereign State and Secular Problematique in Global Environmental Politics

If the modernity's notion of secular sovereign state and its political authority remains confined to the acceptance of non interference of political authority into the religions domain of human beings, then possibility of human beings risen to super conscious stage remain galore. But secularism understood as being mirrored of a fragmented and mechanical material world consisting of multitude of different objects assembled into a huge machine, stands in the way of individuals being transcended from the limitation of atomized egoistic self into super consciousness stage. This is the secular problematique of the sovereign state system based on Cartesian and Newtonian view of matter. Sharing the same ontological edifice with science, the political authority was based on promotion of possessive individualism in terms of production of wealth, inordinate consumption and profligate life style at the expense of nature, other individuals, society and nations. The fulfillment of these materialistic goods remained the criteria of individuals while tendering consent to the sovereign state system. But the future generations' consent to the rightness of political authority to exploit nature, even at their expense taken for granted remained lacking in the legitimation to sovereign state system[72] At present the focus on intergenerational responsibility and inter species accountability in many environmental regimes, particular those addressing issues with long temporal horizons, such as climate change, ozone depletion and the extinction of species points to the relevance of cosmic view questioning the secular world view. Thus, a shift from one sided and single pointed confinement to matter under secular worldview to a universal episteme. Causing new spatial ordering principles, new temporal understandings and new norms of legitimation, is evident in increasing proliferation of a plethora of international agreements on environmental issues since 1970. These agreements put a limit on freedom of authority of sovereign state to continue promoting wealth production, inordinate consumption and profligate life style at expense of nature and others. The states are free to abrogate these agreements but cannot do so at their peril and ignoring pressures from the internal and external sources exerted on them to adhere to the principles of environmental protection. The single point perspective of the sovereign state is being transformed into the multilateral governance, a multi perspective form of organization. The cosmic worldview suggests a movement beyond the multi perspectival and matter confinement to the universality and oneness of spirit. The present globalization ushering in colonisation of the parts by the western view of universe as all matter or economy should not be termed as evidences of an approximation to cosmic worldview. It is an odyssey of transcendence from within and beyond on the part of human beings and their institutions thinking all as subjectivities interconnected and interrelated in the web of spirit. "The current shift in the meaning of sovereignty away from a sole emphasis on rights and towards an incorporation of accountability and responsibility also suggests that secularism's single point perspective is giving way to more inclusive approaches."[73] To hold all, both inanimate and animates as the living presence of spirit is one of the important aspects of cosmic worldview. The extension of rights to non-human species, and recognition of urgency to protect the inanimate represents a rudimentary yet significant shift from secularism's self atomized and individualized human centeredness and anthropocentric presumption in the direction of recognizing the web of interdependence among species and embeddedness of humans within that web. Unless the human beings realize the oneness of spirit in transcendence of matter-spirit dichotomy characteristic of secular worldview, the full-scale shift towards the cosmic worldview cannot be said as in the offing.

The rightfulness of political authority of the sovereign state to promote material prosparity, and universalize matter as ultimate reality not the spirit was derived from the premise provided by science. This faith in science to ensure a materially glittering world is ruptured in the face of deep ecological, social and cultural crisis it fostered. A leap of faith of all scientists, policymakers and human beings in the Cartesian split and mechanistic world for human liberation needs to be shifted to faith in cosmic worldview and its idea of unity and oneness between matter and spirit. Though a shift in the twentieth century science is perceived from this fragmented, mechanized and distorted view of matter to the idea of unity advocated in Eastern Philosophy, it has not been universalized and yet to form the premise of modern sovereign state system. In such a situation the locus of majestas will not emanate not from a secular nation state built upon matter, but from a transcendental vision looking beyond matter and senses. Majestas which commands a sense of majesty or awe has always been an important factor of sovereignty.[74] To persist in such an old Cartesian mechanized, fragmented and distorted view of the universe comes as a testament to our immaturity and failure to identify ourselves with the Real self. From this arrogant rational instrumentality of secular world view emerges the creeping ecological crisis challenging us, the individual human beings and collectivities to evolve body, mind and soul consciously towards the realization of the ultimate truth. The experience of the universe in modern physics as a dynamic, inseparable whole makes the traditional concepts of space and time, of isolated objects, and of cause and effect lose their meaning. Such an experience, however is very similar to that of the Eastern mystics, but very seldom has it been realized that this seems to lead in the same direction, towards a view of the world which is very similar to the views held in Eastern mysticism.[75] The developments in modern physics are nothing new but a reflection of the ancient wisdom. This has been buttressed by no less a person than Julius Robert Oppenheimer:

"The general notions about human understanding...which are illustrated by discoveries in atomic physics are not in the nature of things wholly unfamiliar, wholly unheard of, or new. Even in our own culture they have a history, and in Buddhist and Hindu thought a more considerable and central place. What we shall find is an exemplification, an encouragement, and a refinement of old wisdom".[76] Thus, what remains the greatest challenge is not merely the universal acceptance of the vindication of the Eastern wisdom by the modern physicists but its incorporation into the established political epistemology about state sovereignty and secularism. A political system erected upon a distorted and wrong view of matter as proved by both Eastern seers and modern scientists, needs to be redefined from a cosmic whole perspective. This has been more or so accentuated by the pernicious ecological crisis. The cosmic approach never discards the positive role of matter in heralding revolutionary changes in the living conditions of human beings but its negative and distorted dimension of modernity's secular construction of statecraft. The developments in the conditions of matter started by the physicists in the west for the development of human beings resulted in developments to the surroundings around the human beings, not in them as from rationality to divinity. As said above, the cosmic whole perspective seems the right road map for correcting the modernity's distorted secular worldview on the basis of the ancient insights provided by the East. Eminent historian, Arnold Toynbee, after surveying the story of the entire human race observed:

"It is already becoming clear that a chapter which had a Western beginning will have to have an Indian ending if it is not to end in the self destruction of the human race.... At this supremely dangerous moment in human history, the only way of salvation for mankind is the Indian way..."[77]

In the face of threats stemming from the immoderate devastation of nature, and nuclear holocaust, the only hope for survival of humanity lies in the universal recognition of the radical shift from the methods and values prevalent in modern science and technology to the realization of the Ultimate Reality underlying the ever changing and fleeting universe. The new paradigm in science which views the world as an integrated whole rather than a compendium of dissociated and separate parts, can be called the holistic cosmic whole view in harmony with the Eastern traditions. The cosmic whole view can also be called an ecological worldview because it recognizes the fundamental interdependence of all phenomena and the embeddedness of individuals and societies in the cyclical processes of nature. The ecological paradigm supported by modern science and in harmony with Eastern philosophy is rooted in a perception of reality that traverses beyond the scientific framework to an awareness of the oneness and unity of spirit in all life forms that is like a thread weaves all its multiple manifestations into the cosmic tapestry. Thus, it implies that the cosmic approach is essentially spiritual in its foundations. As Capra points out: "When the concept of human spirit is understood as the mode of consciousness in which the individual feels connected to the cosmos as a whole, it becomes clear that ecological awareness is spiritual in its deepest essence, and it is then not surprising that the new vision of reality is in harmony with the visions of spiritual traditions" [78]. If the modern science has already changed its perception of matter, the view of sovereignty, state and secularism built up on the foundations of the discarded view of matter, needs a rethinking in terms of Eastern values and vision of reality. The western liberal political tradition, which shared the same ontological foundation with Newtonian science, needs to part with it and renew its company with the new paradigm thinking in science in the changing scenario from a cosmic whole perspective.

References

1. Mircea Eliade, The Sacred and the Profane: The Nature of Religion (New York: Harcourt Brace, 1987).
2. Brihadarayanka Upanishad 3.7.15.
3. *Ibid.*
4. Pere Teilhard de Chardin, The Phenomenon of Man (London: Collins, 1959), p. 56.
5. Quoted in Nani A Palkhivala, India's Priceless Heritage (Bombay: Bharitiya Vidya Bhawan, 1986), p. 18.
6. Ernst Haas, "Words can Hurt You: Or, Who said what to Whom About Regimes?" In Stephen Krasner ed. International Regimes (Ithaca, Ny: Cornell University Press, 1983), p. 39.
7. Karen Litfin, "Towards an Integral Perspective on World Politics: Secularism, Sovereignty and the Challenge of Global Ecology", Millennium: Journal of International Studies Vol. 32, No. 1, 2003, p. 31.
8. The Bhagavad Gita, ch-13, verse 15.
9. Sri Sri Paramahansa Yogananda, Man's Eternal Quest (New Delhi: Oxford and IBH Publishing Co. Pvt. Ltd., 1995), 5th edition, p. 57.

10. D. Bohm and B. Hiley, "On the Intuitive Understanding of Nonlocality as Implied by Quantum Theory", Foundations of Physics, Vol. 5 (1975).
11. Sri Aurobindo, The Synthesis of Yoga (Aurobindo Ashram, Pondicherry, India, 1957, p. 993.
12. H.p. Stapp, "S-Matrix Interpretation of Quantum Theory", Physical Review, Vol. D3 (March 15, 1971), p. 1310.
13. W. Heisenberg, Physics and Philosophy (Allen & Unwin, London, 1963), p. 96.
14. Mundaka Upanishad, 2.2.5).
15. N.A Palkhivala, India's Priceless Heritage (Bombay: Bharatiya Vidya Bhavan, 1986), pp. 16-17.
16. Brhadaranyaka Upanishad, 11, 1. 20).
17. Lama Anagarika Govinda, Foundations of Tibetan Mysticism (Rider, London, 1973), p. 93.
18. F. Capra, The Tao of Physics (Flamingo: Harper and Collins, 1975) pp. 221-223.
19. H.Schipperges, "Aspects of an Upheaval in Medicine" in Sieman's Electromedica, 5, 1970, p. 300.
20. Isa Upanishad, Ist verse.
21. Swami Ranganathananada, Science and Religion, (Calcutta: Advaita Ashram, 1979), pp. 77.
22. Thomas Berrry, The Great Work: Our way into The Future (New York: Bell tower, 1999, p. 19
23. Alfred North Whitehead, Process and Reality (New York: The Free Press, 1978), Piree Teilhard de Chardin, The Phenomenon of Man (New York: Harper, 1959).
24. James E. Lovelock, Gaia: A New Look at Life on Earth (New York: Oxford University Press, 1979; Lynn Margulis, The Symbiotic Planet (London: Weidenfeld and Nicholson, 1998), Anne Primavesi, Sacred Gaia: Holistic Theology and Earth System Science (London: Routtledge, 2000
25. Capra, *op. cit.*, p. 130-131.
26. Karen Litfin, Towards an Integrative Perspective on World Politics, p. 35.
27. G.P Gupta and Srinivasan, Sri Aurobindo on Democracy and Secularism (Pondicherry: Sri Aurobindo Ashram Press, 2000), p. 15.
28. Herbert Scheneidan, Sacred Discontent: The Bible and Western Tradition (Berkeley: University of California Press, 1977).

29. Lynn White, "The Historic Roots of Our Ecologic Crisis", Daedalus 1967: 1203-1207.
30. Daniel A.Kealey, Revisioning Environmental Ethics (Albany: State University of New York Press, 1990), p. 14.
31. R.E.J Walker, Inside/Outside: International Relations as Political Theory (Cambridge: Cambridge University Press, 1993), p. 20.
32. Benedict Anderson, Imagined Communities (London: Verso, 1983).
33. Hans Peter Durr, "Episteme: The Meaning of Knowledge in the Natural Sciences and our Experience of Reality", World Affairs Vol. 6, No. 3, July-September 2002, p. 33.
34. Evelyn Fox Keller, Reflections on Gender and Science (New Haven, CT: Yale University Press, 1985), p. 36.
35. David F. Noble, The Religion of Technology: The Divinity of Man and the Spirit of Invention (New York: Knoff, 1997).
36. Yaron Ezrahi, The Descent of Icarus: Science and the Transformation of Contemporary Democracy (Cambridge: MA: Harvard University Press, 1990).
37. Karen Litfin, "Environment, Wealth, and Authority: Global Climate Change and Emerging Modes of Legitimation", International Studies Review, 2000, p. 129.
38. C.B. Macpherson, The Political Theory of Possessive Individualism: Hobbes to Locke (Oxford: Clarendon Press, 1962); See also Karen Litfin, Towards an Integrative Perspective, *op. cit.*, p. 38.
39. J. R. McNeill, Ideas Matter: A Political History of the Twentieth-Century Environment", Current History Vol. 99, No. 640, November 2000, p. 374.
40. Willis Harman, Global Mind Change: The Promise of the Last Years of the Twentieth Century (Indianapolis: Knowledge Systems, 1988).
41. Yoganada Paramhamsa, Man' Eternal Quest, *op. cit.*, pp. 56-57.
42. *Ibid.*
43. G.W.F. Hegel, Hegel's Lectures on the History of Philosophy, trans E. S. Haldane and Frances H. Simon (New York: Humanities Press, 1963) Vol. 1, p. 23.

44. Sri Aurobindo, The Hour of God, Sri Aurobindo Birth Centenary Library (Pondicherry: Sri Aurobindo Ashram, 1972), Vol. 17, p. 7.
45. Hegel, *op. cit.* 34.
46. Karen Litfin, Towards an Integral Perspective, *op. cit.*, p. 43.
47. Max Eastman, Marxism, Is it a Science? (London: Pelican Books, 1941), p. 23.
48. Murray Bookchin, The Philosophy of Social Ecology: Essays on Dialectical Naturalism (Montreal: Black Rose, 1995) and The Ecology of Freedom (Palo Alto: Cheshire, 1982).
49. Swami Ranganathananda, *op. cit.*, pp. 47-48.
50. Swami Vivekananda, Complete Works, Vol. 1, eleventh edition, p. 15.
51. Capra, Tao of Physics, p. 25.
52. Capra, *op. cit.*, p. 332.
53. Eugene Wigner, Symmetries and Reflections: Scientific Essays (Cambridge, Mass; M.I.T Press, 1970) p. 172.
54. Charles Eliot, Japanese Buddhism (London: Routledge and Kegan Paul, 1959), pp. 109-10.
55. Isa Upanishad, verse 5.
56. Karen Litfin, Towards an Integral Perspective, p. 46.
57. Ken Wilber, Tony Schwartz and Dan Spinella eds. A Brief History of Everything (Boston: Shambkala Publications, 2001), pp. 334-35.
58. Srimad Bhagvatam 9.28.
59. Shvetashvatara Upanishad, 2:5.
60. Hegel, *op.cit.*
61. Chuang Tzu, trans. James Legge, arranged by Clae Waltham (New York: Ace Books 1971 ch. 6.
62. Arland Ussher, Three Aesthetic Philosophers, The Listener, 15 April 1948, pp. 623.
63. Paramahansa Yogananda, Man's Eternal Quest, p. 479.
64. J.A. Wheeler, in J.Mehra ed., The Physicist's Conception of Nature (Holland: D. Reidel, Dordrecht, 1973); p. 244.
65. Bhagvad Gita, chapter 4, verse11.
66. Quoted in Capra, Tao of Physics, *op. cit.*, p. 364.
67. E.p. Wigner, Symmetries and Reflections-Scientific, p. 172.
68. Werner Heisenberg, quoted in N. A. Palkhivala, India's Priceless Heritage, pp. 16-17.

69. Arthur Eddington quoted in N. A. Palkhivala, *op. cit.*, pp. 17-18.
70. G.F.Chew, "Bootstrap: A Scientific Idea?", Science Vol. 161, 23 May 1968, p. 765.
71. Kena Upanishad, 1.3.
72. N Gaan, "Global Climate Change, Sovereign State system and the Authority of Science", International Studies 39, 4 (2002), pp. 407-17.
73. Paul Wapner, "Reorienting State Sovereignty: Rights and Responsibilities in the Environmental age" in Karen T. Liffin ed. The greening of Sovereignty in World Politics (Cambridge, MA; and MIT Press, 1998), pp. 275-298.
74. Nicholas Onuf, "Sovereignty: Outline of a Conceptual History", Alternatives16, No. 2, 1991, pp. 420-22.
75. Capra, The Tao of Physics, p. 22.
76. J. R Oppenheimer, Science and the Common Understanding (London: Oxford University Press, 1954) pp. 8-9.
77. Quoted in N. A. Palkhivala, *op. cit.*, p. 1.
78. Capra, *op. cit.*, p. 358.

9

Environmental and Ecological Consequences of War

Arthur H. Westing

Summary

The environmental consequences of war are for the most part deleterious. The adverse impacts of armed conflict can be the unintentional (collateral) result of most routine hostile military actions; or else they can be intentional. Intentional disruption of the environment can be carried out especially in order to deny an enemy force cover and concealment or local sources of sustenance. The release of dangerous forces resulting from attacks on dams, chemical factories, or nuclear facilities (often referred to as 'environmental warfare') can lead to severe environmental disruption of a widespread and long-term nature. The use of land mines, as well as of cluster bombs that leave a residue of unexploded submunitions (bomblets), leads to a long-term impediment to rural post-war reconstruction, moreover, with tragic human ramifications. Unconventional warfare (chemical, biological, or nuclear) is likely to cause extraordinary levels of environmental devastation. Preparations for war also result in a certain level of environmental damage. The environmentally beneficial effects of warfare derive primarily from the sparing of habitats, and the wildlife they contain, by virtue of becoming temporarily inaccessible to human exploitation. Inasmuch as the global biosphere has come under severe threat from the ever expanding needs of the civil sector of society, it is concluded that environmental damage being brought about by the military sector of society must now be recognized as a significant threat to global sustainability.

1. Introduction

Warfare is by its very nature deadly and destructive. The present Section outlines primarily the extent of environmental disruption that can be associated with conventional warfare (*i.e.*, for the most part, warfare that does not involve nuclear or other weapons of mass destruction). Of particular concern here from the standpoints both of nature and of human health and safety are the employment of: (1) environmental manipulations (modifications), especially those that release dangerous forces; (2) forest clearing chemicals and devices; and (3) anti-personnel land mines and cluster bomb submunitions (bomblets). Unconventional warfare (nuclear, chemical, or biological) is dealt with only briefly. Beneficial effects of war and preparations for war are also touched upon, but again only briefly. The adverse effects on nature and humans just alluded to are associated not only with the actual pursuit of conventional warfare, but to some extent also with the pre-war and post-war periods. Thus there is included a preliminary summary of this aspect of the problem.

2. Peacetime (Pre-war and Post-war) Impact of the Military Sector

Hundreds of wars have been fought in this century alone, several dozen of them always being in progress somewhere or other in the world. However, whether at war or peace, most nations maintain armed forces. Such armed forces are maintained by states for various reasons, among them: (a) to deter an attack from outside their borders or, failing that, to defend against such an attack; (b) to threaten an attack on another state in support of some foreign-policy objective or, failing that, to carry out such an attack; and (c) to deter or quell internal uprisings. In fact, most wars in recent decades have been internal (non-international) ones, so-called civil wars fought between government and insurgent forces.

The social and environmental ramifications for states to maintain armed forces for any or all of the above reasons result from: (a) establishing military fortifications and other military facilities; (b) equipping and supplying armed forces with weapons and other military needs, and in turn disposing of these once they become obsolete or otherwise unwanted; (c) training armed forces and testing the weapons they use; and (d) routine deployment of armed forces nationally, in other nations, and in areas beyond any national jurisdiction.

The social and environmental impacts of peace-time military activities are very roughly proportional to the fraction of gross domestic product they represent in a nation, which is now of the order of 2% or 3% for both industrialized and non-industrialized countries. However, it must be recognized that were the military sector in a country made smaller, the human, material, financial, and intellectual resources made available thereby would largely be shifted to the civil sector — presumably to carry out socially more useful activities — but the environmental impact would remain more or less comparable.

3. Environmental Manipulations

Environmental manipulations in wartime can be (a) unintentional, (b) intentional, or (c) intentional for purposes of amplification through the release of so-called dangerous forces.

3.1. Unintentional Manipulations

Unintentional (ancillary, incidental, collateral) environmental manipulations in wartime can result from the often profligate employment of high-explosive munitions against enemy personnel and matériel. Another frequent source of such unintentional manipulations is the use of tanks and other heavy off-road vehicles. Both of these forms of ancillary environmental damage can be especially disruptive of local habitats and the creatures that depend upon those habitats. The construction of base camps, fortifications, and lines of communication can add to the environmental disruption. Battle related activities can also lead to certain amounts of local air and water pollution. Further ancillary wartime environmental damage derives from the often heavy exploitation by armed forces in the field of timber, food, and feed, both within the theater of military operations and beyond.

3.2. Intentional Manipulations

The pursuit of war often involves the intentional destruction of field or forest as a specific means of denying to the enemy the benefits of such components of the environment. The benefits being denied to the enemy include access to water, food, feed, and construction materials. Often even more important, the denied benefits include access to cover or sanctuary, as noted below under 'Forest Clearing' (see Section 4). The long-term environmental impacts of denial (or barrier) operations through the employment of mines is also discussed under a separate heading below (see Section 5.1).

A number of important rivers flow through more than one country, providing an opportunity for a nation upstream to divert or befoul the waters before they reach a downstream nation with which it is at war, a major calamity in an arid region.

The Gulf War of 1991 has gone down in history as the conflict providing the most spectacular example of intentional oil releases, by Iraq in Kuwait, for various hostile purposes. Some of the oil that was caused to escape remained in liquid form; and some was or became ignited, to produce dense clouds of dark soot-laden smoke. Some of the liquid oil was released on land and some into the Persian Gulf. The oil releases into the environment resulted primarily from the sabotaging of about 730 oil wells (of which *circa* 630 were torched), of 20 or so collecting centers, and of 3 or more oil tankers; various storage tanks and pipelines were also breached. Numerous of the sabotaged oil wells continued to discharge oil for many months. The huge resulting releases ultimately amounted to perhaps 10 million cubic meters (60 million barrels). On land, some 200 small lakes of oil were created, leading to the death of much wildlife and to diverse other environmental problems, including the contamination of groundwater. Of the escaping oil, of the order of 1 million cubic meters (6 million barrels) was released into the Persian Gulf, severely contaminating Kuwaiti offshore waters and about 400 kilometers of coastline, primarily Saudi Arabian, thereby disrupting marine habitats and killing much migratory marine wildlife (avian, mammalian, and reptilian). The huge amounts of smoke released into the atmosphere (soot plus various combustion gases) produced a pall that persisted for several months, leading particularly to adverse human health effects especially for those already suffering from respiratory ailments or who were otherwise in a frail condition.

3.3. Intentional Manipulations to Release Dangerous Forces

Under certain conditions, it is possible to manipulate some component of the natural or built environment for hostile military purposes in a way that is intended to result in the release of dangerous pent-up forces. This sort of military effort — which is often referred to as environmental warfare — becomes especially tempting when the hostile manipulation involves a relatively modest expenditure of effort (*i.e.*, of triggering energy) leading to the release of a substantially greater amount of directed destructive energy. Environmental manipulations (modifications) of particular concern with reference to magnified destructive potential involve fresh-water impoundments, nuclear power stations, and to a lesser extent forest lands. Attacks upon certain industrial facilities could also release dangerous forces, in the form of toxic chemical clouds, over a considerable area.

Many hundreds of major dams have been constructed in recent decades throughout scores of countries that impound huge quantities of water. A significant fraction of those dams could be breached with relative ease, either through direct attack or sabotage, releasing the impounded water to cause immense levels of death and destruction. Hostile actions of this nature have been spectacularly successful in various past wars (notably so in such recent conflicts as World War II and the Korean War of 1950-1953); and their social and environmental impacts can take many decades to recover from. Indeed, the most devastating example of a single military — or any other — human action throughout history appears to have been the intentional release during the Sino-Japanese War of 1937-1945 of Yellow River waters. In order to stop the Japanese advance, in June 1938 the Chinese dynamited the Huayuankow dike near Chengchow. Several thousand Japanese soldiers drowned, and the Japanese advance into China along this front was halted. However, in the process, the flood waters also ravaged major portions of Henan, Anhui, and Jiangsu provinces. Several million hectares of farmland were destroyed as were 4000 villages and 11 cities; at the same time several hundred thousand (and perhaps many more) Chinese drowned. The river was not brought back under control until 1947.

Almost 200 clusters of nuclear power stations have now become essentially permanent additions to the human environment, plus a number of additional nuclear reprocessing plants and nuclear waste repositories, distributed in over 30 countries. These sites are amenable to assault, again either through overt attack or sabotage, with the possible attendant release into a surrounding area measurable in thousands to millions of hectares of iodine-131, cesium-137, strontium-90, and other radioactive elements. The most heavily contaminated inner area would become life threatening, an outer zone of lesser contamination would become health threatening, and a still greater zone would become agriculturally unusable. A radioactively polluted area such as this defies effective decontamination. Indeed, it is known especially from the Pacific islands used for testing in the 1940s and 1950s and from the Chernobyl accident of April 1986 that the health-threatening degradation of the land will take centuries to recover.

Under certain habitat and weather conditions, forest fires can be initiated that are subsequently self-propagating and enormously destructive of the forest resource itself, of human artifacts, and of the enmeshed flora and fauna. In killing the vegetation of a forest ecosystem (its autotrophic component), such incendiary warfare leads to substantial damage to the wildlife (its heterotrophic component) as well as to the nutrient budget — the latter via soil erosion and nutrient dumping (the rapid loss of nutrients in solution). Substantial recovery from such unbalancing of a forest system must be measured in decades. Incendiary warfare in grassland (prairie) and tundra ecosystems could, under special conditions, be equally or even more damaging.

The quite widely adopted 1977 Protocols I and II on the Protection of Victims of Armed Conflicts (UNTS 17512 & 17513) include some important specific constraints on the destruction of the environment as outlined above, whereas the less widely adopted 1977 Environmental Modification Convention (UNTS 17119) provides some more or less ineffectual constraints of relevance. The 1998 Statute of the International Criminal Court (UNTS 38544) establishes excessive intentional environmental destruction as a war crime.

4. Forest Clearing

Forests are destroyed during wartime primarily to deny an enemy cover and concealment, and to a much lesser extent to deny the timber resource to the enemy. Forests can be devastated for hostile purposes over huge areas by various means, among them: (a) by spraying with herbicides; (b) by the use of heavy tractors equipped with special forest clearing blades; (c) by saturation bombing; and (d) at certain times and places, by the setting of self-propagating wild fires.

Herbicides (*i.e.*, chemical anti-plant weapons) were employed on a dramatic scale for forest clearing by the USA during the Second Indochina War of 1961-1975 (some 72 million liters sprayed onto almost 2 million hectares), as were heavy tractors (clearing over 300 thousand hectares) and saturation bombing (totaling about 7 million tonnes). Although incendiary attacks are most common, and most successful, against urban and industrial targets, they are also occasionally attempted, with greater or lesser success, against rural grassland or forest targets.

The forest destruction carried out in order to deny the enemy cover and concealment can bring about great damage to upland forest ecosystems and can lead to utter destruction of some coastal ones. In destroying the vegetation of a forest ecosystem, the wildlife is decimated concomitantly primarily owing to a loss of its natural habitat. At the same time, the soil and its nutrients are eroded and washed away, the more so the more rugged the terrain. Depending on the severity of attack, vegetational type, and local site conditions, natural recovery of the assaulted forest ecosystem can take years or decades.

The use of chemical warfare agents, including herbicides, is prohibited by the widely adopted 1925 Geneva Protocol on Chemical and Bacteriological Warfare (LNTS 2138). Protocol III of the 1981 Conventional Weapon Convention (UNTS 22495) includes a modest restriction on the destruction of forests by fire. There are no specific restrictions in the law of war (international humanitarian law) on bombing or on the use of tractors for hostile purposes.

5. Explosive Remnants of War

Singled out for exposition under this heading are the explosive remnants of war (unexploded ordnance, UXO), those resulting from the use in wartime of land mines and other weapons with similar long-term effects, a gruesome and much employed means of warfare that is often taken for granted, but for which at least a partial remedy is available.

5.1. Anti-personnel Land Mines

High-explosive land mines — both anti-personnel and anti-vehicle — are relatively inexpensive, easily employed, and effective means of hindering, slowing down, or channeling the movements of enemy forces as well as of sapping their morale. Land mines are thus widely and heavily employed by both regular armies and insurgent forces, especially so the anti-personnel land mines of particular concern here. Land mines are usually constructed and emplaced so as to defy premeditated discovery, but are of course designed so as to detonate when inadvertently disturbed. Scatterable anti-personnel land mines — now widely employed by technically advanced armed forces — can be remotely delivered in great numbers by various means, including artillery, rocket, and aircraft. The vast majority of all land mines used in warfare are, in fact, <u>not</u> set off by the combatants at which they were directed, and — tragically — most of them remain ready to explode for many decades into the future.

5.2. Anti-personnel Cluster Bomb Submunitions (Bomblets)

High-explosive munitions other than land mines — grenades, artillery shells, mortar rounds, bombs, submunitions (bomblets), rockets, and so forth — are often expended in vastly greater numbers during warfare than are land mines. The increasingly popular explosive bomblets dispensed via air-dropped cluster bombs (cluster bomb units, CBUs) are generally employed in staggeringly high numbers. Whereas most of these many sorts of high-explosive munitions explode as intended at the time of release, a significant fraction (perhaps of the order of 10%) malfunctions, the so-called duds. And, in turn, a significant fraction (perhaps of the order of 50%) of these residual duds remains ready to explode when jolted at some future time. The long-term impact of high-explosive duds is thus quite comparable to that of the residual land mines described above.

The bomblets just referred to are encased in a bomb-like (or rocket-like or shell-like) cannister in groups of several dozen to several hundred or more. The resulting cluster munition can be delivered to a target area by aircraft (fixed-wing or helicopter); or, if appropriately configured, by artillery, mortar tube, or rocket launcher. The bomblets are of various sorts, but are typically charged with a high explosive and constructed for either anti-personnel or anti-tank purposes, or a combination thereof. The bomblets can be equipped with a wide variety of fuses for above-ground, contact, or delayed detonation. Indeed, some fuses make bomblets difficult to distinguish from remotely delivered (scatterable) land mines.

For example, during the Second Indochina War of 1961-1975, cluster bombs were used by the USA as area-denial and anti-personnel weapons. Of the order of 1.5 million cluster bombs appear to have been expended during that armed conflict, or roughly 7% of the total number of bombs dropped. Those 1.5 million cluster bombs contained roughly 750 million bomblets, dropped onto portions of Viet Nam, Laos, and Cambodia over a period of about a decade.

During the Persian Gulf War of 1991, the USA (and, to a lesser extent, also the UK and other members of the United Nations Coalition Forces) used cluster bombs as anti-personnel and anti-tank weapons. Some 60 thousand cluster bombs were expended by the USA alone during that armed conflict, more or less evenly divided between anti-personnel and anti-tank types, together representing about 30% of the total number of bombs dropped. Indeed, those 60 thousand cluster bombs contained almost 30 million bomblets, dropped onto portions of Kuwait and Iraq over a period of about a month.

Other recent wars in which large numbers of anti-personnel cluster bombs were expended include the Arab-Israeli Wars of 1967 and 1973 (by Israel), the Afghan Civil War of 1978-1989 (by the former USSR), the Falkland/Malvinas War of 1982 (by the UK), and the Yugoslavian War of 1998-1990 (by the USA and other NATO forces, primarily in the Kosovo area).

5.3. Environmental Impact of the Explosive Remnants of War

The immensity of the overall problem of land mines and other unexploded remnants of war is difficult to grasp. At present, there are more than — perhaps many more than — 65 million functional land mines emplaced in some 56 countries around the world. Presumably even larger numbers of potentially still explosive dud munitions are to be found additionally in those same and further countries. The records of the International Committee of the Red Cross (Geneva) reveal that these explosive remnants of war are now resulting in more than 800 human fatalities plus further thousands of maimings per month. In Cambodia alone explosive remnants have produced more than 36 000 amputees within the past decade or so; and in Somalia more than 23 000.

The problem of explosive remnants of war exists in many parts of the world, but is perhaps most acute in Africa, where some 18 countries are seriously afflicted with them, including especially Angola, Eritrea, Ethiopia, Mozambique, Somalia, and the Sudan. In the Middle East one must point in this regard especially to Iran, Iraq, and Kuwait; in Asia especially to Afghanistan, Cambodia, Laos, and Viet Nam; in Latin America especially to El Salvador and Nicaragua; and in Europe especially to Bosnia-Herzegovina, Croatia, and Serbia-Montenegro; and even to Poland with its residuum of explosive remnants of World War II, of which thousands are still being found and disposed of each year, but that nonetheless to this day continue to kill or maim several dozen individuals annually.

Human existence and well-being depend upon continuing access to huge rural areas throughout the world for agriculture, horticulture, grazing, forestry, hunting, fishing, mining, and so forth. When a rural area being thus utilized by the local populace becomes a battlefield, the effects of exploding munitions can be devastating. When that rural area has been a theater of military operations that left a residuum of unexploded munitions, this will have severe consequences, both direct and indirect.

To begin with, any remnant clearing operations are themselves apt to be environmentally disruptive, sometimes very much so. Moreover, they are time-consuming, technically difficult, expensive (often prohibitively so), never fully successful, and — above all — exceedingly dangerous.

In many rural areas throughout the world, the local populace is forced by circumstances to continue to utilize the land upon which it has depended, with the result that there is an appalling frequency of fatalities and maimings, both human and livestock. Thus, in former battle zones farming, herding, and forestry become hazardous pursuits. Wood destined for lumber becomes unsafe and troublesome with metal embedded in it. And all sorts of other aspects of local development become equally hampered, including the construction of roads, power lines, and irrigation systems. Income from tourism can be all but eliminated. Moreover, any material and financial resources diverted to clearing, or to remnant-generated medical, veterinary, and other expenses, are lost to productive activities.

The various familial and societal disruptions resulting from the explosive remnants — deaths or permanent disabilities, losses of livestock and other property, reduced opportunities for subsistence food production and for income, forced migrations, and so forth — become a great impediment to the sustainable development of the local economy. To the extent that areas are deemed simply too dangerous to be exploited, the refugees or migrants thereby generated are likely to overburden both the natural and social resources of their sites of destination, whether rural or urban, which is therefore likely to lead to additional, off-site, damage to the environment.

In short, the presence of land mines and other explosive remnants of war makes recovery following armed conflict an extremely onerous matter, thus raising serious social and environmental concerns. Other than eliminating warfare itself, every effort must be made to minimize adverse post-war consequences on humans and nature. In the present context, international cooperation, both technical and financial, is needed to help clear the unexploded remnants of past armed conflicts, something that has been unanimously urged, and to a modest extent orchestrated, by the United Nations General Assembly. Moreover, land mines and every other type of high-explosive munition that are apt to become an explosive remnant of armed conflict should without exception be designed to have a built-in, non-removable mechanism for becoming harmless in due course.

Thus, the long-term post-war problem of land mines and other unexploded ordnance is a singularly grave and intractable one. This is the case especially in view of several factors: (a) the great — and to a substantial extent successful — efforts in mine design and emplacement techniques to prevent their discovery by the enemy; (b) the efforts to keep munitions functional in the face of extremely adverse environmental conditions (quite successful, to judge from their extraordinary longevity); (c) the vast levels of wartime munition expenditures, exacerbated by such recent ordnance innovations as scatterable mines and bomblets; and (d) the emphasis in at least some types of warfare on large-scale area neutralization or area denial.

Existing constraints in international law on the use of land mines and other explosive remnants of war do not as yet provide adequate protection to civilians, either in time of armed conflict or after its cessation. The key multilateral instruments of relevance here are: (a) the 1981 Conventional Weapon Convention (UNTS 22495), 1981 Protocol II of which restricts the use of anti-personnel land mines, especially so its amended (strengthened) version of 1996; and (2) the 1997 Anti-personnel Mine Convention (UNTS 35597), which simply prohibits their very possession. However, none of these three instruments includes restraints applicable to dud bomblets or other explosive remnants of war.

1981 Protocol II has to date been accepted by only one-third or so of all states, and its 1996 amended version has been even less popular (so far with only about one-quarter or so of all states parties). Conversely, the straightforward 1997 Anti-personnel Mine Convention has to date been embraced by more than half of all states (although not as yet by a number of the key major powers).

It is manifestly clear that land mines and such comparable weapons as bomblets should be outlawed, or at least their employment severely circumscribed. First, more states should join the 1997 Anti-personnel Mine Convention, until its strictures become universal. And second, all explosive munitions likely to become explosive remnants of war should be constructed so as to become harmless after their military purpose has been accomplished.

6. Nuclear, Chemical, and Biological Warfare

Unconventional warfare (nuclear, chemical, or biological) has been pursued only rarely in the past, but always remains a possibility. Nuclear weapons have been employed in warfare only once to date, by the USA in two urban attacks against Japan during World War II. Anti-personnel chemical weapons were employed extensively (and openly) by both the Allied and Axis powers during World War I, but not before or since on such a grand scale. (Anti-plant chemical weapons are covered above under 'Forest Clearing'; see Section 4.) Biological weapons have been employed essentially only once in modern times, on a relatively minor scale (and secretly) by Japan against China during World War II.

The possibility for environmental disruption by unconventional warfare is truly enormous, but fortunately prevailing cultural norms seem to make this an unlikely eventuality for the future. Moreover, formal prohibitions are in place to reinforce such social values as regards the use of chemical and biological weapons through the aforementioned 1925 Geneva Protocol on Chemical and Bacteriological Warfare (LNTS 2138); and the 1998 Statute of the International Criminal Court (UNTS 38544) establishes the use of chemical weapons as a war crime. The very possession of biological weapons is proscribed through the 1972 Biological and Toxin Weapon Convention (UNTS 14860). Regrettably, there exists as yet no multilateral instrument that would outlaw the further use of nuclear weapons.

7. Beneficial Environmental Effects of War

Although war and the preparations for war are for the most part detrimental to the environment, some positive effects must be noted. The major wartime benefit that can accrue to nature is reduced exploitation of a rural area owing to the dangers associated with entering war zones.

Another source of benefit is that individuals who might do damage to the environment could be otherwise occupied in time of war. To provide some concrete examples: the severely depleted North Sea fishery was able to recover during World War II since the war largely precluded civilian entry into the area; and portions of the North African desert habitat were able to recover from severe overgrazing because for a time residual land mines and other explosive remnants of war made entry too dangerous. Moreover, various endangered habitats, and the species they contain, find refuge in the typically large off-limits buffer zones surrounding nuclear weapon factories and testing areas as well as those surrounding various other military facilities.

8. Conclusion

Conventional warfare can be devastating, both socially and environmentally. However, it is important to realize that the level of destruction does not, in fact, depend so much upon the modernity of the armed forces involved or upon the sophistication of the weapons available to them. Rather it depends largely upon the objectives, the will, and the tenacity of the parties to the conflict. Improvements in weaponry have followed one upon the other throughout the long sweep of human history, but so far this has not led through time to any discernible increase in the damage brought about by warfare, only in the efficiency with which it is perpetrated.

Indeed by way of example, one of the most socially and environmentally devastating wars in recent centuries was fought with quite primitive arms by the standards of today. In the Chinese Rebellion of 1850-1864 the Tai Ping (Great Peace) movement was ultimately unsuccessful in its attempt to overthrow the ruling Manchu dynasty. The Tai Ping forces pursued their rebellion with continuing violence of a high order and with much pillaging. It was countered by the Manchu forces with equal or greater terror and violence. Among other means, the government forces employed large-scale scorched-earth tactics in order to starve the rebellious regions into submission. The final total number of war deaths is estimated to have been between 20 million and 40 million, representing about 7% of China's total population at the time. The population and countryside particularly of the lower Yangtze River region (Anhwei province plus portions of the surrounding provinces) were truly devastated and had still not regained their pre-war conditions a full century later.

In closing, the global biosphere is being damaged ever more decisively by grossly expanding human numbers and needs — with ultimately disastrous consequences for human and all other life on earth.

It is thus now becoming even more true and more obvious that warfare is an outrageously frivolous human pastime. However if not to be avoided, at least the most perfidious acts and unintentional impacts of war must be minimized. Such restraints must occur for both social reasons and environmental reasons, the latter ones not only because they have an important indirect effect on the health and safety of humans, but also to protect nature and its wild creatures in their own right.

9. Acknowledgment

The author wishes to acknowledge valuable suggestions from Carol E. Westing (Putney, VT, USA).

Glossary

1. Armed conflict: The terms 'armed conflict' and 'war' are used interchangeably in the text
2. Country: The terms 'country', 'nation', and 'state' are used interchangeably in the text
3. LNTS: *League of Nations Treaty Series* (Geneva), forerunner of the UNTS (see below)
4. Nation: See 'country' above
5. State: See 'country' above
6. UNTS: *United Nations Treaty Series* (New York), successor to the LNTS (see above)
7. War: See 'armed conflict' above

10. Annotated Bibliography

Austin, J., & Bruch, C. (eds). 2000. *Environmental Consequences of War: Legal, Economic, and Scientific Perspectives*, 691 pp. Cambridge, UK: Cambridge University Press. [This multi-authored volume is especially noteworthy for its legal coverage of the subject. Environmental guidelines for armed forces during peace and war is covered in Chapter 6.]

Brauch, H.G., *et al.* 2003. *Security and Environment in the Mediterranean: Conceptualizing Security and Environmental Conflicts*. Berlin, Germany: Springer-Verlag, 1134 pp. [This wide-ranging multi-authored volume is a major addition to the literature. For a critical examination of the environmental dimension of the Persian Gulf War of 1991, see Chapter 29.]

Ehrlich, A.H., & Birks, J.W. (eds). 1990. *Hidden Dangers: Environmental Costs of Preparing for War*, 246 pp. San Francisco, CA, USA: Sierra Books. [This highly useful multi-authored volume is the only one available in its subject area.]

Gleditsch, N.p. (ed.). 1997. *Conflict and the Environment*, 598 pp. Dordrecht, NL: Kluwer Academic Publishers. [This multi-authored volume includes coverage of wartime environmental and natural resource degradation and available responses to the problem. Chapter 32 examines the law of war (international humanitarian law) as it applies to environmental disruption, with special reference to several recent armed conflicts, both international and non-international, further analyzing national factors conducive to the acceptance of wartime environmental constraints.]

Goldblat, J. 2002. *Arms Control: the New Guide to Negotiations and Agreements*, 2nd ed., 396 pp + CD-ROM Documentation Supplement. London, UK: Sage Publications. [This is the definitive analysis and compendium of international arms control and disarmament instruments.]

Pittock, A.B., *et al.* 1985-1986. *Environmental Consequences of Nuclear War. I. Physical and Atmospheric Effects. II. Ecological and Agricultural Effects*, 359+523 pp. Chichester, UK: John Wiley. [These two multi-authored volumes provide exhaustive coverage of the presumed environmental impact of a massive nuclear war. For a succinct analysis of the same subject, see *Environmental Conservation* 14(4), 295-306; 1987.]

Roberts, S., & Williams, J. 1994. *After the Guns Fall Silent: the Enduring Legacy of Landmines*, 554 pp + 9 maps. Washington, DC, USA: Vietnam Veterans of America Foundation. [This monograph offers a detailed worldwide survey of the anti-personnel land-mine problem, although it does not address the other explosive remnants of war.]

Schmitt, M.N. 1997. Green war: an assessment of the environmental law of international armed conflict. *Yale Journal of International Law*, New Haven, CT, USA, 22(1), 1-109. [This article provides an extraordinarily thorough analysis of its subject from a military perspective.]

Westing, A.H. 1976. *Ecological Consequences of the Second Indochina War*, 119 pp + 8 pl. Stockholm, Sweden: Almqvist & Wiksell. [This monograph provides the only exhaustive description and analysis of the environmental impact of a war in which attacks on the environment were an integral component of the strategy pursued by one of the belligerents.]

Westing, A.H. 1977. *Weapons of Mass Destruction and the Environment*, 95 pp. London, UK: Taylor & Francis. [This monograph has separate chapters on the ecological impact of nuclear weapons, chemical and biological weapons, and geophysical weapons.]

Westing, A.H. 1980. *Warfare in a Fragile World: Military Impact on the Human Environment*, 249 pp. London, UK: Taylor & Francis. [This is the definitive study of the military impact on the environment for each of the major global biomes during both war and peace in comparison with the civil impact.]

Westing, A.H. (ed.). 1984. *Environmental Warfare: a Technical, Legal and Policy Appraisal*, 107 pp. London, UK: Taylor & Francis. [This multi-authored volume contains separate chapters on hostile manipulations of the atmosphere and of the geosphere, and on the legal ramifications of such actions.]

Westing, A.H. (ed.). 1984. *Herbicides in War: the Long-term Ecological and Human Consequences*, 210 pp. London, UK: Taylor & Francis. [This multi-authored volume includes a history of the use of anti-plant chemical weapons as well as their impact on terrestrial plant ecology, terrestrial animal ecology, soil ecology, and freshwater and marine ecology.]

Westing, A.H. (ed.). 1985. *Explosive Remnants of War: Mitigating the Environmental Effects*, 141 pp. London, UK: Taylor & Francis. [This multi-authored volume covers the history of the use of land mines and other explosive remnants of war, also examining their disposal, and also legal aspects of the subject.]

Westing, A.H. (ed.). 1990. *Environmental Hazards of War: Releasing Dangerous Forces in an Industrialized World*, 96 pp. London, UK: Sage Publications. [This multi-authored volume covers the release for hostile purposes of so-called dangerous forces from nuclear facilities, chemical facilities, and hydrological facilities (dams), and also deals with the legal aspects of the subject.]

Author Biography

Arthur H. Westing is trained as a forest ecologist (Yale University, M.F., 1954, Ph.D., 1959). He served as a combat officer in the United States Marine Corps from 1950 to 1952, has been a Research Forester with the United States Forest Service, and has taught forestry, ecology, and conservation at several colleges and universities. From 1983 to 1990, under contract with the Stockholm International Peace Research Institute (SIPRI) and then the Peace Research Institute Oslo (PRIO), Westing directed the United Nations Environment Programme project on 'Peace, Security, and the Environment', a position which took him to many countries throughout the world. He is the author of numerous publications in that subject area. Westing was on the faculty of the European Peace University from 1989 to 2002. Among the organizations that have recognized his achievements are the New York Academy of Sciences, the Government of Bulgaria, and the United Nations. Westing was named a 'Peace Messenger' by the Secretary-General of the United Nations in 1987, and in 1990 became one of the 500 individuals worldwide to have been appointed to the United Nations Environment Programme 'Global 500 Roll of Honour'. Since 1990, he has been a Consultant in Environmental Security, providing his services to several branches of the United Nations, including UNESCO and the International Bank for Reconstruction and Development (World Bank), to the International Committee of the Red Cross, to the Government of Eritrea, to the World Conservation Union (IUCN), and to various other national and international agencies. He is Vice-President of the International Society of Naturalists (Baroda, India) and is also a member of or advisor to a number of environmental nongovernmental organizations and scholarly journals.

10

Conclusion

Nature was inextricably connected with the life process of human beings, and worshipped with awe and reverence. It used to shape human destiny in their political social and economic relations. The ancient Greek geographer-philosopher Strabo, stated this some centuries ago. The nature had the mastery over human beings. This primacy of nature in human relations did not last long The advent of science in 16thand 17th century and its miraculous achievement reduced nature to a mere lifeless matter to be exploited for the commodious living of human beings. It remained no longer the master and subject of worship. It was viewed as a compendium of raw materials to be expended for the benefits of human beings. It no longer assumed importance in the human concern except that it was to be exploited relentlessly in the name of development. Science, which helped policy makers enslave and tame nature, became the culprit in destruction of the environment to the perils of human beings. When industrialization based on fossil fuel technology reached its peak of development and modernization, nature remained in the evaded periphery of human concern except being a slave attending to its master. As described, policy making at national and international level became denatured. Exploited and despoliated to the hilt nature again occupied the focused primacy in national and international realm when science brought to limelight the devastating consequences of nature being destroyed in the name of development upon the living beings. Thus, what was once at horizon hastened to occupy the core of human concern drawing the attention of all-the policy makers, statesmen, scientists, countries, NGOs, and people of the world to stem the irreversible slide in the degradation of the environment, and redefine what has so far been ubiquitously called as development as à predominant part of western culture being universally clamped on all other cultures. As a consequence, the threats stemming from environmental degradation to the very existence of living beings and future generations provide new insights to contest the very foundations and logic of mainstream political and economic thinking. New planetary ethics and nuances for global governance of environment are felt required to challenge the adequacy of westphalian political system, its legitimation, prevailing pattern of development and approach to life. Proliferation of international agreements and treaties for managing the environment at national and global level points to the fact that there has been remarkably a shift away from the conventional logic and wisdom of realism, which was the guiding lodestar for conduct and formulation of state behaviour in the supposed anarchic international system toward an integral cosmic whole approach in the line of what eastern seers, modem physicists and western idealists have viewed the universe as inter connected, and inseparable part of the cosmic web and manifestation of the Spirit. A detailed analysis of how nature has returned into the international realm to occupy the primacy has already been made. A concept of development, which has excluded in its definition a greater section of the planetary system such as plants, trees, forests, landmass, water bodies, air, and non human living beings as subjectivities is not only one sided but also has been pernicious to both those who have been excluded and included. Once we recognize that environmental systems often exhibit complex, non-linear, interactive behaviour and that environmental scarcity can undermine adaptive responses, we must reintroduce nature into our explanations of social behaviour and political actions.

In the preceding analysis, the Toronto group headed by Homer Dixon developed a theory of causal links between severe environmental scarcity and violent conflict citing various examples and evidences from numerous case studies. According to his analysis, scarcity or degradation of renewable resources can contribute to civil violence, including insurgencies and ethnic clashes which he predicted, would occur with more severity and frequency than in the past, as scarcities of renewable resources, such as cropland, freshwater, forests, air and atmosphere worsen in many parts of the world. Except in some cases where scarcity's role is direct and immediate cause of violence, in other cases scarcity's role is indirect and in interaction with political, economic, and other factors generates severe social effects that in turn create violent conflict. These social effects are decreased agricultural production, economic decline, poverty, migration and weakening of state apparatus. But analysts who disagree with Dixon and other group's conclusion, tend to interpret these social effects as principal causes of conflict, thus underestimating the scarcity's principal role in causing conflict. As analyzed above, the environmental degradation or scarcity, the increased demand for these resources, and/or their unequal distribution, often interact and reinforce each other to produce resource capture and ecological marginalization.

Resource capture is depiction of a situation when the degradation and depletion of renewable resource interacts with population growth to encourage powerful groups within a society to shift resource distribution in their favour which intensifies scarcity for poorer and weaker groups in the society. Ecological marginalization occurs when unequal resource access in combination with population growth causes long term migration of people depedendent on renewable resources for their livelihood to ecologically fragile regions such as steep upland slopes, areas at risk of desertification, tropical rain forests, and low quality public lands within urban areas. The harmful social effects of environmental scarcity in terms of constrained agricultural and economic productivity, migration, social segmentation and state weaking can cause insurgencies, ethnic clashes and coups de'tat.

Skeptics not countenancing the link between environmental scarcity and conflict are of the view that environmental degradation is never a powerful cause of violent conflict. Political, economic and social factors are much more important contributors to violence.[1] Further they argue, these political, economic, and social factors are actually the ultimate causes of environmental scarcity, which is therefore, subordinate to these factors. It never plays an independent role. Consequently, it in no way interests the policy makers concerned about the causes of violence in the world. In response to this, Homer Dixon and his group argue that environmental scarcity produces its effects within extremely complex ecological political system. Further more, environmental scarcity is not sufficient by itself, to cause violence except in certain rare cases where the environmental scarcity of renewable resources such as water and fish has been so severe as to cause direct violence. Otherwise, it always interacts with other political, economic, and social factors. Environmental scarcity's causal role can never be separated from these contextual factors. The relationship between environmental scarcity and contextual factors is interactive. It is often impossible to determine the relative weight or power of environmental scarcity as a cause of violence in specific causes. This does not mean that environmental scarcity is always an unimportant cause. Skeptics underestimate the fact that a large proportion of the world population is fully dependent on local cropland, water and forest resources for their existence.

According to Homer Dixon for these reasons environmental scarcity's role as a cause of violence should not be subordinated to that of political economic and social factors. We should not ignore the fact that environmental scarcity often affects the political and economic character of social systems. For example when it stimulates resource capture by powerful elites, it impels institutional and policy reform. Further environmental scarcity is partly a function of the character of a society's physical environment. If severe damage is done to the environment it can become a permanent source of social stress. Twentieth century stands as a witness to a number of inter-state wars over access to non-renewable resources like oil or mineral. But there have been a few wars over renewables such as cropland, plants, fresh water and fish.The reasons are— First, states cannot easily or quickly translate renewable resources into assets that significantly increase their power. Second, the countries that are dependent on renewable resources are poor. They lack the capability for aggression.

The renewable resource most likely to stimulate inter-state wars is river water. But this occurs in a narrow set of circumstances: the down stream country must be highly dependent on water for its national-well being.The upstream country must be restricting flow, there must be a history of antagonism between the two countries and most importantly the downstream country must be militarily stronger than the upstream country. According to skeptics, since the conflicts arising out of environmental scarcity are not interstate, these are of little concern to policymakers in developed countries. These are of marginal importance to the national security interests of rich countries.[2]

Yet these conflicts generated partly by environmental scarcity, can nonetheless have serious indirect effects on the international community. The changing nature of the international system, heightened economic interdependence, easier access to information, and marvelous revolution in the field of communication resulting in death of distance, make the previously insignificant regions of interest to policy makers. For example, crisis in Haiti, Somalia and Ethiopia often has created serious foreign policy difficulties for developed countries. Flow of refugees due to environmental scarcity to neighbouring countries has often resulted in interstate ethnic violence drawing the attention of international community. Major civil violence within states can affect external trade relations, cause migration, and produce humanitarian disasters that call upon the military and financial resources of developed countries and international organizations for help.

Finally, the skeptics refute the finding of Homer Dixon' s group that environmental scarcity in combination with social effects will generate violent conflict. According to them, scarcity often stimulates useful technological and social change to adapt to rising consequences of scarcity. But in the preceding chapters, it has been shown how poor and developing societies will fail to adapt to crisis because of various constraints. In these societies requirements for genuity to respond to scarcity outstrip supply of ingenuity, making it vulnerable to scarcity's harsh social effects. Homer Dixon is of the view that in coming decades, worsening environmental scarcities in many regions will further exaggerate the world's already widening hiatus between rich and poor societies and between the powerful and weak people within these societies.[3] The world has been so much interdependent that the wealthy nations should not assume that they will able to keep themselves immune from turmoil in societies that do not adapt well to scarcity.

Many analysts and economists place undue faith in the infinite capability of human kind to produce ingenuity to deal with the environmental scarcity. So far as the developing societies are concerned, the supply of ingenuity will not be plenty because of factors and constraints analyzed above by Dixon and his group. There may be a mismatch between the severity of the crisis and the amount of ingenuity needed to adapt to the crisis. This ingenuity gap shall be a common phenomenon of developing societies where the scarcity of resources has been severe. This is the reason why the developing societies are more vulnerable to environmental scarcity than the developed world. The question is not about human adaptation to the environmental scarcity and its social effects whether by suffering, starving and bearing the amount of hardship. The fulcrum of the analysis lies on how to prevent the crisis. This is what comes within the broader ambit of environmental security. It is not that the environmental scarcity shall be allowed to bust into a crisis until a solution is to be found out putting boundless faith in the potential of human ingenuity, as the economists and critics suggest. Human ingenuity is not like a magic wand that unearths a solution out of its sleeve every time when we are spurred by necessity. The crisis shall not be keft on waiting till scientific investments and knowledge come out with a solution. The impact of social effects of environmental scarcity on future generations may have to be more severe and far reaching. Since the poor societies are afflicted by severe environmental scarcity, there will be more ingenuity gap and adaptive failure because of the constraints cited above. In that case the very onus and functions of maintaining intergenerational equity and responsibility may not be properly discharged. The scarcity if let go to be fully blown into a crisis, just keeping faith in the ingenuity of man to reveal a solution, the prospects for social friction and violent conflict not only in the present generation but also in future societies loom large. This analysis is not that of an apologist to put forth arguments linking environmental scarcity and conflict, or it is not that of an economic optimist to wait and see keeping undue faith in human ingenuity which is not plentily available to the poor societies. It is about defining environmental security that includes a pro active preventive measure to avoid the prospects for conflicts as outlined by the dominant environmental conflict paradigm, and efforts to redefine the conventional wisdom about the realist notion of security, and the western pattern of development hinged on fossil fuel based industrialization taking into account the intergenerational equity and intergenerational responsibility.

While analysing the causes and consequences of environmental degradation and depletion of resources, Homer Dixon and others have ignored the role of rich industrialized North countries in causing damage to the environment. As seen from their research studies, their attention has been only confined to the developing countries. It seems as if the environmental degradation is the doings of the South countries, and the rich North countries have squarely put the blame on the burgeoning population of the poor South countries. What is lost sight of is the western pattern of development, its existing economic thinking and life style which have disproportionately used the resources of the earth to the perils of others. The world economic structure presided over by the United States and its allies has been built at the cost of the environment and poor South. The disastrous consequences of environmental degradation in terms of global warming, sea level rise and hole in ozone layer, are the result of western pattern of development, economic thinking and high life style. The victims of these are the poor South countries whose contribution to emission of CO_2 and other green house gases is very negligible in comparison to that of the rich North countries led by the United States. The profligate life style, exorbitant consumption and commodious and luxurious living of the rich North People have been at the root of the environmental crisis and a greater threat to the poor people in South. These non-military threats more devastating than the nuclear weapons have been ignored in the analysis of Homer Dixon and other researches theorizing the linkage between environmental scarcity and conflict. Rejection of

Kyoto Protocol by the United States is suggestive of the fact that America is not willing to compromise its lifestyle for the greater security of the human kind. The process of globalization and militarisation reveals how the notions of free trade, the free market and global security have in reality been an elaborate myth to justify the utilization of violence and state power on behalf of the vested interests. Tom Reifer is quoted to have indicated that" the present model of development is hopelessly flawed, being based on patterns of unjust consumption, exploitations and exclusion which cannot by definition be generalized to all humanity". [4] As pointed out earlier, environmental security is not synonymous with environmental conflict. It is beyond the linkage between environmental scarcity and violence to include the prescriptions for rethinking economic pattern, inordinate life style and exorbitant consumption of the western people. It is not western pattern of development, but sustainable development that addresses the rights of future generations, present generations and also those of the nonliving and living to live a healthy life on this planet on the basis of justice and equity, is to be the basis of environmental security. Homer Dixon and other groups' analysis of environmental conflict lacks prescriptions for the way out of the environmental degradation that has led to violent conflict. Environmental security as pointed out above contains prescriptions in terms of a total overhauling the western pattern of development, established economic thinking and inordinate and profligate life style and consumptive attitude. Intergenerational accountability and responsibility on the basis of justice and equity., sustainable development- and new ethics and vision form the confluence on which environmental security stands to challenge the established frame of mind about security, and sovereign state system associated with the hegemonic mainstream of international relation.

Environmental security is not an appendage to American concept of security built into its system since the industrial revolution. As understood from the viewpoint of the United States environmental security is to assure it access to resources of the earth with the application of military force. Contrary to what is understood by the US, the environmental security does not mean that the poor South countries keep their environment and nature clean and unpolluted to become the resource pool for the rich industrialized North. It is the domestic imperatives shaped by industrial revolution and liberal market economy in terms of production of wealth, profligate consumption, commodious living and inordinate life style that have been built into American concept of security. The entire planet is to be kept ready to fulfill the resource requirement of the North. American is not willing to cast a second look at these imperatives, rather wants that the entire world change according to the domestic demands of the United States.

As seen earlier science and political science share the same ontological foundation during 15th & 16th century when individuals were held in the Newtonian language as particles of motion in the direction of wealth production, inordinate consumption, profligate life style and commodious living. Science helped the individual since industrial revolution seek these goals as sonnum bonnum of life. The liberal market oriented political system emerged then found in the sovereign state system as the guarantor and promoter of these goals to individuals. These formed the basis on which individuals tended their consent and legitimacy to the rightness of action of the sovereign state system to put the earth, and its bountiful bonanza at the service of the individuals. The result is the accumulated emission of CO_2 and other green house gases to the atmosphere due to industrial revolution, profligate life style and the inordinate consumption, which have plagued the entire humanity in terms of global warming, sea level rise and ozone layer depletion. So climate change due to accumulation of CO_2 by the industrialized nations challenges the legitimacy of sovereign state system and the security system built around it. The legitimacy given to the rightness of sovereign state system is not beyond space and time. It has not taken into consideration the very right of the future generations both living and nonliving to live on this earth. Intergenerational equity and accountability has been ignored. The very basis and criteria of giving legitimacy to the sovereign state system in terms of wealth production, inordinate consumption and profligate life style are to be reconsidered, if environmental security is to be assured to entire humanity. In this reinvented criteria is involved the interests of future generations and their right to survival. Thus, the conventional security system built around sovereign state system and its rightness of action in terms of liberal market economy to produce wealth and promote commodious living, has come in for a reversal and overhauling. Science which has helped state system put these materialistic pleasures as objectives before the individuals has become a problem in terms of the disastrous consequences of climate change which also challenges the authority of science to come out with alternatives. The new criteria of legitimacy to the sovereign state system and its political – economic thinking based on recognition of the principle of intergenerational equity and intergenerational accountability will certainly bring out a new configuration of Westphalia sovereign state system and the security system built around it. This would give rise to environmental security to all the present generations, future generations, the living and non-living removing the causes of environmental violent conflict as studied by Homer Dixon and others.

As studied previously, the ethical foundation of environmental security is quest for new vision and planetary wisdom. Man is no longer the Hobbes and Locken possessive individual always in the pursuit and direction of sensual pleasures derived from materialistic aggrandizement. Man as mere a consumer and a cog in the market dominated society is different from man as a whole and complete being. The whole world is a cosmic family in which not only human beings of the present generations, but also of the future, living and non-living are bonafide members. Recognizing each other's right to existence and each other as a part and parcel of the cosmic family will bring about new transformed individuals in whose enlarged self is perceived the existence of all other selves. To transform the body-mind confined individual into a highly enlightened enlarged self encompassing the entire planet, is what is needed to bring modesty to the rapacious nature of the consumerist individuals. As said, a spiritual and political consensus is needed without compromising the secular foundation of the state. The spiritual essence of all religions about the vision of life, nature, cosmos and planet can be weaved into a beautiful ethical tapestry that will constitute the basis of environmental security. The national interest of the sovereign state system defined in terms of self vs. the other the external world and others are to be exploited for the growth of the self-is to be replaced by planetary interests. The recognition of the organic bond that exists between man and nature, the future generations' right to live, the principle of inter generational equity and accountability is what is to be identified as planetary intests. Prioritization of these planetary intests over narrow realist framework of interest forms the ethical basis of environmental security.

Homer Dixon and others have established the linkage between environmental scarcity and violent conflict within the conventional realist military framework associated with the state. The response to the situation arising out of environmental conflict, as pointed out by him is through the military apparatus of state, or violent means adopted by the insurgent groups. Then in what way it is different from the traditional conflict or war so far as the response is concerned? Environmental security as outlined above can address the situation by rethinking the traditional concept of security built around the state. It stands at the confluence of sustainable development or rethinking western pattern of development, recognition of intergenerational equity and responsibility and an ethical resurgence in human beings to recast their inordinate life style, exorbitant consumption. Addressing the causes rather than the symptoms can cure the malaise arising out of environmental scarcity. Environmental security addresses the causes rather than the symptoms. It is beyond the prognostic description of the scenarios of violent conflict that will arise out of environmental scarcity or degradation of resources and is prescriptive about the course of action and, policy needed at the level of individual, society, and decision making structure of state with a renewed vision, wisdom and new planetary ethics to save the earth from the brinks it is being hurtled towards by the mindless, profligate consumption, consumerist market political economy having initiated the entire world into its thesis of development.

As the above discussion shows, despite cataclysmic changes in International Relation, environment and ecology, a dominant group remains unwilling to disrobe themselves of Westphalian straitjacket while understanding the diverse strands and security perspectives, the source of security threats no longer lie embedded in the state.

At the core of this mainstream thinking and portrayal of International Relation remains dominant the ontology of an egoism-anarchy thematic. The boundaries of what is ethically possible are established within a rigid universal closed power politics logic, which not surprisingly, gives politico-ethical legitimacy to great power dominance and hegemonic systems of global order. Thinking beyond this thematic of any unconventional seems to be anathema to this school of thought. The deepening environmental crisis with catastrophic consequences on society and human beings and their views of world hastened to the center stage to challenge the dominance of this statist school of thought customarily inclined to view security on politico-military terms. When the new threats from unconventional sources i.e. from environmental degradation were put to fit into their Westphalia procrustean bed, and could not match their logic and parameters, these are termed as dependable variables and not causal and cannot ascend to the status of national security. Rather view them as predominant and separate security threats from the environmental crisis, they try downplaying these threats and associate these with political and economic factors as Buzan does. Another thing that is mostly ignored is the very assumption that when environmental security is held as national security, it does not mean that it seeks solution to the environmental crisis through the military apparatus of the state only. What is central to the realist logic is that the response to the threats if done through the exercise or use of force, is worth being named as having acquired the status of national security. Deudney, Dalby and others fearing their stand slipping into parochial statism have set all argumentations against bestowal of national security status to environmental threats. On the other hand Homer Dixon and others like Myers, Libiswezski have shown empirically that environmental degradation and security of resources will produce social effects in terms of poverty, decline in agricultural productivity, displacement of people and weakening of political and social institutions i.e. state which in turn will culminate in various violent intra or inter state conflict such as simple scarcity, group identify conflict, insurgencies and other forms of violence depending on the severity of the environmental crisis, the nature of the society and other contextual factors: their mapping out the scenario of violent conflict, from environmental scarcity of resources along its social effects, is not within the politico-military construct of national security. On the issues of environmental scarcity and degradation of renewable resources such as water, the conflict has taken the form of intra-state conflict such as insurgencies, group identity conflict having implications on international security and stability. The thrust of their argument rests on the fact that the environmental scarcity of resources unless properly addressed has the dangers of violent inter and intra state conflict. Hence environmental degradation comes as a non-military security threat to the people of a state to occupy the status of national security.

National security understood in parochial and conventional wisdom needs to be redefined in view of the disastrous transformation and changes in environmental sector of the planet. The referent object of security is no longer the state, but other referent objects have appeared to be taken note of by the security strategists. These are the people, the individuals, the non human beings, future generations, the biotic community and the integrity of the cosmos. The trend towards dissociating security and nation state now clearly visible in world politics has been" strong enough to avoid the dangers of falling down the slippery slope toward a parochial statism that Deudney, Dalby and others fear". [5] The confinement of the debate over whether environment and conflict linkage assumes the status of national security to the Westphalian logic and wisdom cannot be a solution to the environmental crisis. If environmental degradation like the military can be assumed to be a threat and needs a military response, then confinement of the issues to the power politics of the sovereign states system, blurs the distinction between the two and aggravates the crisis. The hegemonic, homogenization and linearity logic typical of world power structure and arrangements comes in to dominate the issue and not to find a solution with different, and alternative parameters that would challenge the above conventional logic and wisdom.

Going beyond the dominant environment and conflict paradigm, the very logic of the concept 'environmental security' suggests a solution not in military but in non-military terms. This means traversing beyond the strict allegiance to the sovereign state system. This is what suggested by Stern:

> **"Blind allegiance to the nation state system and inability to contemplate shifts of sovereignty 'upward' or 'downward' needlessly limit the range of instutionlised or adhoc security strategies, which may be brought to bear in adverting or coping with military and non military threats to individual and collective well being."** [6]

Looking beyond the sovereign state system means assurance of environmental security to all. It is a kind of positive peace not based on violence, or just absence of interstate war but focuses on dismissal of hegemonic, ordering, fixity and certainty connotations of the present international system, which is responsible for much of human fear, suffering and ecological disaster.[7] Ecological ethics and insight on which environmental security is based can offer purpose and direction to human kind by stressing natural cycles as well as the cooperative tendencies of nature.

Environmental security envisages a political project, and reconstruction of human society for human kind in biological imperatives, as aimed by critical theorist but not on ecological insights. It does not assume that human relations are fixed and therefore cannot accept the principle of cultural superiority. In a sense, ecological insights" evoke the notion of natural law, but as a much different sort of essentialism divested of hierarchical preference".[8]

The ecological insight challenges the ethnocentric western paradigm of development, its anti nature and perception of other as different from self, its inordinate life style, and exorbitant consumption and philosophy of life based on pure materialism, commodious living and production of wealth at the expense of others (nature, human beings, non-human living and non living, future generation). Pursuance of this hegemonic ideology and its universalization in the name of liberal economic emancipation, globalization and world order has been the root causes of the pauperization and despoliation of the planet. The proponents of environmental security and its critique and even the critical theorists have never touched upon this point and seem to have displayed the cultural superiority bias of hegemonic mainstream of International Relation. The author in this work stresses upon a new planetary wisdom and vision that will be notably the foundation of environmental security but also the national interests of each and every sovereign state. The imperatives of environmental security must bring to realization of policy makers, that 'emphasizing environmental values at a variety of levels including the national may help drive home the insight that self help nationally based strategies will probably not prove a sufficient basis for coping with the environmental threats now on the horizon".[9]

Environmental threats assume the status of national security on the basis of what Homer Dixon and others propounded, and what Deudney denounced. Dixon's mapping out of inter and intra state conflicts arising out of environmental scarcity and degradation of resources assume the status of national security in Westphalian logic with the emergence of new referent objects of security other than the sovereign state, the environmental degradation affecting these referents will be perceived as security threats demanding not solution in terms military frame work of sovereign state system. The very survival of the people, eco system and bio regions demands new planetary ethics, which ultimately will define the national security interests. The redefinition of national security prompted by environmental degradation replacing the traditional understanding of national security makes the Deudney's disavowal of Homer Dixon and other's analysis discredited, if protection of the people against the threats stemming from non-conventional sources i.e. the environmental degradation –the consequences of which are more disastrous than the war itself.

What emerges significant is to construct a way of rethinking the debate around the environment and sovereignty, which moves beyond what Karen Litfin, calls the geological model of sovereignty being eroded by environmental change and environmental regimes.[10] The image of sovereignty in Litfin's work. The Greening of Sovereignty in World Politics, as a fixed thing, akin to a rock being clearly recognized as socially constructed and consisting of a bundle of rights whose composition and location shift continuously across time. Further, the study suggests that sovereignty should be conceived in terms of three elements-autonomy, control and authority-all of which can be attached to different institutions overtime not necessarily just states, and be constructed themselves in differing ways.[11]

Moving beyond the western straitjacket, the concept 'environmental security' envisions:

- Rethinking western pattern of development, its cultural superiority, hegemonic power structure and universalization doctrine.

- Replacement of mechanical, the other view of nature and human beings by an organicism view which studies human beings, nature, future generations and all interconnected, coordinated in a symbiotic relationship as members as a cosmos.
- Global governance of environmental matters through a coordinated network of NGOs, environmental regimes, norms, regional organizations, and communities cutting across the rigidity of sovereign state system. This means not a proselytization but shifting of sovereignty state system to other centers, at every level. The traditional unidimensional view of sovereignty appears superficially to be inconsistent with the multidimensional requirements of planetary environmental protection.
- Pronouncement of cultural diversities, differentiated civilizational values and not deification of western values.
- An ethical and moral rebuilding of human nature on a spiritual plank to think in terms of an expanded self within a timelessness frame.

As mentioned earlier, the emancipatory goal of the Critical Theory was to deconstruct and expose the imposition of dominant hegemonic discourse of the mainstream of International Relation and suggest the possibilities of new ones different from the existing one. Apart from all the approaches such as dependency theory, feminism, world order model projects and post modernism, is the resistance theory against the cultural hegemony and western straitjacket of the mainstream International Relation. The Critical Theory as seen in Cox's approach travels beyond the limits of problem solving and embraces an historical approach to contemporary hegemony based on Gramscian notion of historic bloc.[12]

Equally evident in dependency theory and in the literature on structuration is the significance of a genuinely global approach to order, recognizing the fluidity of space and evolutionary character of time. The insistence on reproductive social structure and the ontological skepticism in the latter case is quite evident in critical theory.

Post modernism's anti foundationalism and relativism led by Foucault stress on historically specific conditions in which knowledge is generated. The dominant perspective in IR is socially constructed by the people.[13] Ecological theory's deconstructed study of nature as it is in terms of biological imperatives can add to the Critical theory's revolt against the established pattern of thinking.

Ecological approach addresses all those normative positions and contains all elements required by an emancipatory theory of International Relation. Ignoring the organic relationship that exists between human beings and nature to go ahead toward the emancipatory goal the Critical Theory unwittingly endorses the mainstream view of human nature. In the construction of identity with the mainstream of IR so far as the realist and liberal view of human being's nature is concerned, the Critical Theory cannot get rid of if this ecological approach. It will remain halfway in its emancipatory mission.

In this sense ecological approach gets at the very foundation of emancipatory theory by pointing to the relationship between control of nature and the control of man/woman. It does not keep itself limited to defense of any constituency or identity. Freedom is no longer confined to any group at the cost of nature. The 'other' is no longer the external, or spiritless matter-whether living or non-living but the enlarged itself. In other words the emanicpatory approach cannot be emanicipatory without the vision of an enlarged or universal self as suggested earlier by the ecological theory. The identity with the dominant mainstream of International Relation against which Critical Theory rises in revolt can be dissipated only when emanicipatory approach puts stress on a moral reconstruction of human beings that will see in its enlarged self the existence of the nature-the vision of 'Basudheiva Kutumbakam' the whole world is a family – the vision required of man. Constancy, fixity, superiority of culture, clash of civilization or permanence, and spatial exclusion associated with the mainstream of International Relation are considered irrational. Ecological approach addresses a different kind of essentialism that is divested of linearity, hierarchy and elitism evoking the notion of natural law. Everything is in constant flux in this timelessness frame into which both human beings and nature are woven with the warf and woof of cooperation, and coordination. Thus, the political project for human kind is built on the foundation of these ecological imperatives, as outlined above. Nature is not mere a bundle of lifeless raw materials and the sacredness and holism attached to it by ecological epistemology can emanate from a renewed vision and perspectives-at present lacking in emancipatory approaches of Critical Theory. Ecological theory subsumes the Critical Theory offering the vision of an enlarged self, timelessness of evolutionary process, subjectivity existence in diversity and democratic global governance on the basis of Bookchin's municipal confederalism or grassroots globalization. Emancipatory theory seems to have jettisoned the concept of peace aware of its hegemonic and ordering connotations.

The non-military threats diversifying away from state and stemming from environmental degradation can be addressed by ecological approach. It is not synonymous with environmental conflict. It is founded on the confluence of sustainable development, recognition of future generations both living and non-living' s right to life and ecological ethics of enlarged self, renewed vision and an overhaul of the dominant view of inordinate and profligate life style. That nonmilitary threats can be addressed by non-military means can herald positive peace, which is not mere absence of intra state or interstate conflict or violence. It is creation of positive conditions born of ecological ethics, renewed vision about life and universal self without sacrificing the freedom and subjectivity of any whether men, women, future generations or nature. This is what the ecological approach stresses on to be the guiding metaphor for the emancipatory mission of Critical Theory.

In order to make the Earth worth living in, long and long strides have to made away from Hobbessian and Lockean outlook and view of the world. What was conducive to or accelerated the motion of man in the direction of commodious living, inordinate consumption and production of wealth, was considered morally or ethically worth doing. Such a view of an atomized and individualistic self-soaked deep in sense informed materialistic pleasures resulted in a despoliated and ravaged and impoverished earth. Is it worth-naming development if it has made both earth and poor staring at and fed on each other's poverty. So the basic metaphysics of western liberal democratic order based on wealth production and profligate life style comes in for a rethinking. What was true in the context of western civilization, culture and religious value, should not be true in the case of the other. Since the future generation's right, to live on this earth for a commodious living, and consent to the political and economic order are absent in the criteria of the present generation's giving legitimacy to the government, the very criteria of judgment about the metaphysics of liberal democracy while giving legitimacy to the rightfulness of action on the part of state needs rethinking or reordering. Other than what is conducive to one's motion after power, glory and wealth, new ethics and planetary wisdom giving countenance to intergenerational and interspecies equity and accountability are to constitute the foundation of a liberal democratic market based political order. It is not through the unsustainability of both nature and the poor people in South that the economic interests of the dominant class now represented as major dominant players of the North can be perpetuated. Liberal democracy is not a move about forming and unmaking a government, or a collection of rights or proliferation of economic growth, wealth production and luxurious living of the dominant rich, it is more than that which envisions not a mechanistic but a Cosmo centric view of world in which is encompassed the interests of all, the future generations, the living and the non living. A new set of ethics based on intergenerational equity, a new vision of life going beyond the sense derived materialistic framework, a new criteria of legitimacy and shifting of faith in what the liberal market based democratic political order considers as rightful-so far as production of wealth, promoting luxurious life style and inordinate consumption are concerned – are in combination the primary requirements to make both democracy and development sustainable.

New modes of thinking replacing the anti-nature and anti-people syndrome of the liberal market based order, is required that would be based on newfound compassion for the integrity of the planet and for one another. In all likelihood this will spring from a reinterpretation of religious faiths and insights. It is not a diehard or doctrinaire adherence to the secularistic framework of liberal democratic order. Their values lie in recasting of human responsibility for planetary stewardship in contrast to recognition of rapacious human beings to ravage the nature for a luxurious living reminiscent of liberal tradition. An enlightened and eclectic approach drawing from all religions is required where the needs of the natural order of the planet and future generation must have the primacy. The notion that Earth must be seen as a living organism in the sense of a homeostatic equilibrium that demands respect from humanity and other terrestrial life forms has a spiritual dimension on what was initially conceived as mechanistic the scientific base of liberal democracy. As one philosopher of science stated:

> "Instead of viewing the world of nature as onlookers from outside, we now have to understand how our own human life and activities operate as elements within the world of nature. So we must develop a more coordinated view of the world, embracing both the world of nature and the world of humanity."[14]

A rethinking of the human earth cosmos relationship is needed to the established metaphysics of western liberal market built political order based on industrialization, wealth production and sense driven life style and consumption. A new kind of spiritual-political consensus is to take place informing the atomistic individual to change at two levels: the philosophical spiritual level and the level of political secular action. To ensure a sustainable future, the established metaphysics of western liberal market based political order on production of wealth, inordinate consumption and commodious living at the cost of nature and other human and non-human requires a critical look.

The IPCC's report established that there is a discernible human influence on global climate from the accumulation of green house gases in the atmosphere.[15] though there are scientific skeptics who discount the very notion of profound human-induced climate change.[16] The timing and extent of global warming, as well as the effects or resulting climate change, were uncertain. Because the conclusions were so general, there was only rudimentary guidance for policy-makers concerned with how climate change might affect their jurisdiction and their national interests. Substantial uncertainties about regional and smaller scale impacts remain. In such a situation, to push the countries to greater international cooperation to limit carbon dioxide emission will be harder to tick in.

Another dimension added to this is the improvement in the predictions of climate change which name the countries and economic sectors likely to benefit from global warming. Hence, these countries are unlikely to push for greater international regulation to limit climate change. Improved understanding of local and national impacts from climate change may motivate local and regional stakeholders to pressure their governments to do more on the issue of climate change.[17] But the question remains, will there be sufficient perception of risk by political leadership to take action in coming years? In both North and South, concerns about national interest, economic growth and development have too much obsessed their policy makers to pay attention to climate change. Conclusions derived from the Kyoto Protocol suggest that each country's position in the climate change negotiations is driven by a myriad of factors. Among these are important perception of national interest, geographical considerations such as location, landforms, water system and soil types, and existing national and international political coalitions, blocs and friendships. This means climate change impacts assessment of their certainty and expected occurrence combined with domestic and international politics to determine the shape, contours, context and course of international climate change negotiation. Improved assessments of climate change impacts at the local, national and regional levels with greater climate science certainty are essential to the policy at the country level, and can effect international cooperation.[18]

What remains crucial to the success in climate change negotiations is the attitude of the United States and its acceptance of the responsibility for bringing down the level of carbon dioxide in the atmosphere. In addition to this, it needs a change in its energy policy that will decrease its dependence on fossil fuels but there seems to be no change in American energy policy and in its hard-line approach towards the climate change negotiations. Since the signing of the Kyoto Protocol until the New Delhi Conference of the parties (COP-8) to the United Nations Framework Convention on Climate Change the US discourse on climate negotiations had remained the same: developing countries must also commit to reduce or limit greenhouse gas emissions in order for international action on climate change to be effective. The US administration's arguments against the Protocol included unfairness, inefficiency and harm to the US economy. Following in the footsteps of the United States the Russia's vacillation to ratify the Kyoto Protocol is another death blow to the climate treaty.

Another relevant aspect of the negotiations is the shift in interest from mitigation – preventing climate change by regulating GHG emissions- to adaptation. This new focus on adaptation suits policy makers from both North and South countries. The North is supportive because it will not have to undertake costly reforms to achieve its GHG reduction targets. Furthermore, adaptation is a means for developed countries to postpone action. The South views adaptation as an opportunity for additional financial resources from the North from a hypothetical climate change adaptation fund, while leaving its possibilities for economic growth untouched.[19]

As gleaned from chapter seven one of the basic premises on which the issues of human rights are to be sheetanchored and which must be recognized by the North is that the human persons as well as the South have the fundamental basic rights to environment, development, survival, atmosphere, access to resources and use it in fair and equitable denominations. To confine the negotiations going on the environmental front to mere peripheral aspects like transfer of technologies, economic issues and funds, is not only to trivialize the seriousness of the human rights, but also to ignore the basic concerns which contests the very western ingrained economic and political thinking, constituting the very basis of their interpretation of human rights. This is a very pertinent question of equity, which is the basis of all other human rights, not only between North and South but also between and among all the human beings inhabitating this planet.

It involves as much the national sovereign rights of the countries of South over the resources, and their uses as the recognition and enforceability of basic rights of local man, and community to the above without harming anyone and demanding an immediate moratorium on indiscriminate pillage of natural resources and infringement of human rights. It would certainly be demeaning and a blatant mockery of democratic values and human rights, which the West so cherishes not to bring right to environment and survival of the individuals to the fore human rights arenas.

Increasingly, an intense drive for environmental rights not only of individuals but of communities is marked to bring it to the center stage of issues of human rights. The Sierra Club Legal Defence Fund, a U.S. organization that pressed for Human Rights Sub Commission Study, speaks of "an increasingly obvious link between environmental degradation and the health and welfare of communities, whether they be indigenous people, minorities, workers, rural population, villagers or city dwellers". Further, it vouchsafes for an internationally recognized right" of communities, minorities and other affected people" to informed participation in decisions that threaten their health, resources and ecosystems on which they depend for survivals. But the United States opposes this on the ground that it may strengthen undemocratic and oppressive regimes to the detriment of the individuals.

The North countries should not be impervious to this fact that the right to the survival does not concern the South alone. It applies as much to communities affected by nuclear waste in the U.S. and to those affected by the destruction of forests and habitat in the Saami areas of Norway and Sweden and to Yanomami tribals living in the Brazilian Amazon. It is inalienable, indivisible and non-negotiable, and constitutes the basis of all other rights.

To say that a political regime is democratic, because it is elected by the people, it has an elected national assembly or has a constitutionally guaranteed human rights, and to measure democratization of all other regimes around the globe on that score, may be half truth and correct on the surface to satisfy certain political requirements. But if political activities and economic policies of a dominant regime or regimes lead to the destruction of the environment and pauperization of the people in the South, can such regimes deserve being termed as democratic? Thus, the very imperatives and compulsions of an undamaged environment and a sustainable development guaranteed to all not only of the present but also of the future generations, urge to define democracy and human rights not in a narrow political context, but in a broader context transcending political and territorial dimensions. In order to give a concrete shape and realization to human rights, three basic premises are to be given priority:

(a) To define development making it sustainable with nature and environment and other poor human beings, that means, equity not only between man and man, but also between human beings and nature.

(b) To recognize the new global environmental ethics giving top priority to the organic bond between man and the ecosystem. No anti thesis between development and nature.

(c) The Nature may not have rights but human beings have duties towards it.

As of today the issues of human rights so cherished by North and US do not contain the rights of individuals, people and local communities in the South in particular and world in general to survival, environment, development and security. All North's talks of environmental ethics and human rights will be like the proverbial cat who had a record of swallowing a hundred thousand mice, advising them piously about undertaking a holy pilgrimage.

The modem concept of sovereign and secular state, and its legitimacy derived from its people on the criterion of production of wealth, commodious living, inordinate consumption and profligate life style owes its origin to the Newtonian and Cartesian portrayal of the universe as particles in motion. That everything is matter devoid of spirit jettisoned the Hegelian Idea and age-old hallowed view of Eastern mysticism that: everything both animate and inanimate from the tiniest to the greatest is pervaded with, spirit Persistence in such a view held by scientists of the universe as matter in complete disregard of what Eastern seers have intuited through their long experience and wisdom, resulted in a dominant hegemonic culture, which gradually became the universal principle of building the secular sovereign state, and its pattern of development through out the world-The impending environmental crisis is the outcome of this dominant hegemonic culture. Thus, the statecraft and its pattern of development built on "matter" has been the single point or one sided perspective of secularism as it ignored the Eastern insight, western idealism and recent developments in the field of science. It viewed the world as dichotomous, divided, and separate between man and nature. The nature is the other, lifeless and a compendium of raw materials to be exploited for man's commodious living. The subject-object dichotomy falsified the ancient Eastern truth and the recent new paradigm thinking in science that every thing in the universe is connected to the cosmic whole, and cosmic consciousness itself Thus, the ecological awareness and insights is in harmony with spiritual tradition and new paradigm thinking in science. A challenge to the singular or one sided perspective emanates from the cosmic whole approach as mentioned in the preceding chapter. As the cosmic whole approach contains much of the arguments of the ecological movement, new-paradigm thinking in science, and Eastern philosophy, it is pertinent that the view of sovereignty, state and secularism built up on the foundations of the discarded view of matter needs a rethinking. The ecological paradigm in harmony with modem science and Eastern philosophy suggests perception of reality as an awareness of the oneness and unity of spirit in all life forms. Holism and ecological interdependence represent a challenge to the single point perspective of the sovereign state. Thus, the shift from a single point perspective to a universal social episteme requires new spatial ordering of principles new temporal understandings, and new norms of legitimation. The stand point of new paradigm in science, which views the world as an integrated whole rather than a mere heap of dissociated and separate parts, should be universalized as the new basis of rethinking the established political and economic order.

Apart from western pattern of development, its inordinate life style and exorbitant consumption being threat to the environment, as argued by Arthur Westing, the modern warfare with its deleterious impacts on environment has been the greatest threat to the humanity. Unconventional warfare such as chemical, biological, or nuclear has all the ramifications of extraordinary levels of environmental devastations. Thus, military as the greatest factor of environmental degradation needs to be taken note of in international realm while talks on global sustainability continue to put emphasis on the various causes of environmental degradation.

References

1. Ronnie Lipschutz, "Environmental Conflict and Environmental Determinism: The Relative Importance of Social and Natural Factors", in Nils Petter Gleditsch ed. Conflict and the Environment (Dor drecht, The Netherlands: Kluwer, 1997), pp. 35-50 ; See also Wenche Hauge and Tanja Ellingsen, Beyond Environmental Scarcity: the Causal Pathways to Conflict", Journal of Peace Research, 35, No. 3, 1998, pp. 299-317.
2. Jack Goldstone, "Environmental Scarcity and Violent Conflict: A Debate", Environmental Change and Security Project Reports, Issue 2 (Washington, D.C.: Woodrow Wilson Center, 1996), p. 68.
3. Thomas F. Homer Dixon, Environment, Scarcity And Violence (New Jersey / Princeton: Princeton University Press, 1999).
4. Quoted by Audrey E. Kitagawa "Practical Spirituality" in World Affairs Vol. 7, No. I, January-March 2003, p. 106.

5. Eric K.Stern, "The Case for Comprehensive Security", *op. cit.,* p. 145.
6. *Ibid.*
7. On Peace Research and International Relation see Beverly Neufeld, "The Marginalization of Peace Research in International Relations", Millennium Vol. 22, No. 2, 1993, pp. 165-84.
8. Eric Laferriere, "Emancipatory International Relations Theory: An Ecological Perspective", Millennium: Journal of International Studies Vol. 25, No. 1, 1996, p. 74.
9. Eric K.Stern, "The Case for Comprehensive Security", in Daniel H.Deudney and Richard A. Matthew, eds., Contested Grounds, (Albany: State University of New York Press, 1999), p. 145.
10. Karen Litfin, "The greening of sovereignty: an introduction", in Litfin, ed., The Greening of Sovereignty in World Politics (Cambridge, MA: MIT Press, 1998).
11. *Ibid,* See also Karen Litfin, "Sovereignty in World Politics", Merskon International Studies Review, 41, 1997, pp. 167-204.
12. Robert Cox, "Social Forces, States and World Orders", in Richard Little and Michael Smith eds., Perspectives on World Politics, 2nd edition, (London and New York: Routledge, 1991), pp. 444-456.
13. Michael Foucault, The Order of Things: An Archaeology of the Human Sciences (London: Tavistock, 1970).
14. Stephen Toumin, The Return to Cosmology: Post Modern Science and the Theology of Nature (Berkley, University of California Press, 1982), pp. 255-56.
15. J. Houghton et.al., eds., Climate Change 1995: The Science of Climate Change (New York: Cambridge University Press, 1996).
16. S.G. Philander, Is the Temperature Rising? The Uncertain Science of Global Warming (Princeton: Princeton University Press, 1998).
17. Paul G.Harris, "Assessing Climate Change: International Cooperation and Predictions of Environmental Change", Politics, February 2001, pp. 14-15.
18. Paul G. Harris, p. 19.
19. Miquel Munoz, New Delhi to Milan, Down to Earth Vol. 12, No. 14, 15 December 2003, p. 53.

Bibliography

Earthscan, Environment and Conflict, Earthscan Briefing Document 40, London: International Institute for Environment and Development, 1984.

Ferguson H.L.ed., Changing Atmosphere: Implications for Global Security (Conference Statement, Toronto, 27-30 June 1988), New York: UN General Assembly Document No. A/c.2/43/2, 3 October 1988.

Graeger, Nina and Dan Smith, eds., Environment, Poverty, Conflict. PRIO Report. Oslo: International Peace Research Institite(PRIO), 1994.

Lodgaard, Sverre, and Anders H. Afghanistan's Ornas. eds., The Environment and International Security, PRIO Report, Oslo: International Peace Research Institute (PRIO), 1992.

Nadik S, The State of the World Population 1990 (New York: World Population Fund, 1990).

The United Nations Population Fund, The State of World Population 1992 (New York: 1992)

World Bank, World Development Report 1988 (New York: Oxford University Press, 1988).

World Bank, World Development Report 1992: Development and the Environment (Oxford: Oxford University Press 1992)

World Bank, World Development Report 1987 (New York: Oxford University Press, 1987).

World Bank Development Report 1992 (Oxford University Press, 1992)

World Bank Development Report 1995 (Oxford University Press, 1995)

World Commission on Environment and Development, Our Common Future, The Brundtland Report (New York/London: Oxford University Press, 1987), p. 290.

BOOKS

Agnew John, Geopolitics : Revisioning World Politics (London : Routledge, 1998).

Ayoob Mohammad, The Third World Security Predicament (Boulder, Colo.: Lynne Rienner, 1995).

Bahro Rudolf. From Red to Green: Interviews with New Left Review (London: Verso, 1984).

Bennett, Olivia. Greenwar: Environment and Conflict. Washington D.C.: Panos Institute 1991.

Boserup A. and R.Nelid, ed. The Foundation of Defensive Defence (London: Macmillan, 1990)

Boyce James, Agrarian Impasses in Bengal: Institutional Constraints to Technological Change (Oxford: Oxford University Press, 1987).

Brown, Janet Welsh, ed. In the U.S. Interest : Resources, Growth, and Security in the Developing World (Boulder, Colo. : Westview Press, 1990).

Brown Lester R. et al. State of the World 1991, World Watch Institute (India), New Delhi, 1991).

Cantori L.J. and Spiegel S.L. ed. International Politics of Regions: A Comparative Approach (New Jersey: Prentice Hall, 1970).

Crosby Alfred, Ecological Imperialism : The Biological Expansion of Europe, 900-1900 (Cambridge, U.K. : Cambridge University Press, 1986).

Crus Jonathan, ed. Power of Development (London : Routledge, 1995).

Dalby Simon, Creating the Second Cold War: The Discourse Politics (London: Pinter 1990).

Deudney Daniel H. and Richard A. Matthew, ed., Contested Grounds: Security and Conflict in the New Environmental Politics (Albany: State University of New York Press, 1999).

Enloe C. Bananas, Beaches and Bases: Making Feminist Sense of International Politics (London: Pandora 1989).

Fischer Dietrich. Nonmilitary Aspects of Security: A System's Approach, United Nations Institute for Disarmament and Research (UNIDIR)(Alder-shot: Dartmouth Publishing Company Ltd., 1993).

Freeman Peter H. Large Dams and the Environment: Recommendations for Development Planning: A Report for the UN Water Conference, Mar Del Plats, Argentina, March 1977.

Friedmann John. Empowerment: The Politics of Alternative Development (Cambridge: Blackwell Publishers, 1992).

Galtung Johan. "International Development" in Roger A Coate and Jerely A. Rosati, ed., The Power of Human Needs in World Society (Boulder and London: Lynne Rienner Publishers, 1988).

Gilpin Robert. The Political Economy of International Relations (Princeton/ New Jersey: Princeton University Press, 1987).

George P.Castille and Gilbert Kushner, ed., Persistent Peoples: Cultural Enclaves in Perspective (Tuson: University of Arizona Press, 1981).

Giddens Anthony. The Constitution of Society: Outline of the Theory of Structuration (Cambridge: Polity Press, 1984).

Gleditsch, Nils Petter, ed., Conflict and the Environment. Proceedings of the NATO Advanced Research Workshop on Conflict and the Environment, Bolkesjf, Norway, 11-16 June 1996 (Dordrecht, Netherlands: Kluwer, 1997)

Gleick Peter H. "Environmental Resources and International Security and Politics" in E.H. Arnett, ed. Science and International Security: Responding to a Changing World (Washington D.C.: American Association for the Advancement of Science, 1990), p. 512.

Goldsmith Edward and Nicholas Hildyard, "The Social and Environmental Effects of Large Dams" Vol. I Overview, A Report to European Ecological Action Group (ECOROPA) (Cornweli: Wadebridge Ecological Center, 1984).

Grubb M. Green House Effect: Nagotiationg Targets (London: Royal Institute of International Affairs, 1989).

Gurr Ted. Why Men Rebel (Princeton: Princeton University Press, 1970).

Harrison Paul. The Third Revolution: Environment, Population and a Sustainable World (London/New York: Tauris and Co.Ltd. 1992).

Hawley T.M., Against the Fires of Hell : The Environmental Disaster of the Gulf War (New York : Harcourt Brace Javonovich, 1992).

Hillel D. Out of the Earth: Civilization and the Life of the Soil (New York: The Free Press, 1991).

Hollis H.B., A.L. Powers and M. Sommers, ed. The Conquest of War: Alternative Strategies for Global Security (Boulder, Co.: Westview Press, 1989).

Horowitz Donald. Ethnic Groups in Conflict (Berkeley and Los Angeles: University of California Press, 1985).

Hoyt E. Conserving the Wild Relatives of Crops, International Board for Plant Genetic Resources (IUCN) and World Wide Fund for Nature (WWF), Rome and Gland, 1988.

Jacobson Jodi L. Environmental Refugees: A Yardstick of Habitability. World Watch Paper, No. 86, 1988.

Job B.ed. The Security Dilemma: National Security of Third World States (Boulder, Co.: Lynne Rienner, 1992).

Johnston, R.J. A Question of Place: Exploring the Practice of Human Geography (Oxford: Basil Blackwell, 1991).

Kahn H. On Thermonuclear War, edn. 2 (Princeton/ New Jersey: Princeton University Press, 1961).

Kakonen, Jyrki, ed., Perspectives on Environmental Conflict and International Politics (New York, Printer 1992.)

Kaldor M. The Imaginary War (Oxford: Basil Blackwell, 1990).

Kaldor M. and R.Falk, ed. Dealignment: A New Foreign Policy Perspective (Oxford: Basil Balckwell, 1987).

Kononova M.M. "Humns of Virgin and Cultivated Soils" in J.E. Gieseking, ed., Soil Components Vol. I (Berlin: Springer-Verlag, 1975).

Lamb H.H. Climate, History and the Modern World (London : Methuen, 1982).

Lemarquand David G. International Rivers: The Politics of Cooperation (University of British Columbia and the Waterloo Research Center, 1977).

Leonard Jeffery, "Overview", Environment and the Poor: Development Strategies for a Common Agenda (New Brunswick, N.J.: Transaction, 1989).

Lewin T.H.Wild Races of the Eastern Frontier of India (Delhi: Mittal Publication, 1984).

Linkgreen Goran et al., ed., Peace Processes in the Third World Report from the 1991 Advanced International Programme Conflict Resolution (Development of Peace and Conflict Research, Uppsala University, Sweden 1991).

Masters Roger, The Nature of Politics (New Haven, Conn : Yale University Press, 1989).

Moller B. Common Security and Non-offensive Defense: A Non-realist Perspective (Boulder, Co.: Lynne Rienner, 1992).

Montesquien, Spirit of the Laws (original, 1748) (Cambridge : Cambridge University Press, 1989), book 19, section 14.

Nef J.U. War and Human Progress: An Essay on the Rise of Industrial Civilization (Cambridge, Mass.: Harvard University Press, 1950).

Pearce David. Markandya Anil and Barbier Edward B. Blue Print for a Green Economy (London: Earthscan Publications, 1989).

Peters R. and Lovejoy T.ed., Global Warming and Biological Diversity (New Haven: Yale University Press, 1992).

Peterson V.S.ed. Genedered States: Feminist (re)Visions of International Relations Theory (Boulder, Co: Lynee Rienner, 1992).

Rifkin J.Biospheric Politics: A New Consciousness for a New Century (New York: Crown, 1991)

Romm, Joseph J. Defining National Security: The Nonmilitary Aspects (New York: Council on Foreign Relations Press, 1993).

Wachtel Paul. The Poverty of Affluence (Philadelphia: New Society Publishers, 1989).

Walker, R.B.J. Inside/Outside : International Relations as Political Theory (Cambridge, U.K. : Cambridge University Press, 1993).

Walker R.B.J. and S. Mendlowitz, ed. Contending Sovereignties: Redefining Political Community (Boulder, Co.: Lynne Rienner, 1990).

Waltz Kenneth, Man, the State and War (New York : Columbia University Press, 1959).

Westing Arthur H., ed. Global Resources and International Conflict: Environmental Factors in Strategic Policy and Action (Oxford: Oxford University Press, 1986).

Westing Arthur H. Comprehensive Security for the Baltic: An Environmental Approach (London/Newbury Park: Sage, 1989).

PERIODICALS, JOURNALS AND PAPERS

Bachler, Gunther. Conflict and Cooperation in the Light of Global Human –Ecological Transformation, No. 9, 1993, (Bern and Zurich: Swiss Peace Foundation and Centre for Security Studies and Conflict Research)

Boge Volker, "Proposal for an Analytical Framework to Grasp Environmental Conflict", Environment and Conflict Project (ENCOP), Occasional Paper No. 1, Center for Security Studies and Conflict Research, Bern/Zurich, July 1992.

Booth Ken, "Security in Anarchy : Utopian Realism in Theory and Practice", International Affairs, Vol. 67, No. 3, 1991.

Brock Lothar. "Peace through Parks: The Environment on the Peace Research Agenda", Journal of Peace Research Vol. 28 (40)., 1991.

Brown L.Wolfe E. "Soil Erosion: Quiet Crisis in the World Economy", World Watch Paper 60, 1991, World Watch Institute, Washington D.C.:1991.

Brown L.H. "Regional Collaboration in Resolving Third World Conflicts", Survival (London) Vol. 28.1986, pp. 208-20.

Brown Lester R. and Jodi Jacobson. "The Future of Urbanization: Facing the Ecological and Economic Constraints", World Watch Paper 77, May 1987.

Bruyninckx Hans. "Environmental Security: An Analysis of the Conceptual Problems Defining the Relationship between Environment and Security", a paper presented at Budapest on the Workshop on Environment and Security, organized by the European Peace Research Association, 11-16 November 1993, pp. 1-6.

Buzan Barry. "Environment as a Security Issue" in Paul Painchand, ed., Geopolitical Perspectives on Environment Security, Cahier du Gerpe, No. 92-05, University Laval, Quebec, p. 24 quoted in Ole Waver, Securitization and Desecuritization Working paper 5, 1993, Centre for Peace and Conflict Research, Copenhagen, 1993, p. 14.

Byers Bruce, "Ecoregions, State Sovereignty and Conflict", Bulletin of Peace Proposals Vol. 22 (i), 1991.

Dabelko, Geoffrey, and P.J. Simmons, "Environment and Security : Core Ideas and U.S. Government Initiatives", SAIS Review 17, No. 1, 1997, pp. 127-46.

Dalby Simon. "Ecopolitical Discourse: Environmental Security and Political Geography", Progress in Human Geography Vol. 16, No. 4, 1992.

Dalby Simon. "American Security Discourse: The Persistence of Geopolitics", Political Geography Quarterly Vol. 9, 1990, pp. 171-88.

Deudney Daniel. "The Case Against Linking Environmental Degradation and National Security", Millennium Vol. 19, No. 3, Winter 1990, pp. 416-476.

Deudney Daniel. "Rethinking the Link between Environment and National Security Issues", Perspectives on War and Peace, Centre for International Cooperation and Security Studies, University of Wisconsin, Madison Vol. 7, No. 2, Spring 1990, p. 12.

Dixon Thomas F.Homer. "Environmental Change and Economic Decline in Developing Countries", International Studies Notes Vol. 16, No. 1, Winter 1991.

———— "On the Threshold: Environmental Change as Causes of Actue Conflict", International Security Vol. 16, No. 2, Fall 1991.

———— "Environmental Scarcities and Violent Conflict; Evidence from Cases", International Security Vol. 19, No. 1, 1994.

———— Boutwell Jeffery and Rathjens George, "Environmental Change and Violent Conflict", Scientific American, February 1993.

Durning A. "Poverty and Environment: Reversing the Downward Spiral", World Watch Paper 92, World Watch Institute, Washington D.C.: 1989.

Falkenmark M. "Water: The Silent Messenger between Cause and Effect in Environmental Problems", Water International (Lausanne), 9(2), 1984.

Falkenmark M. "New Ecological Approach to the Water Cycle: Ticket to the Future", Ambio (Stockholm) Vol. 13, 1984.

Finger Mathias. "The Military, the Nation state and the Environment", The Ecologist Vol. 21, No. 5, 1991.

Galtung Johan. "Violence, Peace and Peace Research", Journal of Peace Research Vol. 8, No. 3, 1969, pp. 167-91.

Ganguly Sumit. "Ethno-religious Conflict in South Asia", Survival Vol. 35, No. 2. Summer 1993.

Gleditsch, Nils Petter, ed. Conflict and the Environment Proceedings of the NATO Advanced Research Workshop on Conflict and the Environment, Bolkesjo, Norway, 11-16 June, 1996. Dordrecht, Neatherlands : Kluwer, 1997.

Gleick Peter. "Water and Conflict: Fresh Water Resources and International Security", International Security Vol. 18, No. 1, Summer 1993, pp. 79-112.

———— "The Implications of Global Climatic Changes for International Security", Climate Change Vol. 15, 1989, pp. 309-25.

———— "Environmental and Security: The Clear Connections", The Bulletin of the Atomic Scientists, April, p. 18.

Gore Albert. "Strategic Environmental Initiative (SEI)", SAIS Review Vol. 10, 1990, pp. 59-71.

Hall D., Mynick H. and Williams R. "Alternative Roles for Biomass in Coping with Greenhouse Warming", Science and Global Security Vol. 2, 1991, pp. 1-39.

Hare F. Kenneth, "Climate, Drought and Desertification", Nature and Resources Vol. 20, No. 1, January –March 1984.

Johansen R.C. "Real Security is Democratic Security", Alternatives Vol. 16, 1991, pp. 209-42.

Kiessling Kerstin and Nathan Keyfitz. "The Population Debate: Urgency of the Problem", a paper presented at the Population Summit of the World's Scientific Academies held in New Delhi from 24-27 October 1993.

Kaplan Robert D. "The Coming Anarchy", The Atlantic Monthly, Vol. 273, No. 2, 1994, pp. 44-76.

Krasener Stephen D. "International Relations Theory and Global Environmental Issues", Paper presented at the workshop, Global Resources and Environmental: Arenas for Conflict, Opportunities and Cooperation, University of California, Berkeley /Pacific Institute for Studies in Development, Environment and Security, 15-17 March 1990.

Libiszewski Stephan. What is an Environmental Conflict ? Environment and Conflict Project, Centre for Security Studies and Conflict Research, Switzerland, Berne/Zurich, Occasional Paper No. 1, July 1992, pp. 1-16.

Lichbach Mark. "An Evaluation of Does Economic Inequality Breed Political Conflict? Studies", World Politics Vol. 41, July 1989, pp. 431-70.

Lipschutz, Ronnie, and John Holdren. "Crossing Borders: Resource Flows, the Global Environment, and International Security", Bulletin of Peace Proposals 21, No. 2 (1990): 121-33

Lodgaard Sverre. "Environmental Conflict Resolution", Paper presented at the UNEP Meeting on Environmental Conflict Resolution, Nairobi, 30 March 1990.

Lodhi Abdul Charles Tilly. "Urbanization, Crime and Collective Violence in 19th Century", American Journal of Sociology Vol. 79, No. 2, September 1973.

Mathews Jessica Tuchman, "Redefining Security", Foreign Affairs Vol. 68, No. 2, Spring 1989.

Matthew Richard A. "The Greening of U.S. Foreign Policy", Issues in Science and Technology, Vol. 13, No. I, Fall 1996.

Myers Norman. "The Environmental Dimension to Security Issues", The Environmentalist Vol. 6, No. 4, winter 1986.

———— "Environment and Security", Foreign Policy, No. 74, (spring 1989), pp. 23-41.

Norse D. "A New Strategy for Feeding a Crowded Planet", Environment, 34, No. 5, pp. 6-11, 1992.

Porter Gareth, "Environmental Security as a National Security Issue", Current History, May 1995.

———— "Post Cold War Global Environment and Security", Fletcher Forum of World Affairs, 14, No. 2 (1990), pp. 332-44.

Renner Michael. "National Security: The Economic and Environmental Dimensions", World Watch paper 89, Washington D.C.: World Watch Institute 1989.

Rowlands, Ian. "The Security Challenges of Global Environmental Change", Washington Quarterly, Vol. 14, No. 1, 1991.

Springer A.L. "Protecting the Environment: A New Focus for the Atlantic Alliance", Proceeding of the Academy of Political Science Vol. 38, 1991, pp. 124-39.

Stern, Erik. "Bringing the Environment In : The Case for Comprehensive Security", Cooperation and Conflict 30, No. 3 (1995).

Teitelbaum Michael S. "The Population Threat", Foreign Affairs Vol. 71, No. 5, Winter 1992/1993.

Ullman R.H. "Redefining Security", International Security Vol. 8, 1983, pp. 129-53.

Wayne Cornelius Jr. "Urbanization As an Agent in Latin American Political Instability" The Case of Mexico, American Political Science Review Vol. 63, September 1969.

WendtAlexander. "The Agent Structure Problem" International Organization. Vol. 41, No. 3, summer 1987.

Westing A.H. "Environmental Security and its Relation to Ethiopia and Sudan", Ambio Vol. 20, 1991, pp. 168-71.

———— "Environmental Security for the Danube Basin", Environmental Conservation Vol. 16, No. 4, 1989.

———— "Comprehensive Human Security and Ecological Realities", Guest Comment, Environmental Conservation Vol. 16, No. 4, winter 1989.

———— "The Environmental Components of Comprehensive Security", Bulletin of Peace Proposal Vol. 20, 1989, pp. 129-34.

———— "The Atmosphere as a Common Heritage of Human Kind: Its Role in Environmental Security", Scientific World (London), 34(4), 1990.

Widgrin J. "International Migration and Regional Stability", International Affairs Vol. 66, 1990, pp. 749-66.

Wigley, T.M.L., "Impact of Extreme Events", Nature 316, No. 6024, 11 July 1985.

Wilson Edward O. "Threats to Biodiversity", Scientific American 261, No. 3, September 1989.

Winnefeld, James A., and Mary E. Morris, Where Environmental Concerns and Security Strategies Meet : Green Conflict in Asia and the Middle East (Santa Monica, California, Rand, 1994).

Wright Robert, "The Experiment that Failed : Why Soviet Science Collapsed", The New Republic 205 No. 18, 28 October, 1991.

Index

F

J

K

L

O

S